The Scarlet Sisters

OTHER BOOKS BY MYRA MACPHERSON

All Governments Lie!: The Life and Times of Rebel Journalist I. F. Stone

The Power Lovers: An Intimate Look at Politicians and Their Marriages

She Came to Live Out Loud: An Inspiring Family Journey through Illness, Loss, and Grief

Long Time Passing: Vietnam and the Haunted Generation

The Scarlet Sisters

Sex, Suffrage, and Scandal in the Gilded Age

Myra MacPherson

TWELVE

NEW YORK   BOSTON

Twelve
Hachette Book Group
237 Park Avenue
New York, NY 10017

www.HachetteBookGroup.com

Printed in the United States of America

RRD-C

First Edition: March 2014

10   9   8   7   6   5   4   3   2   1

Twelve is an imprint of Grand Central Publishing.
The Twelve name and logo are trademarks of Hachette Book Group, Inc.

The Hachette Speakers Bureau provides a wide range of authors for speaking events. To find out more, go to www.hachettespeakersbureau.com or call (866) 376-6591.

The publisher is not responsible for websites (or their content) that are not owned by the publisher.

Library of Congress Cataloging-in-Publication Data
MacPherson, Myra.
    The scarlet sisters : sex, suffrage, and scandal in the Gilded Age / Myra MacPherson. — First edition.
        pages cm
    Includes bibliographical references and index.
    ISBN 978-0-446-57023-7 (hardcover) — ISBN 978-1-4555-4770-8 (ebook)
1. Woodhull, Victoria C. (Victoria Claflin), 1838–1927.   2. Cook, Tennessee Claflin, Lady, 1845–1923.   3. Feminists—United States—Biography.   4. Women social reformers—United States—Biography.   I. Title.
    HQ1412.M29 2014
    305.42092'2—dc23
    [B]
                                                                    2013027618

In memory of my beloved daughter, Leah,
and for her wonderful daughter, Teagan

Contents

Cast of Characters

THE SCARLET SISTERS: Victoria Woodhull and Tennessee (Tennie) Claflin
CANNING WOODHULL: Victoria's first husband, a doctor and a drunk
BYRON AND ZULA MAUD: Victoria and Canning Woodhull's children
COLONEL JAMES H. BLOOD: Victoria's second husband, a Civil War hero and free lover
JOHN BIDDULPH MARTIN: Victoria's third husband, devoted and rich

The Claflin Clan
REUBEN BUCK CLAFLIN: Father to Victoria and Tennessee, snake oil salesman
ROXANNA CLAFLIN, A.K.A. ANNIE: Mother
UTICA CLAFLIN: Victoria and Tennessee's sister
MEG MILES AND POLLY SPARR: Two older sisters
DR. SPARR: Polly's husband and blackmailer

Suffragists
SUSAN B. ANTHONY: Pushed women's suffrage at the expense of other freedom
ELIZABETH CADY STANTON: Supported Woodhull's free love position
LUCY STONE: Emphatically did not support free love

Lucretia Mott: The *grande dame* of the movement

Paulina Wright Davis: Rich suffragist and Spiritualist

Tycoons

Cornelius Vanderbilt: Thought to be Tennie's lover

Jim Fisk: Flamboyant robber baron

Jay Gould: Fisk's dour sidekick

Daniel Drew: The King of Watered Stock

Henry Clews: Cashed the famous check that began the sisters' career

Abolitionists, Anarchists, Radicals, and Communists

Frederick Douglass: Former slave, nominated by the Equal Rights
    Party to run as vice president with Victoria Woodhull in 1872

Ben Butler: Yankee Civil War general, progressive congressman, friend
    of Lincoln and Grant, supporter of the sisters

Stephen Pearl Andrews: Abolitionist, anarchist, philosopher, linguist,
    free lover, and mentor to the sisters

Karl Marx: International revolutionary socialist and onetime friend

Benjamin Tucker: Well-known anarchist who claimed he lost his
    virginity to Victoria

George Francis Train: Eccentric, controversial, racist millionaire who
    gave money to suffragists

Journalists

Horace Greeley: Editor and publisher of the *New-York Daily Tribune*

Whitelaw Reid: Succeeded Greeley at the *Tribune*

Charles Dana: Publisher of the New York *Sun*

Johnny Green: New York *Sun* city editor and Tennie's boyfriend

The Beecher Dynasty

Henry Ward Beecher: The most famous preacher in America in the
    latter half of the nineteenth century

HARRIET BEECHER STOWE: Beecher's sister, author of *Uncle Tom's Cabin* and of a vitriolic roman à clef about the sisters

CATHARINE BEECHER: Spinster sister to Harriet, author, opponent of women's suffrage

ISABELLA BEECHER HOOKER: Half sister to the Beechers; renegade supporter of Victoria Woodhull

Major Figures in the Tilton-Beecher Scandal

THEODORE TILTON: Handsome abolitionist, journalist, suffragist, thought to be Victoria's lover

ELIZABETH "LIB" TILTON: Wife of Theodore, accused of adultery with Beecher

FRANK MOULTON AND EMMA MOULTON: Major witnesses in the trial

BESSIE TURNER: Former Tilton family servant and paid-off Beecher witness

Rivals to the Sisters

ANTHONY COMSTOCK: Self-appointed one-man Victorian vice squad

THOMAS BYRNES: The "World's Most Famous Detective" of the era

HENRY JAMES: Victorian-era man of letters, fictionalized the sisters

LUTHER CHALLIS: Wall Street financier who sued the sisters for libel

BENJAMIN TRACY: Beecher's meaner-than-a-junkyard-dog lawyer

HENRY C. BOWEN: Brooklyn's Plymouth Church president, who hired Beecher and fired Tilton

Royalty

SIR FRANCIS COOK: Husband of Tennie, one of the richest men in England

SIR THOMAS BEECHAM: Founder of the London Philharmonic, married to the sisters' grandniece

His Royal Highness the Prince of Wales, later King Edward VII

The King and Queen of Portugal, circa 1886

Introducing Two
Improper Victorians

Yes, I am a free lover! I have an inalienable, constitutional, and natural right to love whom I may, to love as long or as short a period as I can; to change that love every day if I please, and with that right neither you nor any law can frame any right to interfere.
— Victoria Claflin Woodhull, November 20, 1871, Steinway Hall

For myself I have at least one financial opinion, and that is that gold is cash. To have plenty of it [gold] is to be pretty nearly independent of everything and everybody.
— Tennessee Claflin, 1871

In 2008 everyone was talking about a momentous historic possibility: the Democratic Party nominating a woman, Hillary Clinton, for president, and an African American man, Barack Obama, for vice president. At the time, I read a squib in a newspaper saying it had already been done, back in 1872. An obscure third party had nominated a woman, Victoria Woodhull, with the famed former slave Frederick Douglass as her running mate.

I started to read more about Woodhull and discovered her younger, sassy sister Tennessee Claflin, and I was hooked. Here were the two most symbiotic and scandalous sisters in American history. They rose from poverty, a trashy family, and a childhood of scam fortune-telling to become rich, powerful, and infamous feminists in the raucous heyday of post–Civil War Wall Street buccaneers and beauties.

Bankrolled by the richest man in America, Cornelius "Commodore" Vanderbilt, in 1870 these strikingly beautiful sisters became the first women stockbrokers in the world, a feat not equaled in America for nearly another hundred years. So amazing was this venture that thousands of gawkers mobbed them when they opened their Broad Street office. However, this was just the start.

The sisters could barely write when they first set out on the road to pursue a divine future. Yet Woodhull became one of the greatest lecturers of her time, with Tennie running a close second. Both sisters were so charismatic that as many as ten thousand people rushed to hear their avant-garde lectures on sex, politics, business, race, prostitution, marriage, divorce, and free love. Even at the age of sixty-four, Tennie twice commanded a sellout crowd of seven thousand cheering fans at London's Royal Albert Hall.

The two shocked the world while racking up amazing "firsts." Half a century before women could vote, Woodhull made her historic presidential bid. Tennie was the second woman (after Elizabeth Cady Stanton) to run for Congress. Woodhull was the first woman in history to address a congressional committee. The sisters became the first women to publish a successful radical weekly that dealt with finance and muckraking decades before Theodore Roosevelt coined the pejorative term for hard-nosed reporting. They fought for women's rights, labor issues, sex education, Spiritualism, and "free love"— a maligned term that could mean anything from fighting for divorce reform to choosing a lover whenever one felt like it. *Woodhull & Claflin's Weekly* devoted itself to the person Victoria Woodhull thought most highly of, herself, and to her quest for fame as the first woman to run for president of the United States.

They were the only women who could cavort with capitalists and Communists alike, from Vanderbilt to Karl Marx. They simultaneously operated on Wall Street, exposed the graft of financiers they observed, and then published the first English-language version of *The Communist Manifesto* in America. They formed the English-speaking section of Karl Marx's New

York International, and Tennie marched at the head of a famed Manhattan parade carrying the flag in honor of massacred Paris Commune leaders.

A bodacious beauty in her early twenties, Tennie stunned audiences when she said that women who married for money were "legalized prostitutes," no better, and in most cases ethically worse, than streetwalkers. The sisters championed sex education for adolescents, called for testing for sexual diseases in clients as well as prostitutes, and advocated for contraception decades before Margaret Sanger—outrageous concepts in this era of stifling hypocrisy. Now, 144 years after they began electrifying the country, their ideas remain controversial. The sisters railed against the restrictions of everything from corsets to all-male law courts. Tennie advanced a cause that still creates a stir: training women for army combat. During Reconstruction, when violence erupted over the status of freed blacks, Tennie scandalized Manhattan by commanding an all-black regiment as its honorary colonel.

The sisters also swore they had a supernatural gift, communing with the dead, and Woodhull became a leader in the immensely popular Spiritualist movement.

For a brief time they were heroines of the militant arm of the suffrage movement, and Victoria, with Tennie at her side, historically addressed a congressional committee on women's suffrage in 1871. The first black male voted in March of 1870, a few weeks after the sisters' historic Wall Street brokerage house opening, but women's suffrage, threatened by fractious infighting, seemed as distant a goal as it was twenty-two years before, when Elizabeth Cady Stanton began her 1848 crusade at Seneca Falls. The sisters annoyed establishment suffragists by arguing that the right to vote was meaningless if it meant electing the same timid or corrupt white males. Women must be elected, yes, but the vote was nothing if it was not coupled with economic independence. Although some laws had changed by 1870, fathers or husbands still essentially owned women.

The sisters not only preached free love—which was also referred to by the more demure name of "social freedom"—but also practiced it, discarding husbands and lovers as they liked. Tennie was the strongest in decrying a sexual double standard, and she defended prostitutes, calling them victims in a hypocritical society where rich men patronized them but continued to be honored as respectable citizens.

In the Victorian age, men made the social as well as legal rules. If a wife conducted a circumspect affair, it was often tolerated, but to break the rules openly with a public lover and to divorce meant punishment, shunning, and ruin for her. In speaking out, the sisters broke a cardinal system by exposing what society wanted hidden.

In nine tumultuous years—1868 to 1877—they went from rags to riches to rags again. They were reviled and loved. They were called tramps, prostitutes, harlots, and, conversely, Joans of Arc: brave, courageous, and misunderstood.

They were survivors, sometimes barely, in a Manhattan that in 1868 was reinventing itself as a center of finance with the emergence of *nouveau riche* and bohemian cadres, and where, according to contemporary police reports, prostitution and crime were unequaled. It was a time when Ulysses S. Grant's administration was famed for being totally corruptible and when Boss Tweed still ruled Albany, Manhattan's City Hall, and all points in between. All this was conducted under a public code of Victorian prudery and a double standard that subjugated women as wifely slaves or mere ornaments.

But the sisters lost any claim to respectability, and a place in the suffrage movement, when they charged in their *Weekly* newspaper and on the lecture stage that the most famous preacher in America, Henry Ward Beecher, had conducted adulterous affairs with his parishioners. One presumed cuckolded husband was Theodore Tilton, handsome Adonis of freethinkers, abolitionist, fighter for women's rights, free love advocate, and on-and-off friend of Abraham Lincoln's. He was also thought to be one of Victoria's lovers.

It was not Beecher's adultery that drove the sisters to expose him, they insisted, but the hypocrisy of a man who preached faithfulness and did not practice it. In the same issue of their newspaper, Tennie penned an article charging a Wall Street financier with raping a virgin, and as a result, both sisters were thrown in jail on the charge of sending obscene material through the mail.

Then, when all seemed lost, the sisters shocked enemies, friends, and probably themselves with a grand final act of hobnobbing with British royalty and enjoying stupendous wealth that lasted for decades.

As for discovering who the sisters really were, while trying to assess the variety of opinions, facts, and falsehoods that exist, I was reminded of a reprobate editor who early on in my journalism career admonished, "Never let the facts stand in the way of a good feature story." I have discovered that this problematic guidance also tempts historians and biographers. After generations of mythmaking, it is difficult, if not impossible, to separate fact from fiction regarding the sisters. Everything written about them is a snarled knot of conjecture, hearsay, fabrication, perceptions of the times, and, yes, some facts.

Historical research is always an investigative attempt to define who people really were, but the Scarlet Sisters—which I have dubbed them for their ability to thoroughly shock Victorians and garner infamy—remain maddening enigmas. The first biography of Woodhull, *The Terrible Siren*, with peripheral attention paid to Tennie, did not appear until decades after the sisters' march on Manhattan and just after their deaths (Tennie's in 1923 and Victoria's in 1927). In the book, novelist Emanie Sachs sought sensationalism over facts, paying anarchist Benjamin Tucker, a friend turned enemy of the sisters, $3,500 to produce his account of losing his virginity at nineteen to thirty-four-year-old Victoria, and to describe Tennie's sexual advances. Tucker was an old man when he told his tale to Sachs, who used his material lavishly and did not divulge to readers the hefty price she had paid for it. Victoria died shortly before the book was published—much to the relief of Sachs, who triumphantly wrote to a friend that families of the dead cannot sue for libel, even if the dear departed were called "prostitutes."

If Tucker's tale is true, it dramatized a freewheeling arrangement that fit the love-for-love's-sake definition of free love, with Victoria's husband looking the other way and sister Tennie ready to substitute for Victoria if Tucker was so inclined. If he exaggerated, there was no one left to complain.

Victoria's mortified daughter, Zula Maud, then in her sixties and living in England, considered suing but decided to devote her life to writing a biography of her mother, an unsuccessful effort.

Sachs's machinations in pursuit of scandal remain paramount factors in the cloudy history of the sisters. She repeated gossip as fact and treated much of Victoria's dubious accounts as gospel. For much of the twentieth century, Sachs's book—which contains no attributions, notes, or index—was followed as fact or used in fictionalized books masquerading as biographies, with made-up scenes and dialogue, but after the 1970s rebirth of feminism, sympathetic portrayals of the sisters emerged by women authors. Historical battles among authors continue. Two recent biographies of the sisters' friend Commodore Vanderbilt tangle over whether he had syphilis or "merely" gonorrhea or neither of these diseases that plagued rich and poor bounders alike in the Victorian era of brothel hopping.

Newspapers in the sisters' heyday showed biases that deflect from balanced accounts. Yet these printed perceptions are vital from a historical perspective, illuminating contemporary attitudes toward crucial events involving the sisters. Sporting magazines, the forerunners to contemporary tabloids, broadcast the sisters' every move, with illustrations that depicted them as hard-featured Jezebels. Forget the idea that celebrity journalism and paparazzi blitzes are relatively modern. A glance at the cartoons, daguerreotypes, blazing headlines, and gossip about the sisters proves that celebrity-chasing was virulent in the Victorian age. The publicity-savvy sisters in turn used the press as much as the press used them. Famous authors Henry James and Harriet Beecher Stowe even immortalized them as shady characters in their novels.

But just as suspect were the sisters' own accounts of their lives. Over the years, they revamped, embellished, or reinvented themselves when it suited their purpose—nothing new in an era where a thief one day could make a fortune the next and needed a pedigree to go with his millionaire trappings.

A crucial example is the "as told to" biographical sketch of Woodhull written by Theodore Tilton, the alleged cuckold in the Beecher scandal. It is lively and lurid, self-aggrandizing, draped in purple prose, and soaked in sentimentality. Victoria orchestrated the tale with several agendas in mind. Paramount was a vendetta against her parents for airing dirty family linen in a court scandal that was wrecking the sisters' fame and future. Victoria also needed to woo the popular Spiritualist movement with declarations of sensational supernatural ghostly powers. She alleged that she was in a trance when, in 1871, at the age of thirty-two, she related the account to her current husband, Colonel Blood, who took notes. Handsome Theodore Tilton, who needed to curry favor with Woodhull, polished this melodramatic extravaganza for his magazine. All too often it has been cited as complete fact.

In this book, for the first time, Tennie is given the attention she deserves, and has been resurrected from a footnote in her sister's life. She played a far larger role than biographers intent solely on Woodhull have portrayed. Contemporary papers gave her more coverage than Victoria before her older sister's drive for the presidency and fame during the Beecher scandal. I have uncovered her fascinating life after Manhattan, previously ignored, including accounts of her married role as doyenne of a London estate and of her castle in Portugal, intimate letters between her and her sister, and accounts of her globe-trotting crusade for women's rights.

The sisters were intriguing characters. They sought riches while pursuing Communist goals, arguing that they had to possess wealth in order to do good. They crawled out of a hustler's childhood of fleecing females as well as males to champion an unheard-of concept in Victorian times: equal pay for women. They fought for female sexual independence when at the same time they may have sold themselves to rich men to earn money for their cause.

They were among the very few Victorian women who knew how to play the male game. As cunning as they were stunning, they crusaded for women's freedom from men yet were nonetheless tough, and sometimes unscrupulous, pragmatists who adopted male rules. They courted and used powerful men in an era when women had no power themselves. With charm and beauty, they turned the tables on males, taking credit while using men to help them in their careers. Yet they were capable of stirring, heroic bravery by espousing unpopular radical humanitarian causes—even as they were recklessly outrageous, extravagant liars, and at times, extremely unprincipled. Initially pushed and prodded by their con artist father, they learned how to survive as fabulists. They moved through life (with men) by their wits, indigenous street smarts, and intelligence, while fighting with feminist fervency for radical causes more than a hundred years ahead of their time.

Theirs was a wild ride through America during and following the Civil War. Along the way, their lives intersected with those of a cast of characters who are real but who, dare I say, read like fiction. Most were famous or infamous during this riveting time in history, and many remain so today (see Cast of Characters).

No American women in history surpass their raging, life-devouring, and life-enhancing journey from pre–Civil War days, through their Victorian battles, down to their final years as two Roaring Twenties *grande dames* having secured their place in history.

Opening Scene: Arriving

On a crisp February morning in 1870, the most dazzling and flamboyant sisters in American history made their debut. Victoria Woodhull and Tennessee Claflin had plotted, cajoled, and advertised and had been written up with besotted fervor in major New York newspapers by male reporters stunned by their beauty and daring.

As their open carriage turned the corner at Wall Street and Broad, the sisters could see the mob moving toward their brand-new Woodhull, Claflin and Co. brokerage firm. Estimates of the crowd reached two thousand and up. One hundred policemen were called out to keep order. Here they were! The first lady stockbrokers in the world! Wall Street had never seen anything like it. Nor would it again for nearly a hundred years.

The buzz on the Street, abetted by the sisters, was that the coarse, ruthless, and immensely rich—in fact, the richest man in America—Cornelius Vanderbilt had bankrolled the young beauties.

Males eagerly grabbed the reins of the high-stepping horses and, as the sisters descended lightly from the carriage, shouts, cheers, jeers, and catcalls shattered the air. The sisters pushed their way through the boisterous crowd held back by policemen, opened the door, and went to work. All day, men peered in the windows and doors of Woodhull and Claflin and whooped with surprise and pleasure if they caught a glimpse of one of the sisters. A doorkeeper guarded the entrance. Nailed on the door was a sign: GENTLEMEN WILL STATE THEIR BUSINESS AND THEN RETIRE AT ONCE.

The mysterious sisters, who seemed to have stepped out from nowhere, had made the splash they wanted. Everything had been staged "to secure the most general and at the same time prominent introduction to the world that was possible," Victoria later admitted.

They had carefully picked their outfits, gambling correctly that a large crowd would scrutinize them on the most crucial day of their lives. Everything matched, as if they were twins, although Victoria, at thirty-one, was seven years older than Tennie. Their skirts were shockingly short, touching the tops of their shiny boots, unlike fashionable dresses that trailed through the muck and manure of Manhattan's streets. Their suit jackets were deep blue wool nipped at the waist but mannishly wide at the shoulders. Rich velvet embroidered the jackets, adding a feminine touch. But gone were the tightly laced corsets that warped a woman's insides and made breathing difficult. Absent, too, were bustles, those steel half-cages filled with horsehair that were strapped to petticoats and draped with heavy brocade and silk that could weigh a woman down by twenty pounds. One cartoon likened the woman who wore one to a snail, with the bustle forming the curlicue shell dragged behind. Instead of ruffles or jewelry, the sisters wore silk bow ties. Their light brown hair had been cut boyishly short; Tennie derided the fashionable nest of curls and chignons as "vile bunches of hair, tortured into all conceivable unnatural shapes." They'd added a rakish final touch: each had tucked a solid gold pen behind an ear, to flash in the noonday sun or catch the gaslight's glow.

The sisters were showstoppingly beautiful, and their unique costumes only added to their allure. Victoria was willowy and gazed at the world through luminous, intensely blue eyes. High cheekbones gave her broad face character, and her proud, chiseled profile could have graced an ivory cameo. Tennie, at twenty-four, was the epitome of the term "pleasingly plump," with a bosom that threatened to burst from her jacket and a sensuous, full mouth that curved into flirtatious smiles. There was mischief in her blue eyes, and she had the exuberance of an untamed colt.

Reporters gushed endlessly about the "Bewitching Brokers" and the "Queens of Finance." They mentioned "their exquisite figures." Reporters seemed astounded that women could be articulate: "They display remarkable conversational powers, Mrs. Claflin [Tennie] in particular talking with a rapidity and fluency that are really astonishing." The gold pens behind their ears were the talk of the "gouty old war horses on the street." The two women were praised, albeit as though they were a P. T. Barnum oddity: with one paper remarking that, at the end of their opening day, the ladies drove away "without any signs of headaches."

Two dandies constantly dropped by the offices of Woodhull and Claflin on opening day, changing hats and outfits to mock the women brokers. Once, the men sauntered in wearing matching dress coats with polished blue buttons, pearl-colored pantaloons, and green kid gloves. When they tried to trap the sisters by asking " 'how Central stood,' Claflin sprang to the [Teletype ticker] and shouted 'Before call 94 ½.' " Remarked the *Herald*, these jokesters "realize for the first time that young ladies can be wise and discreet, and young men rash and foolish." When one visitor told the sisters they would lose money, Woodhull tartly replied they had not come to Wall Street to "lose money, but to make money."

The sisters told the eager Wall Street reporters a disarming tale of fortitude and spunk. Unable to penetrate the exclusive male Stock Exchange, Woodhull said that "solely through agents in the street," they had parlayed business earnings to make about $700,000 before they opened their firm. In today's dollars, that would have made them multimillionaires, if their claim was true. She then remarked with an air of nonchalance, " 'What do present profits amount to when it costs us over $2,600 a month to live?' " The reporter never asked what these staggering expenses could be, in a bad economic period when working-class poor made $200 a year.

Tennie said that "natural aptitude" and early training in business management had equipped her for finance. "I studied law in my father's office six years. My father was once a very successful merchant, and possessor of a large fortune. He lost it mainly in speculation." Their father's financial ruin had made it necessary for them to earn a profitable living, but their "very good education" and legal skills made it impossible to "settle down into the common course of life" of other women. Victoria wove tales of spectacular success in land deals, followed by investments in oil and "railroad stocks," mentioning, among others, Vanderbilt's New York Central and Hudson River Railroad.

The stories told by the sisters made for sympathetic reading: learning law at the knee of a spectacularly rich father, obtaining an education unusual for women at that time, starting a business at a young age. All gave an image of great enterprise.

There was just one problem. Most of it was false.

ACT ONE

CHAPTER ONE

Vicky

Victoria and Tennie's father, Reuben Buck Claflin, was a one-eyed snake oil salesman who posed as a doctor and a lawyer. By the time Victoria and Tennie were born, he was not professional at anything but thievery, blackmailing, and forcing his youngest to join the family quack cure scam. Earlier he had studied some law, but in an era when rigorous policing of the legal profession was unknown, anyone could hang a sign outside his door. Aside from offering legal advice, he also ferried timber down the Susquehanna River and worked in saloons. In 1825, Buck married Roxanna Hummel, known as Annie. She has been identified in books as the niece of a prosperous tavern owner or the illegitimate maid in that establishment. When they moved to Cleveland, Ohio, in the 1830s, construction of the Ohio and Erie Canal brought hopes of real estate riches.

Rough workmen may have gambled in a saloon owned by Buck, but there seemed no legitimate way to make the fortune he claimed to have made. He bragged about making half a million dollars, an incredible fortune, in frenzied real estate speculation. He supposedly lost it all in the 1837 depression, which makes him either a liar about owning this sum in the first place or a very poor manager of money. When Buck settled in obscure Homer, Ohio, some neighbors reckoned he was escaping the law. One legend claims that after selling some horses, he had to race out of one town before it rained and destroyed the horses' shiny coat—of black paint. Buck was approached by a lawman, went another story, while trying to pass counterfeit money. To avoid arrest, Buck ripped the bills up, stuffed them in his mouth, and ate them.

By the time his wife, Annie, had borne ten children—two boys and eight girls, although three of the girls died young—Buck's idea of heavy lifting was making his daughters do the work. As luck would have it, in one of the curious miracles of genetic mutation, the one-eyed Buck and his slattern wife, described by all who met her in later life as an unpleasant old hag, spawned three beautiful daughters among the five living. Buck saw riches in his daughters, starting with the least beautiful and eldest, Margaret, and then her sister, Mary (known also as Polly). There were rumors that he pimped for these two and for Utica, the most beautiful of all the sisters, who was born between Victoria and Tennie.

He touted Victoria and Tennie as fortune-tellers, faith healers, and clairvoyants who spoke to the dead. The sisters themselves professed clairvoyant powers, but Tennie later admitted that she was forced to "humbug" in order to get enough money to feed the family. Throughout her life, Victoria clung to her claim of communion with famous ghosts such as Demosthenes and assorted angels, and of the odd chat with Napoléon, Joséphine, and, when she needed to impress, the spirit of Jesus Christ. An intriguing legend vested mother Roxanna, who could not read or write, with a remarkable gift of memory; it was said that after the Bible was read to her, she could recite entire passages, chapter and verse, from memory.

Victoria was born on September 23, 1838, in Homer, an insignificant hamlet, like many frontier outposts. One lurid, unsubstantiated tale describes her mother, in a wild religious frenzy, babbling in tongues at a revival tent meeting, whereupon Buck dragged her to the back of the tent and fell upon her with equal enthusiasm. Thus Victoria was supposedly conceived in a manner that would have been the devil's handiwork had it not come from passions aroused by religious ecstasy, as some might put it. She was born a few months after Queen Victoria was crowned, so any such consummation was now prettified with the crowning of the child as

"Victoria." When the family was in a good mood the child was referred to as their queen who would someday be famous.

"It is my destiny," Victoria would say.

Tennie, born seven years later, on October 26, 1845, was the last child to survive.

As an adult, Victoria recounted to her biographer, Theodore Tilton, a writer thought to be her lover, a childhood filled with Dickensian debauchery, far from the fancies told to Wall Street reporters. No one could have predicted any life for the sisters except prostitution, domestic servitude, or marriage to drunken wife beaters, trailed by a passel of children. They had no education or social position to pursue anything else.

"She was worked like a slave—whipped like a convict. Her father was impartial in his cruelty to all his children," wrote Tilton. He described her mother—whom Victoria claimed was "never wholly sane"—as having "a fickleness of spirit that renders her one of the most erratic of mortals," and who "sometimes abetted him in his scourgings [*sic*], and at other times shielded the little ones from his blows." Buck soaked braided green willow switches in water to produce a sharp sting, and with these weapons "he would cut the quivery flesh of the children till their tears and blood melted him into mercy." Tilton continued: "Sometimes he took a handsaw or a stick of firewood as the instrument of his savagery." Coming home late and learning of some offense, he would wake the children and "whip them till morning." One rebellious son, Maldon, ran away at thirteen and "still bears in a shattered constitution the damning memorial of his father's wrath."

Victoria did not spare her mother. Wrote Tilton, "She on occasions tormented and harried her children until they would be thrown into spasms, whereat she would hysterically laugh, clap her hands, and look as fiercely delighted as a cat in playing with a mouse. At other times, her tenderness toward her offspring would appear almost angelic. She would fondle them, weep over them, lift her arms and thank God for such children, caress them with ecstatic joy, and then smite them as if seeking to destroy at a blow both body and soul."

Victoria dressed up the Claflin home in her adult account, describing it as a white-painted cottage with a long porch and a flower garden. Homer residents remembered it as an unpainted shack with a porch so rickety the boards rattled when children raced across them.

Neighbors stayed away from the Claflin house, which was ruled by a father with a suspect reputation and a religious fanatic mother given to babbling at a moonlit sky until foam appeared on her lips. Annie claimed distinguished German ancestors. A former neighbor guffawed. "I read of their claims of ancestry: the 'Hummels of Germany.' And who were they? The most ignorant country people of the county were the 'Dutch Hummels' as they were called." Another neighbor remembered, "No properly trained child was considered in good company when associating with the little girls of the Claflin family, therefore my visits to their home were always without leave." She added, "The Claflin house was a little three or at most four room affair...the furnishings and surroundings were of the most primitive possible description."

Revival meetings transfixed Annie, who would twirl in violent religious ecstasy, speaking in tongues and shouting, "Hallelujah!" She would rise in her pew, beginning with a soft clapping of hands, then sway to and fro for a moment before gliding into the aisle and spinning rapidly round and round, "twirling all the way up the aisle, hollering 'aglory!!' She would finally sink down in front of the altar in a state of exhaustion that was called by herself and her family a 'trance.'"

The sisters were not well educated, as they claimed to Wall Street reporters. Tilton's sketch described Victoria's schooling as "less than three years" of broken intervals from age eight to eleven. However, he wrote, she was "the pet alike of scholars and teacher," with "an inward energy such as quickened the young blood of Joan of Arc...The little old head on the little young shoulders was often bent over her school-book at the midnight hour." A few years after Tilton's biography was printed, Victoria strangely and flatly dismissed this. "I am a self made [sic] woman entirely," she declared. "Never spent one year in the school room."

Victoria was not, as Tilton claimed, a popular child. Some in Homer saw her beauty but pitied the fact that she was a Claflin. The woman from whom the children bought milk remembered them running wild, dirty, and hungry, waiting for snacks at her back door. When Buck's brother joined him in Homer, the two large families lived together "in turmoil. Beds were everywhere; in the cellar, the parlor, anywhere room could be found and were never made and rarely changed."

The pre–Civil War years were a time of revivalist "child preachers," who allegedly had a special gift of holiness. Victoria copied them, loving the drama, staring down neighbor children with her intense blue eyes. Already a showman, she faced the "sinners" before her, lashing out at their "terrible sins."

Unquestionably Victoria and Tennie were intuitively smart and quick-witted. Victoria's later great oratorical skills, which kept thousands spellbound, stemmed from her ability to read a page once and commit it to memory. If her mother's talent at memorizing large portions of the Bible, which she could not read, was true, Victoria may indeed have inherited the gift of total recall. Tennie's ebullient street smarts and confidence also won over audiences, well into the thousands. Everyone remarked that the sisters were a decided cut above their squabbling clan, although Tennie was more of a hoyden, and could dip into slang and jokes with ease.

A neighbor recalled that there was something spooky about the Claflins. "The family always bore the reputation and were looked upon by the neighbors as being in some way 'uncanny,' the eldest daughter being mesmerized by several traveling professors and relating marvelous tales of things she had seen and known while 'out of the body.'"

Victoria could not have survived, she claimed, without her visions, her comforting conversations with ghosts during her childhood as a "household drudge, serving others so long as they were awake, and serving herself only when they slept." Her version of her childhood as recounted to Tilton made Cinderella's sound pampered: "Had she been born black, or been chained to a cart-wheel in Alabama, she could not have been a more enslaved slave." Later, living with her older married sister Margaret "Meg" Miles and her family, Victoria "made fires, she washed and ironed, she baked bread, she cut wood, she spaded a vegetable garden, she went on errands, she tended infants, she did everything."

Buck and Roxanna's "eccentricities" were reproduced in all their children—"except Victoria and Tennie," wrote Tilton, singling out the sister partners as noble. The others were "leeches." "They love and hate—they do good and evil—they bless and smite each other...For years there has been one common sentiment sweetly pervading the breasts" of the Claflin siblings, "namely, a determination that Victoria and Tennie should earn all the money for the support of the numerous remainder of the Claflin tribe—wives, husbands, children, servants, and all...Victoria is a green leaf, and her legion of relatives are caterpillars who devour her."

Tales (not mentioned by Tilton) of the Claflin clan's sudden departure from Homer depict Buck as the supreme con man, remembered by neighbors as allegedly setting fire to his empty gristmill to get the insurance money. Small-town folks didn't take kindly to cheating, and there was talk of tarring and feathering him. He vanished in the night, while Homer residents took up a collection to get the rest of the family out of town. After the departure of Claflin, who had been appointed postmaster, the community found undelivered envelopes on which senders had written, "Money enclosed." The envelopes had been opened; the money was gone.

In 1853 the Claflins traveled to the town of Mount Gilead, Ohio, where the oldest sister, Meg Miles, was living with her husband and brood. In Mount Gilead, Victoria soon became a child bride. The marriage between her, scarcely fifteen, and her twenty-eight-year-old bridegroom, Canning Woodhull, was a "fellowship of misery—and her parents, who abetted it, ought to have prevented it," wrote Tilton. "From the endurable cruelty of her parents, she fled to the unendurable cruelty of her husband."

As Victoria was scandalously divorced from Woodhull at the time Tilton was writing her biography, and embroiled in a front-page family ruckus involving her current husband, it was prudent to paint her first husband as dark as possible. She needed to portray herself as an innocent child so tormented in marriage that a Victorian-age divorce would have seemed acceptable.

When fourteen-year-old Victoria became feverish one day, "Dr. Canning Woodhull, a gay rake, whose habits were kept hidden from her under the general respectability of his family connections, attended her. Coming as a prince, he found her as Cinderella—a child of the ashes," wrote Tilton. He invited Victoria to a Fourth of July picnic. She sold apples to buy a pair of shoes for the occasion. On the way home he said to her, "My little puss, tell your father and mother that I want you for a wife."

Victoria is depicted in this sketch as a startled innocent who beseeched her parents to save her. This does not ring true. Canning was a handsome doctor who said he was from a refined East Coast family. Surely to a child who dreamed of power and her own glory, and who fully believed she would one day ride in a fine carriage, he must have seemed a magical escape from her dreary life. Her story continued: "But the parents, as if not unwilling to be rid of a daughter whose sorrow was ripening her into a woman before her time, were delighted at the unexpected offer. They thought it a grand match." Victoria also admitted that she soon looked at the marriage as "an escape from the parental yoke."

On September 23, 1853, Victoria celebrated her fifteenth birthday. Two months later, on November 23, she celebrated her wedding—yet, all her life, she would say she was married at fourteen, to throw an even more helpless cast on the union. "On the third night," her husband "broke her heart by remaining away all night at a house of ill-repute. . . . she learned, to her dismay, that he was habitually unchaste, and given to long fits of intoxication. . . She grew ten years older in a single day. Six weeks after her marriage (during which time her husband was mostly with his cups and his mistresses), she discovered a letter addressed to him in a lady's elegant penmanship, 'Did you marry that child because she too was *en famille?*'" On the day of his marriage, Woodhull had "sent away into the country a mistress" who gave birth to his child.

"He suddenly put his wife into the humblest quarters, where, left mostly to herself, she dwelt in bitterness of spirit, aggravated...by learning of his ordering baskets of champagne and drinking himself drunk in the company of harlots." At this point the couple was residing in Chicago, probably because Canning could make a better living in this bustling frontier city, known in those days as far out West. However, his drinking left him incapable of functioning. Wrote Tilton, extravagantly, "Through rain and sleet, half clad and shivering, she would track him to his dens," compelling him to return. Other nights, she would wait by the window until she heard him "languidly shuffling along the pavement with the staggering reel of a drunken man, in the shameless hours of the morning."

Somehow Canning had found time to impregnate his wife. In retelling the birth, Tilton poured on the pathos: "In the dead of winter, with icicles clinging to her bedpost, and attended only by her half-drunken husband, she brought forth in almost mortal agony her first-born child." For icicles to have found their way to bedposts, the temperature would have to have been mighty frigid, but miracle of miracles, Victoria and even the newborn babe survived. A neighbor brought her food and wrapped the baby in a blanket and took it "to a happier mother in the near neighborhood" to nurse the infant.

Her firstborn child became the real sorrow of Victoria's life, one that would haunt her and spur her lifelong interest in eugenics, her arguments for planned parenting by the most physically and mentally pure, and her fight against loveless marriages. She blamed Canning's drunkenness, and their empty union, for the son she bore on that last day of December 1854: "Her child, begotten in drunkenness, and born in squalor, was a half idiot; predestined to be a hopeless imbecile for life." The son, named Byron, would live a long life. In 1871, at the age of sixteen, he was "a sad and pitiful spectacle in his mother's house...where he roams from room to room, muttering noises more sepulchral than human; a daily agony to the woman who bore him." Byron also displayed an "uncommon sweetness," wrote Tilton, that won "everyone's love, doubles everyone's pity."

One visitor to the brokerage office who often witnessed Byron during the period Tilton described said, "He was almost a complete idiot...

although he had the Claflin beauty...Generally he sat on a lounge for a time, and then would rise and walk *very rapidly* about ten feet, back and forth, mumbling, grimacing and drooling. After five or ten minutes of this he would resume his seat, and remain for a short time comparatively quiet. The alternation went on continually. When his mother was in the office, she at times would seat herself beside him and fondle him. I thought then that she did so out of sincere maternal affection."

Other than Victoria's martyrdom, and the continuing, vain hope that Canning Woodhull would reform, the rest of their time in Chicago is a blank, except for one melodramatic scene after Canning stayed away for a month. He was "keeping a mistress at a fashionable boarding-house, under the title of wife." Victoria "sallied forth into the wintry street, clad in a calico dress without undergarments, and shod only with India-rubbers without shoes or stockings, entered the house, confronted the household as they sat at table." Her tale drew tears from everyone, and the listeners "compelled the harlot to pack her trunk and flee the city, and shamed the husband into creeping like a spaniel back into the kennel" called home.

Victoria no doubt embellished accounts of her husband's behavior, but he did end up an alcoholic and morphine addict. And she was legally helpless to leave him. Like all married women, she was literally her husband's property, as were any children she would bear. In most states, he lawfully had the right to beat her. In a divorce, he had the right to take the children. Even if he had had money, she would not have gotten any if she had instituted a divorce. Though the Claflins were hardly of a social class where a divorce scandal would have tainted the entire family, Victoria was nonetheless crushed, and trapped by the rules of the day.

Tilton gives no date for Victoria's next giant leap: impulsively taking her damaged child and drunken husband with her to San Francisco, during an unspecified time (probably in 1857 or 1858). Victoria was desperate enough, with no money or livelihood, to bravely strike out on a torturous journey that took nearly two months by sea, and more if they went from Chicago in covered wagon through dangerous Indian Territory. Her usually histrionic descriptions are startlingly absent regarding this trip to the coast and their life there. One can even wonder if she might not have made up the San Francisco journey to hide her Midwest life, as here her story becomes elusive. How the young mother who described her Chicago existence as penniless, her clothes meager, and her lodgings squalid found the money for the trip or how they could afford a place to live, or where they settled in San Francisco, are unmentioned. If true, the venture seems to have been an impulsive disaster that lasted less than a year.

In the wake of the 1849 gold rush, San Francisco had grown up. Miners' shacks and shanties had given way to substantial brick houses, the U.S. Mint had built headquarters there, vigilante committees fussed about cleaning up crime in red-light districts, mud streets were being paved with cobblestones and earthquake tremors dutifully tracked. Levi Strauss had opened a store to sell his denims to the miners who still flocked to the surrounding hills. San Francisco had its streets of frontier bawdiness; the Barbary Coast, with its bars and brothels, remained a treacherous den of thieves. Newcomers arrived daily on ships that clogged the harbor, hoping to grab their share of gold.

Canning's drinking continued, and Victoria found herself "support-ing the man by whom she ought to have been supported." Who cared for Byron is not explained by Tilton. Victoria answered an ad for a "cigar girl" in a tobacco emporium, which were notoriously fronts for broth-els. Behind the slim sampling of cigars, girls were supposed to sell favors instead of cheroots. These establishments were routine in large cities. To demonstrate just how vulgar cigar stores were considered, an 1870 guide to Manhattan brothels noted that a cigar girl was low on the list. Custom-ers ranged from fatherly judges to toughly aggressive youths. Newspapers warned impoverished women about the "great evil consequent upon very beautiful girls being placed in cigar stores," where customers "ultimately affect her ruin."

Why Victoria cited this dubious job in an otherwise meager account of her life in San Francisco seems strange, unless it was an attempt to prove herself innocent of prostitution. Tilton wrote that the "blushing, modest, and sensitive" Victoria was fired after one day because she was "too fine" for the job. The proprietor in this sordid occupation allegedly gave Victoria a twenty-dollar gold piece, puzzlingly generous compensation for a young woman he had just fired.

Victoria then became a seamstress, her needle being the "only weapon many women possess wherewith to fight the battle of life," continued Tilton. There are no clues as to how long she performed this job, an exhausting process of hand-stitching, before sewing machines were in general use. One day, "She chanced to come upon Anna Cogswell," an actress, who wanted a seamstress. Victoria complained that she could not make enough money sewing, so Cogswell told her she should go on the stage. Just like that, Victoria was "engaged as a lesser light to the Cogswell star." In those days, actresses were considered part of the shady demimonde, with stage door Johnnies waiting for a trophy in exchange for a late supper.

With Victoria's quick memory, she learned the part, and for six weeks earned fifty-two dollars a week. "Never leave the stage," admiring fellow performers urged. Victoria allegedly said she was meant for something higher. Then, while "clad in a pink silk dress and slippers, acting in the ballroom scene in the Corsican Brothers, suddenly a spirit-voice told her 'Victoria, come home!'" In her vision, she saw Tennie, "then a mere child—standing by her mother," calling her to return. She raced out, still in her "dramatic adornments, through a foggy rain to her hotel. She packed up her few clothes, Canning, and Byron and grabbed the morning steamer for New York." On board, her "spiritual states" produced "profound excitement among the passengers."

Mother Annie, wrote Tilton, had told Tennie—at the same time Victoria saw the vision—"to send the spirits after Victoria to bring her home."

The spirits may have been calling, but it was their mother who wanted Victoria back, to help support the family. With Victoria home, they now had another golden goose to put to work.

CHAPTER TWO

Tennie

When the newly married Victoria moved away in 1853, she had left behind eight-year-old Tennie, who would never know a normal childhood or a schoolroom. Tennessee Celeste Claflin, born on October 26, 1845, was reportedly named after one of the many states the wandering Claflins visited. Or, as another legend has it, Buck named her for the state his favorite president, James Polk, represented while in Congress. As the baby, she was alternately coddled and neglected in this sprawling, squalling family of parents and older sisters who returned with their children, extended families, and assorted husbands between divorces. None of the Claflin clan seemed congenitally able to stay married for long. The fighting continued when the family moved to the home of older sister Margaret Miles. Soon after the Claflins arrived, Margaret's marriage ended when her husband, Enos, the town druggist, caught her in a hotel with another man and chased her down the street with a butcher's knife.

Without Victoria by her side, Tennie became the cash cow for Buck and her mother, whom she later said was "insane on spiritualism." Mary (nicknamed Polly) Sparr, an older sister who picked fights often with Victoria and Tennie, would say that the relationship between their mother and Tennie was "something I cannot explain; something mysterious, unnatural. There is a different feeling between Tennie and my mother than between any child and her mother I ever knew." All her life, Tennie seemed unable to break the bond, even when her mother's outrageous acts threatened to ruin the sisters' lives. She would cry out at her mother's crazy meddling, but say, "I love her dearly anyway."

This strange bonding occurred when Tennie was sold by her mother and father to the public as Buck's "Wonder Child." "Since I was eleven years old I used to tell fortunes with her," Tennie said of her mother. Tennie hated her life, and felt trapped and alone without Victoria. By 1860, when Tennie was fourteen, Buck decided that she should be a solo act in his snake oil "shows." The family rode into midwestern frontier hamlets in a painted wagon, baubles dancing on the bright canopy as the wagon lurched through mud and dirt. Tennie was prominently displayed, sitting up front by her father's side, so villagers could see the smiling blue-eyed girl with golden brown curls and rosy cheeks. Ads were placed in local papers inviting the public to meet A WONDERFUL CHILD! MISS TENNESSEE CLAFLIN.

Born with "supernatural gifts," as the ad read, Tennie could ascertain a person's "former, present and future partners," and "when required will go into an unconscious state." Only a snake oil salesman could have invented the list of ills Tennie could cure: from cold sores to cancer and any disorder that had "baffled the best physicians for years. She may be consulted at her room from the hours of eight a.m. to nine o'clock p.m. Price of consultation, $1.00." Tennie sat there for thirteen long hours a day, learning the art of listening to people, picking up clues, and spinning fortunes that would please. Buck collected the money and sold "Miss Tennessee's Magnetio Life Elixir," a worthless concoction with a picture of Tennie on the label, at two dollars a bottle.

When the Claflin caravan entered Ottawa, Illinois, in 1863, Buck set up an infirmary where he would callously lead Tennie down a terrible path as a "magic healer."

In presenting his daughters as clairvoyants with supernatural powers, Buck was cashing in on the amazing mania of Spiritualism that transfixed the country from the 1850s through the 1870s. Spiritualists became national celebrities and claimed two million members in a country with a population (in 1855) of only twenty-seven million. Their number would grow, by some estimates, to four million.

When Buck saw the incredible fame being lavished on the two young sisters who had started the Spiritualist craze, he could not help but think of his own two treasures, just waiting to be pushed into the movement. In 1848, when Victoria was ten and Tennie three, Margaret and Kate Fox, sisters in the small upstate town of Hydesville, New York, would become so famous that P. T. Barnum would hire them and countless thousands come to see them. Prominent observers such as Horace Greeley, James Fenimore Cooper, and William Cullen Bryant swore the Fox sisters were authentic. Margaret, in her early teens, and her younger sister, Kate, lived with their parents in an old cottage that groaned with strange noises at night, terrifying their mother. An old peddler had been murdered there and his body was never found, so the story went. One night the mother bolted out of bed when she heard loud rapping noises filling the house. The sisters told their petrified mother that the murdered peddler was speaking to them. If the sisters asked a question, his spirit would rap out the answer. Their older married sister, Leah Fox Fish, brought them to her home in Rochester and charged for their "spirit rapping" sessions. The press and traditional clergy cried fraud, but this only added to the sisters' fame, and the awestruck lined up to see them perform. Leah, a savvy promoter, took her sisters to New York, where P. T. Barnum cleaned up as crowds stormed Barnum's hotel.

Greeley—best known today for his admonition to those seeking a fortune to "Go west, young man"—championed the sisters in his *New-York Daily Tribune*. His wife sought their help in reaching her dead son, just as Mary Todd Lincoln would later, in darkened White House parlors, beg mediums to contact her dead son, Willy. In séances across America, spirit rapping, moans, moving tables, weird music, and wispy astral visions ensured the presence of a ghostly power. Printing presses churned out books on Spiritualism at a fast clip. Mark Twain's editor William Dean Howells, an author in his own right, remembered as an Ohio youth that Spiritualism was "rife in every second house in the village, with manifestations by rappings, table-tipping, and oral and written messages from another world through psychics of either sex, but oftenest the young girls one met in the dances and sleigh-rides."

The movement, however, appealed to more than just the gullible who wanted desperately to speak to loved ones on the "other side" or to those who followed it as a popular fad. For progressive reformers, Spiritualism offered something better than the unforgiving hellfire and damnation that thundered from church pulpits. Instead of being terrorized by a wrathful god, they were graced by angels who wanted only good for them. Many humanitarians felt that the "spirits wanted to make themselves felt in earthly affairs and would, in fact, lead mankind to social regeneration." Utopians, many of whom advocated free love, took up Spiritualism, as did many socialists, abolitionists, and suffragists.

Above all, Spiritualism was a breakthrough for intelligent women who loathed their role as silent partners deemed by society as unfit to speak in public. Spiritualism gave such women a platform, because as mediums, it was acceptable for them to speak, as they were not expressing their own thoughts, but acting as conduits for messages from the dead. Savvy women soon took over the movement. They held forth as lecturers and moved into the homes of the rich and famous to conduct séances.

Spiritualism became a religion, with Spiritualist churches springing up across the country as freethinkers revolted against harsh authoritarian Christian orthodoxy. When no traditional churches ordained women, and many prohibited them from speaking out loud at services, Spiritualist churches embraced women's rights and considered them as equal members. While the movement was easily dismissed because of the charlatans and their tricks—disembodied voices, music, spirit rapping, parlor "ghosts"—serious followers believed there was a scientific basis for it. They argued that "reason" demonstrates that life, at least the soul, continues on in some fashion. In an era when the mind was a mystery—"phrenology [studying the bumps on one's skull] and alchemy still passed for science"— the Spiritualist belief in the "science of the metaphysical" seemed rational. Religious Spiritualists believed that there could be genuine manifestations from the other world. This was, after all, just an extension of accepted religions, which told parishioners that the departed existed in "heaven," that they would meet them one day in the "great by and by."

Belief in Spiritualism's power was strengthened by the amazing—some would say miraculous—changes made by the "culture of invention" during the Industrial Revolution. In just twenty years, from the 1840s to the 1860s, machinery and other inventions transformed Manhattan from a nearly medieval hellhole of no sewers, open-hearth cooking, and outdoor privies into homes with running water, stoves, iceboxes, and central heating. After such changes, anything could be believed. For those who could afford it, that is. Poor immigrants and blacks lived in crowded rat-infested wooden firetrap tenements, with stinking outdoor privies; human waste and horse manure mingled in open sewers that spread lethal diseases. Conditions in New York's slums remained appalling for decades.

Radicals among the young, such as the Claflin sisters, were ready for "any sort of millennium, religious or industrial, that should arrive." The invention of the telegraph, which sent unseen messages long distance, floating by seeming magic through the air, bolstered the belief in the supernatural. One leading Spiritualist journal was even called *The Spiritual Telegraph*.

Tennie believed she had the power, but not to the extent promised to the gullible by Buck. One newspaper carried a story about an injured Civil War soldier with a bullet embedded in his foot who sought her services. As she felt his toes, she blurted out, "Why Captain, you were not wounded in battle," and announced that he had been shot by a rebel sniper. The astounded soldier swore that only he had known this.

Spiritualism eventually withered after large-scale fraud was exposed in the 1880s. At that time, Maggie Fox—descending with her sister into alcoholism, drug addiction, and poverty—hastened the movement's death when she told a large crowd at the New York Academy of Music in 1888 that she and Kate were frauds. They had started their rapping as a gag to rattle their superstitious mother, she admitted, achieving the sound by knocking their toes on wood. Despite such assaults on Spiritualism, the federal census in 1890 listed 334 Spiritualist churches in the United States.

*   *   *

Tennie's expertise, she always claimed, lay in her power to heal the sick magnetically by the laying on of hands. The concept of magnetic healing began in the 1770s, when the German physician Franz Anton Mesmer—whose name was the origin of the word *mesmerized*—articulated a "form of psychic healing that included both magnetic healing and hypnotism." He believed that a force or magnetic fluid linked all beings. "This was not so different from Hindu prana or Chinese chi. His method of laying on of hands and giving suggestions to patients led to the development of therapeutic hypnotism." Mesmer presciently believed that mental attitudes often accompanied physical illnesses and that it was vital for physicians and patients to be in sympathy with one another. He used the French word *rapport*—not then common in the United States—to connote "harmony" or "connection."

The prophetic Mesmer has modern-day psychoanalytic and magnetic healing followers. In his times, however, as with most medical pioneers, envious colleagues called him a fraud, and they persuaded the Viennese Medical Council to oust him. But in more liberal Paris, Mesmer treated the wealthy for large sums and the poor for free. He believed that the laying on of hands "had the power to make the fluid flow from themselves into the patient." He claimed that water immersed in iron rods provided magnetic fields. Despite widespread skepticism in America, magnetic healing became popular among Spiritualists.

Tennie believed in her power as a "clairvoyant physician"—saying that she passed positive and negative magnetic waves through her hands as she rubbed patients—and once bragged to America's leading feminist, Susan B. Anthony, that "I was a very good doctor, I cured a much larger percentage than the regular M.D.'s."

Spiritualism became a nationwide craze and a form of solace throughout the sisters' youth. The specter of death was everywhere then: women dying in childbirth; diseases taking infants, children, and adults. In the 1850s, children under five made up more than half the deaths in New York City. When Tennie was fifteen, Civil War slaughters began. Some 750,000 soldiers were butchered or died of diseases and poor medical treatment. Grieving widows and mothers turned to mediums and

Spiritualism in an aching attempt to commune with lost loves. Into this morass of Civil War grief stepped Buck Claflin, with Tennie at his side.

Tennie ran away at fifteen, but the family found her and dragged her back. She briefly married a flashing dandy named John Bortel, but Buck swiftly ended that. By 1863, Tennie was seventeen, soon to be eighteen in October, but in the ads Buck placed in the newspapers, he shaved off three years, gauging that a child administering his treatment would be more trusted. And he had transformed himself into a doctor: the "King of Cancers," to be exact.

Neighbors in the small town of Ottawa, Illinois, sometimes heard screams floating out of the Fox River House, an abandoned hotel rented by the Claflins, where Buck set up an infirmary to treat cancer patients. In addition to the infirmary, he placed an ad in the local newspaper stating that the Fox River House also taught lessons in the "Cult of Love." He never explained his "Cult of Love," but neighbors looked askance at men who showed up there at night. The two oldest sisters, Margaret and Polly, were there with five children, mother Annie, Tennie, sister Utica, and brother Hebern, who, following his father, had become a self-proclaimed doctor.

Buck Claflin, the "King of Cancers," had advertised Miss Tennessee's "Magnetio Life Elixir" at infirmaries in Pittsburgh and Chicago. Until Ottawa, Tennie was treating patients by laying on hands and using the home-brewed magic elixir, thought to contain laudanum, although Buck claimed it was harmless. But Buck was now sliding into criminal territory. Patients came for special treatment from the gifted child. In large type, his ads claimed that "Doctor" Claflin guaranteed a cure—he gave himself an escape clause with this addition: "if patients live up to directions"— and promised "Cancers killed and extracted, root and branch, in from 10 to 48 hours without instruments, pain or use of chloroform, simply by applying a salve of the doctor's own make." Only Tennie, with her magic hands, was allowed to apply the salve. Claflin later said it was a mustard plaster. Authorities said the homemade brew, cooked in an iron vat and stirred by Annie, was heavily laced with lye.

As a lure for more patients, Buck printed fake testimonials in the local newspaper, the Ottawa *Republican*. He disclosed the name of a supposedly recovering breast cancer patient, assuming she would stay silent on the topic in an era when "limb" was routinely written instead of the racier-sounding "leg." The ad read, "Mrs. Rebecca Howe, recovering from a dangerous situation after treatment by MISS TENNESSEE CLAFLIN wishes to thank this remarkable child" and "recommends" her cancer treatment. But Buck did not reckon with the anger of a dying Rebecca Howe. She replied in the *Republican* that her breast had been "wholly eaten away" and that she was in agony, and she called Tennie "an imposter, and one wholly unfit for the confidence of the community."

Following Howe's revelation, when two doctors and the local marshals bounded up the steps of the hotel to raid the second-floor infirmary, they gagged. In the filthy, fetid room they discovered dying and unfed patients lying in their own excrement. But they found no Claflins. The real clairvoyant was Buck, an artist in his ability to escape before police could locate him. This time the whole family vanished. Tennie was not around to be arrested for manslaughter.

The state of Illinois charged that Tennie "feloniously and willfully did kill and slay" Rebecca Howe by placing "upon the right side of the breast of one Rebecca Howe divers quantities of deleterious and caustic drugs by means of which a large amount of flesh" of her breast was "wholly eaten away, consumed and destroyed" by the drugs. Howe languished "in mortal sickness and thereby died" on June 7, 1864. A lesser charge was lodged by a John R. Dodge, who claimed that Tennie sought eighty-three dollars from him "with intent to cheat and defraud" by claiming she could cure him.

Why Buck, the instigator and the adult in this sordid enterprise, was not indicted remains unknown. Probably he smartly put the infirmary operation in the name of another family member. Tennie was now on the lam. She was never caught for the Ottawa indictments, but later in life she would not escape this sensational past.

This scandal might have stopped anyone, but Buck Claflin and family were soon off to newer cities, newer grieving widows and mothers, newer scams, newer charges, and more evictions.

Directed, as she always asserted, by the spirits, Victoria vowed that after returning from San Francisco she was commanded "to repair to Indianapolis, there to announce herself as a medium, and to treat patients for the cure of disease." She took rooms in the Bates House and published a notice in local papers. "Her marvelous performances in clairvoyance" became so well known that people arrived from far and wide. Her rooms were filled and "her purse grew fat." In Indianapolis and then in Terre Haute, she performed seeming miracles: "money flowed in a stream toward her." In city after city, Victoria "supported all her relatives far and near." Victoria claimed she made vast fortunes—nearly $100,000 in one year, $5,000 in one day alone. This has to be a preposterous lie. Her purse-fattening "spiritual art" that made her $100,000 a year would be equivalent to several million dollars today, and $5,000 is still remarkable today for one day's work. Tilton wrote that by 1869, the year after the sisters met Vanderbilt, Victoria's income and the "investments growing out of it" had reached $700,000—many millions in today's dollars. In that year, she was told to discontinue the practice by "direction of the spirits." As Tilton so charitably wrote, "The age of wonders has not ceased."

Despite her vaunted prosperity, Victoria was feeling "inwardly wretched" in the weeks leading up to the Civil War. "The dismal fact of her son's half-idiocy so preyed upon her mind that, in a heat of morbid feeling, she fell to accusing her innocent self for his misfortunes," wrote Tilton. "The sight of his face rebuked her...she prayed to God for another child—a daughter, to be born with a fair body and a sound mind. Her prayer was granted, but not without many accompaniments of inhumanity."

The wandering Woodhull couple had migrated to 53 Bond Street in New York. There, on April 23, 1861, their healthy daughter, Zulu Maud, was born. (Later her name was changed to Zula Maud.) Once again Canning is described as a drunken beast: he kicked pregnant Victoria and assisted her in childbirth with the "feverish and unsteady hands" of a drunk, who "only half in possession of his professional skill, cut the umbilical cord too near the flesh and tied it so loose that the string came off," and soon left mother and child alone. "Nor did he remember to return." But he must have remembered to lock the door, as the following account shows. Despite her claims of wealth, inexplicably no servants were in the house. Victoria's head was lying in a "pool of blood" that had accumulated from "a little red stream oozing drop by drop from the bowels of the child," whose umbilical cord had been so badly tied. Victoria grabbed a "broken chair-rung which happened to be lying near" and pounded for several hours against the wall to summon help. Finally a neighbor, hearing the noise but unable to open the locked front door, removed a grate in the basement window, climbed in, and rescued "the mother and the babe" upstairs. Three days later Victoria, propped up in bed and "looking out of the window, caught sight of her husband staggering up the steps of a house across the way, mistaking it for his own."

At that point Victoria thought, "Why should I any longer live with this man?" Her anti-marriage position began: "after eleven years of what, with conventional mockery, was called a marriage—during which time her husband had never spent an evening with her at home, had seldom drawn a sober breath, and had spent on other women, not herself, all the money he had ever earned—she applied in Chicago for a divorce, and obtained it."

But this stance did not take hold as immediately as Tilton states. Before the divorce, Victoria had set up shop in Chicago, while Tennie migrated to Cincinnati with the Claflins. Victoria had found a soul mate in Colonel James Harvey Blood, a Civil War hero with several bullet wounds to show for it. He was the commander of the Sixth Missouri Regiment and in postwar St. Louis was elected city auditor and was also president of the Society of Spiritualists. The handsome twenty-nine-year-old, with dark eyes, a trim beard, and a soldier's stance, was quiet, intelligent, and content to let Victoria take center stage. His radical beliefs and superior education were guiding forces in Victoria's transformation into a woman of substance. She craved knowledge, and he provided it.

In 1871, Tilton wrote that Blood's "civic views are (to use his favorite designation of them) cosmopolitical; in other words, he is a radical of extreme radicalism—an internationalist of the most uncompromising type—a communist who would rather have died in Paris than be the president of a pretended republic whose first official act has been the judicial murder of the only republicans in France." Here Tilton was referring to the Paris Commune uprising of 1871.

There is considerable confusion as to when Victoria and Blood began living together, but it was before she divorced Woodhull. In 1871, Victoria related that she had lived with Blood for eleven years, but that would have been before Zula Maud was born in April of 1861. On whatever date Victoria met Blood in St. Louis, he was a free lover, an ambiguous appellation that had a racy connotation of discarding partners, even though many "free lovers" were merely advocates of divorce reform to favor wives in abusive marriages. Whether Victoria understood the term or the cult at the time is doubtful, but her independent thinking and sour marriage propelled her to follow Blood's belief wholeheartedly. How much better it would be to live with a true mate, rather than in a wretched relationship sanctified by a piece of paper, she thought. Blood was, "like Victoria, the legal partner of a morally sundered marriage," wrote Tilton. Victoria had advertised herself in St. Louis, and Blood called one day "to consult her as a spiritualistic physician and was startled to see her pass into a trance, during which she announced, unconsciously to herself, that his future destiny was to be linked with hers in marriage."

No time was wasted. "Thus, to their mutual amazement, but to their subsequent happiness, they were betrothed on the spot by 'the powers of the air,'" an unexplained state of togetherness that sounded like the ultimate act of free love.

Different stories are told of their civil marriage, or of whether there was one. Victoria and Blood both gave conflicting accounts of their marital status. Victoria said they were married in a Presbyterian ceremony on July 14, 1866, in Dayton, Ohio. They did file a marriage license before the ceremony, but the minister neglected to file a return, to register the marriage officially. Blood further confused the issue by stating that they were legally divorced two years later, in Chicago, and then "remarried." It is not known whether this was a legal act or whether they were endorsing their belief that true love needed no legal sanctions and that they simply considered themselves married. No matter, wrote Tilton, "the marriage stands on its merits, and is to all who witness its harmony known to be a sweet and accordant union of congenial souls." Victoria saved herself from being Victoria Blood, explaining the avant-garde move to keep the Woodhull name: "she followed the example of many actresses, singers, and other professional women whose names have become a business property to their owners."

The biography, however, skips over crucial moments in the couple's entangled life. Blood dropped his last name and became Dr. J. H. Harvey, traveling as a medicine man with Victoria, known as Madame Harvey, trekking through the Midwest—known in those days as out west—in a ball-fringed wagon, advertising their medical prowess. Eventually they returned to Chicago, where Victoria got her divorce from Woodhull.

Victoria, Blood, and her two children had joined up with Tennie and the Claflin clan at some point during the war. They rode across war-torn fields and witnessed suffering and starving families living survivors' pain. Buck's ads promised a band of healers to cure the body with medicines and heal the soul with Spiritualism's "mysterious revelations."

When the family settled in Cincinnati, in 1865, Tennie advertised as a medium and magnetic healer. By then, at nineteen going on twenty, she had grown into a beauty, her dimpled smile an easy greeting to one and all. Despite the horrors of the manslaughter charge, she remained relatively untouched by life—compared with Victoria, who was then divorced and burdened with a deeply damaged son and an infant daughter. Still, gossip and innuendo followed wherever the Claflins took up residence, and Tennie was soon in the middle of scandalous rumors that she ran a house of assignation and had tried to blackmail one of the clients—who had no reputation to lose, as he was already living with "the most notorious woman in Cincinnati." Meanwhile, Victoria was asked to vacate her Chicago fortune-telling abode when neighbors complained that it was actually a brothel. The stories made the newspapers, but no contemporary official records of arrests surfaced.

Whatever happened in Cincinnati or Chicago became a turning point for Tennie. She had long wanted desperately to escape this life. She later emotionally spoke of her undying love for Vicky and Colonel Blood, who "got me away from that life; and they are the best friends I ever had." She hinted that, in Cincinnati, others came to her rescue: "Some of the first people in Cincinnati interfered to save me." While Tennie denied accusations of prostitution or running a house of assignation, there seemed a desperate need that transcended fortune-telling scams in this fervent thanks for those who "interfered to save me." Years later she spoke of having left a life of degradation.

Vagabond Victoria recounted that her next move was propelled by Demosthenes, the ancient Greek orator, her spiritual mentor, whom she always said instructed her in her trances. Demosthenes told her in 1868 to "journey to New York, where she would find at No. 17 Great Jones Street a house in readiness." Inside, Victoria found it all as she had pictured in her vision, including the table on which the ancient Greek orator had written instructions. In the library, "without knowing what she did," Victoria picked up a book and saw "to her blood-chilling astonishment" that it was *The Orations of Demosthenes*. Tilton does not explain how Demosthenes could write, in English no less, on the table or tell the uneducated Woodhull his instructions. But what was one to do? Move right in. Whether or not Demosthenes beckoned them, the Claflin family leeches soon descended, moving in with Tennie, Victoria, Byron, Zula Maud, and Colonel Blood at the house on Great Jones Street.

At this point, Tennie and Victoria tried to distance themselves from the family. They began practicing together, Victoria as a clairvoyant and Tennie as a magnetic healer. Colonel Blood helped as business manager. Gone were the magic elixirs and harmful cancer medications.

At the beginning of 1868, Vicky was twenty-nine and Tennie twenty-two. They had already lived most of their lives by their beauty, wits, strength, and humbuggery. They could not escape their past fast enough. They had known poverty, the degradation of being unacceptable child pariahs in small-town America, the humiliation of living as drifting outsiders, making a living fleecing people—and they had seen the promise of money. With it, life could change dramatically. Yet the sisters had higher ambitions than being two beauties searching for gold. With their looks, they could have been courtesans to wealthy men who would have kept them in mansions and jewels. They were certainly beautiful enough to become rich men's darlings. But they had more on their minds, a lot more.

Theirs was a deeper drive, an almost impossible one to achieve from their low station in life. They wanted riches, but in order to be independent. They wanted power, especially Victoria. They also wanted to do something meaningful. It would mean using men to serve them, but they wanted to be among the small band of Victorian women who could command their own lives. Like many politicians and public figures, they had competing desires. Altruistic beliefs about changing the world, especially for women, vied with raging ambition. Victoria promised to drive herself until she reached her "Divine Destiny." And Tennie vowed to be there for the sister she felt had saved her from a life of hell. Despite Victoria's messianic peculiarities, self-absorption, and manic fervor, Tennie would devote much of her life to her.

Their horrid childhood and poverty, with its meager pleasures, had been good training, just as it had been for so many of the uneducated men born in poverty whom they would join on Wall Street. The sisters had learned cunning and had known con artists, albeit on a penny-ante scale. Now they were prepared for the big time, unafraid of running with the high-rolling bandits who were forging Wall Street's emergence as the center of the financial world. The sisters headed for their new future with a consuming fierceness that made them an unstoppable force.

ACT TWO

CHAPTER THREE

Wall Street Warriors

The Hudson River was buried in darkness on an icy March night in 1868. No gaslight illumined the shore as a small boat circled wildly. Its two passengers had lost all sense of direction. One was corpulent enough to nearly sink the boat; the other was thin, with a perpetual look of gloom. A ferry loomed out of the curtain of fog, almost capsizing the boat, swamping the passengers with a huge swoosh of water. Then they heard the ominous sound of a paddle wheeler too close for comfort. Clutching at the guardrails of the steamboat as their small boat capsized, they were hauled aboard and soon deposited on the New Jersey shore. They were nearly drowned but were safe now. The two men quickly joined the rest of the directors of the Erie Railroad who had already dashed to the safety of New Jersey—along with $8 million in greenbacks, bonds, and stocks they had hastily stuffed into satchels.

The drenched passengers could have fled Manhattan earlier with the others, but hubris led them to down champagne and oysters at Delmonico's while being chased by the law. The portly and soaked Jim Fisk, who at only thirty-two had scrambled to the top on Wall Street, retold with gusto this farcical moment—among many in the great "Erie War." His companion, Jay Gould, a year younger than Fisk, burned with a great desire to make money and lots of it. Together they had teamed up with the venerable Daniel Drew, swearing to ruin Vanderbilt, who had dared them to a fight by launching a full-throated raid to steal their control of the Erie Railroad.

Drew headed the Erie Railroad board and had made fortunes manipulating the company's stock (long before rules against what today we delicately call "insider trading"). Recently, he had recruited to the board a Boston contingent and the brash unknowns Fisk and Gould.

Vanderbilt, for his part, in 1868 viewed Erie as competition and wanted it either out of the way or under his thumb. (Before Vanderbilt gobbled up multiple railroads to combine them into one system, a passenger could make seventeen changes before getting from New York to Chicago.) By the time of the Erie battle, Vanderbilt already owned the Long Island Railroad, the New York and Harlem and the Hudson River Railroads, and in 1867 had acquired the Central, merging them all later as the New York Central. Still, the Erie line remained competition for passage from New York City to Buffalo, Lake Erie, and Chicago—potentially the single most lucrative line of the era.

Vanderbilt, to weaken his prey for the kill, had taken the preemptive step of procuring a New York judge, the easily bought George Gardner Barnard, a crony of Boss Tweed's, to issue injunctions restraining the Erie crowd from issuing new capital stock. This way, Vanderbilt only had to buy a majority of the shares already circulating to win control, which he had more than enough money to do. He thought he had crafty Drew and his two young partners hog-tied. The Commodore quickly bought up Erie stock, thinking Drew was thwarted, by the injunction, from issuing new stock.

In one of his few mistakes, Vanderbilt underestimated Drew, who was known to "laugh at injunctions." Wall Street had already deemed him the King of Watered Stock for a legendary scheme he'd concocted years earlier as a cattle drover to bilk gullible New York merchants. When he rounded up cattle, he commanded his hands to "Give 'em lots of salt." The thirsty beasts were then given no water until just before they were weighed, and then gulped so much water that their weight, and the sales price, went up. Hence the derivation of the term "watered stock." Now while Vanderbilt was hoarding Erie stock, Drew and his young protégés Fisk and Gould decided to ignore this newest court order. They repaired to a printing press in the basement of the Manhattan Erie Building. Turning blank paper into crisp new Erie convertible bonds, Fisk cracked, "If this printing press don't break down, I'll be damned if I don't give the old hog [Vanderbilt] all he wants of Erie."

It didn't break down, and Drew immediately converted the bonds, still wet with ink, into shares in Erie, which he knew would most certainly be declared illegal by Vanderbilt's judge, since the move squarely violated his injunction against Drew's issuing any new shares. But that problem could wait. Immediately, Fisk and Gould ordered their brokers at the New York Stock Exchange to start selling the oceans of new shares. As soon as Wall Street traders recognized that these several thousand new stock certificates were, in fact, new (easily recognizable as coming straight from the printer), the price dropped "like lead." Vanderbilt had already spent millions to buy Erie shares. He suddenly found their value shrinking rapidly, and stood no closer to controlling the company. If he showed an ounce of weakness at that moment, the bottom would drop out of Erie, creating a panic that could threaten even his vast fortune. The collapse of Erie "would be ruin for him and hundreds of others." So he bought, and bought, and bought, singlehandedly bringing the Erie price back up.

Meanwhile, Drew, Fisk, and Gould, recognizing that Vanderbilt's New York judges stood ready to declare their newly created stock invalid, quickly raced to sell it for cash. They literally stuffed millions in carpetbags and hightailed it to the Hudson River. Some $7 million of their cash had been fleeced from Vanderbilt in his frenzied buying to stave off a major panic. Vanderbilt was stuck with a hundred thousand shares worth far less than what he paid for them. His raid to catch the culprits was a failure.

The furious Vanderbilt got his "injunction" judge to issue arrest warrants against the entire Erie board of directors, but it was too late. His enemies had fled across the Hudson to safety in New Jersey, beyond the reach of New York judges. With great bonhomie, Fisk entertained reporters who had dashed to New Jersey's Taylor Hotel (nicknamed Fort Taylor) to drink his whiskey and laugh at his jokes. Fisk was more expansive than ever, having collected his mistress, Josie Mansfield, known as the best-kept "kept" woman, from her Manhattan mansion—safe from Vanderbilt's contempt citation.

The Claflin sisters, newly arrived in New York, heard all about the Erie War. The conflict had received more coverage than the battle for President Andrew Johnson's impeachment and crystallized in the minds of most Americans the corrupt and heartless financial games proliferating in post–Civil War Wall Street. Soon the ambitious sisters had their minds set on meeting the famously rich Vanderbilt. His belief in Spiritualism was no secret, perfect for two clairvoyants who saw "visions." At this point he was in need of help, spiritual or otherwise, because he faced an inconceivable obstacle. As the Erie crisis unfolded, banks refused to lend to the Commodore, now low on cash. "We can't lend on Erie," a Vanderbilt aide was told; "there is an illegal issue of stock, and Erie isn't worth anything." The aide demanded, "What will you lend on?" The banker said, "[New York] Central—that's good." Vanderbilt's assistant knew that most bankers had broker's loans, which used stock as security. So he snapped to the bank officer, "If you don't lend the Commodore half a million on Erie at 50, and do it at once, he will put Central at 50 tomorrow and break half the houses on the Street!"

Vanderbilt got his credit. Friends had deserted him, but he had stemmed the Erie decline. The battle then went from the courts to the New York state legislature in Albany, where Gould quickly set up shop in Parlor 57 of the Delavan House hotel with a trunk stuffed with thousand-dollar bills. Soon legislators were crowding the suite, where Gould dispensed whiskey and his thousand-dollar gratuities. Since Judge Barnard clung to the view that their stock deal was illegal, the Erie crowd decided that a law must be passed to overturn Vanderbilt's judges and make the stock legal. Boss Tweed, then a senator as well as New York's "King of Corruption," set up his own suite in the Delavan, according to many reports, to aid Vanderbilt on the side of killing the bill. The Erie bill was "a godsend to the hungry legislators and lobbymen" who roamed from one suite to the other looking for the best deal. When Vanderbilt suddenly announced he wasn't going to fight the bill anymore, the bribe-ravenous legislators angrily voted in favor of Gould and Fisk—whose bribes included an estimated half a million in stockholders' money. The legislators, known far and wide for easy corruptibility, nonetheless puffed themselves up as gatekeepers of democratic fair play, roaring that they had voted for the Erie contingent because they could not bear to see a Vanderbilt railroad monopoly.

The crowing Gould and Fisk did not know that Vanderbilt had pulled a decisive ace out of his sleeve. It involved a double cross by Drew, who was only too eager to oblige. In secret meetings, the old battlers agreed on terms necessary to lift Barnard's judicial ruling so that the Fort Taylor gang could return to Manhattan without paying stiff fines or going to jail. In return, Vanderbilt got his money back. Fisk and Gould protested Drew's betrayal, to no avail. The deal struck with Drew included nearly half a million in payment to Vanderbilt for the $7 million in worthless stock he had bought. He soon was back in the game as vigorous as ever. The deal also included a generous golden parachute for Drew. And Fisk and Gould, the newest fiscal celebrities, were left in control of the declining railroad, whose offices they would soon, in 1869, move uptown to Pike's Opera House, their base of many notorious Wall Street operations.

In 1868, at the age of seventy-four, the Commodore remained strikingly handsome, as erect as when he was a young six-foot-tall ferry skipper who could brawl his way to a win on the waterfront. He was known for racing his trotters in Central Park at such a breakneck pace that others got out of his way. His prominent nose gave him the look of a Roman senator, it was remarked, and his blue eyes, with their shrewd squint, bored holes in those who dared cross him. He wore black, and his well-groomed white sideburns reached his stiff white collar with its immaculate white cravat tied snugly at the throat. This old-fashioned attire gave him the appearance of a minister, which of course was a far cry from what the cunning, combative tycoon was. He could not spell; he swore atrociously, mangled his grammar, and used spittoons. But he was impossibly rich. His scrawl on a piece of butcher's paper was good enough for any banker. He also earned a reputation for honesty: "flawed as he was, he was never a liar."

Although he was powerful enough in his youth to beat a belligerent prizefighter to the ground with his fists, "he never launched a war of aggression in all his years as a railroad leader," wrote biographer J. T. Stiles, while still acknowledging Vanderbilt's ruthlessness. One of his most successful methods was price cutting: lowering the cost to passengers, buying up or driving competitors out of business, then jacking the prices up again. With adversaries, he tried diplomacy first but never backed down when a competitor tried to muscle in on what the Commodore considered his—and by the time the sisters met him, this constituted nearly everything in trains and ships.

The Commodore also frustrated anyone who wanted to find out what he was doing by keeping his business deals in his head, not on paper.

Vanderbilt liked fast horses and his share of fast women, and had seen the world from the lowest level to the highest peak. Nothing much surprised him, but he stunned skeptics with his fascination for Spiritualism and mediums.

For all his tough exterior, the Commodore endured private mourning when those few he loved died. He was often cruelly dismissive of his thirteen children, belittling William, the eldest, whom he would eventually choose to succeed him, but he was heartbroken when his youngest and favorite son, George, who had served without distinction in the Civil War, died in 1863 of consumption. Vanderbilt regularly consulted a medium, who would provide answers to questions he wrote to his deceased parents, brother, and wife. Whether the medium told anything that dovetailed with the Commodore's questions is unknown. The Commodore also purchased prescriptions from a Spiritualist healer.

In 1868, the sisters knocked on Vanderbilt's door, calling cards in hand. (Unlike those who had moved uptown, Vanderbilt had clung to the Greenwich Village mansion he had built on Washington Place in 1845, with his stable of fine trotters out back.) When Victoria and Tennie arrived that day, Vanderbilt was definitely ready to embrace their brand of Spiritualism—and twenty-two-year-old Tennie's bewitching charms. He was vulnerable that fall, after his Erie defeat and the loss of his wife, Sophie, the long-suffering mother of thirteen, who had died in August. Vanderbilt was a teenager when they married, and although they had not been close for years, her death reminded him of his own advancing age.

Victoria and Tennie almost certainly had caught wind of Vanderbilt's Spiritualist interest; he was a perfect catch for them. Victoria held out hope that she could please Vanderbilt's obsessive desire to communicate with his long-dead mother.

And he may have heard of them, for when they arrived in Manhattan the sisters had once again widely advertised themselves as "magnetic physicians and clairvoyants" and "charged $25 in advance" for their wondrous cures. Tennessee had made it known that she saw "visions." She pointedly told a reporter "if you doubt it, go and ask Commodore Vanderbilt." Stories made the rounds that Vanderbilt gained stock market tips from the sisters, through their supernatural talents. One woman vowed that Vanderbilt urged her to follow the sisters' advice to buy New York Central stock. Another woman—considered somewhat unreliable, seeing as how she had shot a druggist—stated that Vanderbilt had advised her, "Why don't you do as I do, and consult the spirits?"

Unlike upright citizens who prized demure, quiet women, Vanderbilt loved the sisters' intelligence and boldness. Tennie's magnetic healing, plus her cheery, upbeat presence, helped his aches and pains, earned through years of railroad and horse racing accidents. The Commodore also suffered from an enlarged prostate and complications from a ruptured lung. Tennie frequented his office and, according to the earliest of biographies, it was said that he would jiggle her up and down as she sat on his lap and call her his "little sparrow," while she pulled his whiskers and dotingly called him "old boy." The presumption that they were lovers has lasted for a century and a half. Though the rumor has never been proven definitively, the circumstances and the logic of the situation speak plainly. Tennie would not have blanched at Vanderbilt's swearing, his whist playing, his occasional gin, or his frequent cigars. He would have loved her youth and her freewheeling ability to tell a good story. Although it certainly was never discussed, the two shared the honor of being indicted for manslaughter—she for the Ottawa cancer cure, he for a Staten Island Ferry bridge collapse that killed more than a dozen, although the charge against Vanderbilt was quashed.

Vanderbilt probably sought Tennie in the boudoir between his first wife's death the summer before and his surprise remarriage in August 1869. The oft-repeated "fact" that he asked Tennie to marry him was merely raised later, in 1878, during a sensational fight over his will, by a lawyer trying to prove that Vanderbilt was senile. Disgruntled siblings "proposed to show" that Vanderbilt was of unsound mind during his time with the sisters. The judge ruled this information immaterial, but could not resist a cheap shot at Tennie, to courtroom laughter: "I don't see that the conversation is any evidence of unsoundness of mind. It might be a matter of taste."

A medium once allegedly told Vanderbilt, after two raps on a table, "This is for you, Commodore. It is from your wife." The Commodore reportedly growled, "Business before pleasure; I want a communication from Jim Fisk" (the joke being that Fisk, shot dead in 1872, was someone with whom Vanderbilt could do business even from the grave).

In 1869, however, Fisk was still very much alive. In the months following the Erie War, the sisters credit their good fortune to Vanderbilt's warning them that Gould and Fisk were scheming again. During the Civil War, Fisk had been a Capitol Hill fixture, wining, dining, and bribing whomever he needed to influence government contracts for his product: blankets of an inferior grade of material called shoddy, the origin of the adjective to describe anything substandard. He then cheerfully traded with the enemy, smuggling cotton through the blockades. By war's end, he was a very rich man. He had just turned thirty on April Fool's Day 1865.

Recklessly playing the stock market, he lost it all but swore to return. And by 1869—while the sisters kept a low profile, learning all they could about Wall Street machinations from Vanderbilt, preparing to startle the world with their brokerage move—Fisk was back with a vengeance.

"Manhattan's upper crust" was stricken to find that such a "buffoon," with Boss Tweed by his side, could trample on them and become a "frightening financial and political power." Fisk sailed on, his mustache waxed to rapier sharpness, his red-blond hair marcelled in waves. His diamond-studded vests preceded the rest of him; Fisk seemed to use his girth as his calling card as he swaggered forth.

In 1869, Gould and Fisk tried to corner the New York Gold Exchange's gold market and created the financial panic known as Black Friday. The sisters, by now players in the market, had a lot at risk. The gold-cornering scandal was one of the most famous of many that rocked the Grant presidency. In their attempt to conquer the gold market, Fisk and Gould recruited Grant's brother-in-law, Abel Corbin, to help them socialize with Grant. Over cigars and brandy, Gould argued against the government sale of gold even though the use of Civil War government greenbacks had waned. Grant resisted, but an assistant treasurer of the United States, Daniel Butterfield, agreed to tip off Gould and Fisk when the government intended to sell gold.

Late in the summer of 1869, Gould began buying up massive amounts of gold, causing prices to rise and stocks to plummet. When Grant realized what was happening, the federal government swiftly sold $4 million in gold. On Black Friday, September 20, 1869, Gould and Fisk were foiled. When the government gold hit the market, the premium plummeted within minutes. Panicked investors scrambled to sell. But many were too late. Hysterical sobbing filled the Street and the Gold Exchange as ruined speculators saw their lives collapse in one day.

The sisters were cool customers through it all, relying on Vanderbilt's tips. Woodhull sat in her carriage for four days, from morning until night, operating heavily, a small smile playing on her lips as she watched the frantic movements of men coping with the crisis. At the end of the panic, Woodhull exclaimed, "I came out a winner!" She did not reveal the amount, but the sisters had pocketed a large sum, which Victoria often declared brought their accumulated wealth to the staggering, probably exaggerated, figure of $700,000.

Four months later, on February 5, 1870, they opened their brokerage firm.

CHAPTER FOUR

The Bewitching Brokers

To ensure that the grand opening of their Woodhull, Claflin and Co. brokerage and banking firm would be a sensation, the sisters invited a *New York Herald* reporter for an interview a few weeks before, in their temporary headquarters: two parlors in the posh Hoffman House at Twenty-Fourth and Broadway. The sisters showed startling aplomb by doing business in a hotel, the domain of visiting male politicians, magnates, and financiers.

Nearby was the Fifth Avenue Hotel, which was dubbed handsomer than Buckingham Palace when it opened in 1859. Ridiculed for being built too far uptown, it was the first New York hotel to feature a "vertical railway intersecting each story." This new invention, the elevator, would forever change fashionable urban living. Soon higher floors were prized, paving the way for penthouse clientele. Now, five years after the end of the Civil War and the rush to move uptown, both the Hoffman House and the Fifth Avenue Hotel boasted princes and presidents as residents. Fifth Avenue and Broadway swarmed with potentates and high-priced prostitutes, wealthy matrons visiting Tiffany & Co., theatergoers and diners who patronized elegant Delmonico's, and madams who ran brothels in mansions beside brownstone palaces owned by newly minted millionaires. This circus would soon be the playground for Victoria and Tennie.

The *Herald* reporter eagerly appeared at the sisters' Hoffman House parlor, which was "profusely decorated with oil paintings and statuary." Commodore Vanderbilt stared down from the wall in a large photograph so prominent that the reporter enthused "his spirit is there…as though the mantle of the genial old Commodore had descended upon their shoulders."

When a smiling and buoyant Tennie sailed into the room, she drew her chair close to the reporter's and expressed surprise that he should honor her with a visit, despite the fact that the sisters had orchestrated it. At this point, Tennie needed to appear respectably wed. Her short-lived marriage as a teenager, to John Bortel, was either dissolved legally or simply forgotten. Now she billed herself as a wife: "Mrs. Claflin, though married eight years, is still a young lady of some twenty-four years of age." The reporter termed her "a business woman—keen, shrewd, whole souled, masculine in manner, and apparently a firm foe of the 'girl of the period' creation or those who questioned her novel career."

Asked if she didn't find, as a woman, her new venture "rather awkward," Tennie retorted, "I don't care what society think…Were I to notice what is said by what they call 'society' I could never leave my apartments except in fantastic walking dress or in ballroom costume; but I despise what squeamy, crying girls or powdered counter-jumping dandies say of me…I think a woman is just as capable of making a living as a man… My mind is on my business and I attend to that solely."

When the reporter questioned her experience, Tennie shot back, "I know as much of the world as men who are older. Besides we have a strong [backing]. We have the counsel of those who have more experience than we have, and we are endorsed by the best backers in the city."

"I have been told that Commodore Vanderbilt is working in the interest of your firm," said the reporter. "It is stated that you frequently call at his office about business. Is this true?"

"I know the Commodore and frequently call to see him on business but I am not prepared to state anything as to whether he is working with us." A later story would ridicule the "Queens of Finance" and Commodore Vanderbilt as their "Prime Minister." At that time, Tennie was less discreet, saying outright that Vanderbilt had inspired the "new undertaking."

Before Tennie could say anything more about Vanderbilt, Victoria entered the parlor: a woman with a "keen, bright eye...very plainly dressed, with a single rose tastefully inserted in her hair." Although Victoria wove with ease her false tales of being well educated and a veritable child prodigy in the financial world, the prescient reporter spied a "nervous temperament" beneath her regal control. "It might be apprehended that a serious financial shock would not tell well on her constitution."

Two weeks later, on February 5, their opening day, the sisters joined rush-hour traffic as private carriages, horse-drawn omnibuses, carts, wagons, and horseback riders clogged the way. Everyone in New York complained of gridlock, and accidents occurred regularly—200 horses died daily in traffic accidents—as crowded horses shrieked and reared in panic at the screech of train whistles, the shouts of drivers, and the noise of rumbling carriages. Third Avenue omnibuses built to carry twenty-two passengers bulged with sixty. It could take an hour and a half to get to Wall Street. The first L train (elevated steam locomotive) was not operational until 1871, its ashes falling on pedestrians below, but it helped to allay the congestion.

Underneath the pounding hooves and rolling carts something very new was being inaugurated. The first New York subway, a huge round car propelled by the pneumatic pressure and vacuum created by a giant fan, ran under Broadway from Warren Street to Murray Street at a top speed of ten miles an hour. It closed three years later due to lack of riders.

So New Yorkers continued to rely on horses. By the 1860s, New York's horse population had reached amazing numbers. Some 100,000 horses, said one source, deposited a thousand tons of manure and three hundred thousand gallons of urine a day. Boss Tweed's lackluster sanitation system made a ride on the streets of the city especially fragrant on a sweltering summer's day. Luckily the sisters' big event was taking place on a crisp winter's morning.

Among the mob that watched the sisters drive into Broad Street were many lesser Wall Street regulars, who scorned the women's invasion into this man's world. The sisters, however, had an affinity for the major titans, who, like them, often started poor and had never looked back—men such as the semiliterate Vanderbilt, who began by ferrying small craft in his teens and fought, bribed, and plundered his way to the top of America's shipping and railroad dynasty. Vanderbilt and other gamblers had wrestled one another in fierce financial battles, and in so doing, had created a new America—a land webbed with railroads and teeming with industrial progress and manufacturing might. These men were unquenchable risk takers, addicted to gambling, and they often succeeded with astounding verve, willing to lose it all one day and regain it the next. The game and the power propelled them as much as the money. The Claflin sisters had more in common with these men than they did with the upper-class women who would never accept them or with the middle-class suffragists who, for a while, fancied the sisters, enjoying slumming, as it were, with low-life upstarts.

The sisters had lived a tough enough life to cope with men such as Vanderbilt, Gould, Drew, and Fisk, who was just twenty-nine when he formed his alliance with Vanderbilt's occasional friend but more often enemy, crusty Daniel Drew. Nearly illiterate, Drew habitually used a broken umbrella as a cane, and mopped his face with a red bandana. He seemed unfamiliar with a smile, his thin lips perennially drawn downward. It was said that under that ragman's guise and pious Bible reading there beat "the heart of a shark." Drew is also credited with this ditty: "He who sells what isn't his'n, must pay it back or go to prison."

The other young man partnering with Fisk and Drew, Jay Gould, was a brooding, dark genius who grew up poor and sickly. Gould lived on greed alone at this stage of his long career, fleecing his partners and others. Only the triple-cross bested the double-cross.

For his part, Fisk overshadowed by far all others on the Street with his diamond-studded, mistress-flaunting flamboyance, but he was "no isolated phenomenon; rather, a splendid reflection of the immorality of his time."

Reporters who poured into the sisters' elegant offices at 44 Broad Street throughout their opening week in February 1870 praised the "Bewitching Brokers." Tennie was regarded as the spokesperson; it was said that "Tennie was the Jim Fisk and Victoria the Jay Gould" of the firm.

No matter their reservations, Wall Street's old guard was drawn by the Commodore's name and came out for the sister's opening day. Major brokerage firms sent august representatives to welcome the sisters, including Peter Cooper, for whom Cooper Union is named, and the esteemed Jay Cooke. Bankers had come to laugh, but they left impressed.

The visitor who meant the most to Woodhull, however, was the great writer and poet Walt Whitman, who also paid his respects. She saved for years a scrap of paper on which were written the words he supposedly said to her that day: "You have given an object lesson to the whole world."

Even Drew showed up, growling that he had not aided the sisters and had never met them until opening day. Everyone assumed that his nemesis, Vanderbilt, had bankrolled the sisters. Henry Clews, president of the Fourth National Bank, confirmed that the sisters had deposited a $7,000 check bearing Vanderbilt's signature. Seven thousand dollars was but a teaspoon's dip into Vanderbilt's honeypot, but for the sisters it was a fine sum—worth a good $150,000 or more today—with which to help start Woodhull, Claflin and Co. It could have been just the proceeds from stocks in which Vanderbilt had invested their own money, but the Street thought it was, as Clews wrote, money to put them in business. "Very soon after the Commodore had aided to set up these two women as brokers in Broad Street the firm was known all over the land," recalled Clews.

Delicious rumors circulated about Vanderbilt and young Tennie— even though he had recently taken a second wife with the unusual first name of Frank. Only eight years older than Tennie and forty-three years younger than Vanderbilt, Frank was bent on leading the swearing, womanizing Vanderbilt onto a path of righteousness.

The sisters' friendship with Vanderbilt illustrates how truly pragmatic they were in dealing with anyone who could help them. Vanderbilt could hardly be viewed in the vanguard of feminist support, which the sisters so strongly championed. His womanizing was legendary, and when his first wife, the mother of his thirteen children, balked at leaving Staten Island for his Washington Square home, he had her committed to an insane asylum until she came to her wits and moved to Manhattan.

Vanderbilt's famous signature on their check meant everything to the sisters. More than the money, his power led to their tumultuous renown and notoriety, as did the role Tennie had allegedly played in securing Vanderbilt's support, even though she would later be eclipsed by her older sister's fame. Vanderbilt's biographer Stiles sees the sisters as fleeting diversions in the tycoon's long life, and points out that Vanderbilt soon shunned them and that their brokerage firm did not last. However, without his initial push, the sisters would have been unknown trifles in a class-conscious world. Without Vanderbilt, their ride on Wall Street and their subsequent fame as suffragists, Spiritualists, sex radicals, authors, lecturers, and players in Henry Ward Beecher's adultery scandal would not have happened.

When Clews announced that he had deposited the Commodore's check for the sisters, the Street listened. Jay Gould, the great manipulator, acknowledged that one speculator "paid Victoria and sister Tennie $1,000 a day commission through quite a warm summer spell. I don't happen to know the ladies myself, but in their office things certainly do move smoothly; and I don't doubt at all that it is because of that—exclusively for that—that Commodore Vanderbilt stands for them." Gould did not buy "all this sugary stuff" about a love affair, and he revealed that the sisters had been unwitting foils during his bid to oust Vanderbilt in one scheme: "I picked the ladies' firm myself—without them realizing it—because, you see, The Street when Woodhull and Claflin sold would just naturally jump to the conclusion that the principal was Cornelius Vanderbilt, getting shorter and shorter. Rather neat finesse I thought."

In 1652 the Dutch government of then Nieuw Amsterdam built a wall to keep out English settlers who sought land near a strategic harbor. The wall never kept anyone out, as the Dutch settlers found out when the British invaded in 1664, but the wall gave the Financial District its alternate name. In the seventeenth century, Broad Street was a fetid waterfront canal, and residents were commanded to pave it over. As this rank inlet metamorphosed into the Financial District, the foulness never left; without any regulation, unfettered pillaging made many a war-profiteering scoundrel

fabulously rich. The sisters roared onto the Street in this era of wild speculation, where an unknown shoe polish manufacturer one day might become a
millionaire the next, suddenly striking it rich in a market complete with easily bought politicians and judges. George Francis Train, an eccentric millionaire, wrote a poem that mirrored the easy come, easy go spiral.

> Monday: I started my land operations;
> Tuesday: owned millions, by all calculations:
> Wednesday: my brownstone palace began;
> Thursday: I drove out a spanking new span;
> Friday: I gave a magnificent ball:
> Saturday: smashed—with just nothing at all.

The Williams and Grey firm—which included a forger, bank robber,
swindler, and murderer, a rather concrete example of outlaw days on the
Street—had hastily vacated the sisters' offices, leaving behind furnishings
that the sisters bought at a foreclosure price. The office was "magnificently
fitted up" with heavy walnut desks with gold trim, oak chairs upholstered
in fine green silk, and carpets. "The best Marvin safes are conspicuous,"
said one news account; "...nothing seems wanting to supplement the
boldness, spirit, grandeur and enterprise of the new idea."

Some thirty feet from the entrance, in a smaller office partitioned
off with etched glass and elaborate woodwork, the smiling sisters served
strawberries and champagne. It was said that they had instituted after-
hours sessions of champagne and frivolity on the Street, but their neighbor on Broad Street, jolly Jim Fisk, had preceded them.

Yet no others on the Street entertained as well as they, moving their
after-hours open house to a suite in the Astor House hotel, where they
served up roast beef, champagne, and bonhomie. Some of the famously
wealthy were regulars, and even Clews, who despised the sisters' boldness, couldn't keep away. Among their guests were Arthur Brisbane, the
wealthy Utopian; William Hillyer, President Grant's former chief of staff;
a reverend or two; and the president of the Stock Exchange board. Capi-

talist "presidents" abounded—of Western Union, the Home Insurance Fire Company, the Continental Bank—plus the vice president of the Union Pacific Railroad. And of course, members of the fourth estate. "We like newspapermen," said Tennie. "They are the salt of the earth—and keep everything from spoiling!"

The sisters also cleverly created something amazingly progressive: a private entrance leading to a female-only back room for women stock traders. The sisters' upfront role in the financial world was beyond belief; the ladies' back room sported an unprecedented mix of elderly, sedate spinsters and young "blondes, fair and fresh as pippins," who came to mock but who left thinking that "there were other things to live for besides cosmetics, the toilet, fashion and vanity." Housewives who had managed to save money, madams seeking to grow their portfolios, and feminists also joined the group.

Susan B. Anthony, the prototypical grim-faced Quaker spinster, set out to survey the sisters. Her longtime suffrage partner, Elizabeth Cady Stanton, looked the innocent rotund matron, with silver curls and the heft of having borne seven children. But looks deceived. In addition to being defiantly courageous, both were sharply witty—and both were interested in the swirling gossip within the women's movement.

Anthony was ecstatic when she visited the firm, a few weeks after its opening. She commented on Tennie's striking looks—"a handsome blonde." Tennie had no problem being the stylish businesswoman, despite her tirades about fancy-dressed women. She wore a blue suit trimmed with black astrakhan fur, held her hands in a matching astrakhan muff, and topped her hair with a black velvet hat trimmed with black feathers. Anthony wore black and parted her hair straight down the middle and pulled into a severe bun that did nothing to soften her thin-lipped face or mitigate her slightly crossed eyes squinting behind rimless glasses. She could have disliked Tennie on sight, having no love for idle women of fashion, but these physical opposites hit it off. Anthony was entranced by the younger woman's candor.

"Instead of making shirts at fifty cents each (one per day) for a living, these two ladies (for they are ladies) determined to use their brains, their energy, and their knowledge of business to earn them a livelihood," wrote Anthony in the *Revolution*, the women's rights newspaper she and Stanton published. "Their presence on Wall Street marks a new era." The day she visited the firm, Anthony had picked her way through a crowd of men, and commented with distaste, "Wall Street has been so exclusively monopolized by men that it has not yet got over a bad habit of staring at a passing woman."

Tennie enthusiastically greeted Anthony at the women's entrance, guided her into the inner sanctum, and casually flipped off her hat. Anthony sat on a green silk lounge and got to the point: "What first suggested to you the idea of coming into the rush and tumble of Wall Street?"

"The necessity for earning a livelihood...a knowledge of financial matters, and unfitness for the slow, dreary methods by which women usually earn a living," replied Tennie. "Look at this office! Is it not better than sewing drawers at ten cents a pair?" Tennie's brash comment was refreshing candor to Anthony. "Or teaching music at ten dollars a quarter?"

Tennie bubbled with praise for the "men of influence" who had received them "with the greatest possible kindness." She then mentioned one of Anthony's core topics in the women's struggle: male contempt. "There are a few of the 'small potatoes' sort of men, who never mention the name of any woman, not even their own mother with respect; who sneer, and try to get off their poor jokes on us, but it doesn't hurt us...We shall soon be part of the regular machinery."

Anthony remarked with some surprise that the press "had nothing very dreadful to say against you." The older woman knew full well what newspapers could do. She had endured years of humiliation, described as "an ungainly hermaphrodite...with an ugly face and shrill voice." Eggs were thrown at her when she tried to speak, and she was hung in effigy three times. Recently she had been called a leader "of the delirium of unreason known as the Woman's Cause."

Tennie told her, "No, the worst was that I had been a clairvoyant physician. I did not mind that, it was quite true." Then, she lied, "I never received any money on false pretenses." On a roll, she slipped into slang: "They cannot say that we ever were, or are, bad women, that we ever got tight, or visited disreputable places." She wondered why women could not be judged "for their merits as men are? But if I say I want equality with men, they think I mean, at once, the privilege of getting drunk and being licentious. My opinion is that business, work...and something for it when it is done is the only thing that will put a stop on the social evils."

Anthony warmed to her every word. "You are right," she cried. "Men have everything, most women nothing but what men give them. When women want anything, be it bread or a kind word, they must pay the price that men exact for it, and it is nearly always a 'pound of flesh.'"

"Yes indeed," exclaimed Tennie. "Within the past eleven days we have made five hundred dollars by commissions on sale alone. This is called very good for the beginning."

Anthony agreed, and asked the sisters to join the suffrage ranks.

"Just wait until we get ourselves firmly established in our business and we will show you what we will do for the rights of our sex," replied Tennie.

As she left, Anthony felt a "great throb of pleasure" to see "a waiter from the restaurant, with a tray of hot luncheon on his head," serving Tennie just as if she had been one of the established male brokers. She felt an "augury of better times to come for women—times when they shall vote the right to put food in their mouths, and money in their pockets, without asking men's leave."

After her article on Tennie, Anthony wrote an editorial in the *Revolution* stating that the sisters were stimulating "the whole future of woman": "They are full of pluck, energy, and enterprise, and are withal most prepossessing in personal appearance, in manners, and lady-like deportment; moreover they 'know what they are all about,' and are calculated to inspire confidence by the sound sense, judgment and clear-sighted-ness they show in financial matters." Little did the sisters know that in just a few years, Anthony would become their mortal enemy.

CHAPTER FIVE

Woodhull & Claflin's Weekly

Despite prejudices, so many capitalists and speculators were willing to try the female firm that Victoria and Tennie were swamped in their early days. They had impressed many with their coolness under fire.

Wall Street, however, was but a stepping-stone for the sisters' next venture. Victoria and Tennie had what they wanted: fame and enough money to move on, infuriating Wall Street regulars who saw them as dilettantes. Victoria soon left the daily brokerage duties to Colonel Blood, and sprang a surprise that she had promised in January to reveal "soon."

A week after the opening of the firm, Woodhull had spoken bitterly to a reporter about other women, stating "our own has universally thrown dirt at us." The sisters did not buy the notion that women were "despoiled of most of their rights by the domineering will of man." On the contrary, said Victoria, as soon as women were "prepared to perform" outside their sphere, "the right to do so cannot be withheld." The public was hearing for the first time her ringing cry for freedom: "We propose revolution whenever the chains of conservatism drop too slowly and leave us chafing under their restraint too long."

Six weeks later, on April 2, 1870, Woodhull announced what no woman had ever dared. She was putting her name up for nomination for the presidency of the United States, giving herself a two-year head start to form a political following and organization. She knew she would be ridiculed, but claimed that otherworldly spirits had told her to do so. Her method of disseminating this information, however, was purely of this world: she announced it through the *New York Herald*. The *Herald* called her "The Coming Woman" and cheered, "Now for victory in 1872."

In her letter to the paper, Victoria boldly combined what she saw as her credentials with the plight of women—"As I happen to be the most prominent representative of the most unrepresented class in the Republic..." She stingingly dismissed longtime activists: "while others of my sex devoted themselves to a crusade against the laws that shackle the women of the country, I asserted my individual independence; while others prayed for the good time coming, I worked for it; while others argued the equality of woman with man, I proved it by engaging in business." While other women merely fought for the right to be treated as equals, Victoria scoffed, "I boldly entered the arena of politics [although she had not yet made any noticeable effort] and business and exercised the rights I already possessed. I therefore claim the right to speak for the unenfranchised [*sic*] woman of the country." Woodhull hoped that her candidacy would spur on the fight for women's suffrage and argued that it was overdue, contrasting the inequity for women with that of African Americans: "The blacks were cattle in 1860 and a Negro now sits in Jeff Davis's seat" in the U.S. Senate. She built her campaign on Elizabeth Cady Stanton's novel act. In 1869, Stanton had nominated herself for Congress from New York's Eighth District, arguing that the Constitution said nothing about women not being able to run for office, even if they could not vote. Woodhull's full-bore wooing of the friendly *Herald* led to its publication of lofty position papers, ghostwritten by Stephen Pearl Andrews, an eccentric genius who would soon play a prominent role in the sisters' education.

Following Woodhull's announcement, the sisters immediately made two strategic moves to boost Woodhull's name and their fame. A week later, they leased a four-story mansion in posh Murray Hill, ready to entertain those who could help Woodhull's candidacy. A few weeks later, in May, their *Woodhull & Claflin's Weekly* hit the newsstands. UPWARD AND ONWARD, blazed its masthead, but the sixteen-page newspaper cloaked its radical text in a circumspect format. Victoria for president was a central theme, but far-reaching topics filled its pages. Anthony and Stanton would sell their struggling *Revolution* that spring, after only two years, so the field for a radical paper concerning women's issues was wide open. The *Revolution* had touched on other women's rights issues besides voting, such as liberalized divorce laws, but the sisters expanded this by mentioning the unmentionable: sexual equality for women and participation in politics and finance. Such explosive ideas outraged the male hierarchy of clergy, journalists, financiers, and businessmen. The sisters inflamed them with their frank language on everything from prostitution, sex (in or out of marriage), corruption on Wall Street, defense of the eight-hour workday, coed sex education, vegetarianism, and Spiritualism. Into this mix they added poetry and fiction, including the "immoral" writing of George Sand. There were no salacious cartoons, no blazing headlines. Ads from prominent bankers and brokers were strategically placed on page one, while ads for mediums and clairvoyants and, yes, ever-fraudulent cancer cures, ran inside.

There was no way that the uneducated, unlettered sisters could have penned or, in some cases, even understood the intellectual broadsides to which they signed their names. Once again they used men—Blood to run the brokerage firm and Andrews to craft their words.

Andrews was a visionary abolitionist, an anarchist who argued for individual freedoms such as free love, had taught himself thirty-two languages, and introduced Pitman shorthand to Americans. He also won and lost a fortune as a lawyer. In 1843, while reading Isaac Pitman's phonographic manuals, Andrews saw the possibilities of shorthand as a major learning tool "to teach the illiterate Negro." Because the phonic system taught listeners to record the spoken word accurately—using symbols, not spelling, for the sound of the word—a person unable to read could understand the meaning. Andrews then fought to make shorthand an acceptable course in American schools.

Not content with existing languages, Andrews started his own, Alwato, long before Esperanto was known. His serious work aside, Andrews's fame came through his advocacy of free love, a belief he quickly sold to the sisters, who were already versed in the concept through Colonel Blood. They were eager sponges, absorbing Andrews's knowledge and his introductions to Victorian-era radical thinkers. In 1852 Andrews had engaged in a debate in the *Herald Tribune* with Henry James Sr. and Horace Greeley, on free love, marriage, and divorce. In the debate, Greeley embraced the concept of a conservative straight-laced marriage that could not be dissolved. James argued, vaguely, for a "foggy betweenity." Andrews slammed James for weakness and dismissed Greeley as a bigot.

In 1851, Andrews had helped found Modern Times, a Long Island commune known as the Mother of Free Love, where marriage arrangements were "left entirely" up to the partners. "They could be married formally or otherwise, live in the same or separate houses, have their relation known or unknown." Relationships could be dissolved informally, and it was considered impolite to question anyone about his or her private arrangements, such as "who was the husband or wife of anyone" or "who was the father of a newly-born child."

Such radical communes were not the goal of many free lovers. Many followers were serious reformers hoping to change the contemporary institution of marriage, which they saw as "one of the pillars of the ongoing repression of women." The sisters were among the more outspoken adherents of free love—a distinct reform movement that extolled individual freedoms, beginning with the Utopian culture of the 1820s and continuing through the battle for marriage reform in the 1870s, the fights against obscenity laws in the 1890s, and into the birth control movement of the twentieth century. The sisters' sense of freedom included tolerance for every kind of religion, although churchgoing moralists were among the strongest anti–free love chorus, preaching that marriage was inviolate, that sex should be for procreation only, and that divorce should be forbidden.

The press castigated Andrews's Modern Times, and he himself grew embittered when his endeavor was overrun by "fanatics and faddists," drawn not to his philosophy but to the lure of begetting far into the night. He next attempted to create a Manhattan Utopia for intellectuals.

His brilliance was often eclipsed by convoluted ramblings, but he remained indifferent to critics, who saw him as a "colossal," even "diseased," egotist and "sterile pedant." Yet Andrews held prophetic ideas; he sought to combine original thinking and knowledge into a science he called Universology—one science of the world that "would show how all the other sciences were related to each other...Well before the days of atomic science Andrews had harkened to a subtle echo of sameness that pervaded all things."

He envisioned a "pantarchy," with himself as the "pantarch." His collected philosophers would assemble in several categories—the Grand Order of Religion, Justice, and so on. The Grand Order of Domestic Revolution would work to reduce infant mortality. The only order that became a success was the Grand Order of Recreation, soon reduced to "the Club," a carousing group who took over the upstairs of a saloon at 555 Broadway. A reporter described them as female extremists who wore baggy, ankle-length harem pants and mingled with "perfumed exquisites," a suggestive euphemism for homosexuals. The Club was mobbed, until a vigorous police raid ended the fun in 1855.

When the sisters met Andrews in 1870 he was fifty-nine, a formidable six foot two, with a thin but penetrating voice, bulging blue eyes, and hair "addicted to disorder." Fashionable facial foliage for men had reached topiary proportions by this period, with beards cascading into two points dribbling far down the chest or cultivated under the chin to give a furry muffler effect. (Pictures of Greeley indicate the latter.) Andrews favored the two-pronged cascading beard ending in unkempt wisps.

Just as the sisters needed Andrews to write for them, the renegade philosopher determined to make his mark through the sisters, whom he saw as invaluable celebrities able to speak his words with flair and style in lecture halls far better than he could.

The sisters were perfect blank slates for him: they were eager to stretch their minds and be known as conduits for the outer limits of freethinking. They knew that their woeful education was insufficient. One reporter archly commented, "Possibly Mr. Andrews may understand what he means to say." Whether the sisters did remains questionable, even though they signed as their own the articles Andrews penned for them. Still, the sisters did have definite opinions on one subject, the plight of women, and their feelings came from the heart. Andrews convinced Woodhull that he stood for free love, women's rights, Spiritualism, and the kind of immortality she felt was her destiny. As usual, Tennie came along for the ride, herself vigorously faithful to exposing the double standard in sex, occupations, marriage, and wherever else she found it. So they gave Andrews space in the *Weekly*—far too much, critics would say.

The sisters' grand mansion at 15 East Thirty-Eighth Street, between Madison and Fifth, was both home to a raft of Claflins and a clubhouse for "thinkers and reformers," sustained by the sisters' wealth. Higher than any on the block, it was chock-full of marble pillars, immense gilded mirrors, and massive gold and crystal chandeliers. Ceilings were frescoed in white, green, carmine, blue, and gold, and were painted with frolicking Cupids, seraphs, Psyches, Venuses, Bacchus, Pan, and satyrs. In one suite, purple velvet curtains hid an alcove containing a large bed, its headboard inlaid with elaborately carved ivory. Sachets, wafting perfume, were attached to each cornice. At the top of the winding staircase one of several drawing rooms opened onto a glass observatory filled with singing birds, a fountain, and exotic flowers.

The tour guide for one reporter was none other than Annie, the mother of Victoria and Tennie. The old woman who had lived in shacks with unmade beds sprawled in every room and slept in seedy hotels and at the back of creaking medicine show wagons was now a boastful connoisseur of all things majestic: "What do you think of this parlor? I don't think there is any that can beat it... Don't walk through the mirror, please! You think there is another room off there, but it is only the reflection... Look here," she rattled on, "did you ever see anything more beautiful than this cupola?... it is a Capitol dome on a small scale." Looking up from the lobby, visitors saw a stained-glass dome, surrounded by frescoed images. At night, gas jets illuminated the dome with glowing rays.

If Victoria's spirit guide had transported them to the first home on

Great Jones Street, it was now Tennie's turn. Annie swore that Tennie had seen this same home in a vision, and pointedly added that "one beautiful painting, Aurora," was missing. "It cost her [Tennie] $10,000. She made Commodore Vanderbilt a present of it [a nearly nude figure] and the Commodore has hung it in his back drawing-room." Annie quickly bragged that she herself had dined with Vanderbilt.

If the décor sounds like several interior decorators run amok, plus a brothel touch or two, one must remember that this was the era of cluttered Victorian interiors, although the mansion's contents sound nouveau riche enough, and its occupants and guests bizarre enough, to have disgusted most upper-class Victorians.

The mansion soon glittered with an eclectic mix: financiers and senators, anarchists and abolitionists, journalists and judges, poets and politicians, including President Grant's father, as well as Stanton, Anthony, and other "strong minded women." Andrews compared the soirees to the "salon of Mme. Roland" during the first French Revolution—a rendezvous for "men and women of genius" afire with the ideas of "radical progress." (Madame Roland was a slightly unfortunate analogy, as she met disastrously with a guillotine in the second phase of the Revolution.)

As was their pattern throughout life, the sisters shrewdly snared important male allies. There was little subtlety in their pursuit of handsome Whitelaw Reid, at that time the right-hand man to Greeley at the *New-York Daily Tribune*. He later became the *Tribune* publisher, U.S. ambassador to France and the Court of St. James, and the 1892 Republican vice-presidential nominee. It was not lost on the sisters that Reid's publicity had helped make a star of abolitionist lecturer Anna Dickinson and that he was known to be one of her lovers.

Reid was a different cut from most journalists the sisters knew. With his air of confidence, good looks, and fine manners, he was in demand in New York society, which would never accept the sisters. Following a favorable *Tribune* editorial in 1870 on their Wall Street enterprise, Woodhull sent a letter to Reid indiscriminately name-dropping: the editorial, she wrote, was "entirely satisfactory to our best friend, the Commodore." With a directness that did not go over well, she wrote again asking Reid to "call at my apartments this evening for just a few minutes." She noted later that he had not come. Eagerly pushing her presidential quest, Woodhull invited Reid to one of the sisters' after-hours brokerage soirees. After that evening, Tennie sent him a suggestive letter: "I trust you rested well last night and that you find yourself refreshed there from. For myself I'm lonely today... Love without you / I sigh for one smile—which I hope to see tomorrow"—whether "a.m." or "p.m.," it is not clear in the original. The handwriting of both the sisters' letters appears to be the neat penmanship of Colonel Blood, who apparently had no problem composing forward notes to men for the sisters.

One man whom the sisters did strategically corral was Congressman Benjamin Butler, one of the most powerful politicians in America, who soon became a fixture at mansion soirees. The controversial politician collected an army of friends and a battalion of enemies, and was considered one of the most picturesque and commanding people who "ever figured in American history." Louisianans who lived under his Civil War occupation forever referred to the Civil War Yankee general as "Beast Butler." He won undying enmity when he issued an order that "Confederate women of all social stations" who showed contempt for occupying Yankee soldiers shall be "treated as a woman of the town plying her avocation." Even the British and French governments protested, to say nothing of New Orleans prostitutes, who pinned pictures of Butler on their privies. When one matron pointedly turned her back on Butler, he said loudly, "These women evidently know which end of them looks best."

The sisters' circle could not have been more opposite than those occupied by most of their neighbors in fashionably wealthy Murray Hill. To espouse any one of their ideas was unthinkable to Manhattan's upper class. As Edith Wharton said of her set, they did not encourage "literary leanings"; beyond the "small and slippery pyramid" that comprised their world lay

another "inhabited by artists, musicians, and 'people who wrote.'" The
sisters collected the bohemians, radical writers, politicians, poets, and
thinkers.

Mark Twain's 1873 novel, *The Gilded Age*, satirized the corrupt glitter of the era, which changed the social scenery as "old money" circled
the wagons while nouveau riche Civil War profiteers usurped center stage
with their millions and their corrupt political might. The sisters' osten-
tatious salon and companions such as salty Butler were the epitome of
what established Victorians viewed as nouveau-riche repugnant—partly
because they themselves were not far removed from the same sort of antecedents. The upper crust shuddered at reminders of how their own riches
were acquired. Manhattan's ultimate snob, Caroline Astor, resembled a
walking chandelier when decked out in cascades of diamonds and pearls,
some once owned by Marie Antoinette. She loathed newspaper reminders
that the Astors were descended from German hog butchers or that the
patriarch was a fur trader skilled at fleecing Native Americans. She tried
hard to obliterate the usage of her husband's middle name, Backhouse,
so redolent of the term for a privy, and to ignore the fact that William
Backhouse Astor Jr. carried on the grand Astor tradition as one of Manhattan's major slumlords. Her breathtakingly rich nephew William Wal-
dorf Astor tried to invent an ancestral knight killed in Jerusalem during
the Crusades, only to be laughed at by a leading genealogist who revealed
that—horror of horrors, in America's anti-Semitic blue-blood circle—the
Astors might have, in fact, been descended from Jews.

Nonetheless, Caroline Astor soldiered on, vowing that the new rich
would never enter her mansion. Her tediously dull soirees were a must for
the four hundred so designated as the Only Society That Counted (not, as
it has been claimed, the number of them who could fit in her ballroom).
Most fell into stupefied boredom after a repast of oysters, canvasback
duck, terrapin, partridge with truffles, quail, and stultified conversation;
wit was seldom found amid the "indescribably pretentious" trappings,
which included mountains of flowers, and white-gloved footmen done
up in knee breeches, plush green coats, silk stockings, and vests. It took

a member of this premier set, novelist Wharton, to satirize the wealthy Victorian American caste system that aped the courts of Europe and England's aristocracy: valets and maids dressed them as if they were infants.

Countess Olenska, the nonconformist in Wharton's *Age of Innocence*, set in the sisters' era, mocked the "blind conformity...It seems stupid to have discovered America only to make it into a copy of another country... Do you suppose Christopher Columbus would have taken all that trouble just to go to the Opera with the Selfridge Merrys?"

The lowborn sisters spoke often with contempt about the uselessness of idle, rich young women whose only purpose was to make a proper marriage within "the tribe," as Wharton termed it. Balls, dinners, and parties were all launched by a mother for this sole reason. Few in this set ventured into the suffragist or any other movement. Within the "tribe," hypocrisy ruled: Wives looked the other way at mistresses and at their husbands' trips to the fashionable brothels that, disarmingly, resembled their own mansions. Rippling the social waters with public scandal, rather than enduring a philandering or abusive husband, was out of the question. When Wharton's Countess Olenska plans to divorce, her lover tells her to think of the family and the "vileness" of publicity. "It's all stupid and narrow and unjust—but one can't make over society."

The sisters felt the opposite: that they *could* make over society. They saw chinks in the armor of social decorum and made it their goal to attack this hypocrisy. But in order to change anything, they reasoned, women must be enfranchised. To that end, Victoria and Tennie eyed Washington, planning a suffragist raid on the all-male nation's capital.

CHAPTER SIX

"Madam, you are not a citizen, you are a woman!"

Late in the fall of 1870, Victoria—now a stockbroker, publisher, and candidate for president—set up shop in the nation's capital, among other female lobbyists, who, like any "public women" (the name simultaneously used for prostitutes), were viewed as having dubious reputations. She took rooms in the Willard Hotel, known to every politician as an unofficial branch of government. Grant contemptuously coined the term *lobbyists* after trying to run the gauntlet of favor-seekers who clogged the hotel's lobby from one end to the other. That lobby and the plush dining room and bar, filled with male ribaldry, the fog of cigar smoke, and the smell of whiskey, were the places to do the nation's business after hours. Women were relegated to the second-floor sitting rooms.

With her piercing blue eyes, Victoria observed life at the Willard, watching the after-hours coming and going of congressmen and lobbyists, and later shocked audiences with her observations. "Where is prostitution in its greatest luxury? Washington! Everybody knows what the 'third house' in Washington is. It consists of the lobbyists who are there to obtain legislation—to push this little scheme, or that small appropriation." Lobbyists distributed to brothel madams "ten, fifteen and even twenty thousand dollars." To spellbound audiences, Victoria asked, "Why? To secure their influence with Representatives and Senators. I say it boldly, that it is the best men of the country who support the houses of prostitution!"

As she paraded through the Willard, aware of the male glances at her face and fine figure, Woodhull was secure in knowing at least one extremely valuable ally in the nation's capital, Massachusetts congressman Ben Butler. She had begun a stealthy pursuit of Congress back in 1869, when she and Tennie were unknowns, at which time she sent Tennie down to scout out any members who might be sympathetic to the sisters' suffragist goal. It didn't take Tennie long to cultivate the liberal Yankee. Lincoln had wanted Butler for his running mate in 1864, but had settled for southern sympathizer Andrew Johnson, to balance the ticket. Now Butler was President Grant's favorite congressman.

Everyone agreed that Butler was brilliant—and that he was ugly, with an oversize head on a squat body. He waddled through Hill corridors, resembling a plump bullfrog with drooping eyelids and one eye that wandered off on its own course. But he captivated admirers and bested foes with a scholar's mind and an amazing memory: as a child, he read weighty tomes before entering Exeter at age eight. Butler had grown rich as a lawyer. Butler played hardball politics, but he befriended the working class and poor to build a populist power base. He fought for the impeachment of President Johnson, pushed for an eight-hour workday and the Fourteenth Amendment, and was among the few major politicians who championed the vote for women.

Despite their educational deficits, the sisters were quick studies who captivated brilliant men, not just by their looks but also by their intelligence. Victoria's desire to learn everything, her ability to listen with an admiring, unwavering gaze—all were aphrodisiacs to the powerful men she favored. For her part, Tennie was comfortable with newspaper reporters, who loved her give-and-take, joshing conversation.

Gossip was inevitable when Victoria was seen with Butler. He loved his actress wife, but she was far away in Europe, being treated for thyroid cancer. Butler had openly pursued Anna Dickinson, the charismatic national abolitionist lecturer. At the height of her fame, Dickinson had many admirers, including the handsome *New-York Daily Tribune* editor Whitelaw Reid. Susan B. Anthony also wrote sexually charged letters to

Dickinson, calling her "Darling Dicky": "I hope to snuggle you closer than ever," but fell out with her when Dickinson did not support suffrage.

Victoria and Butler were close friends, but no facts corroborate biographers who use specious evidence to state categorically that they were lovers. Third-hand gossip was passed down that Butler "consented to champion her in Congress in return for an opportunity to feast his eyes upon her naked person." The "evidence" was Woodhull's comment that "I went at night" to ask for Butler's help, something a proper Victorian woman would not do. Yet the ambitious Victoria would have met Butler at any time to reach her monumental goal. She went to see him at night and "asked him to open the [judiciary] committee for me."

The sisters had learned through Butler that the Sixteenth Amendment for women's suffrage was dead in committee, with no one pushing it onto the floor or urging debate. Victoria then formulated her bold initiative. No woman had ever addressed a congressional committee before. Butler agreed to Victoria's doing so and, with his command of crisp legalese, helped draft her unique petition to Congress, called a "memorial."

On January 10, 1871, suffragist Isabella Beecher Hooker anxiously walked the marble halls of Congress, lobbying any member who would listen to her agenda. She had called a women's suffrage convention "on my own… I had to dip into my husband's pockets for the funds."

As she knocked on doors, Hooker heard some news that made her gasp in shock and surprise: "a Mrs. Woodhull had presented a petition to congress and that it had been referred to the Judiciary committee for a hearing on the morrow." Hooker was furious that this stranger had the audacity to upstage her convention, without ever having discussed it with her. She rushed to find Susan B. Anthony, who was in town for the convention and also lobbying the Hill. Stunned, they cornered George Julian, a radical Republican congressman, who verified the story, saying that he would be introducing Woodhull to the Judiciary Committee the next morning. Hooker and Anthony deliberated for three hours. "What were we to do?" Hooker recalled. They decided they had to postpone the convention, at least until the next afternoon, after Woodhull had met with the Judiciary. They hunted down Victoria and talked to her "all that evening." Hooker and Anthony were astounded to find out that Woodhull was operating "on her own." All Hooker's animosity faded; "I was fascinated by Mrs. Woodhull's talent and personality."

On the morning of January 11, 1871, Hooker was among those who stared at the woman who had overnight hijacked her women's suffrage convention, this stranger who was about to make history.

When Woodhull walked into the room to face the committee, she held tightly to Butler with one hand and with the other clutched Tennie, who covered her dark dress with a ruffled green taffeta shawl. Tennie sat protectively beside her sister as Woodhull faced the eight men arrayed in front of her across a large rectangular table. Suffragists crowded behind and around the men in the small room, a makeshift arrangement made when one of the large marble-pillared rooms was unavailable.

As an unsteady Woodhull stood up to address the committee, Hooker thought that Victoria was going to faint. "Her face flushed in patches." "She soon collected herself," recalled Hooker. "Her argument was very ably debated."

During this violent Reconstruction era, when the Ku Klux Klan was growing in strength, women's suffrage was in turmoil. The Fourteenth and Fifteenth Amendments sought equal protection for "citizens." Woodhull was now arguing that the Fifteenth Amendment, which read that no "citizen" shall be denied the right to vote "on account of race, color, or previous servitude," pertained to women as an "inalienable right," since the word *citizens* (not *males*) was used in both the Constitution and the two amendments. Radical suffragists had quickly latched on to the "previous servitude" clause. When a man asked Anthony how women could qualify as having had a "previous state of servitude," laughter and applause greeted her answer: "servitude of the hardest kind, and just for board and clothes, at that."

Woodhull's memorial galvanized what was termed the "New Departure" phase of suffrage. She hammered home the point that the

Constitution and the Fifteenth Amendment made no distinction "on account of sex." She also read portions of the Fourteenth Amendment— adopted in 1868—that stated "no State shall make or enforce any law which shall abridge the privileges and immunities of *citizens* of the United States, nor deny to any *person* within its jurisdiction the equal protection of the law." Her voice gathering strength, Woodhull argued that because Congress "has the power...to enforce the provisions of the 15th amendment...women as citizens should be included" in the right to vote under the protection of the Fifteenth Amendment.

Newspapers played judge and declared Woodhull wrong in her argument that the right of women to vote was "declared by the fifteenth amendment, and invincibly guaranteed by the fourteenth amendment." Sputtered one editorial, "Congress and the States did not intend to do this." Yet the editorial writer was forced to add, "Did they in fact *do* it? This is the question to be argued today."

Woodhull wasted no time in acting out the condescending conversation she had had prior to her committee hearing with representative John Bingham of Ohio, who sat on the Judiciary Committee. "Madam," he told her, "you are no citizen." When Victoria asked him what she was, he sputtered, "You are a woman!"

In fact, the only deviation from the wording *citizen* or *person* anywhere in the Constitution or amendments came in the *second* article of the Fourteenth Amendment's due process clause, written by Bingham. Woodhull handed Bingham a copy of Section 1 of the Fourteenth Amendment. He put on his glasses to look at his own words: "All persons born or naturalized in the United States, and subject to the jurisdiction thereof, are citizens of the United States...No state shall make or enforce any law which shall abridge the privileges or immunities of any citizens." A red-faced Bingham nonetheless remained obstinate, clinging to the Section 2 clause that stated there would be a penalty if the right to vote were denied to "male inhabitants." (Lest there be any confusion about former women slaves having a right to vote.)

Watching the historic moment before the Judiciary Committee, one reporter observed, "The youth, beauty and wealth of Mrs. Woodhull carried the day, and the grave legislators, 'e'en Ben Butler' bowed before these attractions." But they did not bow far enough. The Judiciary Committee turned down Woodhull's petition, with only Butler and William Loughbridge of Iowa in favor. Bingham wrote the majority opinion, stressing that the word *male* applied, citing Section 2 of the Fourteenth Amendment due process clause and ignoring Section 1, thus arguing that the Constitution and the Fifteenth Amendment were void regarding women as "citizens" being able to vote.

Congress weakly fobbed off this hot potato as a states' rights problem. For the next half-century, male legislators and judges decided that whatever kind of citizens women were, they were not voting citizens. Still, it was a decisive personal victory for Victoria, as suffragists applauded.

Tennie, looking on lovingly, won praise for her support of Victoria. Throughout the sisters' years in Manhattan, reporters and observers continued to be enraptured with Tennie's looks, comparing her full face and peaches-and-cream complexion to that of a sweet, innocent child—so in contrast to the risqué rumors that followed her. In fact, Tennie almost stole the show in looks alone during Victoria's famous moment. In a page-one article, a transfixed reporter wrote of Tennie, "She is young, pretty, interesting and quick as a bird both in movement and speech." Her short hair and boyish hat "gives her the appearance of a frisky lad, ready for mischief of any kind. But there is a peculiarly smooth tone to her voice." Her animated movements in any other woman would have appeared "unladylike," but in Tennie, each "lends a positive charm to her conversation and gives an emphasis to her speech that makes her logic irresistible."

Immediately following the hearing, Isabella Hooker asked Woodhull to address the convention the suffragists had postponed to hear her memorial. Hooker became a fervent follower, earning the wrath of and vicious public attacks by her family—half brother Rev. Henry Ward Beecher and famed half sisters Harriet Beecher Stowe, author of *Uncle Tom's Cabin*, and Catharine—the latter, ardently anti-suffrage.

The stir created by Woodhull brought newspaper reporters to a

packed suffrage convention at Washington's Lincoln Hall that same afternoon and evening. At 3:00 p.m. "fresh from the scene of their contest in
the Capitol, wreathed with smiles" came Hooker, Paulina Wright Davis,
Anthony—"the hero of a hundred fights"—and the "two New York sensa-
tions, Woodhull and Claflin." In their matching dresses, neckties, short
hair and "nobby Alpine hats" they were "the very picture of the advanced
ideas they are advocating," wrote one reporter.

Another reporter noted that at times Woodhull sat "sphinx-like." He
watched the "pale, sad face of this unflinching woman...if her veins were
open they would be found to contain ice." But Woodhull was more scared
stiff than ice-cold, petrified of being the center of attention among famous
leaders in the women's suffragist movement. As Hooker rose to introduce
her, Woodhull swayed, and Hooker thought she would fall. Woodhull
had none of the polish or the ringing elocution of later speeches, nor the
background of the educated women steeped in women's suffrage and
equal rights since Seneca Falls. She apologized, timidly saying she was
not used to public speaking and would just read her Judiciary Committee
petition.

Applause filled the packed hall as Woodhull restated her women's
right memorial. Then she and Tennie listened to the intelligent, fiery
speakers who followed, mentally taking notes. Victoria's brief stint on the
stage and Tennie's schooling in disingenuous fortune-telling were good
training for engaging an audience; now they absorbed ways to electrify
crowds with serious arguments. Soon Victoria would be known as one of
the top female orators in the country, and both sisters would later speak to
several thousand in auditoriums.

There was a triumphant air in Lincoln Hall, which was packed with
suffragists and supporters who embraced Woodhull's memorial, feeling
certain that it would recharge the troops and give new life to the struggle. Anthony said that a "poor lone woman" had presented a solution that
had not occurred to those who "had opted to labor on in the old way for
five, ten, fifteen or perhaps twenty years to come, to secure the passage
of another amendment to the Constitution...we were too slow for the

times." Anthony thought this new departure could succeed, thrilled that "the fourteenth amendment is good enough for women."

Actually the idea had first been raised by a Missouri lawyer and his wife, Francis and Virginia Minor, who argued that since the Fourteenth Amendment did not explicitly prohibit women from voting, individual states could not prevent them from doing so. But Stanton and Anthony had seemed unaware that this loophole was a possible tool. Once alerted, they, along with several hundred other women, including Victoria and Tennie, tried, and in some cases succeeded in, casting ballots. Susan B. Anthony, thrilled at casting her vote in the 1872 general election, was gladly arrested, and never paid a $100 fine, pointing out that her sin was merely that of being a woman. The judge, faced with this strong woman, did not make her pay. Both Tennie and Victoria made news when they tried to vote in the fall of 1871, a full year before Anthony.

On the final evening of the convention, Anthony's praise of Woodhull, with a nod to Tennie, was unstinting. "In this age of rapid thought and action, of telegraphs and railways, the old stage coach won't do," Anthony declared. Victoria and Tennie had captured "the spirit of the age" as stockbrokers, an avocation "never heretofore" opened to women and "one of the most difficult avocations that belongs to human kind." Woodhull had helped advance "our cause by as many years at least" as it would take to engineer the "ramifications of an amendment to the constitution."

On that last day, a smitten reporter found that "while women were wasting their breath at the convention," Tennie was off knocking on congressional doors, lobbying as a "worker" ought to "when a favorite measure is before congress. Oh, the irresistible Tennie!"

After Woodhull's electrifying debut before the Judiciary Committee, she became an instant hero to the Stanton-Anthony liberal wing of suffragists, named the National Woman Suffrage Association, or NWSA. Although Congress had refused Woodhull's request to address the entire body, she was now a star. Lecture requests poured in. Following Woodhull's memorial the sisters took full advantage of her celebrity status. They churned out and disseminated several thousand copies of Woodhull's memorial. For maximum publicity they continued to purposely set themselves apart from other suffragists, dressing precisely alike and wearing, as reporters noticed, "masculine coat-tails" on their jackets. They reveled in the validating praise from Anthony: Woodhull was "young, handsome and rich. Now if it takes youth, beauty, and money to capture congress, Victoria is the woman we are after."

Despite her shaky performance at the January suffragist convention in Washington's Lincoln Hall, when Woodhull merely read her position, the group called her back for an encore in the same hall in February. Followers and the merely curious alike flooded the space. When all the chairs were taken, people crushed together in the back. Woodhull, facing the largest crowd ever assembled in that hall, rose to speak. Tennie watched nervously as her sister again began hesitantly. Woodhull's face drained of color, and her pauses were disconcertingly long. Impulsively, Isabella Hooker stood up and put an arm around her. Then the rhythm of her ideas took over, and Victoria was transformed. She always said it was her "spirits" that guided her while speaking.

"I and others of my sex" are controlled by a government in "whose administration we are denied the right to participate, though we are a large part of this country. I am subject to tyranny!" she shouted, loud and clear. "I am taxed in every conceivable way." As a rare businesswoman, she could appeal to the men who had come to the hall to hear this new celebrity: "For publishing a paper I must pay... for engaging in the banking and brokerage business I must pay." She added to this list the taxes that she and other women consumers had to pay for "tea, coffee and sugar," all to maintain a government "in which I have no voice."

Victoria cuttingly said that she was not pleading for those "who are blessed by the best of wealth, comfort and ease," but for "the toiling female millions." She urged women to push for the vote, to petition for rights. She warned Congress that if nothing changed concerning the "utter exclusion of women," there was no recourse than to start a new women's government.

She was hyping her presidential candidacy as much as she was speaking for women's rights. Her voice carrying to the farthest corners of the hall, Woodhull, no longer nervous, shouted, "We mean treason; we mean secession, and on a thousand times grander scale than was that of the south. We are plotting revolution; we will overslough [*sic*] this bogus republic and plant a government of righteousness in its stead!"

The Victorian political world was used to flamboyant hyperbole from men, but not from women. In contrast to Woodhull's fiery call for revolution, the audience response was a heartfelt but ironic gesture. Hundreds of women supporters signaled their approval by a seen-but-not-heard fluttering of white handkerchiefs. This time the press was laudatory: "Mrs. Woodhull has opened her Presidential campaign with a very effective speech," wrote the friendly *New York Herald*. "A brave eloquent and unanswerable argument," wrote Washington, DC's *Daily Republican*. "A masterly argument," wrote the *Chronicle*.

Stanton, who had yet to meet Woodhull, as she was lecturing in the Midwest, read an account of her speech and raved to the young woman in a letter sent from Ohio. Her speech was "ahead of anything, said or written—bless your dear soul for all you are doing to help strike the chains from woman's spirit." The most famous American suffragists—Stanton, Anthony, Paulina Wright Davis, and Isabella Hooker—all bowed down to her.

Victoria and Tennie returned to New York that spring filled with happy dreams for the future. In May, Victoria would make her grand debut in not one but two Manhattan lecture halls. She was invited to give a major speech on labor issues at Cooper Union. In her NWSA address at Apollo Hall, she would use that moment to discuss her presidency.

In a few breathtaking months, Victoria had made such a sensation that the newspapers dubbed the upcoming NWSA Apollo gathering "Woodhull's Women."

CHAPTER SEVEN

Free Love, Suffrage, and Abolition

On Woodhull's big day before Congress, suffragist Lucy Stone was far from the crowd that fêted Woodhull—both geographically and philosophically. Huddled in Massachusetts with her conservative set, the American Woman Suffrage Association (AWSA), Stone seethed at Woodhull's success. Deeply opposed to free love views, Stone regarded Victoria and Tennie—who were being embraced by Stone's enemies Stanton and Anthony—as meddling misfits. When a Stone stalwart, Mary Livermore, swore that AWSA would have nothing to do with a memorial that came from a woman with "unclean hands," Anthony poured out her fury in a letter to a Spiritualist woman friend, underlining vehemently: "Our fastidious Boston friends can't see nor hear of the Woodhull shot…" The Stone group, whom Anthony called the "Boston Malcontents," would rather "women should grovel in the mire of disenfranchisement another whole century [than] be lifted out by what they term unclean hands."

Long before, when Victoria and Tennie were just child vagabonds, Stanton had already staked out a difference that would lead to a future rift in the women's movement; she shocked the sexually repressed Lucy Stone with her graphic comments on sex. When a man sought sex and a woman did not, Stanton railed in an 1856 letter to Stone, "the woman must be sacrificed; and what is worse, women have come to think so too."

In many respects it seemed as if Stone and Stanton would have been permanent allies. Like many women pioneers in suffrage, they rebelled early. Both were whip smart and stung by fathers who belittled their fight for an education. By dogged determination both became well educated. Like other suffragists, they watched mothers reduced to repeated child-bearing and household drudgery. Women of the early nineteenth century, like Victoria and Tennie's mother, routinely bore ten and twelve children. Many suffragist daughters vowed this would not happen to them. Although Stanton had seven children, she never was a docile homemaker, and she continued her tireless suffragist lectures and writing. Both Stone and Stanton were brave abolitionists and outspoken suffragists. Stone showed the same spark of Stanton's rebellion by refusing to take Henry Blackwell's name when they married in 1855. Blackwell also concurred with Lucy's wish to strike the words *to obey* from their vows.

Their joint progressiveness, however, stopped at the bedroom door. Sex so repulsed Stone that her biographer Andrea Moore Kerr surmised that Stone's adult traits mirrored those of women who had been sexually abused as children, in her case, probably by her domineering father, who also beat her when drunk. Among the adult traits Stone shared with sexu-ally abused children, in addition to abhorrence of sex, were a need to feel in control, low self-esteem, and disgust with men. To Lucy's shame, her husband ended up supporting the women's movement in more ways than one, carrying on a celebrated affair with another feminist. His philander-ing hardened his wife's abhorrence of sex. "I have been a disappointed woman...in education, in marriage, in religion, in everything, disap-pointment is the lot of woman," said Stone. She once fiercely vowed to an audience of two thousand, "it shall be the business of my life to deepen this disappointment in every woman's heart until she bows down to it no longer." Some suffragists, viewing a woman so soured by life, understood Blackwell's escape into a celebrated affair.

By contrast, Stanton had an unabashed joy of sex. She once slammed Walt Whitman because he was "ignorant of the great natural fact that a healthy woman has as much passion as a man, that she needs nothing stronger than the law of attraction to draw her to the male." Stanton had known passion in her youth, so in love with her brother-in-law that she considered eloping. Her marriage had no such ardor. The discontented Stanton's shocking battle for liberalized divorce laws long preceded that of the sisters. Unlike Stone, she was among the few early suffragists who, like the Claflin sisters, "insisted that woman's most basic right was to control her body." This included deciding when to have children, which meant (perish the thought) that wives could refuse sex or practice some of the primitive forms of birth control available at the time.

Stanton correctly saw that the "heart of the woman question was domestic and not legal or political." Marriage itself was not the enemy, but the "present form that makes man master, woman slave," she said. Her expanding the fight beyond suffrage clashed not only with Lucy Stone but with her partner Anthony's single-minded pursuit of the vote. Their disagreements would worsen when Stanton embraced Victoria. In 1871, Stanton penned a sharp letter to Anthony: "Men and women dabbling with the suffrage movement should be...emphatically warned that what they mean logically if not consciously...is next, social equality, and next Freedom or in a word Free Love."

The edgy animosity between Stanton-Anthony and Stone burst into a firestorm during the embattled days of Reconstruction, when reformers clashed over whether blacks should get the vote before women. For years, women suffragists and male abolitionists had spoken with one voice; freedom for blacks and women. In 1866 they founded the American Equal Rights Association (AERA). Then, the following year, abolitionists and suffragists tangled when two separate voting referendums, one for black males and one for women, were placed on the ballot in Kansas, pitting against each other two groups that had fought side by side.

Anthony and Stanton stumped for the women's referendum in Kansas with George Francis Train, an openly racist eccentric millionaire fond of using the word *nigger*. They were beholden to him. Train was bankrolling their *Revolution* newspaper. When both referendums were defeated, many reformers blamed Anthony and Stanton. The courageous abolitionist leader William Lloyd Garrison—who once barely escaped lynching by pro-slavery mobs as he was dragged through the streets of Boston—castigated the two women for aligning with Train, "a crack-brained harlequin and semi-lunatic." Lucy Stone was appalled. Anthony defended Train, arguing that he had made possible, with his generous endowment, her dream of publishing a women's rights paper. "If the Devil himself had come up and said 'ladies I will help you establish a paper' I should have said Amen!" Antagonism within the AERA continued until Train left the paper in 1869. (Without his funds, Stanton and Anthony were forced to sell it.)

More hostility occurred at the May 12, 1869, AERA convention in New York. While Anthony, Stone, and many other women argued that women should get the vote before blacks, Stanton's fervency led her down the low road of racism. She and Anthony, propelled by grief, betrayal, and fear that the women's vote would be delayed for decades, vehemently opposed males at the convention who argued that this was "the Negro's hour." Intense shouting broke out on both sides, and Anthony was drowned out when she argued that discussion of the women's vote should be first and the Negroes' last.

No one had fought harder for women's suffrage than Stone, but she was also overwhelmed by the horrific news from the South. The Klan was orchestrating whippings, beatings, lynchings, burnings, and mass killings. When blacks had gathered to demand the vote in New Orleans in 1866, thirty-four men and women were slaughtered. Stone argued that the woman's vote was imperative. Yet, in the end, if the amendment could not be changed for women, Stone conceded, "I will be thankful in my soul if *any* body can get out of the terrible pit."

An enraged Stanton shouted that she did not believe in allowing "ignorant negroes and foreigners to make laws" for her to obey. In no way should women stand aside "and see 'Sambo' walk into the kingdom first." She derided former slaves with their "incoming pauperism, ignorance and degradation" who "wouldn't know a ballot from an order for a mule." Although many women at the convention supported the "women first" concept, Stanton's racist rhetoric was the brilliant leader's flawed moment in history. Once she started, she seemed unable to control her rage. In private she was even more cutting, writing her cousin that she was annoyed at his persistence "in putting Sambo, Hans, Patrick and Yung Fung" before the women. Her partner, Anthony, vowed, "I will cut off this right arm of mine rather than work for or demand the ballot for the Negro and not the woman." But Stanton descended into the worst racist stereotype, raising the specter of rape against white women, warning in the *Revolution* that if the black man got the vote before women it would "culminate in fearful outrages on womanhood, especially in the south."

It was a bristly crowd by the time Frederick Douglass rose to speak. A towering presence at age fifty, the former slave who had taught himself to read and write was a dazzling orator and wrote with burning brilliance. His commanding face with its aquiline nose was set off by a profusion of salt-and-pepper hair. His wide-set eyes searched the hall as he kindly and poignantly acknowledged, "When there were few houses in which the black man could have put his head, this wooly head of mine found refuge in the house of Mrs. Elizabeth Cady Stanton." He said, "There is no name greater" than Stanton's "in the matter of woman's rights and equal rights." Stung and aggrieved, Douglass then criticized her "employment of certain names, such as 'Sambo . . . and the bootblack.'"

Douglass believed that "the right of woman to vote is as sacred in my judgment as that of man." Yet there was not the same urgency as "giving the vote to the Negro." He uttered a chilling comparison that drew thunderous applause: "when women, because they are women are hunted down . . . when they are dragged from their houses and hung upon lampposts, when their children are torn from their arms, and their brains dashed upon the pavement; when they are objects of insult and outrage at every turn, when they are in danger of having their homes burnt down over their heads . . . then they will have an urgency to obtain the ballot equal to our own." Someone shouted, "Is that not all true about black women?" Douglass answered, "Yes, yes, yes; it is true of the black woman, but not because she is a woman, but because she is black!"

Unity crumbled, and at the end of the convention, Stanton and Anthony refused to support the proposed Fifteenth Amendment, which excluded any mention of women's suffrage, while Stone joined the majority of members in support. This ensured the final split between Stone and Stanton-Anthony, a relationship that had been rocky ever since Stanton called for divorce reform and seemed to champion free love, which Stone called "Free Lust."

As moderate abolitionists and suffragists drifted off to join Stone and the Boston conservatives, Anthony and Stanton made up their minds to form their counter National Woman Suffrage Association (NWSA). Theodore Tilton, the blazing abolitionist and Victoria's future biographer, was their titular president, while Stone chose Reverend Beecher. A half year later, in January 1870—just before the unknown sisters made their Wall Street debut—newspapers happily mocked the "Women's War": "in the concededly bitter battle waged between the women of the Revolution and the bucolic Boston cabal headed by Julia Ward Howe, the fight, be it understood, is not for principle, but for position. Lucy Stone and her fast friend, Mrs. Howe, aspire to oust Miss Anthony and Mrs. Cady Stanton from their leadership of the delirium of unreason known as the woman's cause." The reporter called Howe's "Battle Hymn of the Republic" the "Battle-him of the Republic."

Into this messy situation stepped the sisters, committed to free love as well as the women's vote. Now, in 1871, with Woodhull a prominent force following her historic congressional petition and aligned with Stanton and Anthony, the Boston faction remained hostile.

As she approached her all-important New York lectures in May, Woodhull sought every possible support for her presidential candidacy. She made overtures to Lucy Stone but was rebuffed. Although Woodhull tried to dismiss the suffragist battles as petty "teacup hurricanes," the eruptions enveloped her and Tennie. That spring of 1871, leading up to Victoria's Apollo Hall lecture, the sisters and those who championed them were assaulted not only by gossip but by frontal attacks. The long knives were out, wielded by Reverend Beecher, the titular head of Stone's conservative camp, and his two sisters, Harriet and Catharine.

They had begun warning Isabella Hooker, their half sister, to distance herself from wicked Woodhull back in January, when Isabella was moonstruck over Woodhull's congressional triumph. Both Harriet and Catharine were anti-suffrage. Catharine was a fixture among five thousand anti-suffragists who signed a petition to Congress—among them the wife of Gen. William Sherman and wives of senators, representatives, and businessmen. "The Holy Scripture," they claimed, "inculcates for women a sphere higher than and apart from that of public life because as women they find a full measure of duties, care and responsibilities and are unwilling to bear additional burdens unsuited to their physical organization."

Catharine Beecher's national following made her a dangerous enemy of the sisters, as did the attacks leveled by the internationally famous Harriet. Soon gossip about the sisters was rampant. A Midwest AWSA member circulated racy rumors about them and the Claflin family. Disgruntled financiers who had been exposed in the sisters' *Weekly* told more stories. The Reverend Beecher's *Christian Union* newspaper falsely charged that *Woodhull & Claflin's Weekly* printed malicious libel.

By April 1871 the rumors had escalated to the extent that worried suffragists who had backed Woodhull were writing concerned letters to Stanton. She ignored them and gave crucial support to Woodhull, writing to the esteemed elder leader Lucretia Mott that she had "thot [*sic*] much" of "our dear Woodhull, and all the gossip about her and had come to the conclusion that it is a great impertinence of any of us to pry into her affairs. How should we feel to have everyone overhauling our antecedents? Woodhull stands before us today one of the ablest writers and speakers of the century." It was a male trap to pit women against one another, Stanton wrote. The male "creates the public sentiment, builds the gallows, and then makes us hangman." Women had "crucified" outspoken women in the past, and "now men mock us and say we are cruel to each other. Let us end this ignoble record and henceforth stand by womanhood. If Victoria Woodhull must be crucified, let men drive the nails and plait the thorns."

"If all 'they say' is true, Mrs. Woodhull is better than nine tenths of our Fathers, Husbands and Sons," Stanton stated to a male who asked about Woodhull's reputation. She added, "Now if our good men will only trouble themselves as much about the purity of their *own* sex, if they will make one moral code for men and women the world would be much 'nobler'...When our soldiers went to fight the battles of freedom in the late war, did they stop to inquire into the antecedents of everybody by their side? The war would never have been finished if they had." Stanton believed Victoria to be a "grand woman," but even if she were not, "I should be glad to have her work for her own enfranchisement."

In April, as her lecture dates neared Victoria sent a long letter to Isabella Hooker, revealing both anguish and defiant resolve. "Under all the curse and imprecations which are being heaped upon me, strong though I feel, I need some little kindness...I went to Washtn. [*sic*] entirely upon my own account. I did not desire to arouse all the petty fiendishness that has developed." Smarting from the slurs about her "anticedents," Victoria wrote she would not change her course even though "those who assume to be better than I desire it."

At forty-nine, Isabella Hooker at times sounded frantic. Her sisters "nearly crazed" her with letters imploring her "to have nothing to do with [Woodhull]," she wailed to Anthony, asking her or Stanton to "make some examination of this mysterious family." Anthony replied with characteristic sharpness, stabbing the paper with her pen, underlining word after word for emphasis. "Not until we catechize and refuse men—will I consent to question women—And it is only that Mrs. Woodhull is a woman...all of us enslaved class—that we ever dream of such a thing.... what would have been thought of those men [Jefferson and Washington] stopping to trace out every gossip of every revolutionist?"

To another friend, Anthony wrote, "When we women begin to search individual records and antecedents of those who bring influence, brains or cash to our work of enfranchising women—we shall begin with the men. Now I have heard gossip of undue familiarity with persons of the opposite sex"—here she named the reverends Beecher and Thomas W. Higginson, senators Benjamin Butler and Samuel C. Pomeroy, and journalist Frank George Carpenter. "Before I consent to an arraignment of Woodhull or any other earnest woman worker...I shall insist upon the closest investigation into all the scandals afloat about those men."

Anthony's explosive response to Hooker stiffened the younger woman's resolve to carry on her Woodhull support. Yet as Woodhull prepared to take New York in May of 1871, as she had taken Washington with her memorial petition and rousing speech just a few months before, Isabella Hooker worried that Woodhull did not distance herself enough from "Free Lust": "The trouble with Mrs. W is she uses it with a meaning of her own different from this hateful one as she will one day explain I hope." She nervously sought to round off the rough edges on Woodhull, her "darling Queen." Isabella admonished her to stop using "mannish" envelopes from her business stationery, and to "use nice note paper hereafter." As an "accepted standard bearer," Woodhull must be "perfect—exquisite in neatness, elegance and decorum. A lady in every sense of the word." (She also worried about rambunctious Tennie.)

In an era when American class distinctions were locked in place, all the polishing in the world would not have made the sisters acceptable. Suffragists came overwhelmingly from a middle-class WASP (white Anglo-Saxon Protestant) background—the same demographic of women who opposed the movement, such as Catharine Beecher. Woodhull could reinvent herself all she wanted—and indeed she did, to portray a more genteel life—but to most in the movement, Victoria and Tennie would always be déclassé. And they would soon be punished for it.

In May, as Woodhull enthralled her audiences, first at the Cooper Union labor meeting and then, a few days later, at the suffrage convention at Apollo Hall, a personal time bomb was ticking in the shape of her "never wholly sane mother." That she delivered her lectures brilliantly was a testament to how Woodhull could compartmentalize her feelings. The *New York Times* uncharacteristically raved about her Cooper Union Labor Reform League speech, in which she dazzled the audience with statistics and quotations and hammered away at political and business corruption. She was clearly broadening her base for her presidential campaign to include underpaid and overworked laborers.

She also wooed her suffragist allies, winning the support of the esteemed Paulina Wright Davis, who introduced her as the Joan of Arc of the movement, and of Lucretia Mott, the soft-spoken *grande dame* Quaker eminence.

Apollo Hall was jammed to suffocating as people rushed to see the woman who had experienced such a meteoric rise to fame. Nonetheless, windows were shut on this warm May night, the eleventh, because the traffic of horses and carriages crowding in front of Apollo Hall made it difficult to hear speeches. A tremendous mix—politicians, Spiritualists, and laborers—joined NWSA members to listen to Woodhull's keynote address. If Colonel Blood or Stephen Pearl Andrews, or both, had written her words, the thoughts now belonged to her. In the speech, she confronted detractors who saw rank ambition in her presidential bid, which she cast as a gesture for all women, something that would force people to ask "why not" a woman? She coyly added, "This service I have rendered women at the expense of any ambition I might have had" and repeated her cry of women's "revolution" against "tyranny." It was her "firm conviction" that if the major political parties continued to "rule this country twenty years to come as badly as they have for twenty years past, that our liberties will be lost or that the parities will be washed out by such rivers of blood as the late war never produced!" Amid the cheers and handkerchief waving, Woodhull moved to her seat, where she was clasped by Mott. Tears were streaming down the elderly woman's face.

But then Paulina Wright Davis innocently read Woodhull's broader political platform positions, written by Stephen Pearl Andrews. Woodhull called for a one-term presidency, monetary and tax reform, an eight-hour workday, welfare for the poor, national education for children, and a repeal of the death penalty. The platform also included a red flag: "All laws shall be repealed which are made use of by Government to interfere with the rights of adult individuals to pursue happiness as they may choose."

Newspapers quickly labeled this rhetoric on privacy rights as "free love." The rival AWSA seized on the platform for use in its attacks, and NWSA leaders privately tore into Andrews: "We have pretty squally times ahead," Martha Wright Coffin wrote to Anthony. Andrews's "foolish mistimed resolutions have done harm in giving the Philistines a chance to rejoice." Anthony moaned about Andrews's "moonshine impracticalities—oh dear dear what terrible rough seas we do have." The NWSA was incensed that newspapers were falsely implying that the organization had adopted Andrews's resolutions.

The press piled on its disgust of Woodhull, especially the Beecher-friendly *Brooklyn Eagle*, quoting a *Weekly* free love passage: "Who would compel us to prostitute ourselves by compelling us, through your marriage laws, to remain the legal wives of those who have become detestable to us?" The paper then excoriated Anthony, Hooker, and Stanton, who had put Woodhull "forward as the leader." Nervous NWSA members hoped to ride out the gossip and the free love ruckus, but they did not count on the Claflin clan.

CHAPTER EIGHT

All in the Family: "Never a wholly sane mother"

An astounding story about Victoria and Tennie's mother, their sister Polly Sparr, and Victoria's husband, Colonel Blood, made all the papers on May 16, 1871: "[U]pon affidavits of Annie Claflin, Mary [Polly] Sparr and Benjamin Sparr a warrant was issued for Blood's arrest, charging that he had threatened to kill Annie or put her in an asylum and had stolen the affections of daughters Victoria and Tennie."

However, the *Brooklyn Eagle* had a major scoop a week before the trial. On May 7, just as Woodhull was preparing for her Apollo speech, the affidavits from Annie and the Sparrs were read at a pro forma session in the Essex Market Police Court. Surprisingly, Manhattan papers apparently overlooked this, thus sparing Woodhull humiliation before she gave her NWSA keynote address on the eleventh. Blood bowed to the judge. The judge said wryly, "The worst thing specifically charged against you is living with your wife, and not agreeing with your mother-in-law. The complaint is dismissed unless you insist on a trial." Had Blood agreed, the sisters would have been spared mortifying revelations of the family in screaming headlines as far as San Francisco. But Blood asked that "the complaint be not dismissed." He wanted to "disprove the charges against me." With that, the harm done to the sisters' already questionable reputation was about to be enormous.

The trial, which began on Monday, May 15, following Woodhull's stunning NWSA success, resulted in unprecedented coverage of this family feud; it would ruin Woodhull's credibility with the movement, give anti-suffragists fodder for their fight, and cover the sisters in ignominy. Rumors were one thing, and likely to be fleeting, but the stormy assertions and facts about the tawdry battling Claflins were quite another. Victoria, Tennie, and Colonel Blood met with a *Brooklyn Eagle* reporter on May 7 after the court meeting, hoping to defuse the bomb before the trial.

Blood, a spare man of "about five feet eight, with a straight nose, firm mouth and deep blue eyes," impressed the reporter as a phrenologist's fine specimen. Woodhull had a Grecian figure, and Tennie looked like "Byron's Dadu electrified into animation." Blood said that he and Victoria were married "for six years past, and till death doth us part as to the future." Victoria said of her first marriage, "We were legally and duly divorced...by mutual consent" because they "were not compatible." Colonel Blood added vaguely that "in order to effectuate" his divorce, "I left St. Louis for a time. My leaving [with Victoria] is made a great handle of but they will have to prove or swallow all their charges." Blood was referring to an extortion ruse by Polly Sparr and her husband. Blood said, "See how they began this against me six years ago almost," and produced an affidavit signed by another Claflin sister, Margaret A. Miles. She vowed that the Sparrs were going to get a policeman to arrest Blood "for bigamy and get $10,000 or $15,000 for letting him off, which we will divide."

The reporter tried to discuss Annie's complaint, but Tennie interjected: "Now, let me come in right here! My mother is a very old lady, whom I believe to be insane. She can neither read nor write. She did not make that affidavit [on Blood's threatening her life]...A letter like this has been sent to every prominent person with whom we are acquainted," she said, vehemently reading it out loud: "Dear Sir: Your intimacy with Tennie C. Claflin and with Mrs. Woodhull is known...I know also that you have a wife and family. Now I am down on my luck, and I want $300 out of you. You may call this blackmailing. But I have you tight."

Tennie produced a "reply to a blackmailing letter...written to me by a prominent gentleman worth millions of dollars and of high position...:

'My dear Miss Claflin: A pirate has just left this letter with me...an old woman came in who said she was your mother. I believe from what she said that she was crazy. She said that she had been told to get $300 out of me for that letter, but as she couldn't read, I believed that she did not know what she had been put up to. I told her it was no use. That my intimacy with you was honest, square and pure and that all I knew of you was that you were a woman who honestly earned your own living. I gave her three dollars because she said she hadn't eaten anything since yesterday morning, and that she hadn't a cent. I asked her why she didn't go to you. She said Sparr told her that if she did you would send her to the Island.'" Blackwell's Island, now Roosevelt Island, was a nineteenth-century hellhole that housed prisoners, debtors, and the insane. "I write this to you to put you on your guard...the parties behind your mother mean you harm."

In court Tennie charged the Sparrs with extortion, but even her own father was an apparent villain. Benjamin Tucker, a friend who later turned on the sisters, nonetheless noted, "Blackmailers beset them continually, some of these belonging to their own family. One day Victoria handed me a post-card threatening terrible things unless certain demands were met." Tucker went to the address on the postcard, and "through the side-entrance came that frightful old scoundrel, Buckman Claflin." When Tucker reported back to Victoria and Tennie, "the matter was dismissed. They were accustomed to trouble from that source."

These revelations of extortion attempts endured by the sisters explain in great measure why they had tolerated the Claflin "deadbeats." First, they were pulled into nefarious dealings with their parents and family as young girls, and then, when they were famous, they were threatened with blackmail for any activities, real or not. Clearly the shiftless Claflins had no reputations to lose with their extortion schemes, but Tennie revealed the fear that had haunted her and her sister: "When we first started here two years ago, we thought a row in the papers with these people would hurt us." When she tried to evict the "deadbeats" at Great Jones Street, a brawl ensued. "They said if I tried to put them out they would make it hot for us in the papers." When officers came to the home they "told him to clear, else they would throw him out of the window...the marshals had to put them out by force." The sisters' firm paid for hotel expenses, then, responding to their family's threats to ruin them, gave the "freeloaders $1,500 to go West and set up in business...now they are back....they are the blackmailers working through and by my uneducated and feeble-minded mother. We are going to take care of ourselves after this and meet these persons face to face."

The long interview in advance of the trial stimulated the curious. On May 15, reporters and spectators jammed the Essex Market courthouse to view this "Great Scandal." Some papers practically convicted Blood of threatening his mother-in-law's life when they characterized Annie's charges as "revelations" rather than "allegations." Rationalizing its coverage of a trifling domestic squabble, the *Herald* said the story was important because the parties were the notorious stockbrokers, their mother, and Blood, who was the firm's "silent or 'sleeping partner' "—a snide double entendre.

During the sensational trial both sisters testified repeatedly that the only reason the Sparrs and their mother had filed the suit was to get their trump card, Tennie, back telling fortunes to make money for them. However, the main disclosure remembered—and one that would tar Victoria for years as the Jezebel some papers had already labeled her—was that Victoria was living with both a former husband (Canning Woodhull) and a present one (Blood), under one roof. This was hardly a ménage à trois. Canning Woodhull was a drunk addicted to morphine. Victoria tried to explain, in the *World* and the *Times*, that Canning was "sick, ailing, and incapable of self-support," so she felt it her duty to care for him. "My present husband, Colonel Blood, not only approves of this charity but cooperates in it. I esteem it one of the most virtuous acts of my life, but various editors have stigmatized me as a living example of immorality and unchastity." It was indeed an act of compassion. Dr. Woodhull did not live out the year, dying on April 9, 1872.

Her explanation did not matter. What the newspapers headlined was

Colonel Blood's testimony. His statement regarding Canning Woodhull electrified the court: "I see him every day; we are living in the same house."

Counsel: "Do you and Mrs. Woodhull and Mr. Woodhull occupy the same room?"

No answer.

Blood's counsel hastily prompted Blood: "[P]lease tell the Court why Dr. Woodhull lives in the same house, and who supports him." Blood: "The firm of Woodhull, Claflin & Co. has supported the whole of them: Mrs. Woodhull's first child is idiotic and Dr. Woodhull takes care of him."

Annie, a "peculiar old lady, of determined mien and expression," peering with keen little black eyes through gold-rimmed glasses, took the stand and "spoke with a strong German accent and great volubility": Blood had " 'by divers wicked and magic arts and devices, alienated the affections' of her devoted daughters and had 'threatened her life.' " Attempts to keep her on track failed: "Judge, my daughters were good daughters and affectionate children 'til they got in with this man Blood. He has threatened my life several times, and one night last November he came into the house and said he would not go to bed till he had [here the paper capitalized] WASHED HIS HANDS IN MY BLOOD. I'll tell you what that man Blood is. He is one of those who have no bottom in their pockets. You can keep stuffing in all the money in New York; they never get full up. If my daughters would just send this man away, they might be millionairesses [*sic*] and riding around in their own carriages...he has taken away Vicky's 'fection [*sic*] and Tennie's 'fection [*sic*] from poor old mother. S'help me God, Judge, I say here and I call Heaven to witness that there was the worst gang of free lovers in that house on Thirty-Eighth street that ever lived— Stephen Pearl Andrews and Dr. Woodhull and lots more of such trash."

Even her lawyer admonished, "Keep quiet, old lady."

She rolled on: "I was afraid of my life all the time I was in the house; It was nothing but talking about lunatic asylums; if God had not saved me Blood would have taken my life long ago."

Blood denied everything. He never made any threats except one night "when she was very troublesome, I said if she was not my mother-in-law I would turn her over my knee and spank her."

Counsel: "[W]ould you really do that?"

No answer.

The next day, a mob arrived well before the courthouse doors opened, pushing and shoving to get a choice seat to see the sisters. "Physicians, lawyers, social reformers, cooks, chambermaids, brokers, gentlemen of elegant leisure arrayed in velvet and tuba roses thronged the passage ways." They pressed against the railings and stood on the benches to see and hear the "heroines of the hour...as good looks and winning ways generally carry the day, silver-tongued Tennie had all the sympathy," compared to her "more reserved" older sister.

Victoria testified that Blood "is my husband" and Woodhull "was my husband." She shaved her age from fifteen to "near fourteen years" when she married Woodhull. Unless she was living with Blood when she gave birth to daughter Zula in 1861, she misstated that she had lived eleven years with him. Victoria testified that at times she thought her mother "was insane and not responsible for what she said; I never thought my mother in danger of any violence from Colonel Blood." Her erratic mother would sometimes "sit on Mr. Blood's lap and say he was the best son-in-law she had," continued Victoria. "Then again she would abuse him like a thief, calling him all the names she could lay her tongue in... all without any cause whatsoever...The Sparrs were always telling mother that as long as Blood was around" she could not get Tennie back. Her mother was "determined to ruin Blood," recalled Victoria, "saying that she would have him in the Penitentiary before she died."

The counsel asked, "Is the Sparr family poor?"

Victoria said caustically, "They must be poor—they have had to live off two women all their lives."

Tennie caused a stir, greeting her counsel with a friendly nod, and stared the opposing counsel full in the face. "She looked meltingly at the twenty-five reporters gathered to hear her wondrous tale. Tennessee has good eyes and knows her power." She "kissed the book with an unctuous smack...everything that Tennessee did was done fervently. She had evidently inherited her mother's talent for volubility."

With a smile, she teased the opposing counsel: "Now, go on! You may cross-examine me as much as you like. I never knew Colonel Blood to use any violence toward mother. He only treated her too kind, in fact, I don't see how he stood all her abuse." Then she blurted out what was vital to the sisters and what she wanted to convey to a packed court: "Sparr has been trying to blackmail people through mother."

"This is altogether irrelevant!" the Judge bellowed. "If it is objected to I will rule it out."

The counsel said, "I have objected, but I can't stop her."

As laughter filled the courtroom, Tennie raced on, trying to show letters that blackmailed "different eminent persons in this city...written by this man, Sparr!!"

Tennie wanted to reveal the blackmail to explain why the sisters had never totally severed ties with their parents and family. That the parents were willing to ruin their two daughters said everything about the family the women had tried so desperately to escape.

The judge did not care about Tennie's blackmail charges, ruling the letters inadmissible. Tennie persisted, addressing the reporters: "I am the martyred one in this case. Colonel Blood is the best son-in-law my mother ever had...My mother is insane on Spiritualism." Tennie hinted at something worse than just fake fortune-telling: "I have left the degradation of a life where I was almost lost...I have humbugged a great many rich people, Vanderbilt included, but I did it to make money to keep these deadheads [her family]." Tennie swore that she also had real healing ability. The *Herald* capitalized her next statement: COMMODORE VANDERBILT KNOWS MY POWER.

Whatever psychological reasons—misplaced guilt, loyalty to a captor, a vague memory of her mother at her kindest—Tennie felt inextricably bound to her. On the stand, she suddenly cried, "But, Judge, I want my mother," then jumped from the witness box, raced behind the railing, and sprang toward Annie, clasping her in her arms. She kissed her mother so loudly that it echoed in the courtroom, while Polly Sparr tugged on the other side of old Annie.

Spectators stood on tiptoe, craned their necks, and shoved one another in an attempt to see the action. Colonel Blood moved in to soothe the sobbing Tennie, patting her on the cheek and pushing her hair back from her face with gentle hands. He whispered, "Do retire, my dear; you are only making yourself conspicuous." Tennie calmed down. The case was closed that afternoon. Whatever the judge ruled was never reported.

For the sisters—who had lied so beautifully about experiencing a pleasant childhood, acquiring a good education, and learning stocks through their lawyer father—their public image was wrecked. All Victoria's acquired dignity and poise, and Tennie's attempts to be her sister's exemplary partner, were for naught. Now the two were seen as adjuncts to this squalling, trashy clan; the word *tramps* followed them with regularity.

The sisters had a naïve but abiding belief that if they could just tell their story to the press they would be understood and all would be resolved. Yet whatever sympathy they gained seldom offset the traction they gave to more scandal. A few weeks after the trial, the sisters once again held forth for the press. Woodhull revealed her shame at belonging to a family she had tried to hide. The Sparrs, she said, had "forced us to expose our family secrets, which we have been guarding for a long time, and now they can do no more. The skeleton in our closet is exposed." Tennie then said that she was now "free from the Sparrs and their threats: 'we'll show you up. We'll put you in the newspapers. We'll ruin you.' This has been the cry at every attempt of mine toward independence."

Tennie elaborated on her abused childhood: "I was kept down and deprived of all that a child needs, so at fifteen I ran away, from sheer desperation...they brought me back and kept me locked up for a year. I told such wonderful things for a child that my father made from fifty to a hundred dollars a day at hotels, simply by letting people see the strange clairvoyant child...I never had any happiness till I came to live with my darling sister Vicky." Tennie was stalked by her mother, who "has shown an insane determination...to force me to go back to the business...she annoyed everybody at hotels and boarding houses, and I was forced to constantly change my boarding house...She hates Colonel Blood and Vicky because they upheld me."

After this explosive trial, Woodhull furiously sketched her father's viciousness a few months later in the famous biography of her penned by journalist and free love friend Theodore Tilton, describing their father enacting his blackmail schemes: "At times a Mephistopheles...watching for a moment when his ill word to a stranger will blight their business schemes, drops in upon some capitalist whose money is in their hands, lodges an indictment against his own flesh and blood, takes out his hand-kerchief to hide a few well-feigned tears, clasps his hands with an unfelt agony, hobbles off smiling sardonically...and the next day repents." The biography went on: "Victoria's rescue of her [Tennie] excited the wrath of these parasites—which has continued hot and undying against both to this day. The fond and fierce mother alternately loves and hates the two united defiers [*sic*] of her morbid will."

But there was no safe haven for Victoria and Tennie. Horrified at being smeared by association, suffragists clamored for Woodhull's depar-ture from their midst. The AWSA wing gleefully trashed her. When member Mary Livermore accused her of advocating and practicing "licen-tuosness [*sic*]," Woodhull sharply warned (the apparently sexually active) Livermore that those "who live in glass houses shouldn't throw stones, and you very well know that most people do live in these brittle tenements."

As if the trial hadn't been enough, crazy Annie was back in action within days, concocting a tale that made front-page news. She had been kidnapped, yanked into a carriage, blindfolded, taken to a dank place, and given nothing but bread and water for three days, then released. "I believe," she said, that "he [Blood] was the one had me taken off." She told reporters that Victoria was afraid "that some night he may pour hot lead in her ears and kill her if she vexes him, or if she leaves him he may shoot her down in the streets."

By now one would think readers might have tired of the wretched family saga, but a small item created more sensation: DR. SPAR [*sic*] FOUND

DEAD IN A HOTEL. Sparr had registered at a hotel under an assumed name. Finding the door locked the next day, the chambermaid used a stepladder to look through the transom and saw Sparr lying on the floor "in nearly a nude state." The doctor and coroner stated that Sparr "evidently had fallen out of bed and struck his head against the panel of the door with so much force as to partially burst it out...Apoplexy or heart disease may have caused death." The New York *Sun* spiced up its page-one story, hinting that Sparr was the victim of "self-murder...induced by domestic infelicities." An unsigned, incomplete letter written in pencil, found in a satchel in the room, began, "Vickey, [*sic*] Colonel and Tenny [*sic*] included," and referred to "poor old mother, Pa and Polly," warning the sisters and Blood that they "dare not put them out."

The *Brooklyn Eagle* paraphrased whatever Woodhull said about Sparr's death, implying that she was plugging her presidential campaign, thus editorializing that Woodhull was unfit to head the "shrieking sisterhood" whose "most popular leader" had "kicked about the corpse" of a brother-in-law.

For the Stanton-Anthony branch, the arduous task of damage control lay ahead. Victoria drew some comfort from a letter sent to her from Stanton, then lecturing in Wyoming: "The grief I felt in the vile raking of your personal and family affairs was three-fold—sympathy for you, shame for the men who persecuted you and the dangers I saw in the abuse of one of our greatest blessings, a free press." She praised Victoria for her brave speeches: "You have attacked, too, the last stronghold of the enemy—the social subordination of woman."

In the aftermath of the trial's sensational smorgasbord, reporters began to dig into the sisters' past. The *St. Louis Times* wrote about Buck absconding with money from mail at the Homer post office and the suspicion that he had set fire to his gristmill for insurance. The paper also hinted at a tawdry past for Woodhull, yet gave no facts. She ran "a house in Chicago in a grand and peculiar style" and then was the "proprietress of an eclectic institution" in St. Louis. Others did not report but harangued: "Now her shameful life has been exposed, it will follow that the enemies of female suffrage will point to her as a fair representative of the movement." Henry C. Bowen, Beecher's Plymouth Church mentor and publisher of the religious *Independent*, slammed Stanton, Anthony, and Isabella Beecher Hooker for being "foolish" enough "to have given a prominent place to Mrs. Woodhull." The *New-York Daily Tribune*'s Horace Greeley, who was strongly against divorce reform, tore into Woodhull as "one who has two husbands after a sort, and lives in the same house with them both, sharing the couch of one, but bearing the name of the other, to indicate her impartiality perhaps." This was particularly galling to Woodhull and others in the movement who blamed Greeley for his emotionally battered wife and miserable marriage. Woodhull shot back in the *Weekly*: "Mr. Greeley's home has always been a sort of domestic hell."

Perhaps the biggest blow to Tennie was the response of Commodore Vanderbilt to her claims in court that she had "humbugged" him. For a year, the now-married Vanderbilt had distanced himself from the sisters, and he had not been seen as their financial guru for months. Immediately after what he would have considered a stinging insult by Tennie—that she had duped him—Vanderbilt told a reporter, "They h'aint no friends of mine. From what I hear, you shouldn't be associating with such folks."

Other women might have crumpled from the barrage of hostile publicity and invective, but Victoria and Tennie were far from done. They lashed back at the stinging assault from those whose private lives were not as pure as they seemed. Four days after the end of the trial, Woodhull flashed a warning in the *New York Times* and the New York *World*: "I do not intend to be made the scapegoat of sacrifice to be offered up as a victim to society by those who cover over the foulness of their lives and the feculence of their thoughts with a hypocritical mantle." Her sharp threat was aimed at the Plymouth Church's minister, Henry Ward Beecher, revered as the "most famous man in America." Woodhull did not name him, but wrote enough for Beecher to recognize himself among her "judges" who "preach against 'Free Love' openly and practice it privately...I believe in public justice."

Beecher thought, wrongly, that he was safe from Woodhull's threats, but she had just learned of smoldering gossip that was about to ignite.

CHAPTER NINE

Sex and the City, circa 1871

Underneath the Victorian cloak of unctuous morality, sex was everywhere—except in the marriage bed, Woodhull argued. "Marriage," she said, "is a license to cohabit sexually... [yet] the enforcement of this method eventually defeats the original object... it is the common experience among the married who have lived together strictly according to the marriage covenant, for from five to ten years, that they are sexually estranged... I know there are exceptions to this rule but they are the exceptions... Sexual estrangement in from five to ten years!"

On stages across the country, in 150 performances, Victoria delivered this strong brew, addressing the crowd directly: "Marriage," she shouted, "is a fraud upon human happiness!... Think of it, men and women, whom nature has blessed with such possibilities for happiness as are conferred on no other order of creation! Your God-ordained capacity blasted, prostituted to death, by enforced sexual relations where there is neither attraction or sexual adaptation; and by ignorance of sexual science!... from the moment that the sexual instinct is dead in any person, male or female... a person begins actually to die. It is the fountain from which life proceeds. Dry up the fountain and the stream will disappear."

Woodhull confronted the gossip about her head-on: "I have been generally denounced by the press as an advocate of promiscuousness," but she asserted that she was the opposite, a true romantic, and cited what comprised "proper" sexual relations. This was her clearest definition of free love: "First love of each by each of the parties; second, a desire for the commerce on the part of each, arising from the previous love; and third, mutual and reciprocal benefit." She pointedly added for the religious in her audiences who viewed sex as a sin except when for propagation, "Let your religious faith be what it may, if it does not include the sexual act it is impotent." Nothing could be holier than an act that begets children, she said, but she made it clear that sex should be enjoyed for its own sake as long as both parties agreed—a main tenet of her free love position. Her definition of "improper sexual commerce" included that "which is claimed by legal right, as in marriage, second, where the female, to please the male, accords it" as a duty and without love.

Both sisters decried the economic dependency of women that kept them trapped in repugnant marriages. A century and a half before the terms *date rape* and *domestic rape* were coined, Victoria and Tennie shouted to packed houses about domestic abuse. "Night after night there are thousands of rapes committed under cover of this accursed license; and millions—yes, I say it boldly, knowing whereof I speak—millions of poor, heart-broken, suffering wives are compelled to minister to the lechery of insatiable husbands," said Victoria. Nothing "except marriage…invests men with the right to debauch women, sexually, against their wills. Yet marriage is held to be synonymous with morality!" Her voice penetrating to the farthest row, she received boos and cheers as she shouted, "I say, eternal damnation, sink such morality!" She urged men to worship women, "rather than to command or appropriate…Remember that it is a pretension and a fraud to think of ownership in, or control over, the person of a woman."

She chastised the "virtuous women" who abhor prostitutes while condoning their clients. She wove a tale of women reformers who "resolved to visit 'the houses' and learn who it was that supported them, and then afterward to ostracize them." After a week, those in this Women's Crusade "suddenly stopped" their inquiry. The women had "pressed their investigations until they pressed themselves into the faces of the best men of the city, some of them their husbands and brothers," she said archly. "When they found their best men—their husbands and brothers—were supporting these women...they should have taken [the women] home and seated them at their tables beside their companion, and said: 'if you are good enough for our husbands to consort with, you are good enough to sit at our tables with them.'" If enough women organized such homey visits of professional prostitutes, "prostitution, so called, would be abolished at once. It is the women who stand in the way. They, knowing that their husbands visit these women, continue to live on, doing their best to damn the women, but saying nothing about the men."

Tennie defined *sex radicals*, a term that applied to the sisters: "We are engaged in introducing new social views which look to radical and sweeping changes in the present system." This concept included freedom for women to choose their partners, to marry or not, to divorce and be able to retain their children, and to control their own bodies regarding when or even if to have children. "We now stand on the very brink of a social earthquake," she told audiences in her booming voice: "What this earthquake may destroy, who may be swallowed up in its yawning chasm, or whether we ourselves may be swallowed up we do not know. But that great good to the human family will come of it we feel assured." In Tennie's speeches, which were given to audiences around the country and published as a pamphlet by the *Woodhull & Claflin's Weekly* Company, her central theme was sexual equality. Her compassion for prostitutes led detractors to say this was a pursuit she knew all too well. Why were prostitutes arrested while their clients went free? she asked, and threatened to expose clients who were the "best" men in town. Why should an unmarried woman who became pregnant deserve disgrace while the man who impregnated her was never asked to account for anything? she cried.

Tennie, her assurance on the subject a contrast to her youthful face—as "fair as an infants [*sic*]"—related the story of a young beauty who demanded thousands of dollars before she would marry a rich old man. "Now, I say that the poor prostitute, suffering for bread and naked for clothes, who sells herself to some man for a few hours to obtain the few dollars with which to procure them, and thus sustain her life; or the young maiden involuntarily yielding herself up to him to whom her young heart goes out in purity, is an angel compared to this woman who sold herself... to the man she detested, for one hundred thousand dollars.... But such is the force of public opinion" that while the prostitute "would be kicked from the doorstep" and the unmarried girl who engaged in sex with a man she loved would be "turned from her father's home," the designing young married woman is "a worshipped belle of New York—a virtuous woman."

Victoria could certainly be challenged for her assumption that "those who are called prostitutes...are free women, sexually, when compared to married women." Refusal was seldom an option for prostitutes. An estimated twenty thousand prostitutes worked in New York City in 1868, which prompted a Methodist minister to exclaim that Manhattan housed more prostitutes than parishioners. Transplanted impoverished southern belles were forced to choose between starving and whoring along with Yankee girls and mulattos who had once been their slaves.

One male chronicler of the period repeated exactly what the sisters were saying. George Ellington (a pseudonym) estimated that "two out of three men of wealth and fashion and leisure devote time and money to some fair one," and their "female relatives are profoundly in the dark" or look the other way. The "proportion of really happy marriages are exceedingly few, so few," he wrote, that it was a wonder anyone married, and wives of the leisure class routinely had lovers themselves. In a time when a good laborer's wage was $500 a year, the tiny percentage of the very rich, their wealth gained by any means, could enjoy a king's life, including the fairest of those called "Women of Pleasure." Young beauties often were part of the collection of rich men's toys, which included horses, stylish carriages, servants, cruises to Europe, brandy, champagne, the best cigars, and the most elegant garments. These women paraded on Broadway, rode in the finest carriages in Central Park, enjoyed tables at Delmonico's and fine theater boxes, and frequented private supper clubs with discreet back entrances.

Which brings us to *The Gentleman's Companion*, a well-thumbed vest pocket guide to New York brothels published anonymously in 1870. It begins puckishly: "We don't intend to tell the reader where the Central Park is, the Croton Aqueduct...Cooper Institute, or Knox the hatter... we propose" to give the reader "a knowledge of which he could not procure elsewhere."

Pretty maids, tired of earning a pittance in domestic service while being chased around a bedroom by the master, "were the most likely to engage in the sex trade." More than sixty percent of women workers in 1870 were domestics; live-in help worked from dawn until late at night for meager pay. The sisters saw that economics rather than inclination precipitated the exodus from such work into prostitution. Pleasure was often faked; prostitutes were major users of the prevalent opium-based laudanum. Yet they were touted as jolly companions.

The fifty-five-page palm-size brothel guide, its pages decorated with filigreed trim suitable for love poems, detailed the good, the bad, and the just awful dens of iniquity. At $1.50 apiece, the guide was not cheap. It stressed class distinctions and snob appeal. At one end were the "lowest class of courtezans [*sic*]" and "gentlemen who wear their shirts inside out when the other side is dirty." The guide featured far more "first class" brothels among the 125 surveyed, those establishments that catered to the well-heeled men whom the sisters called hypocrites. Madam Jennie Creagh, "a dashing brunette, has splendidly furnished her place...with it's [*sic*] French mirrors, English and Brussels carpets, rosewood furniture, superb bedding." It featured "ten lady boarders, finely dressed and very accomplished and prepossessing." Madam Kate Woods ran a house "better known among the aristocracy as Hotel de Wood." (The sisters knew a wealthy madam named Annie Woods; this may have been her with a different first name.) The three-story brownstone featured a "gallery of oil paintings" that cost $10,000, immense mirrors, and $70,000 worth of furnishings, where "three young ladies of rare personal attractions" were available for "distinguished gentlemen from foreign countries." Other "first class" houses were "visited by some of our first citizens."

To earn high marks, madams had to be fun-loving and friendly, real-life versions of *Gone with the Wind*'s Belle Watling. There was Madam Emma March, with her "inexhaustible stock of good humor," and Madam Ida Thompson and her "lively young ladies...full of fun, love, and fond of amusement." On the other hand, Laura Howard's "power house" got a negative review because "some of its visitors have asserted that it's [*sic*] inmates are of a snobbish disposition." Another house was dismissed with one sentence: the madam and the girls "are as sour as her wine." One house provided a "regular physician." The strangest entry: "There is a report of a bear being kept in the cellar, but for what reason may be inferred." The anonymous author, whose strong suit was not spelling or grammar, was probably paid by madams to promote certain houses; after all, it was routine for madams to pay off the police. The sisters revealed the details of a prostitute's hard life in their 1871 *Weekly*. A first-class prostitute paid her madam $40 a week to use a room and 20 percent of her profits. Towels cost extra. The police made $100 a week in protection money from the madam, and the prostitutes paid patrolmen $3 to $10 a week, plus provided sex on the house. Police captains and sergeants had their pick of girls, gratis. "The amount of degradation and bodily injury" to pay off such rackets "can only be imagined," stated the *Weekly*.

The Gentleman's Companion was very free with establishment addresses and names—most, no doubt, fake—but most madams were spared. Census takers generally recorded them as women who "keep house" or as "domestic servants"—unless they missed their payola payments. Occasionally, police conducted sham arrests, releasing prostitutes after a few hours, once they had paid a fee. The fancier houses produced elaborate calling cards of fine vellum, with name, address, and discreet mention of the number of "lady boarders" in elegant script. Older and drug-addicted prostitutes were reduced to infamous Greene Street. *The Gentleman's Companion* warned its users to avoid Greene Street like the pox, which, the guide inferred, could easily be acquired there: "In the short space of six squares, included between Canal and Bleecker streets there are 41 houses containing barrooms, 8 houses of assignation, 22 houses in which furnished rooms are let to girls and 11 segar [*sic*] stores...the filth and turmoil would lead a stranger to suppose that...old Sodom and Gomorrah had risen from their ashes."

Despite their charms, streetwalkers on fashionable Broadway—"smart, good-looking, well educated, prepossessing"—were also poison. Young "comely females, ages 15 to 25" took their Broadway customers to rented furnished rooms. These "Badgers," or "panel thieves," said the guide with male indignation, "have robbed many an unsuspecting stranger of his all." A married man or well-known public figure was a target; "the presumption is that fear of exposure will prevent him from making a complaint... They are in our public streets what sharks are on [*sic*] the ocean." Public houses where "gentlemen" could meet women included the huge Broadway Garden, extending from Broadway to Mercer Street. A red lamp at 25 East Houston Street marked the establishment of Harry Hill, a "genial and indefatigable landlord."

If a married gent wanted to wander back home, ads in the guide featured Dr. Groves's marriage pamphlets for fifty cents, "with six new illustrations, 310 pages of usable information" containing "all those wonderful, marvelous and mysterious" sex secrets from "the various professions, arts and sciences."

In the nineteenth century it was easy to be called a slut or prostitute. Lucy Stone's father, like many men, called women who engaged in public speaking sluts, including his daughter, remarking that "when the sluts are out, the dogs will bark." When working girls attempted to strike, they were jeered as prostitutes, and foremen threatened to send them to the Tombs, the jail in Lower Manhattan, to await sentencing. Mediums and actresses were considered demimondes. An unmarried society woman who went out at night without an escort could ruin her reputation.

The sensational act of conducting business on Wall Street was enough to cast suspicion on the sisters. Now, as sex radicals, their call for women's sexual emancipation was proof to their enemies. In arguing that a woman had a right to freedom regarding her own body, to choose her mate, to decide when she wanted sex, and actually to enjoy it, the sisters were so far ahead of the era that they were openly called prostitutes in print.

Equally advanced was their shocking notion that "Physiology and hygiene should not stop short of all the uses of the sexual organs. And all this should be taught in every school to both sexes conjointly, so that in early youth children shall not be drawn into the terrible mistake that these organs are indecent, obscene or vulgar," they wrote in the *Weekly*. "At the ages of twelve, thirteen and fourteen years, youth of both sexes begin to experience the sexual desire...it is simply folly; aye it is madness, to pretend to think that a desire so utterly beyond the soul of reason... will be controlled to best results by those who have been kept in the most profound ignorance of its nature and uses....But what has been done to guard or guide this tremendous impulse? Nothing! Absolutely nothing. Neither teachers, parents or priests have opened their lips either to instruct or to warn."

Woodhull's advice included warning children about the evils of masturbation. For all her forward thinking, she shared the Victorian condemnation of the act, saying, "I need not tell you that four-fifths of the children practice self-abuse before they are old enough, of their own wisdom, to know better." Like many in the Victorian hygienic movement, Woodhull viewed this "morbid vice" as sapping one's energy and, for men, wasting precious bodily fluids. When she differentiated "free love" from "free lust," she explained, "Lust is the perverted action of the desire for sexual love." She lumped masturbation in with "free lust" practices such as "sodomy" and "purchased intercourse as in prostitution." She alluded to disgust for homosexuality: "were I to tell you the extent to which Sodomy in man and its antitype in woman have attained, I should shock you beyond measure." Her simplistic and incoherent solution to end free lust evil was free love, with everyone being able to pick and choose his or her true love, providing they did not exhibit what she termed vile behavior.

There were "prostitutes" whom the sisters did despise, but not those mentioned in *The Gentleman's Companion*: they were scathing about the underlying hypocrisy of high-society women who sold themselves for profitable marriages. "What a commentary upon the divinity of marriage are the watering places during the summer seasons!" scoffed Victoria. "The mercenary 'mammas' trot out their daughters on exhibition, as though they were so many stud of horses, to be hawked to the highest bidder. It's the man who can pay the most money who is sought; it makes no difference how he got it, nor what are his antecedents... To him who bids highest... the article is knocked down... this is the ruling spirit, not at watering places only but in so-called best society everywhere. Marriages of love become rarer year after year, while those of convenience are proportionately on the increase... and we prate of the holy marriage covenant!"

Every era breeds some rebellion with the past, and Queen Victoria was crowned in 1838 amid a backlash against an "age of debauchery," when upper-class males routinely kept mistresses. In the Victorian era, the image of the happy family, chaste couples amid the "respectability" of polite society, was acclaimed. And by 1870, reformers were once again fighting crime, obscenity, debauchery, and prostitution as the post–Civil War period mocked much of the Victorian myth. Yet hypocrisy hadn't faded. Despite fashion that paraded plumped-up breasts, women were supposed to be horrified at naked statues in art museums, legs were never to be seen, and the lower half of the body was called the "nether regions."

Only women such as the sisters and a few of the earlier feminists even dared to wear radical dress. Two decades before the sisters cut their hair and wore shorter skirts, Amelia Bloomer, Stone, Anthony, and Stanton wore voluminous harem trousers to the ankles, covered by tunic-length skirts. These "bloomers"—named for Amelia Bloomer—revealed absolutely nothing but made it easier for their wearers to walk. Anthony resisted until she tired of ripping the hems of unwieldy skirts getting on and off stagecoaches and dragging them in the mud.

Stanton added humor as she made her point: "Take a man and pin three or four large tablecloths about him, fastened back with elastic and looped up with ribbons; drag all his own hair to the middle of his head and tie it tight, and hair pin on about five pounds of other hair with a bow of ribbon...pinch his waist into a corset and give him gloves a size too small and shoes ditto, and a hat that will not stay on without a torturing elastic and frill to tickle his chin and little lace veil to bend his eyes whenever he goes out to walk and he will know what woman's dress is."

The ability to walk and breathe freely was no match for the heavy ridicule in newspapers, the hoots and whistles of men, or the rocks thrown by young boys. Stanton told Anthony that "the cup of ridicule is more than you can bear," advising her not to waste her energies fighting it. But Stanton herself held out, even as she embarrassed her husband while he campaigned for reelection to the New York State Senate in 1852. (He was widely depicted as a henpecked man whose wife "wears the britches.")

Twenty years later nothing had changed for the better, and Victoria and Tennie vociferously mocked fashion. "A blind and foolish custom has decreed that women must wear skirts to hide their legs, while they may...expose their arms and breasts," wrote Tennie. She ridiculed coy women who blush "when subjects are spoken of which are of the greatest interest to humanity generally" but "appear at balls and receptions and at the opera virtually naked to the waist." On the contrary, since the "portion of woman's clothing which is supported from the waist" was up to fifteen pounds, Tennie asked, "Are weak backs a wonder? Put on suspenders, girls." Fashionable clothes were "absurd...ridiculous" and "from the health point of view they are suicidal." Tennie spoke contemptuously about a useless upper class: "While women remain mere dolls...it does not matter very much how they dress; but when any of them shake off the shackles of dependence, and become their own support," they should "accommodate their dress to their new modes of life."

However, the sisters themselves ran ads that mocked everything they stood for. BEAUTIFUL WOMEN, beckoned one: "All women know that it is beauty, rather than genius, which all generations of men have worshipped in the sex." A drawing of a woman, with flowing hair, breasts pushed up, touching a potion bottle accompanied the text for the lotion, with the caption "When most men speak of the intelligent women, they speak critically, tamely, coolly." When speaking of beautiful women, "their language and their eyes kindle with an enthusiasm...The world has yet allowed no higher mission to woman than to be beautiful." This lotion promised to smooth out "all indentations, furrows, scars, removing tan, freckles and discolorations...giving the appearance of youth and beauty."

Down through the ages, it was, and remains, an exercise in futility to persuade a large number of women to trade what is deemed fashionable, no matter how torturous, for comfort. The sisters traditionally wore high-necked dresses and little jewelry or makeup, which did nothing to stop male reporters from noticing their beauty and arresting figures. Fashionable women, on the other hand, went to "enameling studios," where the face and bust were coated with dangerous enamel, a semi-paste composed of arsenic or white lead. For $10 to $15, a woman could get a coating that lasted a few days. A shellacking that lasted six months cost between $400 and $600—more than most laborers' annual salary—to retain the dangerous ethereal whiteness. It was not explained how, or if, they'd wash their face after application.

If Mother Nature had not been kind, dentists filled out cheeks from inside with hard composite pads, placed high up inside the mouth. These were not the only "plumpers" in the female sexual armament. If cotton and horsehair padding didn't produce the "very important" bust, "patent heavers" were in vogue. Two rubber bags, miniature life preservers, costing five to ten dollars, were blown up to achieve high-level perkiness. If women seemed loath to perform a tight embrace, it was not Victorian prudery so much as the fear that, under such pressure, one side of the patent heaver would shrink drastically, accompanied by the sound of a deflating balloon. Plumpness was so admired that slim women sewed padding into dress sleeves and added padding to ankles under their hose.

If women were supposed to be chaste, instead of chased, what were all the pushed-up breasts and beautifiers for? Catching a husband and then resisting sex as much as possible was the Victorian ideal. "Ladies" were not expected to enjoy a happy sexual life, but to remain frail and delicate flowers. (In the insanity of the times, some fashionable women were so ashamed of any lust they felt that they even resorted to the extreme measure of removing the clitoris, to be discussed later in this chapter.)

At times, Victoria praised reciprocal monogamous love as the desired "higher order," but she invariably added that it was not possible in most marriages and that "miseries" were "concealed beneath its deceptive exterior." From their radical sex position, the sisters saw marriage as outmoded: "There are two classes only who have anything more than an imaginary interest in maintaining the marriage system: the hypocritical priests who get their fees for forging the chain and the blackguard lawyers who get bigger ones for breaking the fetters" (that is, charging more because divorces were much fewer). Acid dripped as Woodhull said, "Of course 'virtue' must have a legal standard."

Victoria stumbled in her praise of the Oneida Community, a free love commune, saluting it for not permitting "monogamic [*sic*] attachments. If they are found springing up, the parties are compelled to separate." Oneida, however, was not a rosy haven for women, and is viewed by female historians as the "most notorious example of male domination in the free love tradition." It was, in fact, harshly and absolutely controlled by its founder, John Humphrey Noyes.

While other misogynists could well compete for the honor, the Victorian gynecologist was the woman's worst friend. When suffragists pushed for higher education for women, male "experts" in medicine argued that too much education was unhealthy both physically and mentally. The most invidious medical treatment of women revolved around their sexual organs. Freud would have had a field day probing the psychological makeup of the male pioneers in gynecology; they were sexist, misogynist, and anti-contraception. They castrated women who showed signs of neurosis or insanity, husbands being the judges of such conditions, with gynecologists concurring that hysterectomies would do the trick.

An opposite, if impermanent, solution for the purported female disease of "hysteria" called for doctors and midwives to massage the female genitalia manually, arousing a woman to "paroxysm." (*Merriam-Webster's* synonyms are *convulsion* and *spasm*. Victorians did not use *orgasm*.) When Joseph Mortimer Granville patented the first electromechanical vibrator in the 1880s, the stern Englishman proposed using it for muscular aches, and opposed its use for female sexual gratification, but his invention and refined vibrators to come were soon bringing smiles to the faces of many a Victorian woman. And doctors and midwives found it a relief from manual stimulation. Not until 1952 did the American Psychiatric Association drop the term *hysteria* as a disorder from the *Diagnostic and Statistical Manual of Mental Disorders*.

By the 1870s, gynecologists had also begun "to practice surgical treatment of the psychological disorders of women," including "the excision of the clitoris (clitoridectomy) and female castration (removal of the ovaries) to cure 'insanity.'" By far the most common of the two was the removal of ovaries, a surgical procedure that began in 1872.

An esteemed gynecologist, J. Marion Sims, was one of the elite brigade who performed both. For generations, male historians lauded Sims for his work in sterility, for the invention of the speculum, and for surgery that repaired tears in the vagina (vesicovaginal fistulas) often brought about by torturous childbirth or violent sex. Sims was called the "father" of gynecology, and a statue was erected to honor this founder of the Woman's Hospital in New York. Later, female (and a few male) historians exposed the horror of his 1840s experiments. Although anesthesia had been invented, Sims operated on black slave women without it, performing as many as thirty failed operations on one woman over the course of four years. The slaves endured horrific pain, but Sims argued, "I kept all these negroes at my own expense all the time.... this was an enormous tax on a young doctor." When he tried operating on a white woman, the "pain was so terrific that Mrs. H. couldn't stand it and I was foiled completely." This Victorian Mengele bought some slaves expressly for his experiments. He termed them "adequate material." In New York his guinea pigs were uneducated poor women. Only when he had perfected his surgical treatment for vesicovaginal fistula did he operate on wealthy white women.

Sims's success spurred the tendency "toward general, frequent and drastic use of the knife in American gynecology." His motto was "look upon the knife not as the last weapon but as the first."

The director of the American Medical Association and other leaders in the field approved and performed such surgeries as well as Sims, believing that "women's entire psychology was governed by her sex organs." Another excuse for surgery was to cure "oversexed" women, which meant women who had confessed to masturbation. Renowned gynecologists Robert Battey (the originator of hysterectomies for nonmedical conditions) and E. W. Cushing reported that a woman castrated for nonmedical reasons improved dramatically. She had "previously shrunk into a state of profound melancholia on account of her belief that her masturbation eternally damned her." Husbands and fathers unable to enforce what they considered their control over women handed over disorderly women to the gynecologists for hysterectomies. A crusading doctor against the practice, Eli Van de Warker, primarily faulted the medical profession for performing clitoridectomies and removing ovaries; he also described the "collaboration of careless, passive and wealthy women," who found it "fashionable" even to the extent of proudly viewing their scars "as pretty as the dimple in the cheek of sweet sixteen." Twenty years after the sisters' era, in 1893, a hysterectomy proponent still claimed that a woman "becomes tractable, orderly, industrious and cleanly" after having her female organs removed.

When the sisters first arrived in New York, a vigorous battle was under way between clerical-led moralists who fought contraception and those who supported it for overburdened mothers and to stem rampaging venereal disease. Noted gynecologists were often on the side of the anti-contraception clergy. Gynecologist Augustus K. Gardner dedicated his popular book *Conjugal Sins* to the U.S. clergy who were the "great moral lever-power" who "can make this vice [contraception] disgraceful... They can prevent it being the common boast of women that 'they know too much to have babies.'" Class snobbery came into play among doctors such as Dr. William Goodell, professor of clinical and didactic gynecology at the University of Pennsylvania, who feared immigrants would take over the country because they bore so many children. He lectured to WASP cadres that the "unwillingness of our women to become mothers" was one of the "dangers of the hour." Critics blamed as selfish women who, through industrial progress, were now freed from many domestic chores that had kept them from their duty—the "reproduction of the race."

Women were having sex, whether they liked it or not, and many of them resisted male opprobrium in religious and medical hierarchies. They resorted to contraception and abortion, dramatically reducing the birth rate in the last decades of the nineteenth century. The sisters informed women of vaginal sponges but never mentioned their own private habits, although it seems likely that both practiced contraception. Tennie was briefly married in her teens and had at least one "sweetheart" in New York. Whatever relationship she had had with Vanderbilt did not produce children, and gossip about her freewheeling early days was never proven. Whatever liaisons Tennie had, she had no children. After the stressful births of Victoria's two children with Woodhull, she had no more, despite her passionate free love days with Colonel Blood.

Contraceptive devices were called "French Shields for Women" and "Wife's Protector." By midcentury, contraceptive vaginal sponges were increasingly available commercially, with differing views on their efficacy. Critics argued that "quacks" charged five dollars for contraceptive sponges with silk threads attached when all women needed to do was buy a sponge about the size of a walnut, twist together silk threads to make a string, wet it in a weak solution of sulphate of iron, and insert the sponge. After intercourse, the string was used to withdraw the sponge. Douches were common, and the "womb veil," a rubber shield, was the forerunner to the diaphragm of the twentieth century. Lydia E. Pinkham, famous for her "Vegetable Compound and Uterine Tonic," disdained gynecologists and urged women customers to write her, promising complete anonymity, for any help needed and to "let the doctors alone." Her tonic promised to cure everything from menstrual cramps to infertility to prolapsus uteri. Happy matrons had no idea they were downing a hefty slug of booze; the tonic was 20 percent alcohol.

The sisters saw abortion as the inevitable result of a social system that kept women in terrible marriages, forever dealing with unwanted pregnancies. As Tennie wrote in the *Weekly*, "Abortion is only a symptom of a more deep-seated disorder of the social state." Childbearing was a beautiful thing, she said, "but to our faded-out, sickly, exhausted type of women...abortion is the choice of evils." Folk remedies for abortion "survived essentially unchanged over many centuries," but after 1840, abortion became a commercial business. Laws were fairly lenient until 1873, provided that abortions were performed in the first trimester. Mainstream newspapers advertised "female" doctors, and drug firms offered pills touted to induce miscarriage, among them "The Samaritan's Gift for Females." Abortions were slyly mentioned: "LADIES CURED AT ONE INTERVIEW with or without medicine $5." Pills with a promise of producing abortion were touted as "Regulating Pills, $5; sure and safe."

Women resorted to spoons, uterine probes, and abortion instruments that were readily available through the mail and at retail establishments. In 1870 the *Days' Doings* scandal sheet carried ads for seven medicines that left no doubt they were for abortions. Poor women were often the victims of amateur abortions, which produced a death rate 15 percent higher than the maternal death rate.

On the other hand, high-society women could afford famed Manhattan abortionist Madame Restell, who advertised in Manhattan's major papers and lived in a four-story marble-and-gold mansion on Fifth Avenue, a monument built on the money of rich male clientele who brought their mistresses and wives secretly to her private quarters. Tennie referred contemptuously to the hypocrisy of Madame Restell's carriage trade.

Anthony Comstock, a one-man vice squad, dressed in disguise as a destitute man one January night in 1878, entered Restell's basement office and asked for some abortion powder for a woman in distress. As soon as Restell agreed to help, he arrested her. Restell made a decision. She had been in jail before, including in the infamous Blackwell's Island prison, and could not bear it again. Upon her release after posting bail, she went home and, on April 1, 1878, drew a warm bath in her ornate marble bathtub, climbed in, and slit her throat with a pearl-handle knife. She was found the next morning in the cold crimson water, her throat so severely cut that she had severed her carotid artery and both jugular veins. Comstock famously wrote on the police blotter, "A bloody ending to a bloody life." His sentiments were echoed in the *New York Times*, which called Restell an "evil murderer." Restell's success points to a swift business among the rich; upon her death she was said to be worth $1.5 million, the equivalent of several million today.

Male condoms were originally bought as protection against disease from prostitutes, rather than for contraception. Made of skin and India rubber, they offered various degrees of reliability, if price was an indication. They ranged from two dollars to four dollars per dozen, with no explanation for the difference. Ads in *The Gentleman's Companion* spelled out the horrors of venereal disease: "PRIVATE DISEASES. BOTH SEXES CURED WITHOUT MERCURY," blazed one ad featuring "Seminal Pills." One "doctor" offered late services at 651 Broadway until 9:00 p.m. for the convenience of customers. The ad contained a telling comment about symptoms of venereal disease: "For Nervous Debility, $1 per box, or six boxes for $5 by mail or at office." Bachelors were supposed to "sow their wild oats," and doctors were among those who did not ascertain until late in the nineteenth century that venereal disease "constituted a special danger to the family" and had become a massive problem. Too late for countless women and their children, doctors recognized the devastating illness, infant death, and deformities caused by syphilis and gonorrhea.

Tennie, noting that "a long practice in female complaints entitles me to speak authoritatively," excoriated "that class of so-called public servant who affix M.D. to their names—first, for their persistent silence upon this subject; and...secondly their ignorance" regarding "the class of diseases resulting from sexual abuses...never a word do they let drop...that there is such a thing as unfortunate results, which...flow to women from our present marriage system, and to men, from its attendant fact of prostitution." The health system was also skewed for profit. She presciently noted,

"It is the direct interest of the physician that sickness shall prevail, since the people pay the doctors for treatment, not for health." If patients had a "contract by the year for treatment," it would be in the "direct interest of the physician to preserve them in the best possible health," as a healthy patient would be alive to continue paying the annual fee. Instead, there is no "inducement" to battle sexual diseases.

Like Tennie, Victoria was years ahead of the doctors and legislators when she mocked a "Social Evils" bill being discussed in Congress in 1874 that would test prostitutes for sexual diseases. "Now if they really wish to stop diseases and make the business safe, why not register and examine every man who visits these houses before he is admitted? A house of prostitution, free from disease, cannot be contaminated, except through the diseased men. Examine the men, then, and deny admission to the diseased." She added wryly, "How many Social Evil bills would be passed under such conditions?"

In her eugenics discussions, Victoria spoke of the horrors of diseased men creating damaged children well before doctors established this as fact. She hinted at the possibility when speaking of women marrying a man for his money: "It doesn't matter if he is just from the hands of the physicians, cured of a loathsome disease, if he has the cash he is the man." Victoria blamed her husband's alcoholism for their retarded son, but it more likely could have been caused by gonorrhea or syphilis. She never addressed this, possibly because she would have had to face the horrible thought that she may have been contaminated.

The concept that "'profligate' men" could infect their wives and produce damaged children was not prominent until the latter part of the nineteenth century, at which time the idea that innocent babies could be diseased or damaged outraged sensibilities. Long before, in 1837, a French doctor, Philippe Ricord, was the first to establish that syphilis and gonorrhea were not the same disease. By 1876 it was found that severe cases of syphilis could spread to the spine, leading to paralysis and madness. Doctors understood finally that syphilis was much more dangerous than assumed. Yet long after the ravages of syphilis were recognized, doctors continued to view gonorrhea as a milder disorder—and doctors even found a way to blame women for it. Because of the "asymptomatic nature of the disease in women," doctors believed that "a woman frequently gives gonorrhea without having it."

When gonorrhea was thought to be a trifling inconvenience, men saw it as a badge of honor. Actor Edwin Booth had countless lovers, including actress Laura Keene, who was onstage at Ford's Theatre the night his brother, John Wilkes, assassinated President Lincoln. In the 1850s, when Edwin contracted gonorrhea, he termed it the "glorious clap."

By 1879 a better understanding emerged, and gonorrhea, "previously considered a 'trivial disease' now joined syphilis as a serious venereal malady." Studying the effects of gonorrhea on women, one doctor finally understood "why so many healthy, blooming young girls begin to suffer and fail as soon as they enter the bonds of marriage." Virgins before, they were tortured for the rest of their lives by a mysterious malady, including high rates of sterility. An 1886 study gauged that 90 percent of sterile women were married to men who had had gonorrhea.

Not that men got off easily. One well-known physician, Frederick Hollick, wrote a treatise on gonorrhea in 1852, when it was thought to be relatively harmless but carried certain complications. One was that it produced a curvature of the penis, causing a painful erection. Hollick's cure: He placed the penis with the "curve upward on a table and struck a violent blow with a book." If the patient didn't keel over, this would, supposedly, "flatten" his member.

By 1901, doctors recognized what had been hidden in the sex lives of men such as Edwin Booth all those years before. One 1901 study contended that an astounding eighty out of every one hundred men in New York had been infected at one time or another with gonorrhea, which was by then viewed as the most prevalent disease in the adult male population. An estimated 5 to 18 percent of all males had syphilitic infections.

To ease the pain of such diseases, drugs were widely available. In fact, Victorians of all social classes found drugs for various uses accessible everywhere. Large numbers of women of every category used them to ease their lives. Prostitutes used them to dull their existence; housewives, to banish the doldrums of unhappy or boring marriages. Upper-class matrons were often addicted, as doctors liberally prescribed drugs to these pampered, fainting-prone patients. Opium-based laudanum was wildly popular, touted to cure everything from headaches to tuberculosis. Nannies spooned it to cranky infants, sometimes causing their deaths. Ads in newspapers touted opium imported from England. Cocaine was also legal, and everywhere. Cocaine toothache drops for children were popular, required no prescription, and were sold in all drugstores. The rise in cocaine use began in 1850 and quickly snowballed. It was famously found in the original Coca-Cola recipe, and by the turn of the century it was being snorted, which led to serious nasal conditions. Opium, mercury, and lead-based medicines were used everywhere. Implementation of the Pure Food and Drug Act in January 1907, requiring disclosure of a medicine's contents, was the first attempt to control cocaine use.

Laudanum addiction, a fierce and ugly craving, was hard to stop, and wrecked constant users, as did morphine. It was not surprising, then, that at least two in the Claflin clan became addicts, Canning Woodhull and Victoria and Tennie's beautiful sister Utica.

ACT THREE

CHAPTER TEN

Confessions of Sin and Battling the Beechers

In July 1870 the Tilton house in Brooklyn echoed with violent shouts between Theodore and his wife, Elizabeth. "In the heat of passion and in the presence of Miss Anthony, each confessed to the other of having broken the marriage vow." Tilton became so belligerent that Anthony rushed into an upstairs bedroom. "She heard Mrs. Tilton come dashing upstairs, and Mr. Tilton following close after. She flung open her bedroom door, and Elizabeth rushed in. The door was then closed and bolted. Theodore pounded on the outside, and demanded admittance, but Miss Anthony refused to turn the key. So intense was his passion at that moment that she feared he might kill his wife if he gained access to the room. Several times he returned to the door and angrily demanded that it be opened.

" 'No woman shall stand between me and my wife,' he bellowed.

" 'If you enter this room it will be over my dead body,' Anthony shouted back. Tilton then withdrew.

"Mrs. Tilton remained with Susan throughout the night. In the excitement of the hour, amid sobs and tears, she told all to Miss Anthony. The whole story of her own faithlessness, of Mr. Beecher's course, of her deception, and of her anguish, fell upon the ears of Susan B. Anthony, and were spoken by the lips of Mrs. Tilton."

This gossipy morsel, relayed by Elizabeth Cady Stanton—that Theodore Tilton's wife had had an affair with the Rev. Henry Ward Beecher—raced through the women's movement and was added to rumors that had surrounded Beecher for years involving women parishioners. At her angriest, Woodhull depicted Beecher as a serial seducer without conscience. "I am reliably assured that Henry Ward Beecher preaches to at least twenty of his mistresses every Sunday."

Stanton did not tell Woodhull the adultery story until a full year after the incident, in May 1871—the very time Woodhull and Tennie were being pummeled by the Beechers following the Claflin family court brawl. By then, Woodhull's anger at the Beechers had been building for six months, following Woodhull's speech in January before the Judiciary Committee. Not content simply to warn Isabella Beecher against a friendship with Victoria, Catharine Beecher and Harriet Beecher Stowe had spread gossip about Tennie and Victoria and their free love reputation.

Catharine had loathed Woodhull ever since Victoria's first salvo at her in January 1871 when the *Weekly* criticized the seventy-year-old Beecher sister for her anti-suffrage stance: "Is it not possible to drive Miss Beecher for very shame out of her unholy position" that would "deprive woman of her legal right to vote?" Airing her consistent contempt for those who could afford to live in ease, albeit "remaining in bondage" to rich husbands or fathers, Woodhull said of Beecher and her ilk, "Let them remain under it by all means, and lick the dirt from the naked feet of their oppressors; but do not let them interfere with that grand and sublime majority of noble women who prefer freedom and the full rights of American citizenship."

Isabella tried to convince Catharine, the family dowager queen, that if she only met Woodhull, she would love her. The two agreed to meet, and a more improbable duo could not be found riding in a carriage around Central Park on a brisk February day in 1871. Catharine was thirty-eight years older than Victoria. Grief-stricken decades earlier when her fiancé drowned at sea, she had turned from a carefree girl into a "domineering, querulous and eccentric" autocrat. Women's highest and only calling was as mother and wife, vowed Catharine, who had no experience in either. A bitter, virginal spinster, she nonetheless became the nation's wildly popular authority on how to raise children and run a home through her bestselling *Treatise on Domestic Economy.*

Her rigorously religious childhood had held little joy, but Catharine grew up privileged and educated. She could not conceive of the life Victoria and Tennie had known and witnessed, nor share their hardened knowledge of what demeaning jobs poverty-stricken women faced, including prostitution.

The carriage ride through Central Park was a disaster, and at the end of it, war was declared. "I frankly stated my views upon the social question," recalled Victoria, "all sexual commerce not founded on love is prostitution, whether in or out of marriage." Catharine called her doctrines the "rankest of heresies," and said that if a woman had to leave her husband for any reason she should "retire into solitude for life, and never think of another man." Then Victoria told Catharine that she knew that her brother, the reverend, was among those living her theories of "social freedom" but not ready to become an advocate. Catharine exploded. She called her brother's wife, Eunice, a "virago" and admitted that he was unhappy, but she swore he was "nevertheless a true husband."

Victoria shot back, "If you were a proper person to judge, which I grant you are not, you would see that the facts you state are fatal to your theory of faithfulness to marriage." Catharine "became very abusive, calling me many bad names."

Catharine ordered the driver to stop the carriage, got out, and shouted after Victoria, "Remember, Victoria Woodhull, that I shall strike you dead!"

"Strike as much and as hard as you please, only don't do it in the dark, so that I cannot know who is my enemy."

"I will strike you in every way; I can and will kill you, if possible!"

At least, this is Victoria's dramatic version.

Catharine's only public acknowledgment of the meeting was to say that Victoria was "either insane or the hapless victim of malignant spirits." Isabella saw her furious half sister on her return from the carriage ride and could not resist telling a friend, "Sister Catharine, attacking [Victoria] on the marriage question, got such a black eye as filled her with horror and amazement. I had to laugh inwardly…and am now waiting for her to cool down!"

Victoria wrote that after their meeting, Catharine helped kill Victoria's lecture in Hartford, Connecticut, writing letters to the Hartford papers that warned readers not to attend. Meanwhile, Harriett Beecher Stowe, who did not hesitate to brand Victoria "a snake [who] should be given a good clip with a shovel," pounded Victoria and Tennie with a wicked satire serialized weekly in brother Henry's *Christian Union*. When the mortifying Claflin family feud erupted, Stowe happily ripped plotlines from the newspapers: "There's a terrible wash of dirty linen going on," remarks one character in her roman à clef, *My Wife and I*. Her main character, Audacia (or 'Dacia) is called a "tramp," and her newspaper "is not the kind of paper that any decent man ought to have in his house." A demure anti-suffrage heroine sighs that Audacia "makes one ashamed of one's sex," to which another replies that there is no danger of 'Dacia's being a real woman; "she's an amphibious animal."

Stowe's poison dart novel aimed at Victoria often reads more like a distortion of the bolder Tennie; a book illustration also looks like her: "a jaunty, dashing young woman, with bold blue eyes." 'Dacia accosts the book's male hero, aggressively pressing him to buy her newspaper and aid her in her social freedom cause. When he looks amazed, Audacia mocks his naïveté: "You ain't half out of the shell yet"; she tells him she "does just what a man would do" and rants about her right to drink, smoke, and come up to a man's room and "have a good time." He gives Audacia money to get rid of her. In real life, critics accused Tennie of this same sort of badgering to get ads for the *Weekly*. Victoria's presidential quest also is derided by a character in Stowe's book: "What sort of brazen tramp of a woman would it be that could stand it and come out of it without being killed?" The Beecher brigade against the sisters did not stop there. The religious *Independent*, published by Henry Bowen, founder of Beecher's Plymouth Church in Brooklyn, slammed the *Weekly* as unfit reading.

By May 1871 the "brazen tramp" had had enough. With Stanton's tale of the wild Tilton battle over adultery, Victoria now had all the ammunition she needed to fight back. On May 20 she attacked, with a letter to the editor, in the pages of the New York *World* and the *Times*: "I know of one man, a public teacher of eminence who lives in concubinage with the wife of another public teacher, of almost equal eminence. All three concur in denouncing offences against morality. 'Hypocrisy is the tribute paid by vice to virtue.' So be it. But I decline to stand up as the 'frightful example.'" She slapped down the gauntlet: "I shall make it my business to analyze some of these lives, and will take my chances in the matter of libel suits." Woodhull's obvious threat was publicly to accuse Beecher of an adulterous affair with Theodore Tilton's wife if nothing were done to stop the blasts from the Beechers or if the reverend did not openly condone Victoria's free love position, which she said he practiced in secret. The letter instantly hit its target. The Tiltons and Beecher had not figured on Stanton spilling the beans to Woodhull. Tilton rushed into action.

"The day that the letter appeared in the *World*," Victoria said later, "Mr. Tilton came to my office, and showing me the letter, asked 'whom do you mean by that?' 'Mr. Tilton,' I said, 'I mean you and Mr. Beecher.'" Victoria said that it was her "mission to bring it to the knowledge of the world." Tilton begged her not to take any steps now against Beecher— despite the fact that every "impulse urged me to throttle and strangle him," Victoria quoted Tilton as saying. Tilton did not want his wife "dragged before the public." After meeting Tilton's wife, Elizabeth, Victoria agreed to the "propriety of delay."

Woodhull made no such promise for the future, however. It was her avenging angel "mission" to help "destroy the heap of rottenness which, in the name of religion, marital sanctity, and social purity, now passes as the social system." She knew of other adulterous hypocrites, clerical and otherwise, but had picked Beecher because "he is a most eminent man" and has a "great congregation." Woodhull proclaimed, "I am a savior, if you would but see it!"

As in a Greek tragedy, Tilton's ruination was set in motion the day he walked into Woodhull's office on the errand to quell this story of adultery between his pastor and his own wife. The relationship that followed between Tilton and Victoria has been characterized as a steamy love affair. Tilton eventually stated that they were never lovers and that he had been pushed by Beecher to make a friend of this "dangerous woman" so that she would not publicly expose their lurid tale. That task included writing and publishing the fulsome "Victoria C. Woodhull: A Biographical Sketch," printed by his *Golden Age* magazine.

Woodhull alternately vowed and denied that theirs was a great romance. It seems probable that these two beautiful people had enough chemistry to touch off the "amative" impulse that Woodhull often addressed. Even men who disliked Tilton recognized his outstanding looks. He had a charismatic, irresistible "presence," wrote one male dinner companion. "I do not wonder that feminine hearts...break beneath his beaming countenance. His smile is as witching as a woman's, and his laugh hearty and sympathetic." His blond locks hung "in clustery profusion over his shoulders." With all that, Tilton was also a splendid companion. Said the same dinner mate, "I was charmed with sparkling conversation between the Scotch and the oysters."

The sheer audacity alone of taking on the exalted Beechers speaks to the sisters' fearless defiance. Abraham Lincoln legendarily praised Harriet, whose immensely popular *Uncle Tom's Cabin* dramatized the horrors of slavery better than any abolitionist tract: "So you're the little lady who started the war." Her brother's pulpit theatricality enthralled the president, and even a religiously skeptical Mark Twain marveled at Reverend Beecher: "sawing his arms in the air, howling sarcasms this way and that, discharging rockets of poetry and exploding mines of eloquence." When animated, Beecher was a "remarkably handsome man...but he is as homely as a singed cat when he isn't doing anything," noted Twain.

By 1868, the time his affair with Elizabeth Tilton allegedly began, Beecher was fifty-five and overweight, an unlikely looking lover, especially in contrast with thirty-three-year-old Theodore Tilton, who did not follow fashion and shaved, the better for others to see his features. Beecher's pudgy body, full lips, and hooded eyes notwithstanding, he entranced both women and men with his oratorical brilliance and showmanship as he preached his gospel of love—or, as some cynics called it, "the gospel of gush."

He was famous for crying, which he did well. He kissed friends, male and female, with abandon and with boyish vigor, and yet he "smashed the stereotype of the wan, effeminate preacher," wrote Beecher biographer Debby Applegate. Woodhull wrote that he reeked of sensuousness.

Though not as consistently outspoken about ending slavery as Tilton, Beecher could move an audience with dramatic symbolism. Fourteen years before he ever heard of Woodhull, parishioners sat slack-jawed as Beecher spoke of a father willing to sell his own daughter "to go south," adding the unmistakable sexual undertone "for what purposes you can imagine when you see her." Few in those days (1856) spoke openly of the obvious plight of beautiful young slaves, routinely used as concubines by masters and for breeding healthy babies to become future slaves. Yet Beecher's message was all too clear.

"Come up here, Sarah," he beckoned, "and let us all see you."

A light-brown-skinned pretty young woman dressed in virginal white walked up and sank down into the pulpit chair. Beecher commanded her to loosen her hair, which fell in shining waves far down her back. He turned to his flock and shouted, "What will you do now? May she read her liberty in your eyes? Shall she go out free? Let the plate be passed and we will see. How much for her?" Imitating an auctioneer's spiel, Beecher shouted, "Who bids?!"

"Tears of pity and indignation streamed from eyes unused to weeping," recalled Beecher's wife, Eunice. The scene was like old revival meetings. "Women became hysterical; men were almost beside themselves." In a fervent frenzy, they heaped money in the contribution baskets and threw coins and banknotes onto the pulpit. Rings, bracelets, brooches were ripped off and tossed. All this time, Beecher never stopped his dramatics. "He dragged out heavy iron slave-shackles and stomped them under foot."

If Beecher was not a practitioner of free love, as Woodhull charged, he gave a good imitation. A loving God would accept that "one could be true to one's desires without feeling guilty or alone," he preached, ". . . true love could hurt no one; open your spirits to God's beauty." Jesus felt there were "affinities and relationships far higher and wider than those constituted by the earthly necessities of family," he emphasized. Beecher, who was desperately unhappy with his wife, the mother of ten, pointedly told his flock that there were "true kindred" souls to "love" outside the family.

Manhattanites crushed together on ferries, nicknamed "Beecher Boats," to hear his feel-good sermons (while underneath the waters, workmen were laying the foundation for the Brooklyn Bridge, some dying in this dangerous task, which would not be completed until 1883). Three thousand on any given Sunday packed Plymouth Church, with its high-domed ceiling and arched windows, to hear Beecher. He reveled in his release from a childhood ruled by his famous fire-and-brimstone preacher father, Lyman Beecher. His stylish eccentricities were aimed directly at and were an "assault on everything he'd ever hated about his father's religion," wrote biographer Applegate.

The man who was given no toys as a child craved the good life beyond measure—and could afford it. As his fame grew, so did his pocketbook, and at his height, Plymouth Church offered him an astounding $100,000 a year. For a preacher, he became not only wealthy but worldly, fingering the opals he tucked in the pockets of his velvet jackets and flowing capes. He loved European travel, expensive art, and rare books. His passion for lush living reached hoarding proportions: Oriental rugs were piled on top of one another in his Brooklyn Heights home as he bought with no place to put them. He unselfconsciously sniffed violet nosegays, and there could never be too many flowers overflowing the altar on Sundays.

Beecher had the fanciful idea that it was no sin to make people laugh in church. Like a grand actor, he would glide past the pulpit to sit in a chair, as if ready to converse one on one with parishioners. He would mime a "sailor taking a pinch of chewing tobacco and wiping his hands on his pants, a fisherman casting, or a young girl flirting." His rolling-thunder voice moved them, whether he spoke of seeing God at sunset or switched over into a funny anecdote about a horse trader.

At one time, Beecher, Tilton, and Tilton's wife, Elizabeth, were an extremely happy and close trio. Beecher's stern and uncompromising wife, Eunice, was not included. Beecher thought of Tilton as a son, and Tilton thought of Beecher as a father. In the fashion of the times, with no homosexual overtones, they expressed their deep love as soul mates.

The year before the mock slave auction, in 1855, Beecher married Tilton and Elizabeth. Tilton was nineteen, and Elizabeth, a few years older. Young unknowns, they were eclipsed by their pastor's popularity as one thousand guests attended their Plymouth Church wedding. Beecher said they were "one of the fairest pairs that I ever married." The *New York Times* even covered the wedding, thrilling young Tilton, a shoemaker's son who was as ambitious as he was gifted. Everyone commented on the striking couple: she, a tiny dark-eyed brunette nicknamed Lib; he, at six foot three, towering above not only her but most of the men around him.

An unrelenting radical idealist, Tilton became a friend of Lincoln's, then denounced him for not being progressive enough on ending slavery, yet finally pragmatically championed him as the Republican standard-bearer. Tilton cultivated the friendship of famed poet Elizabeth Barrett Browning, turned Beecher's religious *Independent* into a lively progressive newspaper, wrote poetry, and lectured with great force.

Much about Tilton was admirable. Beecher was never so bravely outspoken about either slavery or women's suffrage as his firebrand acolyte. After the war, during the mess of Reconstruction, it became clear that the Republican Party was more interested in being the dominant force in the South rather than revolutionizing the territory for blacks. Few were in a hurry to enfranchise blacks in the North, either; fifteen northern legislatures defeated proposals to expand black men's voting rights. The Republican Party, at their convention in 1866, refused to welcome the great Frederick Douglass, a delegate from Rochester. (Despite the snub to this former slave, the *Brooklyn Eagle* sneeringly characterized the gathering as the "Philadelphia Nigger Convention.") "Only Theodore Tilton, in the face of his Republican colleagues...took his friend's arm and joined the procession through the city." This did not assuage the feelings of the snubbed Douglass, who felt like the "ugly and deformed child of the family," to be kept out of sight. Tilton also led the fight for Andrew Johnson's impeachment. "Those were days of battle," an admirer of Tilton's recalled decades later. "Our present age is one of dazzling decay. He [Tilton] was histrionic; he was vain; he was extravagant; he did love to pose; but, after all, he was an extremely attractive and inspiring man. He did a lot of good."

No stranger to hubris, Tilton felt his pride wounded over the Beecher affair; this drove him to great lengths trying to redeem his name and reputation. The thought of an unfaithful wife was mortifying, but he was equally shaken that his great friend Beecher could have deceived him. Free lover Tilton brooked no such actions from his wife; free love was easy to embrace by males unless they were cuckolded by it. As Victoria caustically remarked when Tilton jealously raged, he was "no vestal virgin." Still, if Lib Tilton was telling the truth in her final confession, a shattered Tilton was sacrificed on the altar of Beecher's respectability. And, as the trial proved, when push came to shove, Beecher had no trouble at all in shifting his gospel of love to the gospel of hate and revenge.

CHAPTER ELEVEN

"Yes, I am a free lover!"

After Woodhull's coded attack regarding the "concubinage" of Beecher and the Tiltons was published in 1871, a desperate cover-up followed. The Plymouth Church "Holy Trinity"—Bowen, Beecher, and Tilton—was forged. Although Tilton burned with revenge, and Bowen eventually sought to wreck both Beecher and Tilton, these strange bedfellows continued to scheme in private and to act their roles in public: Beecher preached, Bowen presided over the church, Tilton wrote and lectured (and quietly separated from Lib).

As the suffragists distanced themselves, Victoria and Tennie searched for new support. To that end, Victoria enlisted Tilton, who frantically needed her silence. Tilton, in turn, corralled his close lawyer friend Frank Moulton and his wife, Emma, to help him in his pursuit of Woodhull's friendship. But if his eagerness was simply to keep Victoria quiet, he certainly performed due diligence. He progressed from formal to intimate notes: "Dear Victoria, Put this under your pillow, dream of the writer, and peace be with you. Affectionately, Theodore Tilton." A "picnic frolic" in the Moultons' library, "graced with Frank's Burgundy," was planned for that evening. "You will stay all night at Emma's." Another indicates that the separated Tilton was staying with the Moultons, but felt it not proper to be there if Frank were absent: "I have a room temporarily at the

Fifth Avenue Hotel, where I shall abide...until Frank's return. I will ride up with you in your carriage this afternoon at 5 o'clock...Hastily T.T."

All that summer of 1871, Tilton spent hours with Victoria, boating on the Hudson, frolicking at Coney Island, watching the stars from her rooftop, and spending at least one night—Tilton sleeping somewhere in that spacious mansion filled with Claflins and Woodhulls but not, they vowed, together. She praised him in the *Weekly* and published his writing, and before things between them curdled, he called her the "most extraordinary woman he had ever met." During his days of bliss with Woodhull, Tilton—who contended in court that it was part of his "services" rendered to mollify Victoria—cobbled together the extravagant morsel called "Victoria C. Woodhull: A Biographical Sketch." A better image for her was imperative to Victoria in order to counter the scandalous court coverage of her shiftless family, newspaper attacks, and the Stowe satire. While hoping to obscure her family's sordid public outbursts, it also pushed her presidency and trumpeted her less than credible supernatural skills.

That summer and fall, with Tilton's help, Victoria tried to form a sizable political bloc of radical reformers—Spiritualists, labor activists, freed blacks, socialists, abolitionists, free lovers, and radical feminists. Victoria found herself facing a paradox of her own making. On one hand, she professed to loathe all that Henry Ward Beecher's hypocrisy embraced. On the other, she was still trying to appeal to the "respectables" who might give credence to her "social freedoms" and Spiritualism. An esteemed male sanctioning those views seemed vital. Her choice was none other than the preacher she threatened to expose; having such an eminent man by her side would be the ultimate prize. She pushed Tilton, who arranged for the nervous Beecher to meet her at Tilton's house.

A confident Victoria left that evening rendezvous certain that Beecher would support her. Beecher was nothing if not gifted in syrupy cordiality and vague promise. Only Woodhull's version exists. She assured readers that Beecher told her he had followed mesmerism and Spiritualism. They met two more times, and according to Woodhull, Beecher expressed a similar view that marriage laws needed reforming: "Marriage is the grave of love." When she allegedly asked why he did not preach such convictions, Beecher exclaimed, "I should preach to empty seats. It would be the ruin of my church."

Still, Victoria held out hope that he would introduce her in November at a Steinway Hall speech, "And the Truth Shall Make You Free," on the principles of social freedom. Agitated by his silence, she penned a threatening letter, one that her foes would cite as blackmail—not for money, but for that Steinway Hall introduction. She demanded an interview with him, unleashing her anger: "Two of your sisters have gone out of their way to assail my character and purpose." Echoing the blackmailing letters her own family had crafted, Woodhull threatened, "You doubtless know that it is in my power to strike back and in ways more disastrous than anything that can come to me. I do not desire to do this. I simply desire justice and a reasonable course on your part will assist me to it. I must have an interview tomorrow," she demanded, as her speech was that same night. She added ominously, "What I shall or shall not say will depend largely on the result of the interview."

This scared Beecher into a meeting. She urged him to come out for social freedom (a.k.a. free love), and that introducing her could "bridge the way."

"I cannot!" Beecher cried. "I should sink through the floor. I am a moral coward on this subject and you know it." He knelt on the sofa, began to weep, and begged her to "Let me off." Victoria said "if I am compelled to go upon that platform alone I shall begin by telling the audience why I am alone and why you are not with me." Beecher was in hysterics, shouting, "I cannot face this thing!" If she was going to expose him, Beecher begged for twenty-four hours' notice "so that I may take my own life." While this tale might be excused as Victoria's extravagance, Frank and Emma Moulton would later testify to remarkably similar histrionics from a pleading Beecher as the scandal unfolded.

Manhattan's streets were mostly empty as heavy winds and slashing rain sliced through the city on the night of November 20, 1871. Yet a vast waterlogged crowd of more than three thousand crushed together, huddling under umbrellas, and pushed and shoved to enter Steinway Hall. They were drawn to giant yellow banners on every side of the hall, announcing Victoria's speech on marriage, divorce, prostitution, and free love. The *New York Times* said it was "one of the largest audiences ever collected together in a public hall in this City," drawn by the "novelty of the doctrines enunciated" and especially the "greater novelty of their expression by a lady."

By 7:00 p.m., an hour before Victoria's speech, the boisterous, impatient crowd jammed the steps, with young men shoving and wisecracking among glowering old women. When the doors opened, "the crowd burst in like an avalanche." The crowd was a mix of old and young, some with "several children of a tender age." A man with long hair and green spectacles had a "decidedly free love look," and "several young ladies of very bad behavior" were "evidently professional." They coexisted with many "respectable looking people." A redheaded girl grabbed a seat, threw off a soggy shawl, and grumped, "I hope, by gosh, I haven't come here for nothing in all this rain." She would not be disappointed.

As the crowd packed every seat on the ground floor and in the two galleries, and stood in the aisles, there was that unmistakable hum of an audience expecting a good show. Backstage, Victoria and Tennie stood together in a small room off a narrow passageway, Woodhull nervously twisting her rolled-up manuscript in her hands. A transfixed reporter said she looked "inspired" and that she put Anna Dickinson "in the shade by the boldness of her utterances." He admired her small waist, little feet, and her "dark eyes burning with suppressed fire," and underestimated her age as twenty-seven; she had recently turned thirty-three. A watch chain pendant dangled from the neck of her simple black dress, and a fresh tea rose at her throat "enhanced the fairness of her skin."

Tennie, also wearing black, talked at a typically fast pace; her quick movements swirled her skirt, revealing galoshes. Victoria flushed with anger as she anxiously waited, checking her script. Tilton "the blond poet," friend Moulton, and "the Great American *Pantarchist*" Stephen Pearl Andrews arrived, followed by "a large number of Free Love ladies and gentlemen, most of the latter being very homely." Still, there was no

Beecher. An agitated Victoria cornered Tilton for a private talk. He told her Beecher had half-promised to come, if he could muster the courage. Woodhull paced, cheeks burning, her fury mounting by the second.

Out front, the waiting crowd could read a memo, written in the third person, placed on each chair. It explained that Woodhull was giving this speech "for the express purpose of silencing the voices and stopping the pens of those who, either ignorantly or willfully, persistently misrepresent, slander, abuse and vilify" her because of her "outspoken advocacy of, and supreme faith in God's last and best law. She wishes it to be distinctly understood that freedom does not mean anarchy in the social relations any more than it does in religion and politics; also that the advocacy of its principles requires neither action nor immodest speech." The circular exhorted Horace Greeley, among her "defamers," to sit with her on the platform, while her "lesser defamers should secure front seats."

The crowd grew restless as 8:00 p.m. came and went. Finally Woodhull gave up waiting for Beecher. As she, Tennie, and Tilton moved toward the stage, Moulton cried out, "Are you going to introduce Mrs. Woodhull to the audience, Tilton?" " 'Yes, by heaven,' said Tilton, 'since no one else has the pluck to do it.' " Andrews hovered at the foot of the stage, holding the script he had written. As Tennie began to move toward a nearby balcony, she shot a parting warning to her sister: "Now Vicky, be calm." The towering Tilton walked onstage, quieting the rowdy audience; he took an anonymous swipe at Beecher, condemning "several gentlemen" who had refused to introduce Woodhull, because of objections to "the lady's character" and "her views." He had planned to come only to hear "what my friend would have to say in regard to the great question which has occupied her so many years of her life" and was introducing her because she was going to have to face the audience "unattended and alone." Tilton defended her character: "I know it and believe in it and vouch for it." The audience could judge for itself about her views. He then uttered a backhanded compliment, stressing her right to speak. "It may be that she is a fanatic; it may be that I am a fool—but, before high heaven, I would rather be both fanatic and fool in one than such a coward as would deny to a woman her sacred right of free speech!" He struck the right chord, and the audience applauded. Tilton ended with a flourish: "with as much pride as ever prompted me to the performance of any act in fifteen or twenty years, I have the honor of introducing to you Victoria C. Woodhull, who will address you upon the subject of social freedom!"

The next day, the *New York Herald* bannered a headline, VICTORIA AND THEODORE. No last names were necessary. The tier of headlines stated MRS. WOODHULL CLAIMS THE RIGHT TO CHANGE HER HUSBAND EVERY DAY IN PRESENCE OF THREE THOUSAND PEOPLE. The *Herald* characterized her speech as "the most astonishing doctrine ever listened to by an audience of Americans." For some reason, Woodhull spared Beecher. Instead, she exposed herself with words that followed her for life and beyond.

As Woodhull walked timidly onstage, she was greeted by a blast of applause and shouts from every corner of the hall. "A hundred ravenous male bipeds leaned over the platform, standing up in front of the audience." Woodhull bowed and began her two-hour speech in a clear and pleasing voice. She read several thousand mind-numbing utterances about a "trinity in all things," before emphasizing a feminist position that was genuinely hers: "the principle by which the male citizens of these United States assume to rule the female citizens is not that of self-government but that of despotism."

For those who questioned her intelligence or saw her as a mere puppet for Andrews, Victoria's ability to electrify, either with her words or those written for her, was exceptional—especially regarding radical women's rights. She would stride, her face illuminated by stage gaslights, ignoring the written speech in her hand. Some lines were so well memorized that she took the stage like a diva, speaking without notes in a clear voice that carried throughout the hall, modulating her cadence, eyes flashing, color flushing her cheeks.

The audience perked up when Woodhull got around to freedom from bondage over sexual relations, and hissing erupted as she continued on her central theme that sex conducted in a marriage without love was a form of legal prostitution. These passages were from her heart: "I have

seen the most damning misery resulting from legalized prostitution...
thousands of poor, weak, unresisting wives are yearly murdered [referring
to death in childbirth] who stand in spirit life looking down upon the
sickly, half-made children left behind, imploring humanity for the sake of
honor and virtue to look into this matter...and to bring out into the fair
daylight all the blackened, sickening deformities that so long have been
hidden by the screen of public opinion and a sham morality." (Woodhull's
flawed eugenics—that forced sex in an unloving marriage bred deformed
children—could not be confirmed or denied in an era just beginning to
study reasons for stillbirths and deformed children.)

Woodhull tried to praise good marriages, "a very large proportion"
of which are "commendable" and "as good as the present status of society makes possible." As for the marriage certificate, she added archly, "no
grosser insult could be offered a woman than to insinuate that she is honest and virtuous only because the law compels her to be so." When she
insisted that "good and commendable" marriages would "continue to exist
if all marriage laws were repealed tomorrow," half the immense audience
leapt up and hissed vehemently, while the other half cheered as loudly. Tilton stepped forward to rescue her, but his shouts were hissed down. Victoria stamped her foot and moved into her premise that harmonious and
loving partners, whether in or out of marriage, produced healthy children.

Then came the bombshell that, with few exceptions, was all that the
contemporary papers covered and that many books to follow would discuss. As Woodhull tried to "excuse the stain of illegitimacy," a beautiful
woman who kept shouting from her box seat jumped up and faced the
audience. She shouted to Woodhull, "How would you like to come into
this world without knowing who your father and mother was?"

Woodhull stared up at the woman in the low overhanging balcony
and shouted over the noise, "I assert that there are as good and noble men
and women on top of this earth suffering from the stain of illegitimacy as
any man and woman before me." She added a possible rueful attempt at
humor: "God knows I do not know how many illegitimate men or women
are in this hall tonight." At that, the confusion and shouting became so

great that no one could hear Woodhull. Pandemonium ensued for ten minutes, forcing Woodhull to stop her speech.

Tennie, who well knew that the woman shouting from the box seat could be drunk or on drugs, tried in vain to push through the mob to the woman's side. "I am her sister!" the woman shouted, refusing to sit down and looking defiantly at Woodhull and then the audience. At that disclosure from Utica Claflin Booker, Victoria and Tennie's sister, the audience cheered Utica wildly. Several women seated next to Utica, fearing a riot, retreated to the back of the inner box. Tilton, ever the free speech advocate, promised, "You shall all be heard if you only give us time. I must say, however, that this lady"—referring to Woodhull—"has hired the hall, and she is entitled to be heard first." Many shouted for Utica to take the stage. Bedlam ensued when a policeman bolted through the door to Utica's box, grabbed her wrist, and tried to drag her out. The entire audience rose up at this highhanded attempt, some with hisses and groans and others cheering Utica's exit. The policeman was forced to leave the box. Utica sat back down.

Woodhull then continued "at race-horse speed, and as if she feared that something would again interpose." Here reports break down. Either she was asked or she posed the rhetorical question "Are you a free lover?" "Yes, I am a free lover!" she shouted. "I have an inalienable constitutional and natural right to love whom I may, to love as long or as short a period as I can, to change that love every day if I please!" Hisses grew louder, but Woodhull continued: "and with that right neither you nor any law you can frame have any right to interfere; and I have the further right to demand a free and unrestricted exercise of that right, and it is your duty not only to accord it, but as a community to see that I am protected in it. I trust that I am fully understood, for I mean just that, and nothing less."

At this, "wild young men cheered most tumultuously." Woodhull tried to elaborate, "I believe promiscuity to be anarchy and the very antithesis of that for which I aspire. I know that there are degrees of love and lust, from the lowest to the highest. But I believe the highest sexual relations are those which are monogamic [sic] . . . But I protest, and I believe every woman who has purity in her soul protests, against all laws that would compel her to maintain relations with a man for whom she has no regard. What can be more terrible than for a delicate, sensitive woman to be compelled to endure the presence of a beast in the shape of a man who knew nothing beyond the blind passion with which he is filled, and for which is often added the delirium of intoxication? I protest against this form of slavery."

Woodhull's evening was marred by Utica, who stayed to have the last word. Stepping to the front of her box, she bowed to the cheering audience and shouted, "I would ask her," looking at her sister, "how can we reform the Greene Street women she speaks of, and at the same time teach them to live promiscuously with men?" Prolonged cheers for Utica followed, and it was hopeless for Victoria to continue. Tilton came forward to halt the evening as the gaslights were turned out.

Throughout Victoria's career, the curious were never able to find out about her private life regarding free love. There was never any proof except her union with Colonel Blood before her divorce from Woodhull was final. No lovers ever came forth; no one found any love letters. The Tilton relationship remains a probability, not fact. Only after Victoria's death did one ancient alleged lover, Benjamin Tucker, surface with a tale that was a half-century old; at nineteen he had sex with thirty-four-year-old Victoria.

Woodhull's "I Am a Free Lover" anthem made an indelible impression on Tucker, then an eighteen-year-old MIT student, who watched her from the front row when she delivered the same line to a packed Boston Music Hall in early 1872, shortly after the Steinway Hall sensation. (This was proof, wrote Tucker, that reviewers of her Steinway speech were wrong to label it an extemporaneous remark.) A year later, in February 1873, Tucker helped a radical group find a Boston hall for Woodhull's lecture when respectable halls refused to rent to her. As she raced for the train afterward, she realized she had left behind her shawl. Tucker caught up with the train, dashed along the corridor, and handed her the shawl, whereupon Victoria "kissed me squarely on the mouth." Tucker leapt off the train "a much excited and wondering youth." Months later, he ran into Colonel Blood in the reading room of Boston's Parker House, and Blood invited the eager youth to help manage Victoria's New England lecture tour. Tucker's subsequent meeting with Victoria left him a virgin no longer.

Tucker demurred that, despite the money he had been paid to tell all, he was not "striving to damage Mrs. Woodhull's character...She deserves, not injury, but honor. It was part of her doctrine, as it is a part of mine, that in cases of sexual attraction, the initiative may be taken as properly by the woman as by the man" and to be done so "frankly, modestly and unmistakable, rather than by arts and wiles and coquetry."

The evening of their first intimate moment, when Tucker was visiting Woodhull and Blood in their Parker House suite, Woodhull "came forward, her face wreathed with cordial smiles, and her two hands, both outstretched, clasped mine, and shook them warmly." When Blood left the suite, Woodhull turned the key and artfully "hung a wrap upon the knob to cover the key-hole. Then, always in a quiet, earnest, charming manner, she marched straight to the chair in which I was seated, leaned over, and kissed me, remarking then: 'I've been wanting to do that so long!' "

The next day's meeting progressed to the point that "after some conversation, Victoria said 'Do you know I should dearly love to sleep with you?' Hereupon any man a thousandth part less stupid than myself would have thrown his arms around her neck and smothered her with kisses." Yet Tucker only replied, "It would be my first experience in that line. She looked at me with amazement... 'How can that be?'...Soon 'my ruin' was complete, and I, nevertheless a proud and happy youth." With the acceptance of Colonel Blood, Tucker said he had sex twice with Victoria, including a night when Blood "pulled the lounge into the bathroom...and went to bed, leaving the sleeping room to Mrs. Woodhull and myself. At one o'clock in the morning I left, in order that Col. Blood might not be obliged to pass the entire night so uncomfortably."

After that, Tucker joined the Woodhull-Claflin-Blood entourage for more than a year, until late in 1874, but his accounts never referred to any more sex with Victoria. When Victoria's biographer Emanie Sachs fished for dirt about Victoria's love life, Tucker said, "She showed no tendency to promiscuity." She was "not vulgar in her love-making, simply enraptured and happy...She was never very gay, but almost always cheerful and charming...Her interest in Free Love was sincere and intelligent."

If Tucker was telling the truth, Blood seemed comfortable with an open marriage. "I never saw the least evidence of ill-nature in the relations of Vicky and the Colonel." Tucker underlined, *"I always found Col. Blood to be an honest, whole-souled, open hearted, open-handed, generous gentleman."*

Contrasting Victoria with the rest of the Claflins, Tucker wrote, "I never heard V. utter a coarse or profane word. Meg Miles was a case... The Claflin cleverness, the Claflin perversity, the Claflin vulgarity were there in full bloom." Victoria was mortified when one day Miles "broke into a noisy and violent quarrel" with Tennie, Victoria, Colonel Blood, and Zula, "which ended in her dashing out of the room, slamming the door and shouting: 'you can all kiss my ass, everyone of you!'"

CHAPTER TWELVE

From Spirit Ghosts to Karl Marx

When the American Association of Spiritualists met in September of 1871, in Vineland, New Jersey, just two months before Victoria's "I Am a Free Lover" declaration, portions of Victoria's biography by Tilton were read aloud at the meeting. Whatever her actual Spiritualist beliefs, Victoria had a calculated reason to wildly exaggerate her power, leading Tilton to write that "she straightened the feet of the lame; she opened the ears of the deaf." Cynical readers hooted, but Victoria scored with the audience she was targeting. Losing ground with suffragists, she turned to other radical groups to push her presidency—among them, Spiritualists. Enthralled by Tilton's sketch, the Spiritualists elected her president of their association at a second September meeting, in Troy, New York.

The sketch attributed everything she had ever thought, written, said, or accomplished to messages from the Other World. From early childhood, "angels" were her "constant companions. They abide with her night and day. They dictate her life with daily revelation... she goes and comes at their behest." Victoria was but a vessel. Colonel Blood, the "reverent husband of his spiritual bride," recorded what Victoria said in her trances, when a "mystical light irradiates from her face... Her enterprises are not the coinage of her own brain, but of their divine invention." Trances took the place of sleep: "Seldom a day goes by but she enters into this fairyland, or rather into this spirit-realm." In good weather she sat on the roof

Victoria Woodhull

Tennessee Claflin
(Courtesy of New York
Public Library)

Annie Claflin
(John Miles Thompson, Jr. Papers)

Buck Claflin
(John Miles Thompson, Jr. Papers)

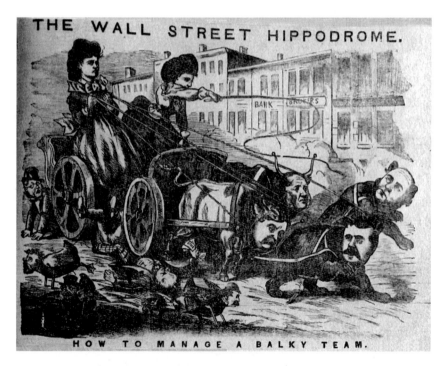

Sisters on Wall Street cartoon (Courtesy of New York Public Library)

Tennessee Claflin
(Courtesy of Library
of Congress)

Cornelius Vanderbilt
(Courtesy of Library of
Congress)

Victoria Woodhull

Colonel James Blood

Benjamin Butler
(Courtesy of Library
of Congress)

Victoria Woodhull at House Judiciary Committee
(Courtesy of Library of Congress)

Frederick Douglass
(Courtesy New York
Historical Society)

Drawing of
Woodhull and
Douglass as
minstrel act from
Pomeroy's Democrat,
May 25, 1872

Theodore Tilton
(Courtesy of New York
Historical Society)

Henry Ward Beecher
(Beinecke Rare Book &
Manuscript Library, Yale
University)

Beecher-Tilton scandal cartoon (Courtesy of Library of Congress)

of her stately mansion "communing hour by hour with the spirits...her simple theology being an absorbing faith in God and the angels."

For someone who professed to remember nothing she dictated in a trance, Victoria was an adamant editor. She refused to let Tilton cut what he knew would make him the butt of cynical journalists' jokes, if the rest of his florid outpouring had not already done so. He fought, she resisted, and what she said ran—most notably, the story of resurrecting her son when he was declared dead. According to this account, Victoria exclaimed, " 'No! I will not permit his death.' And with frantic energy she stripped her bosom naked, caught up his lifeless form, pressed it to her own, and sitting thus, flesh to flesh, glided insensibly into a trance in which she remained seven hours; at the end of which time she awoke...the child that had been thought dead was brought back again to life." The spirit of Jesus Christ wrought this miracle, wrote Tilton.

Her primary muse was Demosthenes, who came to her almost daily for years, wearing a Greek tunic, but never telling her his name until he wrote it on the table that miraculous day at Great Jones Street. It was, she vowed, Demosthenes, not Senator Butler, who helped craft her famous memorial to Congress. Apparently in the throes of something himself, Tilton wrote, "If Demosthenes could arise and speak English, he could hardly excel the fierce light and heat of some of the sentences which I have heard from this singular woman in her glowing hours."

Hoping to appeal to moderate social reformers as well as free lovers among Spiritualists, Tilton wrote, "her theories are similar to those which have long been taught by John Stuart Mill and Elizabeth Cady Stanton...that marriage is of the heart and not of the law, that when love ends marriage should end with it." Tilton added: "finally, in religion, she is a spiritualist of the most mystical and ethereal type."

Woodhull's announcing herself as candidate for president the year before was "mainly for the purpose of drawing public attention to the claims of woman to political equality with man," wrote Tilton. But now the "Victoria League" (organized by Victoria) was clamoring for her. Tilton linked Vanderbilt to the cause—although the sisters' former mentor had recently publicly castigated them following the family feud scandal. Nonetheless, wrote Tilton, the league was "popularly supposed, though not definitely known, to be presided over by Commodore Vanderbilt, who is also...imagined to be the golden corner-stone of the business house of Woodhull, Claflin, & Co."

The New York press mercilessly mocked Tilton's screed. The *World* headlined its tirade "The Queen of Quacks" and Tilton's words "hideous rubbish." *Harper's Weekly* hooted: "If apples are wormy this year, and grapes mildew, and duck's eggs addle...it may all be ascribed to the unhallowed influence of Mr. Tilton's Life of Victoria Woodhull."

Many critics saw Tilton hopelessly besotted over Victoria—yet his biography of her reads almost as if he was deliberately damning her with so much overwrought praise that it could be seen as a satire. Whatever the reason for such extravagance, Tilton never lived it down.

Nonetheless, the biographical sketch served Victoria well with the American Association of Spiritualists, for whom praising Jesus Christ, God, and a belief in a spirit's living on after death were movement touchstones. She also won the hearts of dedicated Spiritualists when her *Weekly* took on the charlatans with their spirit tapping and table lifting as tarnishing the religious-oriented movement. As their elected leader, Woodhull quickly sought their aid in her presidential campaign. While not expressly political, Spiritualists were reformers and humanitarians who could garner support.

While embracing the Spiritualists, the sisters simultaneously sought the support of laborers, joining up with Karl Marx's International Workingmen's Association (IWA) in the spring of 1871. The following December the *Weekly* became the first American publication to print the English version of *The Communist Manifesto*, translated by Stephen Pearl Andrews. Their support of radical labor unions, the bête noire of America's ruling capitalists, solidified the end for the sisters among influential Wall Streeters and the establishment press, even more so than their free love advocacy.

One could argue a possible hypocrisy in the sisters' ardent support of labor. They had gained their own financial independence on the same Wall Street they were now vilifying. However, Victoria consistently said that they had pursued riches in order to finance their humanitarian causes, which included downtrodden laborers. Additionally, they had more recently faced extreme ridicule from mainstream wealthy quarters, and Woodhull pragmatically realized she had to find a new base of support. Also the sisters were still under the influence of Andrews, and by the summer of 1871, Tilton was a constant presence, touting the cause of laborers. For the sisters and other Victorian radicals, the labor movement was indeed a natural extension of their democratic causes. Furthermore, as underdogs for most of their lives, with the exception of the last few years, the sisters sympathized with the working poor. As Woodhull explained, "I never objected to the accumulation of wealth...but I always shall, until it is remedied, object to a certain few holding all the wealth, while the producing multitudes barely escape starvation." After their brokerage firm had failed, Victoria cast the venture as a symbolic mission: "We went unto Wall Street, not particularly because I wanted to be a broker...But because I wanted to plant the Flag of women's rebellion in the very center of the continent."

With Andrews leading the way, the sisters—"this pair of enigmatic and remarkable radicals"—within a year became the hub of the major IWA Section 12, labeled "The Yankee International," for its broad-based egalitarian departure from other IWA sections that were controlled by and comprised mostly immigrant laborers and trade unionists. Dominated by the "independent political activities of the sisters," the Yankee International held its meetings in the offices of the *Weekly,* which became the official English-language organ of the American IWA.

At first, the sisters' relations with IWA founding member Karl Marx were cordial. They published an interview with Marx, who wrote back, thanking them for sending an edition of their "highly-interesting" paper.

The sisters' unique section attracted "some of the most eccentric and garrulous personalities to ever call themselves Internationals." Crusaders of abolition, feminism, socialism, and Spiritualism saw Section 12 as a "beacon of reform." But to traditional labor organizers, the two women were an embarrassment. This constituency may seem disparate at first glance, but they were natural allies. Spiritualists were found among abolitionists, suffragists and in Free Love communes. "Nearly the entire leadership of the abolition movement espoused Spiritualism at some point in their careers." Suffragists were not so receptive to Spiritualism, but there were many among them, including Isabella Beecher and Paulina Wright Davis. Stanton and Anthony wrote favorably, the "only religious sect in the world... that has recognized the equality of women is the Spiritualists."

Like many in their eclectic following, the sisters fought for a socialist form of democracy that included equality for women, freed slaves, American Indians, and anyone else excluded from the privileged white male order. Once again the sisters behaved uniquely and historically, pushing for reform for blacks and women and fighting for the eight-hour day and equal pay for women in factories.

To the man Marx had appointed watchdog over the IWA's sections, a German immigrant named Friedrich Sorge, the sisters' cadre disrupted his single-minded goal to organize white male trade unions. Sorge devoted himself to undermining and discrediting the sisters' section, appalled at their fight for working women and blacks. "The battle for the soul of the American International was waged over section 12," wrote Marxist historian Timothy Messer-Kruse.

Like many American reformers in 1871, the sisters were propelled into action after the battle that crushed the Paris Commune in May. Following France's defeat in the Franco-Prussian War, Paris workers rebelled against the new Third French Republic, formed under humiliating peace terms. Monarchist leaders of the Republic fled Paris, and workers and socialists elected the Paris Commune as an independent government. The Communards called for labor reforms, separation of church and state, and free education for all, with emphasis on girls' schools, since women had been so deprived of education.

On March 26, 1871, French workers cheered as the socialist red flag waved atop the Tuileries Palace. The Commune lasted less than three months against the army of the Third French Republic. Communard cannons were set amid barricades made from cobblestones and mattresses, some on the steep hills of Montmartre. The last barricades were smashed during the "Bloody Week" massacre beginning May 18. Immediate executions, death in prisons, and exile followed. "An orgy of killing took place. Many innocent were killed," mistaken for Communards, including chimney sweeps "on the assumption that their hands had been blackened by gunpowder." In two prisons, some 2,300 were said to be shot in two days. As reprisals continued, even anti-Communard newspapers implored "Let us kill no more!"

Some 25,000 Communards were allegedly killed, another 6,000 were executed or died in prison, and 7,500 were exiled.

In the aftermath, the question of wages, hours, equity, and poverty were fervently discussed on both sides of the Atlantic. The establishment press routinely portrayed the workers who declared their independence from the Versailles government as rampaging, murderous mobs. But former abolitionist, Spiritualist, and other radical papers supported the Commune. Here Tilton and Woodhull were politically aligned; his *Golden Age* magazine supported the Communards, as did the *Weekly*. In December of 1871, Tilton and the sisters were among thousands marching in a mock funeral parade to honor the French workers massacred in Paris that May. The sisters, as always, were newsworthy. The parade came a month after Woodhull's "I Am a Free Lover" speech, and she was even more in demand as a celebrity.

Curious bystanders turned out in record numbers, shoving close to marchers, climbing trees and lampposts, and leaning out of windows all along the two-and-a-half-mile route. A majority of newspapers surprisingly treated the procession with respect, as did the spectators, praising the Skidmore Guards, a "magnificently uniformed" black military band. Even the Fifth Avenue rich tumbled out of hotels and clubs to watch, surprising the procession by cheering heartily; out of respect, the prestigious Manhattan Club lowered the American flag to half-mast. However, preliminary scuffling with a Zouave band, which refused "to march in front of the 'niggers,'" held up the parade. Leaders eventually forged a compromise with honor guards and an American flag carrier placed between the two bands. During the delay, as the sisters waited in the street, gangs cornered them, jostling and badgering them with cries of "Which is Tennie?" "Lor' ain't she homely?" "Let me through, I'm a free lover." Each jeer was greeted with uproarious laughter. No police came to the sisters' aid. The two women bravely stood their ground, and Andrews and Blood "exerted themselves like Trojans to prevent their fair charge from being squeezed to death."

As the marchers turned onto Broadway, huge cheers for the women surpassed any of the day. All the spectators stared at Victoria and Tennie. Marching in front, the sisters wore matching dark blue jackets "cut tight to the figure, black dresses, white collars, Alpine hats and each wore a broad crimson scarf." Tennie led the women's group, carrying a heavy red flag on which was written I.W.A. SECTION 12, COMPLETE POLITICAL AND SOCIAL EQUALITY FOR BOTH SEXES, although the weight was so much that she had to give up the banner after walking a half mile. Victoria walked behind her sister, but for a portion of the parade she rode in a carriage at the rear. The *World* praised the IWA for honoring the martyrs of a "great idea," and noted their banner: THE WORLD IS OUR COUNTRY—TO DO GOOD OUR RELIGION.

Meanwhile, Henry Ward Beecher used the parade and the IWA's eight-hour-day battle to hector the working poor from the pulpit. Fewer hours would tend "to make men feel that work is not a good thing… hard knocks, and a good many of them" were the only way to "carve out independent fortunes." Beecher admitted that underpaid workers could not make enough in an eight-hour day to advance from their lowly state at their present pay, but he neglected to denounce the owners who paid them so poorly. Working longer hours was his Christian solution.

In February 1872, Victoria gave a rabble-rousing "Impending Revolution" speech in the hall she loved the most (for its fine acoustics), the Academy of Music. She could be heard in every corner, with little strain on her voice. No longer Wall Street darlings, the sisters were now causing capitalists to shudder at their message as they declared a pox on high finance and the corruption that went with it, untrammeled by laws, and the exploitation of the many for the wealth of the few. And the masses came to listen.

An estimated twelve thousand showed up—and six thousand were able to push into the hall for Victoria's denunciation of capitalist power.

Most New York newspapers used such phrases as "motley crew" to describe the immense audience, and infuriated Woodhull by concentrating on the mob scene and not the content of her speech. She now larded her messages with passages from the Bible, preaching that her view was not antagonistic to religion and arguing that Jesus was a beneficent socialist (a point made by modern liberation theologists). The sisters' pointed message was that Christ "commanded the rich to 'go sell all thou hast and give to the poor,'" but their biblical interpretations did not sit well with wealthy church brethren.

The red meat that had her audience cheering for more came when Woodhull attacked individual capitalists. This resulted in a counterattack from the pro-capitalist *New York Times*. "It is a crime for a single person to steal a dollar," she said, her face flushing with enthusiasm, "but a corporation may steal a million dollars, and be canonized as saints. Oh, the stupid blindness of this people! Swindled every day before their very eyes, and yet they don't seem to know that there is everything wrong, simply because no law has been violated."

She even attacked a hand that had once fed her. "A Vanderbilt may sit in his office and manipulate stocks, or make dividends, by which, in a few years, he amasses fifty million dollars...But if a poor, half-starved child were to take a loaf of bread from his cupboard, to prevent starvation, she would be sent first to the Tombs, and thence to Blackwell's Island." Woodhull took on William Backhouse Astor, Manhattan's predominant slumlord: "An Astor may sit in his sumptuous apartments, and watch the property bequeathed him by his father, rise in value from one to fifty millions, and everybody bows before his immense power...But if a tenant of his, whose employer has discharged him because he did not vote the Republican ticket, and thereby fails to pay his month's rent to Mr. Astor, the law sets him and his family into the street...and, whether he dies of cold or starvation, neither Mr. Astor or anybody else stops to ask."

The *New York Times* editorial attacked her character: "Victoria C. Woodhull has been married rather more extensively than most matrons, and hence it might be deemed inappropriate to style her a 'foolish virgin'; but by her inconsequential method of reasoning, Mrs. Woodhull closely resembles them." As a person, she was of "no possible consequence" and her presidential candidacy a "feeble travesty." However, her "Communist fanaticism" and "hostility to accepted social morality" could inflame the "hostility of the poor to the rich" and foster "the conviction that capitalists have no rights which working men are bound to accept."

The editorial incorrectly slammed her for omitting Vanderbilt "among her rich oppressors of the poor. Mr. Stewart [owner of Lord & Taylor], she asserts, has no right to his wealth, because he never produced a dollar of it by his own physical labor; and Mr. Astor, who received his fortune by inheritance, is even a worse criminal." Woodhull should be asked "upon what title her own claim to hold property, wear dresses, and accumulate jewels and chignons rests...she does not profess to have earned them by manual labor...has she a right to receive the proceeds of a newspaper which she does not write and bank which she does not conduct, if Mr. Stewart has no right to the revenues of a business which he has created and continues to manage?" If "Mr. Astor should surrender his houses to the carpenters who built them, and Mr. Stewart his goods to the shopmen who sell them, by all means let them also insist that Mrs. Woodhull... should be consistent and heave her best black silk and her jaunty sealskin jacket, her diamond rings and her golden necklaces, her dainty high-heeled boots, and her most cherished chignons" into a bonfire. "She ought to consent to mingle a little consistency of action with her rhetorical malice, and her mendacious abuse of men who have made her no presents."

This sneer about "presents" was of course aimed at the sisters' Vanderbilt connection. The *Times* refused to print Woodhull's response, citing the press of other news. She was forced to print it in the *Weekly*, first attacking the *Times* for its incorrect statement regarding Vanderbilt. She challenged the newspaper to deny her point about Stewart's poverty wages; his underpaid sewing women were building his fortune by "coining their blood into money, drop by drop, stitch by stitch to pay for it." Tackling railroad "kings," Woodhull condemned "a system of law which will permit them to 'water' their stocks...the

Times would have the people continue to think...that the laws which permit such thieving are just and right...A single line of railroad leading from this city to Chicago, takes from the people to pay dividends on fictitious stock, more money every year than Tammany has stolen from the city."

As for the personal attack: "I see no comparison." As she often did, here Victoria switched back and forth from first and third person, and this may well have been written by Andrews. "Mrs. Woodhull does not monopolize dresses, jewels, or chignons; since of the first she only possesses sufficient to render her comfortable, while with the last two she has nothing to do." Nor was there any similarity between her small enterprises and the tycoons she described: "When Mrs. Woodhull conducts her paper and bank under cover of legal contrivances, so that she shall enslave a million people and be enabled to tax the entire country, to increase her possessions from the common necessities of life to many millions more than her demands require, then the *Times* may consistently put her in comparison with Mr. Astor and Mr. Stewart."

Meanwhile, Woodhull was being honored—if that could possibly be the word—in the Thomas Nast Hall of Infamy. The famous political cartoonist portrayed her as a demon titled "Mrs. Satan." The ominously dark illustration shows Woodhull in the foreground, wearing horns and massive clawed bat wings, holding a sign that reads, BE SAVED BY FREE LOVE. She is looking back at a woman in rags, carrying a drunken husband and several children on her back. The trudging woman, stooped over by the weight, vows, "I would rather travel the hardest path of matrimony than follow in your footsteps." Suffragists and free lovers saw the irony in the cartoon; such a terrible version of matrimony could hardly be an appealing alternative. The damaging tag of Mrs. Satan, however, stayed with Victoria far into the future.

CHAPTER THIRTEEN

Being Tennie

One evening after working at their brokerage firm, the two sisters entered famous Delmonico's. They strode across the plush carpet, under the soft glow of gaslit chandeliers, sat at a damask-covered table, and ordered soup for two. The owner, who catered to money, old or new, and to celebrities, fair or foul, glided over. He bowed low enough to whisper that he would swiftly walk with them to the door so that other diners would think the sisters had merely come to have a business chat with him. Surely, he said to the sisters, they knew the rule: women were not allowed to dine without a male escort at night. Tennie jumped up and hurried out the door, and commanded to their coachman, "Come down off your box and come here." She herded the embarrassed driver, in crimson coat and polished high boots, top hat plucked off his head, into the restaurant and sat him down.

"Soup for three," she ordered.

This response was pure Tennie. As Victoria pushed her presidential campaign, Tennie acted like the younger sister who was no pretender to the throne: determinedly rebellious. Throughout 1871 and 1872, she kept a beaming smile, tossing her curls, flirting, and pushing her own political agenda. The sisters were such a force that the *New York Times* remarked sarcastically, "That there should be two such, jointly working at the same time, would surpass belief, did not the fact stare one in the face."

Unlike most Victorian maidens, Tennie was easily at home with the saucy retort. When she experienced an uncomfortable railroad journey in France in 1874—there were no toilets on the train, which meant getting off and on at station stops—Tennie declared vehemently that, had she to travel longer in France, she would not stand for this at all; she would carry with her a large tin cup. With animated gestures that made others laugh, she said that she would fill it…and that at the first convenient chance she would toss the contents out the window. One of her fellow travelers said, "What I have known and seen of Tennie convinces me that she would have been as good as her word. Very good humored as a rule, she nevertheless was not a person to trifle with."

On a sleeting day in Manhattan, Tennie shocked a male visitor as she entered the *Weekly* office, throwing off her sodden outer garments. " 'Isn't this weather terrible? Just look at this!' Up went her skirts to a point midway between her knee and waist." The revelation of drenched stockings and underwear that came to just above the knees—and revealed nothing of Tennie—nevertheless unnerved the visitor.

From the moment the sisters stepped onto Wall Street, Tennie captivated reporters. She possessed "the impulsive gaiety of a gypsy," wrote a *Sun* reporter. "She is all verve, and vivacity, full of imagination and excitability, very free in her modes of expression." Gossips were appalled at her habit of sitting close to men when she engaged them in conversation. One story made the rounds that when a wife admonished her husband for being so taken with Tennessee, he replied that what on earth could he do when a woman so charming leaned that close to him? When she stood on platforms to speak, young men in the audience warbled, "Oh that Tenn, Tenn, Tennessee."

Tennie enjoyed entertaining reporters at the sisters' Thirty-Eighth Street mansion, plying them with champagne and amusing conversation. They eagerly came to interview her following the 1871 publication of *Constitutional Equality of the Sexes*, a scholarly treatise under her name, widely thought to be the work of Stephen Pearl Andrews. Authenticity mattered little to the reporters greeted by Tennie: "She is all animation, talking not only with her tongue, but with her eyes, face, hands, and all over. One would think her whole physical structure was inlaid with a thousand sensitive spiral springs." Having "mingled largely and freely with men of the world, she will say and do the most outré things, but with an air of the most childlike and unsophisticated innocence."

Tennie treated them to her premise on the sexual double standard: "Take, for instance, Hester Prynne—she darted a quick look at Col. Blood—'it is Hester Prynne, isn't it?' If she is forced to wear a scarlet letter A, then so should her reverend seducer." Asked what "Reverend Seducer" she had in mind, Tennie winked and said, "Draw your own conclusions."

While Victoria scandalized with her radical views, she also maintained a controlled and regal image, seldom displaying the carefree abandon of her sister. Even in private she showed decorum, while Tennie let fly with her thoughts. Once, when Tennie referred contemptuously to a man as "that old cock," Victoria darted a warning look, recalled Benjamin Tucker. Tennie said, "Oh Bennie knows very well that I was not referring to his private parts."

Tennie was great fodder for cheap "sporting news" papers such as the *Days' Doings*, read in saloons, barbershops, and sporting men's clubs. The public drew on tabloid celebrity coverage to form their opinions about the famous, swearing with knowing looks that the stories were true, as surely as if they were happening to next-door neighbors, simply because they had read them in the scandal sheets. Lurid headlines and drawings in gossip rags added to the criticism heaped on the sisters in the mainstream press. The *Days' Doings* made Tennie a cover girl, with drawings that depicted her in low-cut dresses, although she seldom wore them. The New York *Evening Telegram* wrote that Joan of Arc was never as well known as Tennie, and quipped, "Joan of Arc never had her name in the newspapers once, while Tennie Claflin's name is in the newspapers all the time."

Taking their cue from such coverage, the Beecher sisters Catharine and Harriet exploited Tennie in their determination to destroy Woodhull. Catharine referred to them as the "two prostitutes." As the Beecher sisters tried to investigate the scarlet sisters' past, Tennie's actions added to the low-class portrayal they loved to depict, as in Stowe's roman à clef, *My Wife and I*.

On occasion, Harriet and Catharine had ammunition. When the sisters opened the brokerage firm, Tennie was lavishly lauded in the press for her ability to spot the purveyor of a fraudulent check, expertise no doubt gained from her long experience with Buck Claflin. But her publicity drew the attention of some Chicago merchants who swore that a woman who owed them money looked a lot like Tennie, thus exposing a small crack in the prim and proper tale the sisters had told Wall Street reporters. The debt was $125.70, for medicines bought in her spiritual healing days. Tennie denied having been in Chicago, and when a lawyer read a description that fitted her exactly, she said, "with a smile which would have rivaled Cleopatra's," that she had often been mistaken for a lady who looked like her and had been obliged to pay her debts. Shortly after they opened the brokerage firm in 1870, Tennie had gone to court to answer charges on the unpaid bill, wearing a black silk-and-velvet dress, a chignon, and a fashionable hat. She smiled engagingly at the judge, but when he demanded she pay the bill, Tennie flounced out of the courtroom with a slight sway of her upholstered derriere.

Tennie had borne the brunt of their father's larceny from childhood throughout her teenage years; when she was a young woman, skipping out on a debt and lying about it was a normal way of life. Still, this public notoriety was enough for Vanderbilt to begin distancing himself from the sisters. The New York *Sun* reported that Vanderbilt "denies all knowledge of her and her partner." This was disingenuous, because the Commodore certainly had known them and helped them for two years.

The truth about Tennie scarcely mattered, because sporting newspapers used "almost any excuse to lampoon the sisters, whose images had wide commercial appeal." Tennie's political ambitions were mocked in illustrations with vicious stereotypes of the kind of people who would follow her. In one, Tennie stands aloft in a low-necked gown, a glass of champagne in hand, while the men ogling her include a thick-lipped African American, a Chinaman with a long braid and an opium pipe, and a large-nosed bearded man who fit caricatures of Jews in that era. Splashed on the cover of one *Days' Doings* was an improbable scene: Tennie is depicted as an unbridled harpy, pummeling a male drama teacher with her fists as he

begs for mercy on the floor. This silly illustration was printed without reason or relevance; what mattered to the editors is that the sisters sold well.

Both sisters were savvy enough to know that as a team they enhanced
their power, adding a special allure. Dressing alike was their showman's
trick, giving the intriguing impression of a twinlike personality. Tennie
recognized that they were not of the norm, once saying defensively, "We
have queer theories, queer opinions, queer manners and queer dresses, but
we are pure-minded women, trying to do business just like men."

There is no indication that Woodhull, with her proper manners and
high ambitions, ever tried to restrain her lively sister. A friend who saw
them constantly for nearly two years said that they always seemed fond of
each other. The two were inseparable. In private, Tennie assumed a pro-
tective, almost motherly role when her older sister let down her guard and
collapsed in fatigue. Victoria sorely needed Tennie's unwavering support,
for public scorn and upper-class condemnation weighed heavier on Victoria than her fiery rebuttals indicated. Victoria appeared impervious while
striking back in print or at the lectern; only later would her private letters
and musings reveal how deeply she was wounded.

At times, however, Tennie pushed for separate recognition. In the summer of 1871, when Theodore Tilton was Woodhull's devoted camp follower,
Tennie felt left out and unsatisfied. "I will tell you confidentially," she wrote
in a decidedly not confidential *Weekly* article, "that since Mr. Andrews is
chief of the pantarchy and Victoria is chief of the Cosmopolitical Party,
I have taken it into my head to be 'chief of something.'" She might enlist
the help of "my friend the Commodore, Rothschild, or whoever else has a
few hundred thousand to spare" to bankroll an enterprise to show "what
my own genius can design and realize." She would leave the mansion, she
said, and have her own "grand city home" and salon filled with "men and
women of letters and genius, great artists and the like...leaders of reform."
She would call it the Republican Court. This never happened, but Tennie
did indeed make a solo splash the following year.

Still, Tennie always remained eternally supportive of her sister. After
Woodhull's "I Am a Free Lover" speech in November 1871, Victoria was

much in demand as a lecturer, setting off on a wearying journey in towns throughout Michigan, New York, Ohio, and West Virginia. This time Tennie stayed home to defend her sister and carry on the fight to lambast sexual hypocrisy. She published a letter from a madam named Mary Bowles, complimenting Victoria for a speech that "touched the hearts of thousands of degraded women with a thrill of joy and hope...your lecture has awakened a soul in me which I thought was dead. If your views could prevail, virtue and happiness could be again mine. God bless you for your honest effort for women even though it should fail." About to retire from her lucrative business, Mrs. Bowles offered to expose her clientele: "I will give you access to my two big books," which would reveal the names of "all classes—from doctors of divinity to counter jumpers and runners for mercantile houses. Make what use of them as you please."

Tennie published a disingenuous reply in the *Weekly*: "My sister and myself have scrupulously adopted the policy of avoiding personalities when possible." Then she added, "But the time may come when that policy will have to be abandoned, for our enemies do not scruple to resort to them in the most scandalous manner." As always, Tennie, more than Victoria, spoke of and to prostitutes from a deep well of sympathy. "I shall be happy to receive you at my home at any time," either alone or "with others of your class. It is enough for me that you are human beings, and such as Christ loved and associated with."

The trick in all this was that there was no "Mrs. Bowles." She was Tennie's invented madam. All the correspondence was fake. Posing as "Mrs. Bowles," Tennie seethed with rage at the way men treated prostitutes and poorer women, and she declared (as Mrs. Bowles) her "intense indignation, amounting almost to hatred, for society which had condemned and excluded me, and for men especially in their mean and hateful treatment of women of our class—intimate with and caressing us in private and coolly passing us by without recognition before the world." If Tennie was referring to herself, this is a deeply revelatory passage, and the most telling of all her comments. Nowhere else had she expressed such vehement private feelings: "almost hatred for society" that had "condemned her"; the "mean and hateful treatment" of men "caressing us in private" and shunning them "before the world." More than anything said about the sisters, her venom gives the impression that Tennie may have been a young prostituted victim of the Claflin tribe, ignored by day by men who had sought her at night. If so, it would go a long way toward explaining her unrelenting crusade regarding the sexual double standard.

While viewed by some as a shadow sister in the Woodhull machine, Tennie was stalwart in her fight for women's independence. She was the one who procured Vanderbilt's crucial support and start-up money for the brokerage firm, the one who hounded businessmen for *Weekly* ads. Tennie was the better salesperson, cutting deals through her bold pursuit and unwavering confidence. She was thus criticized for possessing persuasive powers that were considered attributes in men. She was also the sister who first scouted Capitol Hill for their suffrage fight. She managed to wangle a meeting with President Grant, parlaying a chance encounter in her youth with Grant's hardworking tanner father, Jesse Grant, into a White House invitation. Jesse lived in Covington, Kentucky, across the river from Cincinnati, when the Claflins were plying their clairvoyant medicine trade in the 1860s. Old Jesse sought out Woodhull to spiritually heal his aches and pains and near deafness. He spent an afternoon with the sisters and became so entranced with Victoria, sister Utica, and Tennie that he composed a poem citing their peculiar names: "Three sisters fair, of worth and weight / a queen, a city and a state." The visit must have been jolly; his poem ended, "Each bewitching gypsy / got that day a little tipsy."

Tennie was a solid partner as advance woman and warm-up act, and when her sister suddenly became ill or too exhausted to perform, Tennie substituted for her. One time, Tennie stood alone, a pretty young woman, but with none of her sister's commanding presence or name recognition, facing an overflow crowd at the Academy of Music. The murmurs of disappointment changed when Tennie charmed them with her "inimitable freshness and vivacity." She could bellow with such tremendous volume that she had sometimes frightened the audience. One critic, who had heard Tennie speak earlier, said, "Her voice is something astounding to hear when at its full capacity"; she could go from high C soprano to "melodious contralto" and down to "tremendous thunderings" of a "basso profundo." But this time, Tennie kept her voice in check and won over the packed house. She was no shadow.

Despite Tennie's reputation and the rumors surrounding her, there is little evidence of a freewheeling sexual life in Manhattan. Outside of Vanderbilt, and of Tennie's easily discarded first husband, and of a suggestive letter to the influential Whitelaw Reid, little is known. Even the gossip papers never located lovers. One dashing young man was known as a steady companion and "Tennie's sweetheart," the city editor of the New York *Sun*, Johnny Green. He was "a tall, handsome, smooth-faced chap of about 30, with an olive complexion that made him look like a Portuguese," one acquaintance noted. Green was " 'all gone' on Tennie" and showed up often at the offices of the *Weekly*. When Tennie or the family wanted to broadcast anything, Tennie fed it to Green.

The only suggestion that Vicky and Tennie had an unusually charitable relationship concerning shared beaus came from the gossip-for-sale Tucker. "One afternoon, when I was walking uptown with Victoria, from the office, she [Victoria] said to me suddenly: 'Tennie is going to love you this afternoon.' I looked at her wonderingly. 'But,' I said, 'I don't care to have her.' 'Oh! Don't say that,' she answered, 'Nobody can love me who doesn't love Tennie.' " Tucker relates that he ducked "numerous hints and opportunities" from Tennie.

Tucker remarked that Tennie had "some intelligence, some force, some humor, and a little education"; her beauty "was of a sensuous nature. I think that the love that she inspired was generally of a sexual nature."

While her most defiant public gesture was seen by tens of thousands in December 1871—carrying the large red IWA banner for a portion of the parade honoring the martyred French Communards—she made other scandalous news on her own.

In August 1871, soon after Tennie confessed that she wanted to become "chief of something," she ran for Congress, representing the primarily German American Eighth District, speaking in German to several hundred members of the German-American Progressive Society. An "attentive and appreciative audience, composed largely of the better class of German citizens with their wives and daughters" and also "many of Miss Claflin's broker and banker friends," was there. Even Henry Clews, who had been so disparaging about Tennie, and Jim Fisk lent their support, along with progressive politicians and "reform agitators." A large lithograph of Tennie decorated the hall, in addition to German and American flags.

Deafening applause greeted the smiling Tennie, who wore a plain black organdy dress with a small print pattern. Her short hair hung loose and bushy about her forehead and temples. Coached by Andrews, the master of languages, Tennie spoke in a clear, strong voice in German. It was a long speech for any politician to finesse in a foreign language. She flattered the crowd, noting that she was "descended from the German stock," and outlined the "New Departure" argument for women having the right to vote. She then asked if anyone thought "things could go worse in the administration of our national affairs than they now do?" This view in the wake of Grant and Tammany Hall scandals was cheered. Tennie suggested they "try the experiment merely of entrusting a woman with the performance of official duties." If she failed, they could "retrieve their mistake."

A beer-drinking cadre shouted, "Bravo," and applauded her reference to temperance actions and Sunday drinking laws: "just as the religious American has the privilege of going to his church on Sunday, so must the right be equally secure to you to seek your recreation on Sunday…and to drink your glass of lager beer in peace and quietness, so long as you do not disturb the public order." German admirers followed her home to serenade her at the mansion, complete with a full military band, once more startling staid Murray Hill. Tennie appeared on the balcony, like royalty, thanking them. Nothing more came of her attempt, but she was unstoppable. Her next campaign was to seek the colonelcy of the Ninth Regiment of the National Guard.

Her military bid began with one of the century's most famous murders. Jim Fisk's most disastrous move in his checkered life was introducing Edward "Ned" Stokes, a handsome gambler and flashy dresser, to Fisk's mistress, Josie Mansfield. Soon they became lovers. When Mansfield proposed that they all three be friends, Fisk replied, "No, Josie, it won't do. You can't run two engines on the same track in contrary directions at the same time." Fights ensued between Stokes and Fisk over their partnership in an oil refinery as well as over Josie. Then Josie and Stokes "decided to extort money from Jim Fisk's deep pockets." She demanded a settlement of $25,000 and tried to blackmail him with love letters that might disclose nefarious business deals. Fisk countered, and had Stokes arrested for embezzlement; Josie then had Fisk arrested for libel, Stokes sued Fisk for malicious prosecution, and the press went wild.

Late on a Saturday afternoon, January 6, 1872, Fisk was on his way to meet a friend at the Grand Central Hotel. He started up the broad red-carpeted staircase toward the mezzanine. Standing at the top was Stokes, pistol poised. The life of Jubilee Jim, the exemplar of a financial era marked by capricious fortunes, greed, and corruption, ended on the steps of the hotel. Stokes shot twice, hitting Fisk in his arm and the hard-to-miss abdomen. Fisk crumpled, his crimson-lined cape and diamond stickpins lying in an oozing puddle of blood. He died early the next morning. He was thirty-six.

"Not since the memorable night that Abe Lincoln was shot," remarked the *Herald*, "was there such excitement throughout the city." Fisk was a rascal, but he was the people's rascal. They loved his bonhomie, and his charitable contributions, which included a generous donation to Chicago after the famous 1871 fire. More than twenty-five thousand people jammed Manhattan's streets for Fisk's funeral parade, which featured a brass band and members of his Ninth Regiment.

The Reverend Beecher intoned that Fisk was a man "absolutely without moral sense." This infuriated the sisters. The *Weekly* knocked "the sanctimonious, long-faced, orthodox saint" who would "shriek aloud about the immorality of Fisk...We are no admirers of the vain, vulgar display Fisk made of his wealth. The well-remembered 'Black Friday'...is doubtless the best instance of his 'sharp practice'...but he had grand virtues also. It is said that the last act of his life, with his pen, was a generous gift to the needy and deserving poor." The paper sent a message to Beecher: God would judge the good in Fisk and punish the follies of the "loudest professing saint on earth."

Three months later, Tennie published a letter requesting that she be considered for the still-vacant position as colonel of the Ninth Regiment. "There can be no objection to me, save that I am a woman... Joan d'Arc was also a woman. While I do not make pretensions to the same military genius she possessed... it has always been my desire to become actively connected with the service." While her request would "occasion incredulity... permit me to assure you I am deeply... in earnest."

The *New York Times*, fresh from exposés that brought down Boss Tweed and his Tammany Hall gang, poked fun at Fisk, who also "finally fell, if not precisely in the front of the battle." Sarcasm dripped as it editorialized, "There could be found a no fitter successor for the dead Fisk than the living Claflin... Of course no citizen of character and social position would care to wear the metaphorical stars of Col. Fisk." The sisters cheekily excised the sarcasm and reprinted "there could be no fitting successor" as praise from the *Times*.

Of the two sisters, the *Times* acidly editorialized, "the more erratic and dashing Tennie... cites Joan d'Arc as a reason why she should be elected... we admire Miss Claflin's logic quite as much as we admire her modesty." The *Herald* mocked Tennie's request as a typical publicity stunt: "For two years past two women of the same family have managed in this city to attract—by very gratuitous system of advertising—the attention of all persons to their every word and action." Papers across the country joked about Tennie's attempt. One of the illustrations published shows her in a can-can dancer's corset outfit, stepping into gigantic trousers that the hefty Fisk would wear. Another shows her erratically riding a horse to demonstrate her military ineptitude. All this was nothing compared to the reaction of Tennie's next jaw-dropping accomplishment. After being turned down by the Ninth, she was named colonel of New York's Eighty-Fifth, the only black regiment in the state.

Only the New York *Sun* treated Tennie or the regiment with any respect, possibly because of the smitten editor, Johnny Green. The *Sun*'s owner, urbane Charles A. Dana, who had been a close friend of Lincoln's, also no doubt favored the coverage. Dana assumed a worldly, cynical air but also produced a liberal paper famous for its style, human interest stories, and proletariat message. Its motto was "The Sun Shines for All."

The paper published a long and deferential front-page article about the black regiment, remarkable at the time for mainstream papers. No one was lavishing money on these soldiers; due to an unpaid forty-five-dollar gas bill they had inherited from previous tenants, the armory was dimly lit with ten coal oil lamps when Tennie appeared. Accompanied by Colonel Blood and a captain of the regiment, Tennie sat onstage, in a large armchair, wearing a plain black dress with a white frill at the neck and a blue necktie. Woodhull sat in the darkened audience, not wanting to steal her sister's thunder. Tennie "exhibited a pluck that was truly remarkable. Her bright, beaming eyes wandered about the large room, and here and there she nodded to her friends."

An officer stated that they had become "tired of inviting colored men and white men to assist them" with no results. It would be an honor to accept Tennie. One captain got to the heart of the matter. "He was willing to be led by a man or woman if either would uniform the regiment." Great laughter followed. But the senior officer said he would oppose Claflin. Smiling at the audience sweetly, Tennie said she did not mean to oppose his authority. Reminding the audience that the struggle for an eight-hour workday had already led to bloodshed—in 1866, President Grant issued a proclamation for an eight-hour workday, but only for government workers; in reaction, laborers fought bloody battles in strikes and riots well into the twentieth century—Tennie said she was ready to be in the "advance column fighting for that right."

Tennie knew how to work a room. Applause thundered as she vowed, "I would rather accept the colonelcy of a colored regiment than that of one composed of white men." The approbation increased to a roar when she added that she could "pick out more white men than blacks who would run from the field of battle."

As the captain politely insisted that a black should be its leader, Tennie said she would defer to him. Arguments became so vehement that a riot seemed imminent. Tennie tried hard to control herself, but "her beautiful eyes were filled with tears." In the end she was overwhelmingly chosen as the first and only American white woman to be elected colonel of a black regiment. She already had her uniform and promised that she would outfit the six-hundred-man regiment in grand style.

Predictably, the *New York Times* led the ridicule of Tennie and the black regiment in offensive racist tones. "The colored race has a tropical fondness for brilliant colors and provided Col. Claflin selects a uniform which shall consist largely of red and yellow," how they are arranged would not be a "matter of much consequence." She must be prepared to exchange "the cosmetics of the Caucasian woman" for "burnt cork." Other papers followed suit with more sarcastic references to "burnt cork," which was used by white actors to don blackface.

African American soldiers had struggled for years and had finally gotten the word *white* erased from the state's militia code; black companies could now combine into "Tennie's" regiment, which was poised for incorporation into the National Guard. This historic move represented a potentially major social and political victory for the black community. "The decision to invite Tennessee to assume the high profile post...could not have been taken lightly." Yes, money for uniforms was important, but Tennie "had earned the respect of New York's black community through her own actions, through her association with the Yankee International and her participation" as a member in Victoria's Equal Rights Association, which had nominated Frederick Douglass a few weeks before Tennie's regimental victory. Due to the chaotic events that followed, which left the sisters nearly destitute, Tennie was never able to provide funding for her regiment and was never commissioned.

The sisters' direct assault on masculine ego and tradition hit a nerve; furious indignation lay beneath the snide humor directed at these women who audaciously mocked the power that made men feel superior. The *Times* slammed Tennie as unnatural, no longer a woman, mentioning that she would have to wear the long riding habit of "her 'former' sex or adopt the trowsers [*sic*] and saddle of the masculine sex, since nothing is more preposterous than an equestrian fringed about with a five or six-inch skirt." The New York *Evening Telegram* chortled, "If Miss Tennie would select a mule to ride on, the picture would be more lively and fascinating."

If her feelings were hurt, Tennie could take solace in box-office receipts as she spoke to packed houses. Even before her astounding dash for the colonelcy of the black regiment, an enormous crowd turned out on March 20, 1872, to hear her speak at the Academy of Music, drawn by her notoriety and a prominent ad in the *Weekly* touting her lecture as the "most searching analysis of present conditions." The lecture was titled "The Ethics of the Relations of the Sexes: or, Behind the Scenes in Wall Street." The crush mirrored the mass of people at her sister's "Impending Revolution" speech a month before. The crushing mob outside, pushing and shoving to enter, reached riot proportions. The sisters were accused by some of selling more tickets than the house capacity.

"A mob of ten thousand persons—rich and poor, high-toned and rough, elegantly-dressed ladies of acknowledged respectability, and loudly attired women, whose opposite standing was equally apparent, bankers, brokers, merchants, hack-drivers, gamblers, pickpockets, bootblacks and every other class of society—pressing, pushing, squeezing, crowding to get into the building to hear Tennie C. Claflin."

Police rushed in but could not stop the surging crowd that blocked the streets, halting carriages and nervous horses. Ushers were pushed aside by the crowd that overran the house from the orchestra to the topmost gallery. With the house packed, the doors were barred to avoid suffocation. "Such a spectacle is seldom witnessed in this city," noted a reporter, "and certainly no lecturer, however popular, has ever succeeded in creating such an immense furor." The mob remained in the streets and pounded on side-door entrances for an hour, furious that tickets had been oversold.

When Tennie walked alone on stage, a wave of "rollicking, rolling, noisy outburst of applause" from men lasted for several minutes, while baskets of flowers "poured in upon her from every direction." Tennie, in a simple white dress, eventually got to the advertised subject of her speech, "Behind the Scenes in Wall Street," but first gave a "rather rambling and sophistical argument," extolling her "peculiar views," which condemned marriage "as it now exists."

The *World's* sentiment was in the article's title: TENNIE CLAFLIN'S LECTURE: ANOTHER POLLUTION OF THE ACADEMY OF MUSIC. The *New York Herald* also kissed off her performance, headlining it TENNIE'S TIRADE. She discussed the relations of the sexes with "biblical plainness and boldness of speech unfit for its readers," so the *Herald* paraphrased her lecture: "Women should be free to disown her wedded husband, for cause, and free to turn the tables upon a man when he went after strange women." Then she attacked capitalists, ticking off the lower wages that women made as cooks, tailors, and saleswomen. "There is no single kind of labor that is performed by both women and men for which men do not receive much the higher rate of pay, even at typesetting."

Tennie described the discrimination she experienced in the brokerage business. Once, after entering a firm "upon a purely business matter," the head of the firm said, " 'Tennie, see here, I don't want you to come here so much; it will be remarked on the Street' . . . as though my visits must mean something wrong, against which these immaculate men stood in fear." She relayed that a female servant then entered with a tray of drinks for the bankers.

" 'Does this woman come here every day?' " Tennie demanded.

" 'Yes,' the banker replied.

" 'Why don't you make the same rule for her that you require me to follow? Are you not in danger from her, and from those who daily mop your floor and dust your office?' " Tennie looked out at the thousands listening to her. "You see, the real objection to me was that I was attempting to stand upon an equality with them, to transact business, while these other women were their slaves, to wipe up their vile tobacco puddles."

The *New York Times* was beside itself, with a sexist defense of its practice of paying more for male linotype operators than females: "The latter do not work as well as the former." Women "lack the patience to acquire the careful thoroughness characteristic of good workmen." As reporters, they received the same pay as men, stated the *Times*, a dubious premise to those familiar with newspaper practices. Nor did it mention that women were relegated to social news and "story writing in our magazines."

The *Times* came close to calling Tennie a whore; when a woman "tries to gain business favors in exchange for familiarities too freely offered to be attractive, the ordinary man of business is annoyed and disgusted." It cited Tennie's attacks on marriage and her advocacy of free love. "She must not be surprised if her acquaintance is not regarded as desirable by men"—here the *Times* italicized an attribute not overly noticeable among males on the Street—"*with reputations to lose*."

Men of Wall Street, many of whom had come as friends to hear her the summer before as a congressional candidate, were now bitterly opposed to Tennie and her sister and their pro-labor rhetoric. Life on Wall Street as the sisters once knew it had indeed come to a limping end.

CHAPTER FOURTEEN

Future Presidentess

At the beginning of 1872, despite the free love fracas, family scandal, and divided loyalties in the women's movement, Victoria was still supported by many in the NWSA wing. She drew long and enthusiastic applause at their Manhattan convention in January of that year. Her speaking tour had garnered enough money to pay for the convention program, but this gesture to aid the ever-strapped NWSA came with a string attached: Anthony must treat her with respect. Anthony was not enamored of Woodhull's growing presidential ambitions. Yet she was trapped to some degree by Woodhull's largesse.

At the convention Anthony gave an unscheduled speech, which was an adroit act. It flattered Woodhull but rippled with warning; NWSA would back either the Democrats or Republicans, depending on who supported women's suffrage. She emphatically rebuffed Woodhull's bid: NWSA did not endorse "any sect, breed or political power" including Spiritualism and labor reform. "Now," she asked the crowd, "do you understand our platform?"

Anthony continued to both praise and belittle Victoria: "I have been asked by many: 'why did you drag her to the front?'" Then she said, "She was 'not dragged.'" She came from Wall Street with a "powerful argument" in her memorial to the Judiciary Committee and "lots of cash." A bit of a knife cut received loud applause and laughter: "I bet cash is a big thing with Congress." If "youth, beauty and money" were needed to capture Congress, "Victoria is the woman we are after." Anthony never mentioned intelligence or dedication.

A few months later, Anthony's pique at Victoria turned to rage when she heard gossip from anti-Woodhull suffragists that Woodhull was threatening blackmail and that she would publish the sexual liaisons of well-known suffragists who maligned her while they hypocritically practiced free love. Of course this tidbit was much bruited about among the women. Anthony, who deplored Woodhull's unceasing drive to run for president, believed the rumor and told Ezra Heywood, a friend of Victoria's, that Woodhull had "resorted to blackmailing intentionally."

Woodhull vehemently denied blackmail. She saw no blackmail, just retaliation, and her answer to the rumor contained no subtlety: "I concluded to shut the mouths of a clique of loose and loud-tongued women who were continually stabbing me." She justified her actions, noting that she had sent the women on the list proof sheets of the projected article, giving them a chance to desist in their actions, before she used it. "The filthy fountains suddenly ceased to vomit forth their slime." She did not publish, but warned that, if need be, "I shall not hesitate to do so."

Even her protectors in the movement chided Woodhull when they heard of her proposed article, called "Tit for Tat." The elegant and wealthy Paulina Wright Davis wrote from Europe, where she was convalescing, thinking the piece had already been published: "My dear Victoria, driven to bay at last you have turned, poor hunted child, and dealt a cruel blow... everyone of these women you name has been hounded by men and now it suits them to make cat's-paws to hunt you... dear child, I wish you had let them pass and had taken hold of these men whose souls are black with crimes and who set up to be the censors of morality."

Throughout the winter of 1872, the sisters kept up a bold front—even to the point of funding the NWSA's January programs—sensing the vulnerability of their position if they were perceived as sinking financially. By April, unable to pay the rent on the Thirty-Eighth Street mansion, the sisters and their entourage moved out, but they were missing one member: Canning Woodhull had died on April 6, at the age of forty-eight. Woodhull buried her first husband with a gushing *Weekly* obituary, despite her damaging portrayal of him in the past.

Once again Victoria was in the position of trying to defuse family scandal, this time caused by her drug addict sister Utica, who came to the house upon learning Canning was dying and raised "a great fuss," until sister Meg Miles called the police to get her to leave. Utica wanted to give Canning morphine. "She takes it herself—as much as 30 grams a day," revealed Miles. Utica demanded an autopsy, which found that Canning had died of "congestion of the lungs." Meg Miles said that he had been cared for lovingly until the end: "People will find out sometime that Tennie and Victoria are the two best girls in the world."

The Murray Hill mansion, a shimmering sinkhole of excess, the home of dazzling and expensive dinners and salons, was now but a memory. Much of the furniture must have been rented; at least there were no articles of a public auction, an event that would surely have caused the New York press to scavenge and salivate over the sisters' turn of fate. Gone were the massive gilt-edged mirrors, the yards of purple velvet drapes, the incense discreetly placed, the art and statuary, the Oriental rugs, grand piano, tinkling champagne glasses, and political chatter.

Without the aid of Vanderbilt, the brokerage firm was also crumbling. If it was true that he had helped subsidize the *Weekly* for two years, as the sisters intimated, time had run out on that, too, with no expectation of further assistance. They continued to make money through lectures and, like celebrities, sold their autographed photos through the mail, but it was all slim pickings compared to their glory days. The sisters moved in with sister Meg, who ran a magnetic healing institute on West Twenty-Sixth Street. There Woodhull nurtured her presidential obsession, gathering her coalition of laborers, African Americans, abolitionists, Spiritualists, and suffragists under the umbrella of social change and reform.

The *Weekly*, the campaign's publicity arm, was now run by Blood, as Woodhull and Tennie kept up a frenetic pace speaking to interested groups and urging labor unions to come on board. If Woodhull's quest ever came to votes, male union backing would be a necessity. Women suffragists could attempt only symbolic voting, and the eclectic Spiritualists often bowed to a higher order than the voting booth.

Woodhull had dreamed of becoming president, even practicing her unruly scrawl until she could compose the fanciful signature "Future Presidentess," a weird combination of president and princess. Now, as the May NWSA convention drew near, Woodhull had a grand scheme to turn the gathering into a nominating convention for herself. Moreover, she had Stanton's backing. A furious Anthony saw that Stanton had added her own name to a list of Woodhull supporters without her knowledge. Anthony stormed at Stanton for backing Victoria and vowed to stop her.

Stanton fought back and both she and Isabella Hooker accused Anthony of being "narrow, bigoted and headstrong." Stanton quit as president but defied Anthony in her keynote speech by urging NWSA members to join Woodhull's People's Party. Anthony, now president, "positively refused to allow" Woodhull's use of Steinway Hall, which had been rented in Anthony's name. Woodhull then engaged Apollo Hall for her new party convention. Anthony thought the crisis was averted, but "just as she was about to adjourn the first evening session, to her amazement, Woodhull came gliding in from the side of the platform and moved that 'this convention adjourn to meet tomorrow morning at Apollo Hall!'" An ally of Woodhull's quickly seconded the motion, while Anthony "refused to put it," but Woodhull herself shouted for the motion and her stacked hall of followers carried it overwhelmingly. Anthony shouted that the "whole proceeding was out of order" as the majority of voters were not members of NWSA, but Woodhull raced to the front of the platform and began a full-throttled speech. Furious at Woodhull's attempt to highjack her meeting, Anthony bellowed in vain over the "Woodhull for President" party claque, then tore out of the hall, found a janitor, and ordered him to turn out all the gaslights in the hall. First the gas footlights, then all the lights went dark. Woodhull was forced into silence as the women clutched one another, searching for the aisles and groping their way toward light.

Woodhull had made an implacable enemy of Anthony. "The next day, almost without assistance and deserted by those who should have stood by her," Anthony went through the motions of conducting three sessions and then closed the convention. That night Anthony moaned in her diary, "all came near being lost. Our ship was so nearly stranded, we rescued it only by a hair's breadth..." The fight created the worst split in her twenty-four-year-old partnership with Stanton. Anthony was "never so hurt" by anything as "this folly" of Stanton's "demoralizing" embrace of Woodhull.

Without NWSA backing, Woodhull swiftly turned the People's Party into the Equal Rights Party—taking the name from the party formed in 1866 by the coalition of abolitionists and suffragists. She hoped to build a populist base at a time of widespread revulsion over the Boss Tweed and President Grant scandals, such as the gold-cornering scandal and Tweed's extensive fraud and bribery empire. As delegates assembled in Apollo Hall on the morning of May 10, they were tagged the most "heterogeneous gathering that assembled in any city in any age." One male speaker voiced his sentiment amid cheers: The Republican and Democratic parties had destroyed themselves by corruption. The present administration was rotten and "its financial system a failure. The country could not stand another Black Friday." Now was a "golden opportunity for a reform movement." The Equal Rights Party proved that it could be as long-winded as any political party, with twenty more speeches lasting until 4:00 p.m. Banners draped throughout the hall reflected the party's support for radical working-class issues: GOVERNMENT PROTECTION FROM THE CRADLE TO THE GRAVE; PUBLIC EMPLOYMENT A REMEDY FOR STRIKES. Blue silken banners on either side of the platform included one with gold writing: JESUS SAID: GIVE TO THE POOR.

Some mainstream newspapers surprisingly gave the convention fair and prominent page-one coverage, but others vied for the most caustic reporting. The Democrats' New York *World* was the most antagonistic, degrading the participants by writing, "So far as dress and appearance went, [they] could be classed with either sex. There were all varieties of color and complexion." The women's faces had "hard, angular masculine expressions," while the men, "most of whom were very old," bordered on the "feminine," with the men "growing their hair as long as possible, while the women cropped theirs almost to the usual masculine shortness." Even the *Herald* headlined its convention piece, VIC SAYS: "I WILL STUMP THE STATES WITH TENNIE," cuttingly called the six hundred delegates "strange looking people" who were ready to support African Americans and Native Americans and liberal issues far different from the white, male-controlled Republican and Democratic conventions. However, the Associated Press praised the party's platform, which stated that "monopolies should be abolished...wars should be abolished by international arbitration." It called for representation of minorities, free trade with all nations, and an end to capital punishment.

When Victoria showed up with Tennie on her arm, both dressed in black silk, the smiling sisters were swarmed by hugging and kissing delegates, but Tennie "objects to kissing, and would not have it." The night session was packed with delegates and the curious who had come to gawk. Woodhull, looking "extremely pretty," prophesied, "From this convention will go forth a tide of revolution that shall sweep over the whole world."

Woodhull waited until the roar of applause died down, then gave an hour-long firebrand speech, denouncing politicians and the U.S. Constitution. "Some may call this a revolution. Well, and if it does mean revolution what then? Shall we be slaves to escape revolution?" Her voice rising, she shouted, "I say, never! I say, away with such weak stupidity...let us have justice, though the heavens fall!" To tremendous applause and cheering, she called for a united movement to purge the country of "political trickery, despotic assumption and all industrial injustice." A new constitution was needed to replace an inadequate, "blood-stained document." In the din, a delegate jumped up and swiftly nominated Woodhull for president; this was followed by a five-minute standing ovation. The uproar was so great that crowds rushed in from the street. Rumors that Woodhull had fainted were quelled when she reappeared onstage. Her bosom heaving and her voice trembling, she said, "I thank you from the bottom of my soul for the honor you have conferred upon me tonight."

The vice-presidential choice was not so unanimous. IWA dele-
gate Moses Hull nominated Frederick Douglass. Thundering shouts of
"No!" were followed by shouts of "Yes!" A delegate nominated a Native
American named Spotted Tail, saying, "The Indians were here before the
Negroes." Some accounts said he used the word *nigger*. Another said if
Douglass didn't accept, they should nominate a "heathen Chinese."

When Douglass was chosen, newspapers outdid themselves in deroga-
tory headlines: THE HIGHLY COLORED HUMAN TICKET. The "venerable and
colored" man coupled with the "young and painted creature in petticoats."
The *Philadelphia Inquirer* simply tagged the delegates "semi-lunatics." Nothing could compare to a western paper, the *Guard*, which named Woodhull
and Douglass A SHAMELESS PROSTITUTE AND A NEGRO. The racist New York
Pomeroy's Democrat drew Woodhull and Douglass as a pair of ugly minstrels,
looking like distorted dolls with tiny legs, riding on two costume ponies,
Douglass's pitch-black face next to Woodhull's grim white one.

However joyous the crowd, there was a general rush for the door when
the house was asked to contribute to Woodhull's campaign. In the land of
the left-out radicals, there was little money to offer.

Male reporters and politicians viewed Victoria's campaign as self-
aggrandizing lunacy. Yet Woodhull earned a footnote in history as the
first woman to be nominated for president, although her candidacy was
stillborn. Her name was not on the ballot, but a few states wrote it in. If by
some fluke she had won, she would have been ineligible because she would
not have reached the constitutionally mandated age of thirty-five. In her
quixotic and symbolic quest, Woodhull had hoped to gain attention and
support for her equality-based coalition in a time of dissatisfaction with
the two major political party candidates.

No group was more discouraged than NWSA suffragists, who had
hoped to throw clout behind the best major candidate but had found little to praise in either. The race was indeed a mess. Republican president
Grant was faced with a rebellion, albeit ineffective, when a group calling
themselves Liberal Republicans defected and backed Horace Greeley on

the Democratic Party ticket. The *Tribune's* Greeley was pummeled by the press for his "shameless and corrupt bargain" to head this hybrid ticket. The women's movement had no horse in the race.

Anthony must have been furious when the NWSA convention, held the same day as Woodhull's, took second billing in all the newspapers. But Woodhull and the NWSA were at least in alignment regarding Greeley; the sisters had loathed him for not supporting suffrage and for his repeated attacks on them. Woodhull called him "this pettifogging pretender to honest journalism." At the NWSA convention, Isabella Beecher Hooker scathingly attacked him, stating, "He has no backbone. When he gets into a pinch he always backs out... He has stamped upon us."

The Republican convention in Philadelphia did not endorse suffrage, but the platform added a weak plank recognizing that "the honest demands of any class of citizens for equal rights should be treated with respectful consideration." As tame as this was, the reference was the first to women in any major party platform. Wit intact, Stanton referred to the Republicans' women's plank as the "Philadelphia Splinter" whittled to a "toothpick."

ACT FOUR

CHAPTER FIFTEEN

Down and Out in Manhattan

Victoria's glorious moment in June of 1872 as the first woman nominated for president of the United States was simply that, a moment. The house of cards propping up the sisters and hiding their financial vulnerability was collapsing. To conserve money, the *Weekly* moved into cheaper brokerage quarters at 48 Broad Street. Their firm was failing. Their high-risk gamble of speculating in gold on margin, which Tennie had touted, was disastrous in a volatile gold market. The firm had been "guessing wrong more often than right," and clients closed out their accounts.

Woodhull's Equal Rights Party had no money to fuel a campaign. She tried selling bonds, but few of her "oppressed" followers could afford to buy them. In a long-winded *Weekly* article, she thanked the party for nominating a duo representing America's "two oppressed and repressed classes" but did not tell her readers that Douglass had never responded to the party's nomination. Douglass seemed to have no interest in joining this radical group, but at the time the nominations were ratified, on June 15, Douglass was also preoccupied by a "very grievous loss." On June 2, his Rochester home was burned to the ground (arson was suspected but not proved). His family was safe, but twelve volumes of his writing were "devoured in flames." Crucial years of antislavery history, from 1848 to 1860, were destroyed. "The loss is immeasurable," wrote Douglass. In the fall, he was stumping for Grant, not Woodhull.

As if to solidify the oppressed and repressed nature of the party, the Grand Opera House in New York barred them from holding their June ratification meeting following the nominating convention. After accepting payment for its rental, the Opera House decided that the party's class of people "would damage the house irreparably." Damaging its reputation was an absurdity; the house was the massive marble edifice built by Jim Fisk and still owned by his former partner, Jay Gould, of the rapacious Erie Ring. Woodhull charged that barring her was the work of "Greeleyites," and vowed a "day of reckoning." The party members followed the sisters to the Cooper Institute and boisterously ratified the nomination.

Back in the winter, the *Weekly* had wittily protested violation of the separation of church and state by religious groups that wanted to put God in the Constitution. "We have no evidence that God has any desire to get into the Constitution, nor yet that it should be agreeable to either of the remaining members of the trinity...badly as the constitution needs improvement, we don't think this movement is of that character." Now, in the summer, the sisters had a candidate to ridicule on the God front. Greeley's vice-presidential running mate, B. Gratz Brown, called for overthrowing "civil and religious liberty" by "incorporating the name of God in the United States constitution." Like many politicians, Woodhull mentioned God in speeches, but was appalled by this, especially at the proposed wording that exalted "a Christian nation." The *Weekly* attacked: "The free-thinking German, the Jew, the materialist, the Atheist have equal rights with Christians under our present constitution, but Brown would rob them of civil and religious liberty."

Woodhull was also furious at Tilton for having left her side to support Greeley. Tilton was a turncoat who had deserted the women's movement and was now "urging as a candidate the very man whom he had recently so severely castigated with his most caustic pen." Greeley "denounces the greatest of all reforms—the enfranchisement of women."

By June, the *Weekly* had increasingly taken on a beleaguered tone. The paper counterattacked when Lucy Stone argued that Woodhull had lost the battle for suffragist supremacy. "We hope the suffragists have got rid of the Free Love incubus which has done incalculable harm to the cause of woman Suffrage," said Stone, adding, "Women, like men, are 'known by the company they keep.'" The *Weekly* mused, "How can Lucy Stone ever again claim to be an honest, truthful woman" after her "barefaced attempt to misrepresent" the Equal Rights convention and Woodhull?

During the 1872 general election, Anthony practically begged Stone to join ranks with her at a public meeting so the world could see a united women's suffrage movement. When Stone did not, that was the last straw for Anthony. She and Stanton had nothing to do with Stone's AWSA until the two groups united in 1890.

For the sisters, wrangling with Stone was a mere flea bite compared to what they faced in their personal and professional lives. They were now desperate for money, jilted by capitalists and Communists alike. Their anticapitalist winter speeches signified the public demise of their Vanderbilt connection, which had ended privately well before, after Tennie broadcast during the Claflin family feud trial that she had "humbugged" Vanderbilt for money. The sisters' continued feeble attempts to cite his influence in the *Weekly* were just window dressing. Without Vanderbilt, Wall Street support had long vanished.

Still popular with laborers, who cheered their speeches, the sisters lost favor with Marx, who saw their egalitarian inclusion of women, blacks, and democratic freedoms destructively at odds with his ideology. It did not matter that the *Weekly* had reprinted a thousand copies of Marx's treatise on the Paris Commune, an interview with Marx, and *The Communist Manifesto*. Nor did he consider their devoted support of wage reform, the eight-hour workday, and strikes. Free love, women's suffrage, and a call for a universal language—Stephen Pearl Andrews's mystifying contribution—were all just too much for him. The end of the sisters' Section 12 of the International Workingmen's Association came at the IWA's international convention in the Hague, in June 1872, when Marx refused to recognize their delegate. Pausing to adjust his monocle, Marx leveled assaults at Woodhull as the "president of the spiritists" [*sic*], and as a "general humbug" who "preaches free love, has a banking business." The sin of "bourgeoisie" thinking hung over Section 12, he said, adding that it "agitated especially for the women's franchise" and talked of "personal liberty, social liberty [free love]." He demanded the section's immediate expulsion, calling its members "riffraff."

While some Marxist historians blame the sisters and their eclectic makeup for causing the American IWA's downfall, others fault Marx. He did not see the "great potential of the Yankees to adapt the International to their own situation and spread it among experienced American radicals," wrote historian Timothy Messer-Kruse. Killing the sisters' section spelled defeat for Marxist orthodoxy in America. "The tremendous gains" in recruitment made by the sisters came to a halt. "Yankee radicals simply had no reason to join an organization that was torn by faction and treachery" or follow a leader who did not hold their democratic values dear. The sisters finished Marx off in the *Weekly*, calling him a fallen despot.

Despite their inglorious end in the IWA, the sisters remain honored by liberal historians; they and Section 12 were considered to have "made greater strides toward bridging America's racial divide than had any radical movement since abolitionism." But for this, they paid a large price.

Publicity about Woodhull heading a "Red Party" with a "Negro" as a running mate, and Tennie's honorary leadership of a black regiment, plagued them everywhere they tried to find housing. Temporary lodging in sister Meg Miles's home was insufficient for Victoria, Tennie, Colonel Blood, Byron, and Zula Maud. The Hoffman House, where they had begun their glorious climb just two and a half years before, had now banned them. Under assumed names, they found rooms in Gilsey House, at the corner of Broadway and East Twenty-Ninth, but were soon recognized and asked to leave when four black lieutenants called to take Tennie for an inspection of the regiment. The manager told Tennie, "If you go off with those niggers you need never come back here." Tennie turned around and jumped into the carriage. Later that afternoon, Victoria, Blood, and Tennie found Zula Maud and Byron standing on the sidewalk surrounded by luggage.

Victoria took aim at the hypocrisy: "We might have lived there as the mistress of any man; but we ought not to talk out loud in the halls and parlors about social reform. They told me that they admired us for the course we had taken, but to have it known that Woodhull and Claflin were living in the hotel would frighten away all their family boarders."

Tennie was even stronger on the issue. "Hotels have virtually adopted the motto—'best of accommodation for the worst of men, the best women not admitted.' If however they are accompanied by any of the aforesaid men, no questions asked." She and her family were evicted "because, forsooth, we hold social theories and have the courage to advocate them that do not quite suit the hypocritical pretenders to a virtue they do not possess, and because we publish a paper to advocate advanced ideas of reform."

After the Gilsey eviction, the clan trooped to the brokerage firm, hoisted Zula over the transom, waited while she unlocked the door, and slept on the office floor. Even this shelter would be temporary. The landlord had upped the rent by $1,000 a year. Anguished, the sisters were forced to suspend the *Weekly*, and the campaign was abandoned.

Just before their eviction from the Gilsey House, a desperate Woodhull wrote to Henry Ward Beecher: "Dear Sir, the social fight against me being now waged in this city is becoming rather hotter than I can well endure longer, standing unsupported and alone as I have until now. Within the past two weeks I have been shut out of hotel after hotel and am now, after having obtained a place in one, hunted down by a set of males and females who are determined that I shall not be permitted to live even, if they can prevent it.

"Now I want your assistance. I want to be sustained in my position in the Gilsey House, from which I am ordered out and from which I do not wish to go—and all this simply because I am Victoria C. Woodhull, the advocate of social freedom. I have submitted to this persecution just so long as I can endure. My business, my projects, in fact everything for which I live, suffer from it and it must cease. Will you lend me your aid in this?"

Beecher was not in a magnanimous or, for that matter, a very frightened mood. He remained a colossal success, and it had been over a year since Woodhull first threatened to tell all. Perhaps it was just talk, he may have thought. Still, he appealed to Frank Moulton to make Victoria understand that he would not "take a single step in that direction, and if it brings trouble—it must come."

Dismissing Woodhull was not the most prudent act. She was "a proud, wounded, unlettered creature with some vigor of mind, the more vigorous for her ostracism," observed Moulton. Throughout the cover-up, Moulton and his wife, Emma, sympathized with Woodhull, yet eventually felt they could not suppress or control her; she would give way to the "adverse influence" of the "persecution she was to suffer." The proud Woodhull felt deeply humiliated. Tilton had been mocked unceasingly for his fulsome Woodhull biography, but now he was redeeming his reputation on the lecture circuit while supporting Greeley. Beecher, who had disdained to answer Victoria's plea, was riding high, named to a teaching post at Yale and celebrated by his adoring flock at Brooklyn's Plymouth Church.

Forced to temporarily suspend the *Weekly*, the sisters editorialized bitterly in a later edition when they resumed publishing in the fall of 1872. Woodhull complained that the press, "divided between the other two great parties, refused all notice of the new reformatory movement." This was routine for mainstream journalism: covering campaigns as horse races and dismissing third-party also-rans, no matter their message. Yet it stung Woodhull deeply. Her nomination "seemed to fall dead upon the country; and to cap the climax, a new batch of slanders and injurious innuendoes permeated the community in respect to my condition and character. A series of pecuniary disasters stripped us, for the time being, of the means of continuing" the paper and "forced us into a desperate struggle for mere existence." Now there was no way to broadcast her broadsides at enemies, her opinions and goals—even to "my own circle of friends."

All this travail was leading to an eruption of anger, revenge, outrage—and a desire to justify her actions. The American Association of Spiritualists met in Boston in September for its annual meeting. Woodhull was not popular with the conservative faction, and she felt there would be trouble.

Tired but "dragged by a sense of duty," she was prepared to resign her presidency. She was greeted not by "hostility or unfriendliness" but by a feeling of "painful uncertainty and doubt." As she faced her audience, "I was seized by one of those overwhelming gusts of inspiration which sometimes come upon me, from I know not where...some power stronger than I"; this power made her "pour out into the ears of that assembly, and, as I was told subsequently, in a rhapsody of indignant eloquence, with circumstantial detail, the whole history of the Beecher and Tilton scandal." This was the first time Woodhull had uttered the details in public. She added coyly, "They tell me that I used some naughty words. All that I know is, that if I swore, I did not swear profanely." That they reelected her president was proof she had not "shocked or horrified" her audience, she defensively remarked.

Woodhull was in command of her oratorical genius that night, according to one Spiritualist, Mrs. E. A. Meriwether: "A sort of electric shock swept over the assembly; striking it to a dead stillness...Mrs. Woodhull tossed back her hair, in high tragic style, and poured out a torrent of flame. It made our flesh to creep and our blood to run cold...two crimson dots burned on her pale cheeks and a lurid light filled her eyes...she has all the action and fervor of a tragic actress...Her face, the saddest I ever saw, tells of wrecked hopes and a cruel battle with life." To Meriwether, Victoria's speech was not obscene, but "fiercely denunciatory, fiery and scandalous."

Only the Spiritualist group heard this first public revelation of the scandal. The Boston press said her words were too obscene to print. Woodhull attacked them for suppressing what she'd said and for insulting her as a "slanderer." She threatened that she would now have to unveil the complete facts for all to read. Thus the long-private Beecher-Tilton scandal was born in a special edition of the *Weekly*. This time it would be a story heard around the world.

CHAPTER SIXTEEN

Unmasking Beecher and a Masked Ball Rape

The *Weekly*'s staid format buried what most papers would have blazed on page one, if they'd dared print it at all. The Beecher "thunderbolt" began on page 9, and then only with a singular headline, THE BEECHER-TILTON CASE, this in an era when papers routinely stacked run-on headlines that consumed a good quarter of an article. Small type followed: "The Detailed Statement of the Whole Matter by Mrs. Woodhull."

The article promised to expose "one of the most stupendous scandals which has ever occurred in any community." She roundly slammed the esteemed Beecher as "a poltroon, a coward and a sneak." The tale had been whispered "for the last two or three years," and now, wrote Woodhull, "I intend that this article shall burst like a bomb-shell into the ranks of the moralistic social camp."

But first she announced her central theme: that marriage "as a bond or promise to love another to the end of life, and forego all other loves or passional gratifications, has outlived its day of usefulness." Woodhull then jumped into her role as the aggrieved bearer of free love truth and claimed to be astounded that she was "denounced by the very persons" who privately followed her doctrines: "astonishing disclosures" about these lives were "laid open before me" and "included spiritualistic and social reformers...leading lights of the business and wealthy circles, and of the various professions, not excluding the clergy...It was nevertheless from these very quarters, that I was most severely assailed."

Ignoring the threats she had used for months, Woodhull claimed to have "wholly abstained" from responding to such abuse. She was now acting on a reluctant but deep sense of duty, she assured readers. Those who snatched up the *Weekly* at every newsstand had to wade through an exhausting twelve-thousand-word treatise on love and adultery, written by Stephen Pearl Andrews, proving that even sex in the abstract can be boring.

For the first time, the public was reading the account of the stormy night when Elizabeth Tilton raced to her bedroom after allegedly confessing an adulterous relationship with Reverend Beecher, followed by her husband's hair-tearing jealous rage, his pounding on her locked bedroom door with Susan B. Anthony standing guard.

Woodhull now wrote that Tilton was struck by "the terrible orgies— so he said—of which his house had been made the scene, and the boldness with which matters had been carried on in the presence of his children—'these things drove me mad,' said he, 'and I went to Elizabeth and confronted her with...the damning tale she had told me. My wife did not deny the charge nor attempt any palliation. She was then *enciente*, and I felt sure that the child would not be my child. I stripped the wedding ring from her finger. I tore the picture of Mr. Beecher from my wall and stamped it in pieces. Indeed, I do not know what I did not do. I only look back to it as a time too horrible to retain any exact remembrance of. She miscarried the child and it was buried. For two weeks, night and day, I might have been found walking to and from that grave, in a state bordering on distraction...I stamped the ring with which we had plighted our troth deep into the soil that covered the fruit of my wife's infidelity.'"

What shocked many of America's "good citizens" was not so much that Woodhull had charged the famous preacher with committing adultery as that she was using free love reasoning for exposing him: it was not the adultery, it was the hypocrisy! It was only normal that the

Reverend—with his "demanding physical nature" and "immense physical potency," coupled with enduring a harpy wife—should seek love elsewhere, wrote Woodhull. His "physical amativeness" is what "emanates zest and magnetic power to his whole audience." There was no reason to condemn him and Lib Tilton for their passion; Woodhull's reasoning was "indeed the exact opposite" of that for which "the world would condemn him." Theirs was adultery; hers was hypocrisy.

Beecher had "helped to maintain for these many years that very social slavery under which he was chafing, and against which he was secretly revolting, both in thought and practice...he has, in a word, consented, and still consents to being a hypocrite...failing, in a word, to stand shoulder to shoulder with me and others who are endeavoring to hasten a social regeneration which he believes in."

The unanswered question is whether Woodhull would have publicly exposed Beecher had he introduced her at Steinway Hall, given her money when she was destitute, or prevailed upon his sisters to stop vilifying her. Would her sense of a crusade have been so keen? Despite her noble reasons, Woodhull's revenge for being dismissed by Beecher did play a part. She later admitted that she was operating with the vengeance of the old bromide "Hell hath no fury like a woman scorned."

In this fashion, she also took on Theodore Tilton, saying his display of jealousy and wounded manhood were caused by "bogus sentimentality" driven by the inculcation of "sickly religious literature and Sunday School morality, and pulpit phariseeism" [sic] which had "humbugged him" into thinking he "ought to feel and act in this harlequin and absurd way."

In the same issue, sister Tennie weighed in with an even more salacious article of seduction at a French masked ball by a Wall Street banker named Luther Challis. But first she scathingly assailed the double standard of courts and the public. "Put a woman on trial for anything—it is considered as a legitimate part of the defense to make the most searching inquiry into her sexual morality, and the decision generally turns upon the proof advanced in this regard." Defending her duty to expose male sexual conduct, Tennie wrote, "even the President of the United States, a governor of a state and a pastor of the most popular church, president of the most reliable bank, or of the grandest railroad corporation, may constantly practice all the debaucheries known to sensualism [*sic*]—many of which are so vicious, brutal and degrading as to be almost beyond belief—and he, by virtue of his sex, stands protected and respected, so much so that even the other sex cry shame on the exposer [*sic*] . . . and the newspapers pretend not to know that anything detrimental to public morality has transpired."

Again Tennie defended prostitutes: "But let a woman even so much as protect herself from starvation by her sexuality . . . and everybody in unison cries out, 'down with the vile thing'" while newspapers make it their "special business to herald her shame . . . utterly forgetting that there was a man in the scrape."

There was only one solution to this man-made hypocrisy: "The tables that have so long been completely subsidized in favor of immunity for men must be turned upon them." It was no "light matter to be pioneers in any reform," but someone had to vindicate women's rights and redress "their wrongs." Her next sentence filled many a Manhattan male reader with dread: "We propose to take leading personages from each of the several pursuits of life and lay before the world a record of their private careers, so that it may no longer appear that their victims are the only frightful examples of immorality." First out of the box was "Mr. L. C. Challis," a rich broker. A lawyer in his celebrated fight against Tennie would nickname him This Poison Challis.

The annual masked French Ball, organized by the Société des Bals d'Artistes, was held at the distinguished Academy of Music. Newspapers described it in a jocular "men will be men" fashion as a bacchanal filled with "three thousand of the best men and four thousand of the worst women." In the *Weekly*, Tennie said their account came from an anonymous participant: "We have her name and can command her affidavit at any moment." Once again, Tennie resorted to the ruse of claiming her information came from another person. In actuality the sisters were the witnesses at the ball. Unknown to Colonel Blood, the two had dressed as shepherdesses, wearing white masks, and repaired to a red damask-draped box, remaining "closely dominoed," as they observed the action.

This was in December 1869, just before they had become famous stockbrokers. By exposing the incident three years later, the sisters revealed yet another unsavory past, admitting that they had attended this orgy, shared a personal association with prostitutes, and, as Tennie put it, their "whoremongers that may marry a pure woman, move in good society and be generally respected." For three years this had bothered her conscience, she wrote. It was time to let the world know of the "wrongs these women suffer and the men who inflict them."

Men smoking cigars and guzzling champagne in boxes watched a mob of scantily clad dancers below. As midnight approached, the scene grew wilder. "One of the women is caught up by the crowd and tossed bodily into a proscenium box, where she is dragged over the sill." Her dress flew up, and the men roared with laughter as they looked at "what small vestige of raiment" showed. Another pretty young woman is "thrown up, tossed over, her skirt flying up, and then thrown again." A hefty woman was not so lucky; thrown from a box, she fell "heavily on the floor" and was picked up and carried out by the police. "There is not a whisper of shame in the crowd, it is now drunken with liquor and its own beastliness."

Tennie saw Challis and another man with two young girls "not more than fifteen or sixteen years of age," schoolgirls from Baltimore who had "fallen in with these middle-age roués, and had in their innocence been led by them in the ways that lead to ruin." Tennie knew Challis, and they all gathered in one box. The girls "were plied" with drink. "I remonstrated and begged them not to drink anymore. My effort...was met with an insulting request from the men to let them alone...they were seduced by them...They were taken (along with two other young girls) to the house of a woman we will call Molly [Molly de Ford, who was a client of the sisters' brokerage firm], a first-class house of prostitution."

There the young girls "were robbed of their innocence by each of these scoundrels." The next sentence in the *Weekly* would astound, disgust, and become the center of a court battle: "And this scoundrel Challis, to prove that he had seduced a maiden, carried for days on his finger, exhibiting in triumph, the red trophy of her virginity. After a few days these Lotharios exchanged beds and companions, and when weary of this they brought their friends, to the number of one hundred and over, to debauch these young girls, mere children."

The *Weekly* vowed "every word here written can be proven." As for a skewed standard, the sisters did not indict the madam for the heartless, criminal if true, gang rape of underage girls by more than a hundred men. Rather than utter a horrified word about Madame de Ford, Tennie continued: "The children he [Challis] has seduced and debauched have now no way open before them than the prostitute's road to hell." She reasoned that the young women would have had no chance in court; "had a woman brought this case to court, he would have been believed and she would have been considered a perjurer no matter the truth. And this is the justice that is meted out to women, this case being the rule and not the exception." Tennie added a personal indignity. While the trustees of the Academy were aware of such "scenes of lechery, the manager now refuses to lease it for the performance of 'The Merchant of Venice' because Miss Claflin, in connection with it, is to make her debut as Portia."

The sisters were clairvoyant enough to foresee the commercial appeal of their story, initially printing 31,000 copies of the issue, dated November 2, 1872, which hit the newsstands on October 28. "I crowded my way through the army of newsboys and news dealers which actually blocked up Broad Street for hundreds of feet . . . Hundreds of dollars per hour were flowing into their coffers," recounted a *Chicago Times* reporter. "The sisters were "jubilant—the terrible expose had gone off like buttered hot cakes." The first run of 100,000 sold out, the sisters said, adding that copies sold for as much as forty dollars.

The sisters scarcely had time to savor their success. They were quickly carted off to jail and faced court battles over two charges—one for obscenity, the other for libel—that would drain them financially, physically, and spiritually for nearly two years.

As soon as the shocking *Weekly* issue appeared, members of the Plymouth Church leapt into action. Either they contacted a young former dry goods salesman, Anthony Comstock, or he contacted them. Either way, it was a happy marriage as Comstock, who had made a small name for himself as a police informant exposing booksellers dealing in erotic literature, was aching to be the czar of vice. He instructed two clerks associated with Plymouth Church to buy copies of the *Weekly*, specifying they be sent through the mail. When the issues arrived, the United States district attorney for the Southern District of New York, Noah Davis, another powerful Beecher friend and Plymouth Church parishioner, quickly issued an arrest warrant for the sisters. Although federal law made it illegal to send obscene material through the mail, it was up to the courts to decide what was obscene, thus the sisters had to wait for a trial.

News of the sisters' arrest tore through Wall Street, and bankers, brokers, and clerks all rushed from their busy Wall Street offices to see the police escort Victoria and Tennie into their carriage. In his haste, one officer stumbled into the carriage, plunking down on Tennie's lap. Some three thousand copies of the damning issue of the *Weekly* were reportedly found in the carriage and destroyed.

Comstock, as a one-man vice squad, preened over his sensational coup, wanting all the publicity to the extent that he said the Plymouth Church was not involved. He would continue to hound the sisters for years, becoming their Inspector Javert and arresting them three times as he sought their conviction. Comstock, a dry goods salesman, aligned himself with the Young Men's Christian Association (YMCA) and named himself the head of his creation, the New York Society for the Suppression of Vice. Comstock was so eager in his pursuit of obscene material sent through the mail that he became an unpaid U.S. postal clerk prior to any knowledge of the sisters. His shiny Vice medal depicts a man, presumably a seller of obscene literature, being arrested on one side; on the other, a man stands over a pile of burning books that are releasing an incendiary swirl of smoke.

CHAPTER SEVENTEEN

Jailbirds and the Naked Truth

By the time the sisters' carriage reached the commissioner's office for arraignment, dense crowds in a "fearful rush for seats" dashed into the courtroom, while the unlucky piled up in the corridor. The sisters wore matching plain dark suits of alpaca, with silk purple ties and jaunty hats. "Tennie was flushed like a rose" and smiling. Woodhull's facial expressions were never so predictable as Tennie's, and could change dramatically depending on her moods. In the throes of a lecture, Victoria radiated an intelligent, rather haughty beauty. Her slightly heavy-lidded eyes could convey a sultry expression or one of noticeable sadness. In repose, not smiling, she could look commonplace, as she did this day in court.

Victoria and Tennie were nearly eclipsed by their famously flamboyant counselor, William F. Howe, who wore plaid pantaloons, a purple vest, a blue satin scarf held in place with an immense glittering diamond pin—just one of his collection of diamond rings, cuff links, vest buttons, and stickpins. Legend followed him everywhere. He once shot at a burglar who had dared enter his home, later quipping that "I don't object to burglars as clients—they are pretty good clients—but I seriously object to them operating at my house." Courtrooms were stages, violent death his specialty. He was so versed in courtroom crying that adversaries suspected a newly chopped onion was buried in his handkerchief.

The sisters' case was a natural for Howe, filled with the theatrics he craved. Here were "two women, who, from their education and intelligence, ought to be models of virtue and purity, charged with sending filthy, vulgar, indecent and obscene publications through the mails."

When the sisters' carriage pulled up to the Ludlow Street Jail after their arraignment, a mob watched as the prisoners tripped lightly out of their carriage and were met by the jailor. "No womanly exhibition of tears was visible" as they passed through the heavy doors. The sisters' cell was in the ironically named Fifth Avenue block. They were given royal treatment on their first night: dinner of broiled chicken in the warden's dining room. Visitors poured in, including their father and quarrelsome sister Polly. Zula Maud, now an attractive girl of twelve, sat with her mother on her cot. The sisters affably met other inmates, including a notorious forger. In honor of their presence, fellow inmates refrained from smoking.

The charge of sending obscene matter through the mails was weak in this case—except in the eyes of Comstock, who saw sin in nearly everything written, including great literary works and anatomy drawings in medical books. Only one year older than twenty-seven-year-old Tennie, he seemed like a man who had never been young. His diary is consumed with torturous guilt. While a young soldier in the Civil War, Comstock faced ridicule as he tried to save his drinking, smoking, and swearing companions from perdition. He continually chastised himself in his journal: "Again tempted and found wanting. Sin, sin. Oh how much peace and happiness is sacrificed on thy altar....Seemed as though Devil had full sway over me today, went right into temptation...how sinful am I. I am the chief of sinners...Sin, that foe that is ever lurking...Today Satan has sorely tried me; yet by God's grace did not yield...This morning—severely tempted by Satan and after some time in my own weakness I failed."

These entries and confessions about the "fierce trials" to which the devil made him submit, even while still a farm boy, easily leads one to think that he was speaking of masturbation—or "self-abuse," as it was termed among Victorians. However, Comstock was reticent in describing what temptations the devil threw at him. Confessions, even in the privacy of his diary, seem astoundingly innocent: "Spent part of day foolishly as I look back; read a Novel part through."

Comstock, like the sisters, felt he could further his causes through publicity, and Comstock, like them, felt the ends justified the means. Just as the sisters felt that threatening to expose as hypocrites those who secretly practiced free love was not blackmail, Comstock had no scruples about the entrapment he performed to ensnare his victims. No ruse was wrong in capturing culprits who sold, by his definition, filth. "Obscene literature...breeds lust. Lust defiles the body, debauches the imagination, corrupts the mind, deadens the will, destroys the memory, sears the conscience, hardens the heart, and damns the soul. It unnerves the arm, and steals away the elastic step."

Woodhull dismissed Comstock as an "illiterate puppy," but his fanatical quest did great damage to free speech and education in America well into the twentieth century. An unknown stalker of sin when he attacked the sisters, Comstock used his notoriety following their sensational publicity to persuade Congress to pass a tougher obscenity act, known as the Comstock Law, which disregarded the First Amendment and censored all manner of literature. Adored by religious extremists, the vindictive Comstock was responsible for at least two suicides, one of them of abortionist Madame Restell. Later becoming an object of ridicule, one cartoon showed the rotund, balding Comstock pointing to a startled woman standing with him before a judge. "Your honor," said the Comstock figure, "this woman gave birth to a naked baby!"

But at the time he tangled with the sisters, the press and public saw a noble young crusader against evil. The New York press overwhelmingly treated the sisters as if Comstock's charges were true, calling them harpies and omitting the vital word *alleged* in coverage of their case.

L. C. Challis, stung by Tennie's masked ball depiction, quickly introduced a parallel indictment, charging the sisters with libel. Henry Ward Beecher, however, remained so silent that even fans wondered why he did not publicly deny or sue. Some felt he was showing how trivial the sisters were, but others questioned how an innocent man could refrain from defending himself.

As the sisters sat in their cell, Ulysses Grant was celebrating his massive reelection, having swamped Greeley. Victoria wrote an appeasing letter to Susan B. Anthony; the latter did not reply. Stanton, who was one of the few suffragists to have backed Victoria, now lied, trying to save Elizabeth Tilton's honor, denounced Woodhull, and disavowed passing on the adultery tale: "Mrs. Woodhull's statements are untrue in every particular." Woodhull was stunned by her friend's betrayal at such a crucial time. Too late to help, Stanton later verified the details she had told Woodhull.

Meanwhile, the sisters' nemesis, Greeley, was very ill, a defeated and humiliated candidate. A group had conspired to wrest control of the *Tribune* from him, and Whitelaw Reid had him committed to an asylum, where he sank into a coma and died. The sisters were in jail when Grant and other dignitaries listened to the effusive-as-ever Beecher eulogize Greeley. Victoria did not share Greeley's last request: "Be kind to Tilton. He is foolish—but young."

The sisters had to simultaneously battle two charges, the obscenity matter led by Comstock and the libel suit brought by Challis regarding the masked ball article. Colonel Blood was detained in another prison, awaiting a court decision as to whether he had been a participant in the articles. Stephen Pearl Andrews falsely claimed he had had nothing to do with the articles, and was not charged. When the sisters appeared as witnesses in the examination of Colonel Blood on the libel charge Challis had brought, the *Herald* termed it the "Sensational comedy of free love."

The courtroom was crowded to suffocation with people curious to experience drama that "has seldom been surpassed for filthiness of detail," wrote the *Tribune*. Howe's "shamefully absorbing" questions would "bring a blush to almost any woman's face." Spectators stood up to see what effect the words had upon the sisters. They did not flinch, leaning forward to suggest new questions to their lawyer. After this tease, the *Tribune* gave no details, citing the tenderness of its readership.

Comstock took the stand to testify about his arrest of Tennie, the author of the Challis article. When asked to identify Tennie, Comstock pointed to her and said, "The individual at your left, sir."

"What?!" Howe asked sharply.

"The individual at your left."

Howe appeared deeply offended. "Your honor, when I represent a lady in the court of law I would like to have her treated as one." Jeering laughter filled the room until the judge called for order.

Buck Claflin took the stand and, as usual, made the situation worse for his daughters, this time displaying his enmity for Blood. He claimed the Colonel had told him to "shut his venerable mouth" when Buck advised against the *Weekly's* printing the Challis article. Although the near-deaf Buck cupped his ear to hear in the courtroom, he declared that he had heard through a closed door what he "thought" was Blood talking about "Challis." Buck said Blood declared, "[W]e believe it and we mean to publish it." The sisters, who had been trying to save Blood so that one of the trio would be free to run the *Weekly*, were crestfallen. They clutched nervously at Howe's sleeve, whispering to him. Tennie twisted her gloves restlessly, and her face flushed an intense red. Victoria lost all sense of composure, her face ashen as she listened to her father's damaging testimony.

Challis then took the stand, and Howe quickly set out to make him the kind of cad who would debauch a virgin. In so doing Howe further ruined what reputation Tennie had by suggesting such a familiarity that Challis gave her a present of underwear. Contemporary accounts never explained or expanded on why Howe would so damage his client in such a way. Apparently Howe was trying to prove that they were on such friendly terms that Tennie could not have blackmailed Challis, as he charged.

As much was deemed "unfit for publication" many newspapers didn't mention the underwear present. Howe tried to expose Challis's social habits, but Challis's counsel objected to his questions as a "violation of the decency of the Court." The judge agreed. Howe extracted that Challis had seen Tennie at her office and five or six times at her house. If readers were now salivating, it did not matter; newspapers refused to print "the disgusting scene in the courtroom."

As soon as Challis said that he had met Claflin "at the French Ball," Howe pounced.

"French Ball!? Indeed! French Ball did you say, sir?"

Howe forced Challis to admit that he was familiar with the demi-monde, and that he saw about fifteen women at the ball whom he had met before. When Challis admitted that there were two young girls in his French Ball box, Howe, grandstanding to make his point, joked that he, himself, certainly "had an interest in these girls."

Much of the examination fell into a he said, she said contretemps. Challis said Tennie had called him to her cell, begging that if he ceased the prosecution she would swear in an affidavit that the story was false. Woodhull, rather than Tennie, took the stand to defy Challis. Trying to control her emotions, she emphatically denied that Tennie had tried to bargain with Challis. Instead, she said, Tennie had told him "every word of it was truth and could be proven." Challis had visited their house after the French Ball and boasted about seducing two young girls, Woodhull swore. As she tried to describe in the courtroom the particulars of the "terrible debauchery," she was repeatedly stopped by the judge for presenting indecent material. "Although both sisters swore that Blood had had nothing to do with the masked ball article, the judge ruled that he was complicit in the publication and would stand trial.

Blood was released on bail, but the sisters were kept in jail, with an inordinately large bail to pay and no sign of a trial, for the entire month of November. They finally made bail, paying $16,000 to walk out on the third of December into fresh air. Thirty days in jail had taken their toll. Broken and in despair, Woodhull had refused to eat for three days. In her weakened, fasting state, she swore that Jesus had visited her; Tennie slept through his appearance. No other women of the sisters' ilk could have spoken of the horrors of prison conditions: wading in water up to their ankles in cold cells, downing wormy biscuits and foul-tasting coffee. Instead of being cowed by the experience, though, the sisters breathed fire and were ready for battle again. Comstock, however, was waiting for them, already plotting ways to ship them back to jail.

The sisters, burning to tell their story of life in prison and the injustice meted out to them through "Moral Cowardice," set up lectures. Victoria planned to speak first in Boston, but Harriet Beecher Stowe used her influence to make sure "those vile jailbirds" were banned from there.

Meanwhile Comstock, who had vowed on New Year's Day to do "something every day for Jesus," began his entrapment scheme to nail the sisters once again, on a second charge of obscenity, for sending the same material through the mails. Using the fake name of J. Beardsley, he sent a money order for six copies of the infamous November 2 issue of the *Weekly* from a Greenwich, Connecticut, post office box. He had ridden through snow on a sleigh from New York to rent the box. He then rode to Norwalk and used the name of a friend there to purchase six more. When he had collected the twelve copies he obtained warrants for the sisters' and Colonel Blood's arrests for sending obscene material through the mails.

Blood was arrested at the *Weekly* office on the afternoon of January 9, 1873, and that night the sisters were scheduled to speak together at the Cooper Institute. Blood managed to get word to them that Comstock was on the chase. When U.S. Marshals searched their house, they came up empty. Tennie was under their noses, hiding under a large upturned washtub. Victoria had fled with her bondsmen to the Taylor Hotel in New Jersey, as Jim Fisk and his cronies had done back in 1869.

The sisters had placed advertisements for their lecture, calling it "Moral Cowardice and Modern Hypocrisy—the Naked Truth—Thirty Days in the Ludlow Street Jail." Before the doors opened, more than a thousand people, most of them women, clustered around the entrance. Laura Cuppy Smith, their faithful friend and a Spiritualist trance speaker, greeted the audience in their stead.

A carriage drove stealthily down Third Avenue. A lookout slipped past waiting marshals to the carriage and whispered that the passengers would be safe if they mingled with the crowd pressing through the front door. A little old Quaker lady stepped out of the carriage, her drab silk bonnet projecting several inches beyond her face, which was concealed by a thick gray veil. She huddled under a black-and-white shawl and hobbled down the aisle. People offered to help, but appearing deaf, the woman spoke to no one as she moved closer to the stage.

Then, with a quick, nervous step, she ascended the platform. In an instant, "old age, coal-scuttle bonnet and gray dress disappeared like magic" and Woodhull stood before them, "an overwhelming inspirational fire scintillating from her eyes and beaming from her face." The Quaker costume lay coiled at her feet. Breathing in heavy gulps, she raised her arms high and threw back her head defiantly, her hair tumbling down. The crowd went wild. Victoria waited for the hollering, shouting, and applause to die down, then created further bedlam with her greeting: "Friends and Fellow-Citizens! I come into your presence from a cell in the American Bastille, consigned by the cowardly servility of the age." People in the front row instantly put their feet on the iron railing surrounding the stage to prevent any attempt by the marshals to grab Victoria. She disarmed the audience when she apologized for her heavy overshoes, explaining that they would be useful on her trip to Ludlow Street Jail.

"Her voice rose in clear and piercing tones, like a song of love, blended with the war-cry of battle, and the pent-up forces of her soul rushed forth in an impetuous and irresistible torrent of burning, glowing words." Woodhull marched through a tour de force for an hour and a half, outlining her obscenity defense, ridiculing Comstock, and extolling socialism, free love, and religious freedom. She positioned herself as a First Amendment fighter for free speech and equality in every possible arena—from the boardroom to the bedroom. She sprinkled her speech with historical references to the goddess Diana, to Acts of the Apostles, and to Caligula.

Woodhull mocked the "cowards" who had suppressed the *Weekly* "by violent and illegal seizures," arrested her and her sister, and ransacked and destroyed files and equipment in their office. She accurately reported that when the "New York *Herald* boldly and unhesitatingly reprinted the 'most objectional [*sic*] matter'" from the *Weekly*, no one, including Comstock, had lifted a hand to charge the powerful *Herald* with obscenity. Woodhull engaged in a lengthy tirade about how the passage most objected to—"the red trophy of her virginity"—was less inflammatory than many in the Bible. Surely the YMCA fellows should know that, she taunted, or could it be that they didn't know their Bible? "The fellow Comstock is, I think, too conceitedly egotistic to realize the position into which his action has placed him. He is also, I think, just enough fool and knave combined" for buying the papers and having them addressed and sent to the post office on his account, by a person "having no right or authority to act for my sister and me."

She tackled the criticism of her free love speech, now a year and a half old, in which "I said something to the effect that I have the right to change my love every day or every night if I choose to do so," and the response of the press and public was "Mrs. Woodhull confesses that she lives an utterly abandoned life; she lives and sleeps with two or three or five hundred or some other egregious number of men...All this is very absurd." Nothing she ever said, or that others knew of her life, would show "whether I live the life of a nun, or whether I live as the exclusive wife of one man, or whether I am what the cry [of the public] indicates." Her friends were eager to "assure the public that I am one of the most exclusive and monogamic [*sic*] of matrons." As always, Woodhull laced references to her personal behavior with enticing ambiguity: "I have been perfectly willing that the world should think just the other way." She saw herself in the front lines as a martyred saint, taking the bullets if it would help condition the world for others "who might want a broader social sphere than I do and to give the world just this lesson—it is none of its business." She could not understand why "affectional [*sic*] as well as religious freedom should not be tolerated in this free government."

At the close, Woodhull surrendered to the waiting marshals.

This time, she and Blood were allowed to sleep together, in cell 12 at the Ludlow Street Jail.

While briefly out of jail and awaiting trials on the charges of libel and obscenity, Victoria and Tennie tried to reconstruct their ransacked office and wrecked equipment in order to resume publishing. Less than two weeks after Woodhull's "Naked Truth" speech arrest, they were stunned when they were arrested for a third time. Everyone seemed dazed by now.

"I thought we had been arrested often enough to satisfy everyone," said a caustic Woodhull to the two deputy sheriffs. "What have we done now?"

They were told that it was "for libel," but no one knew who had sought it. The indignant sisters sent messengers to their lawyer and bondsmen before entering the carriage with Blood. When they arrived at the district attorney's office, they discovered that he and his clerks had gone for the day. Their lawyer learned that Challis was arresting them, again on charges of libel, because the masked ball issue of the *Weekly* was still in circulation. Their bondsmen were ready to sign the bail bond, but no one was in the office to accept bail. Woodhull angrily railed at the "outrage" of being arrested so late in the day, obviously "so that they could not give bail." This time the trio was sent to a prison worse than the Ludlow Street Jail, the massive, foreboding prison known to all as the Tombs because its architecture resembled an Egyptian mausoleum. Charles Dickens called it a "dismal fronted pile of bastard Egyptian."

By now their frequent incarceration had taken its toll on the sisters; even Tennie wore no smiles. Howe was a studied performer, but he was also genuinely livid at the numerous arrests. He challenged the "persecution of his clients by an obscene person, one Comstock." He had twice caused their arrest, and while they were clamoring in vain for a trial, Comstock had arrested them for a third time, all to "satisfy the malice of this man [Beecher] who won't come into Court to make his charges good." Howe also attacked the excessive bail—"these women simply for an alleged misdemeanor, are under $60,000 bail [because of the accumulated arrests] which was more than bail set for the infamous and recently arrested Boss Tweed."

After many delays, Howe was finally allowed to quiz Comstock, in a hearing to ascertain whether the charge should be taken to trial. Howe blistered Comstock in court, reading, line for line, from the masked ball article and pausing repeatedly to ask Comstock, "[I]s this obscene?" "No," replied Comstock to all the passages.

Then came the crux of the challenge, the three-line sentence in the Challis article containing the "red trophy of her virginity" phrase. The hyperbole of the writing—the disgusting implication that Challis would not have washed his finger "for days"—notwithstanding, Howe declared that the phrase was not obscene. When asked, Comstock declared it was. Howe triumphantly opened the Bible to Deuteronomy 22:15 and read, "Then shall the father of the damsel, and her mother, take and bring forth the tokens of the damsel's virginity unto the elders of the city in the gate."

Now, asked Howe, "Is this portion of Holy Scripture obscene?" Comstock said no, he didn't think so. "Even if they say the same thing?" pressed Howe. "Yes, even so," said Comstock.

Comstock's case was severely weakened. Howe and the sisters continued to protest loudly against their enemies and the cowards who had hounded two women, destroyed their business, and suppressed their newspaper. Howe demanded a lowered bail and, after so many outrageous delays, an immediate trial. The judge lowered the bail to $2,000 for Blood and $1,000 each for the sisters. But a trial was still far off, delayed by the prosecution for months.

By now the sisters were garnering defenders who saw something terribly wrong in their treatment. In her "Naked Truth" speech, Woodhull flatly charged that Comstock, Beecher, Bowen, and other members of Plymouth Church, the district attorney, and the commissioner, backed by Challis and the judge, had engaged in "personal and vindictive persecution." People were beginning to believe it.

Even a *Brooklyn Eagle* editorial attacked the sisters' long incarceration as an outrageous act of the U.S. government. In fact, the paper saw their persecution as a dangerous erosion of free speech, when they were first thrown in prison: "Without having generally known it, the people of this country are living under a law more narrow and oppressive than any people with a written Constitution ever lived under before." Why had the law continued "to play with Woodhull and Claflin as a cat plays with a mouse? If they are to be prosecuted, let the suit be pressed," demanded another New York City editorial. Papers throughout the country showed more spunk and skepticism in denouncing Beecher and Comstock.

The YMCA was ridiculed in the press, but no one could match the acid tones of the sisters, who called the organization "the Young Men's Christian (Christ forgive the connection) Association." The sisters attacked in the *Weekly* (after managing to restore their equipment). Comstock's YMCA was fit for the "title of the American Inquisition." Although, "We should no more think of comparing Comstock...with Torquemada, than of contrasting a living skunk with a dead lion."

The "living skunk" prevailed for another half year as the sisters nervously waited without a trial until the summer of 1873. Challis's libel case moved even more snail-like, not reaching a trial until March 1874. In the meantime, the sisters continued to slam Beecher, Comstock, Challis, the YMCA, and Plymouth Church, keeping the scandal alive and causing the public to ask if Beecher was so innocent, why he was keeping silent.

The ordeal of prison and bad publicity had shattered the sisters more than their fierce façade revealed. Without money, backing, or friends, they tried to weave together a semblance of a life. They subsisted on lecture fees as the curious across the country paid to see criminal celebrities. They kept the *Weekly* afloat throughout the spring of 1873, but money was now a constant problem, and Victoria soon became sick in mind and body.

CHAPTER EIGHTEEN

Life and Death

As the months passed with no resolution on their trials, money worries and exhausting efforts to keep the *Weekly* running plagued the anxious sisters. By May of 1873 there seemed no end to the delays to their final days in court in their libel and obscenity trials. Tennie held up better than Victoria. The pressure on Victoria had left her mind in turmoil. Her bondsmen were weary and gave signs that they might desert the sisters. The hearings upon hearings had worn her out. The tension of endless waiting to find out their fate turned into desperation on June 6. The sisters had endured two days of hearings in a stifling, crowded courtroom on Comstock's obscenity charge. The judge made no decision, and once again the case was set aside.

As Victoria rode home with Tennie that night, she brooded about her constant persecution. As she walked up the stairs to the house, she clutched her chest and told Tennie she was not feeling well. Victoria had a cup of tea with her family in the dining room but said she was tired and scarcely ate. Blood walked with her upstairs toward her bedroom. On the landing, she suddenly fell with such a crash that Tennie and their mother raced from the dining room and up the stairs. Blood, Tennie, and Annie managed to drag Victoria to her bed. She was unconscious and could not be revived. A messenger was sent for a doctor. Woodhull's face was ashen. A sobbing Tennie telegraphed her boyfriend, Johnny Green, city editor of the New York *Sun*, wailing that she thought Victoria was dead.

The *Sun* had an exclusive the next day, splashed on page one and then across the country on the wire service. Papers flashed the DEATH OF THE GREAT REFORMER. At the time of Tennie's message, the *Sun* had reason to believe Victoria was dead. The family tried everything to revive her. They felt no pulse. They held a mirror to her face, and there were no signs of breathing. Victoria was unconscious for thirty minutes. Then a trickle of blood oozed from her mouth. When the doctors arrived, they saw little hope. As she moved her head slightly, doctors told her to lie absolutely still. Mustard plasters were applied, and her hands and feet were immersed in hot water. The doctors feared she would die before dawn. Tennie and Blood, the only two allowed with her, sat beside her throughout the night. Woodhull remained unconscious and in critical condition all through Saturday. The doctors thought a blood vessel to her lungs had ruptured and that she may have had a concussion from the fall. On Sunday she regained consciousness but was too weak to leave her bed for days.

Two weeks later, the *Weekly* stated, "Tennie, in her grief, telegraphed to an intimate friend that Victoria was dead." This error was corrected after Woodhull was revived and "it is very much regretted that it occurred." This did no good with unrelenting foes. The *Chicago Daily Tribune* had announced that the death report was a hoax to garner sympathy.

A few days before Victoria fell ill in 1873, astonished *New York Times* readers gasped as they read about an astounding cover-up involving adultery, greed, jealousy, and power within the Plymouth Church that had begun as far back as the mid-1860s. This bombshell would have great bearing on the sisters' obscenity trial and would finally convince the public that the two women may have been telling the truth about Beecher a year and a half before after all. The article in the *New York Times* was a paid announcement, bought by Beecher's friend Samuel Wilkeson for the purpose of exposing and tarnishing Henry Bowen, Beecher's wealthy patron and president of Plymouth Church. Wilkeson, who had bankrolled Beecher's latest book for a whopping $10,000, used the pseudonym "Suffolk," but was soon identified. GALVANIZING A FILTHY SCANDAL WAS the *Times* headline on the Wilkeson story, which depicted Bowen as a two-faced manipulator. "It is high time that the torrent of slander against Henry Ward Beecher be arrested," wrote "Suffolk," a.k.a. Wilkeson. He wrote about the trio who had colluded in the great cover-up and who had signed a tripartite covenant: Beecher, Tilton, and Bowen.

Ten years previously, in 1863, Bowen had burned with jealousy and revenge when his wife, Lucy, told him on her deathbed that Beecher had committed adultery with her. Bowen's sense of betrayal was immense; he had brought the dynamic preacher east in 1847, paid his old debts, and housed and clothed Beecher and his family. In exchange, Beecher had ignited Bowen's parishioners and became the golden goose Bowen could not afford to alienate. Still, Bowen could not hold his tongue at this revelation from his dying wife, and told young Tilton the sordid tales of Beecher's adultery with Lucy and with other parishioners' wives; some possessed private keys to the preacher's study.

Tilton could not forget Bowen's lurid tale about Edna Dean Proctor, a budding author who was living in the Bowen mansion during the 1850s. Beecher was alone in Bowen's home with young Edna, who planted a kiss on Beecher, who then "threw her down on a sofa, accomplished his deviltry upon her and left her." Bowen charged that "it was 'no less than rape'" or "something very nearly like ravishment." The ever-charitable Beecher said he was sure Proctor was no virgin anyway, but denied that he had violently assaulted her. Beecher's relations with "certain ladies of the church" was such common talk in the 1860s, Bowen revealed to Tilton, that congregational leaders had confronted Beecher, who promised there would be no further cause for gossip.

Meanwhile, in the late 1860s, Tilton was acting out as the problematical wunderkind of the church paper, the *Independent*. He printed essays satirizing solemn orthodoxy and advocated women's rights. He defiantly said his views were the same as Beecher's, but the preacher, backing influential church factions hostile to Tilton, denied he shared Tilton's ideas and sharply rebuked him.

With his eyes always on the collection plate, Bowen stalled; he could not get rid of the popular preacher who may have seduced his wife, but Tilton's talent and growing fame were also too precious to kill. Relations between Tilton and Beecher had quickly soured after Tilton quarreled violently with his wife, Elizabeth, in the summer of 1870 over *her* alleged affair with Beecher. Tilton stewed, ranted to his female suffragist friends, and penned an editorial (published on December 1, 1870, in the church paper) arguing the free love view that loveless marriages should be dissolved.

A month later, in January 1871, Bowen fired Tilton. Machiavellian money maneuverings, however, necessitated that no more bad blood be spilled, although all three men remained bitter toward one another. Wrangling continued, and like wary nations attempting to avoid all-out war, the three signed their secret "tripartite covenant" more than a year later, in April 1872, in which they agreed to keep mum about their spiteful little secrets. But the snarling did not stop, and just a few weeks before the sisters' 1873 obscenity trial, the *New York Times* was printing these spicy details of adultery and cover-up. The *Times* tried to have it both ways, publishing prurient details while professing high-minded purity. This "very disgusting controversy" should have been left to "circulate among the organs of the slums with which it originated"—meaning, of course, the *Weekly*. "Slanders upon the character and habits of Mr. Beecher," wrote the *Times*, first appeared in "an obscene newspaper."

The tripartite agreement was innocuous compared with the blistering accompanying letter, written by a furious Tilton to Bowen after he had fired Tilton in January 1871, which Wilkeson had obtained. Bowen had sandbagged Tilton by discrediting him to Beecher as a dangerous radical. Tilton's letter fingered Bowen as the one who had spread the Beecher adultery stories. As the public read the damaging letter, now two and a half years old, Beecher was too scared to face his congregation. He composed a letter of resignation, went to Frank Moulton's wife, Emma, and wailed that he "might as well go out of life." As always, Beecher's theatrical despair faded, and he was soon back at the pulpit.

Meanwhile, the press was hounding Bowen so fiercely for scandal details that he frantically sought the very sisters he had so often attacked.

A strange gathering occurred on the night of June 25, 1873, when several dignitaries and Plymouth Church brethren trooped up the stairs of a Manhattan brownstone and were met by Woodhull, Tennie, their mother, sister Utica, lawyers, and a newspaperman.

With grim satisfaction, the sisters faced the humbled Puritan potentates. Assailed by newspapers for trying to wreck Beecher and certain that Beecher was planning revenge, Bowen desperately needed evidence. Woodhull had claimed she possessed damaging letters, and Bowen now wanted her treasure trove. He had hoped to keep the meeting secret, bringing his own stenographer, but the sisters had made sure that it would make the next day's papers.

An *Eagle* reporter grilled the sisters after the meeting. Bowen said he had come for "corroborative evidence against Mr. Beecher...to vindicate his honor," recalled Woodhull. "I said to him that I was astonished that he should come to me to vindicate his character...'you knew of some of these facts years ago, and yet you have kept silent' she scolded him." Despite Bowen's admission that he was scrambling for evidence to save himself, Woodhull suspiciously thought this was a trick. "I believe that you are here in the interest of that gigantic fraud, Henry Ward Beecher," she told Bowen, and denounced him for abetting in her harassment. Tennie spoke up: "If you had no hand in my persecution how is it that you sent for those papers which were used against me?" Bowen weakly responded that he had purchased the scandal issue that led to the obscenity arrest because, when he saw "anything interesting or spicy in our paper he was in the habit of sending for three or four copies."

When Bowen asked for letters, Woodhull teasingly told him, "after several month's [*sic*] intimacy with Mr. Beecher, being with him frequently and alone, that our correspondence was not one of mere platonic affection." She knew from "personal experience that Mr. Beecher is a free lover." She had no "personal enmity" against Beecher, whom she had just called a "gigantic fraud."

She also referred to the crux of Bowen's revenge: "I said to him that I could not understand how he could go to church Sunday after Sunday, and look in the face of this man who was reported to have debauched his wife, and then sit with sealed lips." Bowen replied that he had "felt in honor bound to keep silent" then, but now "his lips were unsealed." She gave Bowen a swift peek at Beecher's signatures on two letters, but not the contents. (The letters were a bluff, relating only to Beecher's not attending a suffrage convention and to her Steinway Hall speech.) Woodhull's game contained an underlying quid pro quo: if Bowen could swing the obscenity trial in their favor, she might cooperate with him.

Five days after the meeting, the sisters won their startling victory in court against Comstock. The sisters, who had claimed all along that the church was behind their persecution, now felt sure that it was the Plymouth Church lawyers who had pulled strings to settle the long-overdue trial. The judge suddenly ruled that the statute under which the women had been arrested did not specify newspapers—a decision that certainly could have been reached months before had not the prosecution presented roadblocks. Even the *Brooklyn Eagle* excoriated the prosecution as an "Inglorious Failure."

Ironically, Comstock had defeated himself. Earlier in 1873 he had succeeded in getting a tougher federal obscenity law passed, one that *included* newspapers. This new provision was proof that the law had *not* covered the sisters at the time he arrested them in 1872.

Comstock lost his big prey but was able to escalate future convictions, severely damaging free speech and tyrannizing the literary world well into the twentieth century. He confiscated works by Walt Whitman, Theodore Dreiser, and George Bernard Shaw. When he stalked Shaw's plays, the playwright blazingly attacked him, coining the word "Comstockery. . . . it confirms the deep-seated conviction of the Old World that America is a provincial place, a second-rate country-town civilization after all." Comstock referred to the Nobel Prize laureate as the "Irish smut dealer." In 1914, birth control pioneer Margaret Sanger fled to Europe when Comstock tried to arrest her. Comstock died the next year, but his law, particularly as it pertained to curbing contraceptives, lived on for decades.

As for Beecher, the public humiliation—disclosures of alleged adultery, church leaders trudging to the scandalous sisters seeking Beecher sex secrets—finally forced the scared preacher to print a public denial a few days after the sisters' obscenity trial victory. All the "stories and rumors" are "utterly false," he wrote.

Despite the obscenity acquittal and revelations of the tripartite agreement, the sisters were in no mood to celebrate. They still faced the Challis libel trial, with no date in sight. Also Woodhull was barely recovering from her illness. The June 21 *Weekly* was filled with tributes to Victoria, a narcissistic preoccupation so extreme that it signaled emotional troubles. Articles saluted her bravery, purity, and truthfulness, combined with numerous passages of self-pity. She wrote that her "present physical state" began when she first "heard the click of the lock that confined her to a 'six-by-eight' cell" eight months before. She felt "keenly the month's imprisonment," and felt the "stabs" to the heart when friends who knew she was telling the truth deserted her, causing constant suffering.

Then, in July, within weeks of their obscenity trial victory, their tormented thirty-one-year-old sister, Utica, died. One of her last acts was once again to attack Victoria, Colonel Blood, and Tennie. Arrested for being drunk and disorderly, Utica charged the sisters with having beaten her. Soiled family linen was again aired in the papers as Woodhull revealed that Utica had attacked sister Meg Miles with a chair and "began her insane and disorderly conduct." Woodhull sounded paranoid when she claimed in a statement to the *New York Times* that Utica's "purely malicious" complaint "was made to affect the public against me." A few days later, Utica was dead of Bright's disease, her kidneys failing from years of alcoholism. The *New York Herald* did not spare Utica: "She would take brandy, whiskey, gin, rum, wine and beer." She even downed "draughts of bay rum" and was also a morphine addict. "The result was that at times she was a raving maniac" who pursued her frightened sisters.

Woodhull decided to tell all in a eulogy, which alternated between writing about her dead sister and defending herself. The family had not realized that Utica's violent behavior was caused by her dependence on alcohol and "stimulants," Victoria wrote disingenuously. "We now understand" that Utica "was a fit subject for an asylum, either for ine-briates or the insane; but as the victim of a series of circumstances that conspired to make a lamentable ruin of one of the most divinely gifted of human beings, she deserved the keenest commiseration of every one, and their most compassionate endurance." Victoria blamed Utica's death on two disastrous marriages that made her a "sexual slave" to marital con-formity. Woodhull wrote, "Indeed what might be said of her, 'Cut off at thirty-one by marriage.'"

Yet thoughts of herself filled the *Weekly*. As she looked at her dead sis-ter, Victoria was said to cry out, "Do you wonder...that I feel desperately in earnest to reform the evils of our social life when I remember what I have suffered in my own family? Opposed and misunderstood by my par-ents and sisters, compelled to bear an idiotic child by a drunken husband, O, my God! And the world thinks me only ambitious of notoriety!" The article then proceeded once again to denigrate her family, even Tennie: "She has unbounded benevolence, an exuberance of animal spirits, and a ready tongue, but seems to lack the interior life and inspiring power" of Victoria. Only Blood got off unscathed: "a nobler man never lived."

Whispers of poison and rumors of the sisters' imminent arrest filled Victoria's mind, along with the idea that Comstock's YMCA was at work. She requested an autopsy of her sister's body, which revealed that Utica's kidneys were enlarged to twice their natural size and "much decomposed." Her uterus and vagina were pronounced "free from disease and as natural as those of a virgin." Given that Utica had been arrested for soliciting and had had two marriages, the "virgin" comparison was a stretch, but the sisters clung to the "free from disease" phrase, since "remarks had been made" that an examination "would reveal the fact that the deceased was rotten with sexual disease."

Reflecting some of the bitterness they felt over constant rumors and assumptions, Tennie and Woodhull rejected the "outward exhibition" of customary funerals. Utica was dressed in a pink silk wrapper, with a white flower at her breast, and laid in a plain casket, while Tennie and Victoria, wearing white roses on their dark dresses, were surrounded by "many of their literary friends." A plain hearse and four carriages took the casket and family, with Tennie weeping, to the cemetery.

The sisters brought the body of Canning Woodhull from another cemetery to lie near Utica, offering no explanation for the joining of the two hapless addicts who had died of the same disease.

During this period, there seems little doubt that Woodhull was either on the verge of a nervous breakdown or experiencing a full-blown collapse. Her writing and speeches contain an unnerving fixation. Yes, she was persecuted, but her preoccupation—with her imprisonment, unfair judges, the Comstock-Beecher brigade, and hectoring newspapers—became uncontrollable. In the past, reporters had described glimpses of high-strung fragility lurking behind her masterful control onstage. Now Victoria wrote at times as if only she, and not Tennie and Blood, had endured jail and castigation. The *Weekly* suffered from this self-absorption. Finally, in the fall, Victoria showed some of her combative spirit. She took on adversaries at the annual Spiritualist convention in Chicago, following a fiery speech at their August event in Vineland, New Jersey. There, Woodhull faced social freedom critics who said future children would suffer if mothers could leave bad marriages. Why, she asked, should such naysayers "be so terribly concerned about the children who are to be, when they have no concern whatever for those who *are*... Go to the fifty thousand houseless, half starved, wholly untaught children of New York City, who live from the swill barrels of the rich Christians, ask what is becoming of them and they will tell you they don't know. But it is plain to be seen that they are going to the bad, surely."

Woodhull no longer was invited to speak to suffragists. She and Tennie were no longer queens of laborers or, conversely, capitalists. Ads in the *Weekly* now reflected a narrower audience: "Psychometric Readings"; "Botanic Physicians" who promised "no poison used"; a painting for sale of the Fox sisters' home, the "Birthplace of Modern Spiritualism."

The *Chicago Daily Tribune* stingingly portrayed the Spiritualists at their September 10 annual meeting in Chicago as an insignificant band of misfits, mocking them as old women, and men who looked like "old women too," with a smattering of homely young women. The "Woodhull doctrines" were a last resort for "shelved virgins" or those "whom nature has denied even a modicum of the charms of the sex."

However, Woodhull was praised both for her keynote speech—"A Slashing Address by the Presiding Genius"—and her final speech. Freed from the convoluted rhetoric of Stephen Pearl Andrews, she was electrifying the crowd with more personal language. At her first appearance at the three-day convention, the audience saw an unsteady, ghastly pale Woodhull, who was introduced as having been very ill. She appeared dazed and disconcerted by a hostile minority of conventiongoers, but recovered to attack them with fire: "As I sat listening to these terrific denunciations from the male virgins and immaculates [*sic*]," she related a story that revealed an uncharacteristically lighter sense of humor.

Woodhull had taken a Broadway stagecoach that was filled with several "gentlemen." She sat down beside "an elegantly dressed lady" who quickly put her fan to her face and whispered in Victoria's ear, " 'For heaven's sake, Mrs. Woodhull, don't recognize me here; it would ruin my business!' I then recognized her as the keeper of a fashionable house of assignation, to which I had been upon an errand of inquiry . . . it soon occurred to me that some of the gentlemen present were her customers, who seeing that she knew me, would never again dare to visit her house." As some of the Spiritualists laughed, Woodhull added, "So you see I am ostracized by those whom the world calls prostitutes almost as fearfully as I am by those whom I call the real prostitutes—those who come before you with a sanctified look, and with meek voices parading their virtue, which they profess to be in deadly fear of losing should social freedom prevail." She would obey no man-made laws that subjugate women, "and especially will I spit upon" their social laws.

At an afternoon session, a heated confrontation with a Mr. Cotton ensued when he demanded to know if she had "prostituted herself sexually" to carry out her "glorious work." Woodhull stared him down. "I want to fully understand you . . . what is it that you want me to explain?"

She looked at the rest of the audience. "I am thinking whether I shall lose any of my womanly dignity to answer this man...A *man* questioning my virtue!" Cotton drew some laughs when he said he was not "worth the powder to shoot at," but said he had details of Victoria's private life he would share with the audience if she didn't. Woodhull, her voice stronger, let fly: "If this Convention wants to know anything about my sexual organs let us have it understood!"

A man asked her if Cotton was telling the truth.

She stared at Cotton and referred to herself in the third person. "Has Mr. Cotton ever had sex with Mrs. Woodhull?"

"No," he replied.

"Do you know any man that has?"

"No."

"Then what in the name of heaven can you prove?" asked an affronted Woodhull. How dare he come before this convention and "arraign me for hypocrisy? I hurl the intention back in your face, sir, and stand boldly before you and this Convention, and declare that I never had sexual intercourse with any man of whom I am ashamed to stand side by side before the world with the act." This was a study in ambiguity, but still the frankest comment she had given regarding a personal embrace of free love. "I am not ashamed of any act of my life." Her words echoed as the audience sat silent. *"At the time, it was the best I knew. Nor am I ashamed of any desire that has been gratified or any passion alluded to"* [emphasis added].

Brushing Cotton aside, Woodhull discussed how she felt about being ostracized. Why had this group made her their president? "Is it because I have shown any cowardice during the last two years? Or is it because I have gone through the very depths of hell to give you freedom? I want to know! Is it because I have been a coward, or is it because I have braved the penitentiary and every other damnable thing that could be put up to hinder me giving you the truth?"

Ignoring Tennie's role, Woodhull was caught up in her go-it-alone theme. Victoria had always thought of herself as a singular queen, the charismatic center of the Woodhull machine, and indeed she was. Tennie was her helper and partner, one who lectured engagingly and sometimes upstaged her, but Victoria did the dictating. Victoria showed this tendency when she wrote or spoke about the two of them, often unconsciously shifting into "I." It was not a matter of her purposefully distancing herself from her younger sister as much as it was thoughtlessness and an overriding belief in "her destiny" as a leader. "When I came out of my prison I came out of it a beggar." She had appealed to Spiritualists and reformers to send money to keep the *Weekly* afloat. "But did you do it? No! You left me to starve in the streets, you left my paper to die...Hence I went to your bankers, presidents of railroads, gamblers, prostitutes, and got the money that has sent you the paper you have been reading."

Then Woodhull resorted to a tantalizing vagueness that detractors would view as proof: "I used whatever influence I had to get that money and that's my own business, and none of yours and if I devoted my body to my work and my soul to God, that is my business and not yours... suppose I have been obliged to crucify my body in whatever way to fulfill my duty, what business is that of Mr. Cotton?"

Victoria would do "whatever is necessary" for her cause, "even if it be the crucifixion of my body in the manner for which I am now arraigned. If you do not want one to be forced to that extreme, come to my rescue as you ought to have done before and not let me fight the battle all alone." She should not be "subjected even to the possibility of a thing so utterly abhorrent to me as to submit sexually for money to a man I do not love."

After this last statement, clearly abhorring prostitution for herself, Woodhull could not resist leaving her audience wondering, neither confirming nor denying whether she had sold herself to keep the *Weekly* running. "If Mr. Cotton, or if any of you are so terribly alarmed lest I may have been obliged to do this, let him and you manifest your alarm by rallying to my support to insure that no such exigency shall ever again rise."

When asked if she herself had "boasted" of prostitution to carry on the *Weekly*, Tennie answered with "a brazen-face impudence, 'If you spiritualists had done your duty, we should not have to do so, but what are you going to do about it? How are you going to help yourselves?'"

The scene was intense, and Colonel Blood stood with the sisters to protect them as this ugly session ended. Despite this altercation, Woodhull gave a final electrifying speech that so awed the *Chicago Daily Tribune* reporter who covered the meeting that he declared, "She is one of the most active, energetic, and eloquent speakers that ever appeared in this city, and it may well be regretted that so highly gifted a woman should not have devoted herself to a more worthy cause." Her lecture was "devoted to a really eloquent and exhaustive discourse... upon the evils, physical, mental, and social, that result from the present system of marriage and sexual relations." The paper, however, decided the speech was "not of a character to be published in these columns."

Woodhull was overwhelmingly reelected president of the American Association of Spiritualists. This did not stop detractors in the group from saying the election was rigged.

Soon Woodhull's self-involvement would be subsumed by a far larger crisis. On Thursday, September 18, 1873, Jay Cooke and Company in Manhattan, the nation's most powerful banking house, closed its doors, signaling a monumental financial crash. Like everyone else, the sisters would be absorbed in the Panic of 1873 that shook the world.

CHAPTER NINETEEN

Panic and Victory

Ever since Jay Cooke became known as the Union "savior" who had helped finance the Civil War, his banking firm was seen as the citadel for security in the world of finance, and Cooke himself was known as the Rothschild of America. Cooke was said to have "bought congressmen, bribed two vice-presidents, built churches" and helped penniless preachers; he "combined the qualities of money-getting, corruption, farsightedness and piety in such successful proportion that he was venerated by the public, feared by politicians, and considered by all the country's leading banker."

Unlike some of the very rich, Cooke had given generously to the poor, albeit from his fifty-three-room mansion that was light years away from the life of hod carriers, bricklayers, and domestics and from the slums of America's cities. Everything ended—for Cooke, the middle and lower classes, and those at the very bottom—on Thursday, September 18, 1873. With tears in his eyes, Cooke gave the order. Customers were ushered out of his Wall Street branch. The massive bronze doors were bolted. The unbelievable had happened. Jay Cooke and Co. had gone bankrupt, precipitating a nationwide collapse.

The twenty-first-century financial disaster eerily echoed the causes of the 1873 crash—ungoverned and rampant real estate speculation, easy mortgages and lending, and bank failures. Corruption at the top had caused credit to dry up and banks to go under. An epidemic of foreclosures followed, farms failed, factories closed, and thousands upon thousands of unemployed and homeless roamed the streets.

The failure of Jay Cooke and Co. "came like a thunderbolt." Even Vanderbilt and Jay Gould were pressed to the wall. Henry Clews, the arrogant detractor of Tennie Claflin a few years before, closed his banking house. Men walked the Street with blanched faces, swearing, weeping, staring. As another of the "richest and soundest" banks went under, a run on the remaining banks ensued. This was not a "mere Wall Street panic but a nationwide collapse." People hoarded greenbacks and the Cooke failure caused a "veritable paralysis" in several industrial regions. As the depth of the disaster began to register, the New York *Sun* attempted an analysis: Construction in railroads and housing had "been done on credit." A prime example was the collapse of Cooke's expensive gamble, the Northern Pacific Railroad.

The day after Cooke folded, brokers sloshed through heavy rain to the Exchange floor screaming, yelling, and running pell-mell in an attempt to sell, but no one was buying. Wall Street still hoped for a correction. Then, the next day, Saturday, the twentieth, for the first time in history, the New York Stock Exchange closed, and stayed closed for ten days, a financial disaster still unparalleled.

The sisters hurried back from Chicago's Spiritualist meeting to a city marked by fear and terror. They had nothing to lose on Wall Street. Their brokerage firm had faded. They were living at sister Meg Miles's crowded house in Manhattan, assembling the *Weekly*, surrounded by a bickering contingent of Claflins.

Despite their own financial straits, the sisters were invigorated, back on a mission, fired up by suffering laborers and the gross inequities between rich and poor. "We shall lift up our voices to advocate the rights of the 'Lower Million' against the Upper Ten!" was their proletariat battle cry. Underdogs all their life, they found their natural inclination surfacing. By December, 105,000 unemployed workers, about a quarter of New York City's population, were roaming the streets. Exhausted charity workers fed 7,000 a day, yet this was but a dent in the masses seeking food or shelter. The sisters strived to turn those statistics into people, to make their readers and audiences feel the suffering, printing stories that showed the city's "terrible conditions."

"The demand for shelter of really respectable-looking, deserving men, is so great," wrote the *New York Herald*, which the sisters splashed on their pages. These were the newly down and out, not the usual handful of vagrants. Quiet, hardworking men presented themselves with cast-down eyes. Speaking of the fifty-eight hungry men crowded into the Fifteenth Precinct, the squad captain said, "There ain't a man in this room but is willing to work and has tried hard to get it. Do you think they'd come here if they had any other place; no sir, they would not."

"I walked the streets for four nights before I could bring myself down to come in here, but the cold and the want of clothing drove me to it at last," sobbed one man. He had sold his possessions "one after another to keep the children together. Two or three of us married men club together what we squeeze out during the day to pay for a room for the women and children to sleep in... Where it is going to end, heaven only knows." A younger man came in, having eaten nothing for twenty-four hours. A maker of paper boxes, he drew out of his pocket two crumpled letters of recommendation from bosses who themselves no longer had their jobs; showing them around to salvage some pride. "I'm willing to take a job at anything for anything, but I can't get one." An older man jumped up and said, "What chance have I to feed my five children, my mother and my wife against that young man!?... what am I to do? Lie down and starve, and see my children do the same thing? Great God! And in America!"

Such hunger, pain, and humiliation formed the basis of an angry Populist Party that surged briefly during this depression, which was the forerunner to the powerful turn-of-the-century socialist movement. The sisters once again found their voice and an audience—among restless laborers. The halls of New York had been "closed against us for nine months," the two women shouted, but now "we shall lift up our voices to advocate the rights" of the poor against the rich and to thunder against "the monopolies which starve the laboring class." A *Weekly* ad promised that "Victoria C. Woodhull and Tennie C. Claflin will both speak in the large hall of Cooper Institute on Friday evening, October 17."

That night, "every available inch of room in the great hall of the Cooper Institute was occupied," while hundreds more never got inside. The restless audience hissed and booed until the man giving an introduction gave up and turned the stage over to Woodhull; Tennie waited her turn nearby. A flushed Woodhull begged for the rowdy crowd to act like "ladies and gentlemen." She stood alone, waiting for the prolonged applause to stop, dressed in her familiar lecturing outfit of a plain black dress with a single rose, this time red, pinned at her throat. For a change, she was almost no match for the crowd, some of them a heckling clique who had come to disrupt. She apologized for her voice, weak and husky from a cold. Everywhere in the country, people were crying, "Give me back our riches or we will take them," she exclaimed. She preferred reform to revolution, but "if the former were denied," she would use "all her influence to bring about the latter." Applause and hisses followed. Woodhull gained strength, and soon she was mesmerizing the audience. She had named herself the "Queen of the Rostrum" and had her reputation as a major orator to uphold.

She attacked the fraud and corruption that were "everywhere," the culmination of a rotten system of government. She recited a long list of charges against the government, and her audience shook the hall with the "violence of their applause" as she shouted that the "country is on the high road to a monarchy in which Grant would be Dictator." She urged the audience to vote against every incumbent running, "for there was not one of them fit to pick out of the gutter." Loud laughter followed with cries of "That's so!"

Her pleas for starving children and women oppressed in marriages were impassioned, and at times she strode quickly back and forth on the stage as she kept up for an hour and a half. Woodhull flailed away at a perennial favorite, the press, which she said had already "tried to kill me, but was not able to do so." The crowd loved this. Woodhull jumped into the need for prison reform; the system was a "disgrace."

Although the sisters—Woodhull more than Claflin—spoke about

their own spiritual feelings and God, Victoria said to her agreeing audience that Christian platitudes did not help: "How many poor in New York who for the past twelve days had listened to the fervent utterances of the Evangelical Alliance would be able to purchase coal for the coming winter?" Again there was a storm of applause. The audience was so clearly for the downtrodden that it sympathized with poor women possibly forced into prostitution. Cheers broke out when Woodhull said that, rather than religious banality, she wanted to know how thousands of her "suffering sisters would be able to procure the necessaries of life without falling into vice" that could not be solved by their learning "the worn-out song of Christianity which had been sung for the last thousand years." Except for throwing the rascals out, she offered few remedies to clean up government and business, only warning that if reform did not happen, revolution could result.

As Woodhull ended the lecture the applause was deafening, reminiscent of rowdy political conventions; no one was in the mood to quiet down. When Woodhull bowed, she quickly declared the meeting adjourned, cutting off her sister's advertised speech. The audience clamored with shouts of "TENNIE!" But the disorder and shouting, along with Woodhull's abrupt adjournment, gave Tennie no chance to get to the stage.

In the winter of 1873 and the early days of 1874, Woodhull took this show on the road to the Midwest. Her daughter, Zula, was her warm-up act. Woodhull no doubt thought that a child reading a noncontroversial poem would have audience appeal, and newspapers generally did refer to Zula favorably. Blood introduced mother and daughter. If Tennie was present, newspapers did not record any speeches by her.

Woodhull combined her speeches on the ills of government, corporate America, and organized Christianity with frank talk about the "social question," mainly parental neglect in sexual matters. Papers throughout the country wrote how shocked audiences were that Woodhull was not the "coarse and rude" woman they had expected from what they had read about her. She still astounded many, to be sure, when "she launched hot thunderbolts at the hypocrisies of priests, churches and law-makers." Recognizing that Woodhull was "telling the truth" but "telling it far in advance of the readiness of the people to act upon it," the *Republican* of Sparta, Wisconsin, nonetheless praised her for her courage, as did many other newspapers that championed free speech, although "we cannot subscribe to her doctrine." This reporter had heard Stanton, Anthony, and Anna Dickinson, "but none of these can approach Mrs. Woodhull in the eloquence and the power of her oratory."

Then, at one of her lectures, Woodhull announced that she must race back to New York. Challis's libel suit was finally being tried.

Despite depression woes, or perhaps because of them, an overflowing crowd, many no doubt unemployed and seeking entertainment, mobbed the courtroom during the sisters' eight-day trial in March 1874.

"The defense was conducted in magnificent style by Charlie Brooke," remembered Benjamin Tucker, the young anarchist who claimed to have lost his virginity to Victoria and remained part of the Claflin family entourage. He took Victoria twice to Brooke's home office for evening consultations as he prepped her for the courtroom. Brooke was a "dashing young Irish lawyer, who after making a reputation in Philadelphia, had transferred his practice to New York under the wing of Tammany Hall."

When the sisters eagerly arrived in court, they learned that one of their bondsmen had withdrawn his security. After the first day of trial, without time to gather bail, they and Blood were once again locked up in the dank Tombs. Brooke gained sympathy when he argued that this showed "palpable oppression" and that he needed his clients free for consultation. The judge denied his request. After their second day locked up, there could be no mistaking the judge's partisanship. When Brooke asked that bail be reduced, the judge refused.

After three nights in the Tombs, one of New York's worst, rat-infested jails, Woodhull was called to testify. Stunned by her prison stay, she nervously burst into tears on the stand. She swore to the truth of the entire article and said she had published it to show that if women were ostracized or rebuked for their behavior, men should be as well. Loud applause bolstered her and angered the judge, who tried to gavel them down several times before the crowd quieted. It was imperative to argue, as Brooke did, that the article's facts were true and therefore not libelous. The sisters were extremely worried; many who had sworn they saw Challis with several women at the masked French Ball had run for cover and could not be found to testify. However, Brooke was able to establish that Challis had been at the bawdy ball, drinking wine in a box with several women.

Brooke needed to show that Challis was hardly the upright citizen his categorical denials purported him to be. Just as attorney Howe had tried in earlier court sessions, Brooke had to convince the jury that Challis was close enough to Tennie that she might have asked for money for her lecture, not as blackmail but as a gift from a rich friend. To that end, Meg Miles, the older Claflin sister, took the stand and was asked if Challis had come to the Woodhull residence so intoxicated that the family put him to bed, where he vomited on the bed and floor. The court ruled out the question, so that Miles was not able to answer. Displaying Claflin wiles, Miles passed by the jurors after her testimony and declared in a voice loud enough for them to hear: "I had to wipe up the vomit."

Tennie swore on the stand that a letter with her signature asking for $200 for her lecture was genuine, but the other—which Challis vowed was a blackmail threat accompanying a page of her article—was a forgery, or "at the least was not sent by her nor by her authority."

On the eighth day of the trial, as the judge instructed the jury, the nervous sisters stared intensely at the white males. While "the punishment for libel was comparatively trifling," said the judge, he "considered that the present case…was of very great importance." His instructions were dire regarding the sisters' contention that their masked ball article had been written for the worthy cause of exposing hypocrisy. The judge told the jury that there was no way that its being published with "good motives" was a justifiable argument. After seven hours, the jury returned, still puzzled about the "good motives" argument. The judge practically ordered them to convict: "It would be absurd," he said, to judge that something is "not libelous because a person causing it to be published thought he had good motives." The still-deliberating jurors were locked up for the night.

The next morning, a large crowd waited for the verdict. The exhausted sisters and Blood, friends, and family whispered anxiously. The jury filed in to a breathlessly silent courtroom. The sisters stared at the jurors.

"How say you: do you find the prisoners guilty or not guilty?" asked the clerk.

The foreman answered in a clear voice heard throughout the room: "Not guilty."

The crowd leapt up, and tumultuous applause continued for several minutes while court officers yelled for silence in one of the most extraordinary scenes ever enacted within that courtroom. After all the waiting, the fear in response to the judge's instructions, the public displays of fortitude, the nights in jail, the destitution, the sisters broke down completely, sobbing so hard that they could not speak for several minutes. "Blood appeared scarcely less agitated." The judge was not pleased. It was the "most outrageous verdict ever recorded," he sputtered. "It is shameful and infamous, and I am ashamed of the jury who rendered such a verdict." The jurors agreed, stating they had been loath to vote for acquittal but had reasonable doubt.

The *Brooklyn Eagle* had assumed the sisters would be convicted, and it lashed out at "these notorious women" who "seem to have reached the end of their crazy career." The lesson was that "sufferings will ever attend the woman that unsexes herself." But the sisters had won, and continued to say and write more about the famous preacher whom the *Brooklyn Eagle* had so assiduously befriended.

After the trial, Victoria and Tennie rented a floor, furnished, in a house on the East Side, where they lived with Byron and Zula; somehow Colonel Blood and feisty Annie also coexisted in this dwelling. At this point Buck was not around, but his absence went unexplained, and there was no indication of where he was. The six lived in a condition of bohemian disorder.

During hot weather, one of the family members routinely carried a large pitcher to a Third Avenue tavern to fill it with beer. Callers were few; friends had deserted them.

At that time, publishing the paper was a struggle. They begged for donations in each issue. George Blood, Colonel Blood's loyal brother, did some of the writing along with Blood and also undertook the care of Byron. A professor, Robert W. Hume, a "stout and mild-mannered Scot," wrote editorials on economics. Although the sisters were briefed on what was running in the paper, Benjamin Tucker, who was present during these days, contended, "Not once did I ever see Victoria have a pen or pencil in her hand. Tennie could scrawl a page or two, but on serious subjects nothing in the least worthy of attention." However, they were clear advocates of the free love position and women's issues. The ability for extemporaneous speech lifted their thoughts with eloquence, but their court ordeals and prison sentences had drained that spark from both.

Suddenly, Victoria suggested a vacation in Europe for the entire brood, a trip that raised great suspicion that Beecher had paid them to leave the country just as the Tilton-Beecher scandal was exploding again. Victoria issued a notice that Beecher had nothing to do with the trip. With their having little money, however, it was hard to believe they were paying their own way. Tucker said, "Tennie, who was always chosen for such errands...visited the various steamship offices to ask reduced rates for the trip as journalists, and finally succeeded in engaging passage...at half the regular fare" for him, Blood, the sisters, Annie, and Zula. However they worked it, the sisters were out of the country in July 1874, when the Beecher fireworks began in earnest.

CHAPTER TWENTY

The Star Chamber

Beecher was finally frightened deep in his soul, and the most famous reverend was collapsing. His friend Wilkeson, in his foolish public ploy to wreck Bowen, had done Beecher incredible harm the previous May by exposing the tripartite agreement and Tilton's revelations. The follow-up meeting instigated by Bowen with the sisters had also been a publicity disaster for Beecher and Plymouth Church. The press and public clamored for explanations. Something was decidedly sour about the tripartite agreement, cried newspapers. Beecher "hugs to his breast the two men who have pronounced him the ravishers" of their wives, while Bowen and Tilton, "self proclaimed cowards...promise never to allude to his crimes again...Verily a sweet-savored trio, this."

Hoping to end this "filth," church leaders expelled Tilton from the church for "slandering" Beecher. Then, in April 1874, a preacher friend of Beecher's lit everything on fire by delivering a parable aimed at Tilton using the words *knave* and *dog*. Tilton finally went public, accusing Beecher of committing an unspeakable "offense" and demanding that Beecher clear his, Tilton's, name.

In the summer of 1874 the desperate but ingenious Beecher staged an investigation loaded with six handpicked church leaders who would surely clear him of this volcano of erupting gossip. Tilton, Stanton, and many others called this investigation a "star chamber," a reference to the sixteenth-century English court that meted out brutal punishment without a right of appeal or juries.

Beecher's friends, on the other hand, saluted the public venting. Months before, Mark Twain had written a friend, "I think the silence of the Beechers is a hundred fold more of an obscene publication than that of the Woodhulls and the sad silence is a thousand-fold more potent in convincing people of the truth of that scandal than the evidence of fifty Woodhulls could be." A concerned Twain wrote, "the nation will gradually form itself into the verdict that there is *some* fire somewhere in all this smoke of scandal."

The church tribunal gathered in secret in July, but it was a leaky crew: six clergymen and two of Beecher's counselors fed details to newspapers, read by a hungry public across the nation. No fiction or theatrical production could match the racy tales of illicit sex and mangled marriage involving the Great Preacher, handsome Tilton, and "Lib," his dark-eyed, petite wife. "This most marvelous of human dramas" was, of course, compared to Hawthorne's *The Scarlet Letter*, written in 1850, but one paper judged this real story as "greater in plot, development and effect." Victorian readers had never seen anything like this verbal slugfest between a Good Christian Woman and her husband. Elizabeth portrayed Tilton as insanely jealous as Othello and as manipulative as Svengali.

Elizabeth was now living with friends of Beecher's and had so joined his side that Benjamin Tracy, the preacher's lawyer with a cutthroat reputation, coached her on her testimony. She dutifully gave the church committee rich fodder: Tilton was a vain and cruel narcissist, so insanely jealous that he would lock her in a room for hours while accusing her of infidelity "with one and another, and with Mr. Beecher particularly...many times, he had said that he did not know whom his children belonged to."

Elizabeth was spilling her venom to millions of spellbound readers. Tilton's "morbid jealousy" came at a time he was "giving up his religious faith," in 1870. He "laid the cornerstone of free love" in their house; it was a "godless" atmosphere, "impure for my children." She said Tilton confessed to having affairs with "several" women and that "he wished me to understand that...if he desired the gratification...he would do it." He mocked her in the presence of his women's rights friends and told her at one gathering, "'I would give $500 if you were not by my side,' meaning that I was so insignificant that he was ashamed of me." Her friendship with Beecher grew: "With Mr. Beecher I had a sort of consciousness of being more; he appreciated me as Theodore did not."

Elizabeth said Tilton had a mesmerizing evil power over her: "I never had any will around him." She concluded: "I affirm myself before God to be innocent of the crimes laid upon me; that never have I been guilty of adultery with Henry Ward Beecher in thought or deed." Nor had the pastor ever offered her an "indecorous or improper proposal."

Tilton fashioned himself as noble; concern for his family had kept him from telling the truth. Now, because Beecher has publicly affected "ignorance and innocence," and Elizabeth, "lately my wife" now sides with Beecher in "denying the truth," he had no obligation to remain silent. He dumped 208 letters of passionate devotion between him and his wife into the pages of the *Chicago Tribune* to show he was not the monster Elizabeth depicted. Newspapers around the country picked them up. A riveted public now read breathless love letters written by his wife to Tilton while he was gone for weeks lecturing: "Ah, did man ever love so grandly as my Beloved?" she gushed. She loved Theodore "with the fervency of my whole being." "My beloved...my waking thoughts last night were of you. My rising thoughts this morning were of you. I bless you; I honor you; I love you." Tilton noted that the date of this last letter, January 28, 1868—was "only a few months before her loss of honor."

Many mainstream papers belted Tilton for "parading before the world these sacred treasures of wifely affection" to "enhance the picture he would paint of his own magnanimous moral beauty." They eagerly printed them, however. The letters, including Tilton's sending his wife endless affection, proved that the couple had at one time been in love and gave some credence to Tilton's case that Beecher had wrecked a loving marriage. In fact, Elizabeth's testimony slaughtered her husband to such a degree that, in the face of this demonstrated past devotion, it seemed exaggerated for Beecher's sake. Elizabeth told the committee, "The implication that the harmony of our house was unbroken" until Beecher became a frequent visitor "is a lamentable satire." Tilton "lived to crush out Beecher."

Heading into the Plymouth investigation, the sixty-one-year-old Beecher cutely said that his statement would show he had "not been a bad boy." In his testimony, he attacked Woodhull and Tilton and cast himself as an innocent avuncular figure, beloved by the Tilton children. He was only giving Elizabeth "strength and encouraging her" at a time when Tilton was "sliding into dangerous associations, and liable to be ruined by unexampled self-conceit." Woodhull—who had become involved in Beecher and Theodore Tilton's efforts to silence the scandal after threatening that she would tell all—was attacked by Beecher. Tilton's adoration of her—as "priest of her strange cause"—precipitated Tilton's fall from grace, making him "bankrupt in reputation, in occupation and in resources." Beecher ignored the fact that Tilton lost the support of Beecher's political and religious center well before he met Woodhull.

Beecher blamed everyone but himself. He had once "loved him [Tilton] much," but he now termed Tilton a disloyal liar, encased in "insatiable egotism," a man who "starves for want of flattery." Elizabeth Tilton was not spared, despite her earnest demolition of her husband. The preacher polished her off as a lovesick fool, blaming himself only for "want of prudence and foresight" when she "thrust her affections upon me unsought." Beecher admitted that he had promised Tilton "not to betray his wife," but "I meant only that I would not betray the excessive affection, which I had been told, she had conceived for me and had confessed to him. It certainly did not refer to adultery." Tilton, in turn, vowed that Beecher had aggressively pursued his wife. Beecher's "criminal intercourse" had happened only "after long moral resistance by her."

Although Woodhull was among the first, many other observers later asked if Beecher was so innocent, why did he go to tortuous lengths for four years to cover up "nothing"—rather than stoutly deny the charges? Now forced to admit his part in the cover-up, Beecher testified that his desire to keep a lid on the scandal was because a famous man of the cloth could be wrecked even by false gossip. "The great interests, which were entirely dependent on me, the church, which I had built," the book he was writing, his family, his good name—everything—"seemed imperiled. It seemed to me that my life work was to end abruptly and in disaster."

This excuse sounded hollow to many who heard his lawyers consistently declare that Beecher's sanctified and unblemished past proved his innocence. If that was the case, surely this lofty paragon could immediately and successfully have squelched the "scurrilous" gossip of a "prostitute"—as his lawyers called Woodhull—and a vengeful husband. However, most major papers rushed to denigrate Tilton and Woodhull and to heap praise on Beecher. He was the "victim of a monstrous conspiracy," wrote one paper, typical of the exoneration by the press.

Beecher's lawyers grilled Tilton endlessly about his relationship with Woodhull. Backpedaling as fast as he could, he denied having been intimate with her or having told her details for the *Weekly* scandal story. But his wife dropped another gem for Beecher's defense. Elizabeth said she believed her husband was "the author" of "the shameless slanders against Mr. Beecher," in collusion with Woodhull, a woman of "that class," whom she refused to allow in her home on the Sabbath.

During the Plymouth Church investigation, an article for the *Chicago Times*, devastating to Tilton's case, put him in bed with Woodhull: "He was my devoted lover for more than half a year...A woman who could not love Theodore Tilton, especially in reciprocation of a generous, impulsive, overwhelming affection such as he is capable of bestowing, must be indeed dead to all the sweeter impulses of our nature...for three months we were hardly out of each other's sight...he slept every night for three months in my arms." Woodhull always swore that this conversation never happened, but writers nonetheless have passed it down as truth for more than a century. The veracity of the story is questionable because of crucial discrepancies. The alleged interview was two years old. Why was the paper just now publishing this explosive story, linking it to the church investigation? Two years before, such an interview would have been red-hot copy; the *Weekly* Beecher article was electrifying the country at that time, and the sisters' trek to Ludlow Street Jail would have ensured a large readership. So why was it not printed then, when it would have caused a sensation? The author of the piece wrote that he had talked to Wood-hull just before the sisters went to jail in 1872. He signed himself simply "Historian," gave no explanation for the two-year delay, and said, "I give you the interview substantially as it occurred, from notes recorded at the time." Among other errors, he described Victoria and Tennie as living in a palatial mansion while they were in fact hard-luck boarders at their sister's home. Suspicion rises at a mystifying description of Tennie—something never seen in any other public or private accounts, never remarked upon by reporters covering her speeches, never mentioned by close friends: she lisped. As she supposedly came into the room to break up the interview, "Historian" quoted her thus: "Thister Vic., have you tholen ofth here by yourthelfths for the whole evening?"

Also, it hardly seems that Woodhull would have spoken so rapturously of Tilton in the fall of 1872. Six months before, she had blasted Tilton for rejecting her presidential candidacy and repudiating universal suffrage to campaign for Greeley's misbegotten alignment with Democratic Southern sympathizers. They had parted angrily and forever.

Beecher's lawyers, however, crowed at this morsel, a supreme example of a free-loving Tilton. The term *free love* was employed throughout the Beecher scandal as the overarching destroyer of marriages, vilified in newspapers, testimonies, and cross-examinations. Beecher's lawyer, Benjamin Tracy, grilled Tilton for four days as to whether he had committed adultery with free lover Woodhull or any other women. Tilton refused to answer, and shot back to Tracy, "Have you ever committed adultery?" Tracy said he was not charging his wife with it. Tilton said he would accept the word of his wife on this matter but that it was none of the business of men defending Beecher. Using the *Chicago Times* piece as a springboard, Tracy asked if Tilton had ever lived with Woodhull. "I never lived with her," he replied. Asked if his wife had been told he lived with

Woodhull, Tilton said, "I never heard about it until now. I saw something about it the day before yesterday in a salacious paper."

"The *Chicago Times*?"

"Yes."

Tilton testified that he spent only one night at Woodhull's mansion, but on a couch, while finishing his biography of her. Victoria's esteem for Tilton had long curdled by 1874; nonetheless, she declared the same in print, perhaps because she desired to see Beecher convicted. It was a complete repudiation of "he slept every night for three months in my arms."

Woodhull was a "total stranger to me," said Tilton, until they met after she had published the "concubinage" threat. He swore that he sought Woodhull's "goodwill" only to keep her from publishing her "grossly distorted" story and from writing anything that would harm him or his family. Tilton's wife "had a violent feeling against her. She had a woman's instinct that Mrs. Woodhull was not safe," he ruefully testified.

Elizabeth Tilton stuck to her claim of innocence, and said Stanton had misrepresented the 1870 confession of her, Mrs. Tilton's, adultery. She vowed that she had not confessed, only that her husband had accused her of it. Stanton told the press that Elizabeth was lying, and said she had "not the slightest" doubt that Elizabeth had confessed to Susan Anthony, "Susan always speaks the truth."

"This was a confession of a criminal intimacy with Beecher?" asked a reporter. "Yes," Stanton replied, "criminal is the word as generally understood. Mrs. Tilton did not look upon it that way."

Stanton's wrath was reserved for Beecher and his church committee, which were determined "to impeach the integrity of every witness against him." Beecher's team produced Bessie Turner, a young former servant in the Tilton home, who told lurid tales of being sexually accosted by Tilton. Bessie had been packed off to a school out west because she knew too much about Beecher's sojourns at the Tilton home when Tilton was away, which terrified Beecher. The preacher professed to have scant knowledge of Bessie's departure from New York and her schooling, but Moulton's records proved Beecher had financially supported Bessie's schooling. Now she was back to testify for him, painting Tilton as black as possible.

Bessie even tried to tar Tilton's suffragist friends; the elderly Stanton played chess with Tilton until 3:00 a.m.; stern Susan B. Anthony was "sitting on his [Tilton's] lap on one occasion and she jumped up pretty quick." Stanton slammed Turner as a lying "self-confessed tool for whomsoever might choose to use her." Pursued by reporters, Anthony joked, "Well, that was my only lapse from rigorous virtue. All the men had declared that Susan was so sour and I thought I could show them that I could sit on a young man's knee just like any foolish girl." When the reporter pressed her about the scandal, Anthony attacked men in general and Beecher in particular. "When a woman gives herself to a man...he will trample her into the dirt to serve his own ends...Old Adam said 'The woman tempted me and I did eat.' Beecher says, 'The woman tempted me and I did not eat.' Either way the woman gets blamed."

The *New York Herald* denounced the committee for allowing Bessie's testimony. "Whose reputation is safe...when even Miss Anthony cannot escape suspicion...crush Theodore with your scorn, if you wish, but oh! spare us the reputation of Susan."

As the church tribunal continued, no suffragist voice of protest was louder than Stanton's. "What a holocaust of womanhood we have had in this investigation!" she declared in a long letter in the *Chicago Tribune.* "What a football the committee, the lawyers, Mrs. Beecher, and her husband, have made of Elizabeth R. Tilton!" She mockingly termed Beecher "The Great Preacher," who, dismissing Elizabeth "like a wilted flower...casts her aside and tells the world 'she thrust her affections upon him unsought'—the crowning perfidy." NWSA members, "in common with the rest of the world...heard and repeated the scandal," and for that, Beecher "dubs them 'human hyenas' and 'free lovers.'" Isabella Beecher was "presented as 'insane,' 'deluded' and 'weak-minded.'" Stanton did not mention talk of the latter's "unnatural" attraction to Woodhull, a lesbian inference that Beecher allowed his lawyer to make about his own sister.

Stanton also defended Tilton and Frank Moulton, the urbane merchant who had acted as mediator. Moulton had balked at spilling all to the church committee "in a last despairing effort for peace." For this, pro-Beecher newspapers called him a coward. Beecher had once called Moulton a treasure "sent by God," but now denounced him as a liar, blackmailer, and conspirator. Moulton, a sudden celebrity, proved a feisty adversary, vowing to restore his blackened name. A fastidious fact keeper and an honest man, Moulton had a mile-long memory of his meetings with Beecher and a huge leather satchel full of letters and documents. He dumped his load of incriminating evidence into the newspapers, and readers devoured sensational letters that did great damage to Beecher. So, when a character in a popular New York play delivered the line "What should I do about the letters?" the crowd howled as a joker in the audience shouted, "Give them to Moulton!"

Tilton and Moulton were "not the base, unreliable men represented in Mr. Beecher's statement," wrote Stanton. It was a travesty, she said, that as soon as Moulton "opened his mouth to tell the whole truth, he became a blackmailer and conspirator" and that "a refined gentleman and scholar like Theodore Tilton" could "become the target for the jibes and jeers of the nation, without one authenticated accusation of vice."

Yet Stanton acknowledged that even "in the face of facts...justice is not possible...[Beecher's] position will be maintained for him, as he is the soul and center" of financially greedy church leaders who would prop up their kingpin. "The whole investment hangs by the eyelids until Mr. Beecher is whitewashed."

Predictably, the Plymouth Church investigators decided on August 22, 1874, that Beecher was a victim of the "vicious and vengeful actions" of Moulton and Tilton. Elizabeth Tilton was guilty of pestering the innocent preacher with her "inordinate affection."

One limerick summed up a popular view:

Said Beecher, "the Voice of the Nation
Is Loud for an Investigation
So I say 'find me six friends'

Who are pledged to my ends
And from them get a full vindication."

Tilton immediately charged Beecher with alienating his wife's affections. Finally the open trial that people had clamored for was on the docket, scheduled for four and a half months later, in January 1875.

CHAPTER TWENTY-ONE

Wickedness in High Places

Few, if any, Americans could resist the sensational trial that began in January 1875. Manhattan ferries churning through the icy East River to Brooklyn were jammed with spectators hoping to see the greatest show on earth: Step right up! A churchgoing matron swearing on the Bible that the Great Preacher threatened to kill himself with poison! Beecher's frantic cover-up with two men he now calls liars and blackmailers! Former servants swearing that Tilton spent nights with Victoria Woodhull! Piles of incriminating letters! Husband sees reverend touching his wife's ankle! It was better than P. T. Barnum's circus.

Much of the case had been spelled out that past summer in the farcical investigation by the Plymouth Church, but now there was a chance to see the characters before their eyes, in a real trial in the City Court of Brooklyn. The courtroom seated three hundred, but the standing-room crush brought the number to a suffocating five hundred. The trial lasted six months. During the winter, spectators brought blankets to stay warm in the frigid courtroom. In the summer, some fainted in sweltering heat. When the East River froze, ferries could not navigate, stranding counsel and witnesses in Manhattan and halting the trial.

Officials issued tickets, which were often scalped for five dollars apiece. As many as three thousand people a day were turned away, to the delight of neighboring saloon owners. The well-heeled arrived in carriages lined up as if in front of an opera house, while working-class men trudged on foot. With many New York laborers still unemployed following the Panic of 1873, they ruled the upstairs gallery in rowdy disorder, spitting peanut shells and tobacco juice on the floor, laughing, and applauding as if at a Bowery saloon performance. Politicians, diplomats, bankers, and social leaders fought for grander seats below and, like the common folk, either brought lunches or purchased sandwiches from vendors; no one risked losing his seat at lunchtime. Opera glasses were sold for close-up viewing of the expressions of witnesses.

When Mark Twain appeared, the crowd shoved and ogled. A friend who accompanied Twain chuckled that many in the audience mistook him for the star witness, Frank Moulton, as both sported shocks of red hair hanging down their foreheads and large handlebar mustaches. It was "a good joke on Mark," who had disliked Moulton's looks "exceedingly." Under different circumstances the satirical friend of Beecher may have enjoyed Moulton's savoir faire: "He lived up to his reputation as a man of the world by discussing Beecher's adultery with what was described as 'the manner of a listless gentleman giving his verdict upon a novel brand of champagne.'" When asked if he had said Beecher was a "damned perjurer and a libertine," Moulton answered, "I don't know whether I told him he was a damned perjurer and a libertine. I may have told him he was a perjurer and a libertine, which he is."

The stale air of sweating crowds was partially perfumed by the large banks of flowers that daily covered Beecher's table. Like an Elizabethan duke warding off the plague, Beecher often pressed a small bouquet of violets to his nose. Tilton's fans one day presented him with large and elegant bouquets, putting him "upon a horticultural equality with Mr. Beecher, at last." Far more alone than Beecher, often contemplative, Tilton blushed at this attention.

The crush of reporters was unprecedented. European newspapers reported eagerly, if sometimes in baffled confusion. *Le Journal de Marseille* headlined L'AFFAIRE BEECHER-STITON, ET VICTORIA VODULL [*sic*]. The culprit was "Madame Breechertow," said to be "the mother of Uncle Tom."

Woodhull as Mrs. Satan (Courtesy of Library of Congress)

Image of Anthony and Stanton from a private collection in New York, cited in Mary Gabriel's *Notorious Victoria* (Alberti and Lowe Collection)

Illustration in Harriet Beecher Stowe's *My Wife and I* (American Antiquarian Society)

THE ADVANCED WOMAN OF THE PERIOD.

"'You go in for the emancipation of woman; but bless you, boy, you haven't the least idea what it means—not a bit of it, sonny, have you now? Confess?' she said, stroking my whiskers coaxingly."

Image of Tennessee Claflin in Fisk's pants and other derisive
depictions of her leading troops and riding a horse

A PLACE WHERE MEN AND WOMEN OF THE MOST DIVERSE STATIONS IN LIFE MAY MEET—IN FACT A REPUBLICAN COURT.

Depiction of Tennessee Claflin in a low-cut gown with champagne and insulting stereotypes of men from *Days' Doings*, July 22, 1872

Anthony Comstock
(Originally published in *Anthony Comstock, fighter: some impressions of a lifetime of adventure in conflict with the powers of evil* [1913] by Charles Gallaudet Trumbull)

John Biddulph Martin (From a private collection)

Tennessee Claflin, also known as Lady Cook, holding flowers and surrounded by adoring suffragettes (Courtesy of Library of Congress)

Tennessee Claflin
(Courtesy New York
Public Library)

Sir Francis and Lady Cook at Monserrate (Jane Brabyn Collection)

Victoria, Byron, and Zula in car at Norton Park
(Country Life Photo, Holland-Martin Family Archives)

Monserrate
(Gerald Luckhurst)

Norton Park with Victoria Woodhull and Zula Maud on the terrace
(Country Life Photo, Cite at Holland-Martin Family Archives)

In Atlanta, tavern arguments became so violent regarding Beecher's guilt or innocence that bar owners banned all discussion of the trial. Cartoons flooded newspapers; one pictured a man in a top hat stuffing his wife into a large bank vault. The caption read "one man in Brooklyn who was determined to find his wife at home when he returned from business." Newspaper coffers filled rapidly, with the New York *Graphic* selling as many as four hundred thousand copies of key printings.

Although Victoria Woodhull made but one brief appearance during the six-month trial, her name, reputation, and actions were "woven into the warp and woof" of the proceedings, and the word *prostitute* was flung at her in the opening remarks of Beecher's lawyer, Benjamin Tracy. As they had already shown in the Plymouth Committee sham investigation six months before, the main goal of Beecher's lawyers was to smear Tilton and Moulton—as blackmailers, liars, conspirators, and participants in all things nefarious, especially due to their relationship with Woodhull. Thus, they argued, Beecher had to be innocent of adultery with Elizabeth Tilton because nothing her libertine husband and friend said could be credible.

Although Tracy had warned the legal team that this tactic might backfire—that "painting Tilton black can't make Beecher white"—he nonetheless decided that Woodhull was his trump card. Tracy needed to show that Moulton, the avowed "heathen," had bonded with Tilton to attack Beecher in pursuit of revolting "new social theories" promulgated by "loose women," particularly Woodhull. Moulton and Tilton had compelled their own wives "to become the mere ministers to their lust," expounded Tracy. It was Moulton, not Tilton, who sent "his wife to bring home in a carriage the most notorious prostitute the world has ever known." Emma Moulton's lips "were smurched [*sic*] by the filthy kiss of Victoria Woodhull." Although the *Brooklyn Eagle*, New York *Sun*, *World*, and *Herald* all quoted the words *prostitute* and *filthy kiss*, the final printed text sanitized the phrase. Instead, Woodhull became the "most notorious *preacher and practitioner of free love*," not a "prostitute." The

Brooklyn Eagle had received advance copies containing the words *prostitute* and *filthy kiss*, and dispersed them to other papers that used this version. Other newspapers that were not privy to the advance copy used the final version with the words *prostitute* and *filthy kiss* expunged.

Woodhull excoriated Tracy in the *Weekly*, then took on the embarrassed lawyer in person. Subpoenaed by Beecher's lawyers to produce private (and innocuous) letters at the trial, Woodhull went unwillingly. Tracy came forward and began an apology for his prostitute reference.

"I shall accept no apology from you, sir," said Woodhull. "The only one that you could make should be made as publicly as was the insult that you offered."

"But," protested Tracy, "I knew of you only from what I had read in the newspapers..."

"That will do, sir! I wish to hear no more. You grossly maligned me without cause, and I can accept no apology." She turned her back on him, leaving the voluble Tracy speechless for once.

This one appearance of the infamous Woodhull created a sensation. Many rose to their feet to gawk. Counsels on both sides swiveled in their chairs to stare. Jurymen whispered to one another, casting curious glances at her. As she pushed through the crowded aisles, Woodhull appeared to shrink from the universal notice she had attracted. She had been ordered to turn over letters in her possession. She bowed and addressed Judge Neilson. "Your honor... they are letters, which are entirely creditable to myself as well as the gentleman who wrote them." She spoke of having been "imprisoned several times for the publication of this scandal. During that time my office was ransacked, and all my private letters and papers taken away. I have reason to believe that some of my letters are in the hands of the defense, as well as of the prosecution."

Woodhull opened her purse and turned over the letters. As the lawyers pored over them, in obvious disappointment, she waited in a chair. Tilton "pursed his lips and peered at Victoria in an inquiring way as though he was puzzled to see her in the courtroom at all." At one point Woodhull and Tilton "looked steadfastly at each other for nearly a minute, and

Victoria's face flushed slowly but vividly." In another account, "Mr. Tilton turned his face toward Mrs. Woodhull and watched her intently with an anxious, half despairing look." All reporters searched Eunice Beecher's face. "Insensibly her mouth closed firmly as she surveyed the woman... and then her lips curled and a bright glitter grew in her eyes." When Woodhull was excused, she quickly strode through the crowd.

A new dilemma—the presence of women in the courtroom—had emerged for the all-male jurors, counselors, and the frowning judge. Several women were "listening eagerly to words that no woman should hear without a blush," declared the disapproving (Mobile) *Alabama Register*. Beecher's lawyers, however, needed to shore up their client with these respectable women from Beecher's church. Some reporters felt that Eunice Beecher's delicate ears should not be subjected to such words as *sexual intercourse*, but she was the prize sideshow for Beecher's lawyers—a steadfast, daily reminder of a faithful wife, seated in an oak chair, her snow-white hair surrounding her grim, thin-lipped face.

When Elizabeth Tilton arrived on the second day, the crowd craned their necks to see. Tilton looked nervously at the door as his wife entered wearing a black silk dress, a dark velvet cloak, and a black velvet hat ornamented by an ostrich feather. Removing her veil, she glanced at her husband for a moment. Eunice Beecher pointedly walked over to Elizabeth Tilton in a show of solidarity. As spectators gawked, the wife and the alleged adulteress talked congenially. At other times, Beecher, who kibitzed easily with lawyers on both sides and greeted spectators with smiles, boldly walked his wife over for a chat with Mrs. Tilton.

Spectators and reporters warmed to soft-eyed, petite Elizabeth, the perfect Christian woman who would not cause any man trouble unless he deserved it. Yet they were more intrigued by a puzzling specimen of a good Christian matron. A member of Beecher's church since age sixteen, Emma related that she could not bear to attend church ever since her favorite minister had confessed to her his adultery.

More than any witness, Emma presented an unwaveringly impressive denunciation of Beecher. Despite the attempt to tar Tilton with his Wood-hull association, the heart of the matter centered on damaging actions and letters Beecher had written. Emma recounted a meeting with the distraught preacher, whom she repeatedly vowed had confessed to her his adultery with Lib Tilton and then threatened suicide, which enforced the concept of his guilt. In fact, her story of Beecher's unfettered morbidity was similar to the hysterical meeting Woodhull had described two years before, in which the preacher knelt on her sofa, tears streaming down his face, and begged her not to ruin him. But Victoria was a dreadful free lover peddling "gossip," while Emma was a good Christian. So the whole courtroom listened in respectful, jaw-dropping silence.

Under cross-examination, Emma Moulton never flinched: "[H]e told me very positively that he should take his life and I believed him when he said so." She said Beecher told her, "I have a powder at home on my library table which I have prepared, which I shall take, and shall sink quietly off as if going to sleep without a struggle." She testified that Beecher came to her in June 1873, following the exposure of the tripartite agreement, sobbing that he was utterly without hope and relayed his suicidal plans.

Everything Emma Moulton said was "pure invention," Beecher countered, but Tilton's lawyers showed that just days before this alleged meeting, Beecher had written that Emma was "noble...one of God's comforters." Why would this noble woman tell lies? It made no sense. In this letter praising Emma Moulton, Beecher had also hinted at suicide: "I have a strong feeling...that I am spending my last Sunday and preaching my last sermon."

In one correspondence, famously tagged the "Ragged Edge Letter," written in 1872, Beecher had written that "to live on the ragged edge of anxiety, remorse, fear, and despair, and yet to put on all the appearance of serenity and happiness, cannot be endured much longer." He wrote that Tilton had begged him "with the utmost earnestness and solemnity not to betray his wife, nor leave his children to a blight." Asked the *Times,* "Supposing Mr. Beecher to be innocent how could he have betrayed Tilton's wife? What was there to reveal?" William Fullerton, one of the best trial lawyers in New York and head of Tilton's legal team, set a trap for the unwary Beecher, who had stated that such written agonies were due to his fear of apoplexy attacks. He had denied having suicidal thoughts or possessing poison powder. Tilton's lawyers had to show the opposite: that Beecher's "remorse" and "fear" and suicidal thoughts were tied to a dreadful act of adultery with Elizabeth Tilton. Fullerton let Beecher expound on what he stated were recurring attacks of apoplexy, then triumphantly whipped out for exhibit a policy of Beecher's life insurance. Beecher was in full health, the policy stated, and had "no tendencies whatever toward ailment or disease of any kind." The *New York Herald* editorialized, "Here was contrast of fiction and fact that was most striking."

Attitudes in the press changed sharply after a stumbling Beecher took the stand for several days in April. He resorted nearly nine hundred times to phrases of "uncertainty, forgetfulness, or evasion," according to one source. His temporary amnesia included not remembering the term *nest hiding*, which he had coined in his novel, *Norwood*, and which Elizabeth Tilton had used as an expression for secret meetings in a letter to him.

The conservative *New York Times*, which would have given the benefit of the doubt to a famous man of the cloth against a free-loving Tilton, thundered, "Every theory advanced by Mr. Beecher during the trial is expressly contradicted by his own former admissions and letters." Other papers were tougher: "Beecher penned his own condemnation" (*St. Paul Dispatch*); "He is a hypocrite and a criminal of the first water" (*Petersburg* [Virginia] *News*); Beecher has fallen "beyond the hope of resurrection" (*Dayton* [Ohio] *Journal*); "He is as guilty a man as walks the earth" (*Bloomington* [Illinois] *Pantagraph*). The sisters happily reprinted these opinions in the *Weekly*. Even the president of the *Brooklyn Eagle* had had enough of his paper's sycophantic coverage and yelled at his editor that his coverage was making the paper look ridiculous "in the eyes of every man of sense." Crowed the *New York Times*, "It is a remarkable fact that yesterday afternoon's issue of the *Eagle* did not contain a word that might be construed in favor of Mr. Beecher or adverse to Mr. Tilton."

Central to this disbelief were the "Five Memorable Days" that set the entire scandal in motion. After listening to Beecher's response to questions about these days, the *New York Times* editorialized that Beecher was guilty of perjury and probably adultery. The Five Memorable Days began the day after Christmas in 1870 and ended on New Year's Day. On Monday, December 26, 1870, a stewing, cuckolded Tilton sent his letter to Beecher demanding that he immediately quit the church "for reasons you explicitly understand." Three days later, Thursday, December 29, Elizabeth wrote an adultery confession. She testified that her husband forced her to write it. The next day, December 30, hearing of the adultery confession, Beecher immediately slogged through a snowstorm to Elizabeth in her sick bed and forced her to "retract her charge." The next day, Saturday, New Year's Eve, Frank Moulton went to Beecher's house and demanded he hand over the forced retraction. Beecher handed it over, stating at the trial that Moulton had threatened him with a pistol. Tilton's lawyers caught him in this lie by producing an adulatory "Dear Friend" letter Beecher wrote to Moulton just weeks after Moulton had supposedly threatened him at gunpoint.

The last of the Five Memorable Days, Sunday, New Year's Day 1871, was the clincher. Beecher dictated his damaging "Letter of Contrition" to Moulton: "I ask through you, Theodore Tilton's forgiveness and I humble myself before Theodore Tilton as before my God." Tilton "would have been a better man in my circumstances than I have been under the circumstances."

Why on earth would Beecher have begged forgiveness and humbled himself before a man who had just called him an adulterer? Why would Tilton have been a "better man" than Beecher had been? Beecher blamed Moulton; he had distorted what Beecher had dictated to him. Under stiff cross-examination, Beecher weakly admitted that Moulton had "substantially" recorded his views. Why, asked critics, would Beecher have been so contrite if he was so innocent? Even his counselor said any man would be justified in "burying a knife in Tilton's heart" at an accusation of adultery. And why was he dictating thoughts to Moulton, a man who had threatened him with a pistol? And calling him a dear friend?

Beecher's reasons for such overwrought repentance were flimsy at best. One, he had guided Elizabeth regarding a separation from Tilton, and two, he had backed Bowen's desire to fire Tilton. Few could understand his possibly begging Tilton's forgiveness for these reasons. The *Times* concluded that Beecher "has told a dozen different stories in explanation of his letters and conduct—and every one of them crushes the other."

Throughout the trial, Woodhull was used as a smokescreen to hide the feebleness of Beecher's testimony and to damage Tilton. In his testimony, Tilton on occasion showed dry humor. When asked repeatedly about their trip to Coney Island and whether he had been bathing with Woodhull, he replied to laughter, "[N]o sir, I was never in the water with her, except in the hot water in which I have been put these last few years." Moulton was grilled repeatedly about Woodhull and his friendship with her. Beecher's lawyers produced a letter of Tilton's urging a friend and his wife to read his biography of Woodhull, gushing that it "praises and rates Victoria on too low, rather than too high a scale." The defense's purpose was to show that Tilton was proud of his biography and had written it "*con amore*," not as "a matter of compulsion to keep the woman's nails from the throat of Mr. Beecher." One of Tilton's lawyers, William Beach, returned to Tracy's opening remarks calling Woodhull a prostitute. Slamming Tracy as governed by a "loose principle, and by a looser morality," Beach berated Beecher's lawyer for smearing Moulton as a friend of "prostitutes." Beach did nothing to cast Woodhull in a respectable light; Moulton had met with her only "for the sake of the honor of the church and the good of society" and would not "dream of associating with prostitutes for his own pleasure!"

So once again in this trial she was called a prostitute. Since neither side dared call her to the stand, she was forced to defend herself in the *Weekly* and the *New York Herald*. Woodhull fumed when a former servant testified that Tilton was in Woodhull's office in the fall of 1872, treating her in a "lover like" manner and telling her that they could get $100,000 in blackmail from church leaders to scuttle the Beecher scandal issue.

Woodhull countered in the *Herald* that the servant had described an office the sisters did not occupy in 1872, that there was no talk of bribes or a "lover like" tableau, as she had not seen Tilton in six months at that time. (Under cross-examination, the servant could not remember even the seasons in which incidents allegedly occurred.) When servants testified that Tilton had slept over, Woodhull countered with specific details; her family filled the rooms, there was "no spare room," and the house did not even contain the "sofa-lounge" Tilton allegedly slept on.

Everyone knew, wrote Woodhull, "I am my own mistress…and I would not lie either for myself or for anybody else—that is if Mr. Tilton and I had occupied the same bed those two nights I would never deny it." Woodhull snapped that Beecher's defense was in dire straits if it had to resort to "supposed 'amorous glances' and 'tender embraces' and 'preparations for retiring at night.'"

The *Herald* remarked, "There is a charming frankness about this lady, who at least has the courage of her conviction." The paper clamored for her to take the stand: "In view of the charges she brings" against the servants, "she cannot well be left out of the case much longer." Beecher's terrified lawyers made sure she did not testify, except for the brief handing over of harmless letters. Had she been able to testify, her countering of the testimony of the servants would have been crucial for Tilton; if the servants were believed, their testimony would make him a perjurer.

Since she couldn't take the stand, Woodhull defended Tilton in a letter she wrote that was published in the *Herald*. "I owe Mr. Tilton a too great depth of gratitude," she wrote, to remain "silent when such testimony as this is offered." "No matter how inconsiderately he has treated himself—not me—in regard to his relations with me, I forgive him heartily all this intended harm, now that the defense are making use of those relations to crush him in this case."

Her magnanimous view was quickly smashed when the *Herald* next printed a letter Woodhull had intended to destroy. Written during the trial, in the white heat of anger, this furious letter had been impulsively put into type for the *Weekly*. Then, on "mature consideration," Woodhull had changed her mind. Obtained "through the treachery or carelessness of a third party," the letter was now splashed in the *Herald*. Tilton was very lucky that the public, not the jury, was reading this immensely damaging assault.

This letter was written after Tilton had one day during his testimony directly faced the jury and said, "I wish distinctly to say that my relationship with Mrs. Woodhull was a wrong one and a foolish one and I do not ask any man to defend me for it, but to blame me for it." Then he added, "I say here before God that Mr. Beecher is as much responsible for my connection with Mrs. Woodhull, as I am myself."

In the letter Woodhull regretted writing, she tore into Tilton. Hiding behind Beecher, he had resembled "a little schoolboy's sniveling—'He made me do it; if it hadn't been for him I shouldn't have done it.' To resort to such an escape, and to continue to pretend to retain any of the elements of manhood, ought to make him a laughing stock for every true woman...Mr. Tilton would make quite a man if he should live to grow up."

Woodhull ticked off "untruths" in his testimony. The most devastating, which lent credence to Beecher's defense that Tilton had acted out of malice, came close to saying that Tilton had helped with the publication of the Beecher scandal. "He would have consented to aid in its publication in a way that could have made Mr. Bowen responsible; 'If I should be made to appear as the authority for it, I could not live with Elizabeth afterward,' was his argument."

But Woodhull seemed most betrayed as a woman scorned. She came close to admitting that theirs had been a passionate love, and poured out her heartfelt anger like a lover's lament. She slashed at Tilton's "strenuous effort" to say their bond was "solely to suppress the scandal"; this was "utterly fallacious, utterly false, and has been concocted by Mr. Tilton." If he had only been with her to suppress a scandal he would not have been the confidant who would "bare his soul [to her] with all its imperfections as well as its beauties; he would not entrust her with his own inmost secrets...he would not entrust her with the means to ruin his reputation, his honor, his all, as he has done all this with me." She wrote that they had laughed at "foolish" women who fashioned he was in love with them. "Such things as I have recounted are not favors. They are bestowed only when and where the most powerful of all motives move men and women to venture everything, transforming the cool, cautious, calculating man into the hot-headed, inconsiderate lover."

So Elizabeth Tilton was not the only one shattered by a man's testimony, and Woodhull asked plaintively what she had ever done to make Tilton speak "as if I had been a contemptible creature?" She challenged him to produce a "single thing...This is the deepest infamy that can be cast upon any woman, and were you to live a thousand years and have a thousand lives, every one of which should be devoted to undoing the injury that you have wrought for me, you would still fail to wholly repair the wrong that I have suffered from your erratic course."

After this letter was published in the *Herald*, and widely publicized, Woodhull had the embarrassing chore of backtracking in a third letter the paper published. When she read Tilton's words denouncing his relationship with her, "they seared into my soul. I saw myself held up by him to the public gaze as a despicable thing, as an intriguing, treacherous, vulgar, and untruthful woman...it was in this feeling that I wrote the letter." Just before publishing the letter, Jesus, she wrote, had stayed her hand. She tried to convince readers that the laudatory first letter, meant to establish "the falsity" of her former servants, "was a wholly different affair from that of my personal feelings against Mr. Tilton." Now in her third letter, Woodhull was trying to explain how she could have written two such different letters about Tilton. The tempestuous second letter "contains nothing but the truth, made sharp and bitter, to be sure by an outraged woman's soul." She saw little contradiction. "One was prepared under a sense of personal injustice, the other under the spirit of impersonal justice, with self expunged."

At least Stanton was back in Woodhull's corner, chastising Tilton for having derided his association with Woodhull, and championing her bravery. Woodhull "had done a work for woman that none of us could have done. She has faced and dared men to call her names that make women shudder, while she chucked principle, like medicine, down their throats. She has risked and realized the sort of ignominy that would have paralyzed any of us who have longer been called strong-minded."

In the end, despite Beecher's feeble defense, Tilton had little evidence to prove adultery. For the jury, his charge of alienation of his wife's affections was not sufficient without that. Tilton had but two descriptions of his wife and Beecher exhibiting unusual behavior: Once, while the two sat on the floor looking at a photo album, Tilton said he saw Beecher furtively reach inside his wife's long skirt and touch her ankle and lower calf. Another time, Tilton came home to find them behind a locked bedroom door with Beecher sitting in a chair with his vest off. Elizabeth told him they had locked the door because the children were making noise and they wanted to talk. Her own brother reluctantly testified that when he entered a room in the Tilton home, an embarrassed Elizabeth hastily jumped back from Beecher's side.

Elizabeth and Beecher said these incidents never happened. Tilton admitted that the only proof he had was his wife's confession, which she continued to recant. With both Elizabeth and Beecher standing fast, there was no "beyond a reasonable doubt."

The jury deliberated for eight days and returned deadlocked, unable to reach a decision. The first vote was 8 to 4 in favor of Beecher; the last, 9 to 3. The defense's closing argument stressed that Beecher, a man of such religious magnificence, could not possibly be guilty as charged. Nine of the jury bought this.

Other lives were ruined, but Beecher kept his pulpit. The grateful church gave him $100,000 to pay for legal expenses. Nothing was settled, but Beecher's faithful flock declared victory.

CHAPTER TWENTY-TWO

Beecher's Revenge

The reverend was out for retribution, and it came swiftly. Emma Moulton was dispatched with lightning speed, expelled from the Plymouth Church. She demanded a hearing before an ecclesiastical council. Once again, delegates were selected for their allegiance to Beecher. Once again, newspapers called the deliberations a farce. The proceedings sounded like ancient inquisitions. Emma was not allowed to testify or have a representative. The council ignored her husband's letter that he was prepared to attest that Beecher was guilty of adultery and perjury. Emma fumed that it was a "clerical kangaroo court" with a preordained decision.

Henry Bowen's head was next. When Bowen demanded a right to speak before the church, the building was packed with Beecher fans. As he rose to speak, Bowen was assaulted with hisses and shouts to sit down. He had built this famous church, hired Beecher, and paid his expenses when Beecher was ill, Bowen reminded them. He reiterated the story he had told for years: the horror of his wife's deathbed confession of adultery with Beecher. Only, Bowen never mentioned her by name, or other women he alluded to, except for the now-public Elizabeth Tilton. The *Brooklyn Eagle* had viciously attacked Tilton for publicly exposing his wife. Now the paper despicably attacked Bowen for the opposite: his gallantry to a dead woman. "By not naming names, it was clear that Bowen "knows nothing." Bowen spoke of an anonymous church lady who had a key to Beecher's study where they met for trysts. "Then one day she saw another woman coming from Beecher's study, who also had a key." The knowledge that she was not alone among his loves eventually "killed her." If Bowen was referring to his wife, she died at age thirty-nine, having given birth to her tenth child. Bowen said, "My knowledge is so certain that it can never be shaken by any denials or protestations or oaths, past or future."

Realizing his fate before he faced the church committee Bowen printed for posterity in the *Independent*: "The Rev. Henry Ward Beecher, without even a shadow of doubt in my mind, is guilty of the awful crimes of adultery, perjury and hypocrisy." Winding up a long speech before the committee, Bowen repeated that Beecher was an adulterer, a perjurer, and a hypocrite; he added a "blasphemer for calling on God and heaven so solemnly to be witness to a lie." For "falsely" accusing Beecher, the church founder was excommunicated in May 1876, in a style worthy of medieval popes banishing heretics. As the *Eagle* intoned: "From now until the coffin lid closes upon his dead face, Henry C. Bowen must go through the world with the finger of scorn pointed at him."

Elizabeth Tilton's turn came in 1878. She was living with her mother and, since the trial, had been teaching music to earn money. On April 16, 1878, she addressed a letter to her lawyer and requested that it be published in newspapers across the country. "After long months of mental anguish," she had told a few friends "whom I had bitterly deceived, that the charge brought by my husband, of adultery between myself and the Reverend Henry Ward Beecher was true, and that the lie I had lived so well the last four years had become intolerable to me. That statement I now solemnly reaffirm, and leave the truth with God, to whom also I commit myself, my children and all who must suffer. I know full well the explanations that will be sought by many for this acknowledgement; desire to return to my husband, insanity, malice—everything save the true and only one—my quickened conscience, and the sense of what is due to the cause of truth and justice."

Beecher, to no one's surprise, pushed the insanity explanation: "Poor woman," he clucked. He had heard the "rumor" that she was in a "morbid and self condemnatory state of mind." His attorney Benjamin Tracy gouged away: "I think there is something radically wrong in her mental operations." A few weeks before, several papers had printed rumors that the couple was reuniting. Now they editorialized that this confession was proof that Elizabeth was under Tilton's control again. Snapped Beecher's lecture agent, J. B. Pond, this "confession is the price she pays for a reconciliation."

Everyone searched for a pat explanation, because almost no one took this reversal seriously in light of her previous confession and recantations. This would mean that she had lied repeatedly and publicly. Newspapers discredited anything she said and reprinted her previous protestations, her ardent avowals of innocence, including her standing up at the trial and begging that she be heard to clear her name. What had possessed her now to subject her children to the knowledge that their mother was an adulteress, a terrible burden in Victorian times? Frank Moulton provided an interesting theory: her reversal was caused by an ultimate disillusionment with Beecher. "She is a religious fanatic, and so long as she believed she was protecting a saint she could say things that were not true." This same fanaticism could have caused the confessional "mental anguish" for all those past lies, if she was now telling the truth. Elizabeth stayed with this confession in her letter to the church's examination committee: "The acknowledgement of adultery with the reverend Henry Ward Beecher, pastor of Plymouth Church, was the truth and nothing but the truth." Having "previously published a false statement denying the charge, I desired to make the truth as world-wide as the lie had been." The two hundred parishioners at the meeting voted unanimously to excommunicate Elizabeth.

She never spoke of it again, banished newspapers from her house, and enjoyed a "wide circle of friends." When she was near death in 1897, newspapers had to explain who she was: "At one time," wrote the *Brooklyn Eagle*, she and her husband "were more talked about than any other private individuals in the whole civilized world." Blind for years, a recent operation had restored her sight. During Elizabeth Tilton's last days, a friend called her a "living exemplification of Christian charity and fortitude." When she died on April 15, 1897, the *Eagle* was respectful but sparing in its praise, noting that she "never lost, to her blessed comfort and to their great credit, the loyalty and love of her children." She and Tilton never reunited.

After the trial, Theodore Tilton spoke at the Brooklyn Academy of Music to a sell-out crowd of three thousand. He had not lost his handsome allure. Many ladies "were present and his clever and witty speech on the Human Mind was interrupted often with laughter and applause." The audience loved his political references. The body had progressed beyond the mind, Tilton said, cleverly gesturing, painting a picture of gymnastic prowess. When a bouquet was brought onstage, Tilton quipped, "These are the tuber roses which they scatter over graves. Let it be the monument and the sweet memorial of the death and burial forever of the un-American idea of any third term" for American presidents, which had recently been discussed among politicians.

The *Eagle* was astonishingly laudatory, given its past treatment of Tilton: "The lecture is characterized by the felicity of expression, the delicacy of fancy and the oratorical skill" for which Tilton was noted before "the late unpleasantness. It is pleasant to see that Mr. Tilton has lost none of his old time skill." He need have no fear of "drawing a goodly company together at any time in Brooklyn."

Tilton ignored Beecher and the scandal in his lecture, but "he turned an Arabian proverb at the expense of the editor of the *Eagle*." Obviously referring to the editor's closeness with Beecher and his minions, Tilton quoted a proverb: "A wise man keeping the company of the vicious at last becomes an idiot." The *Eagle*, in response, could not resist a dig at Woodhull: Tilton "ought to lay the Arabian proverb in question of his own heart…when the Woodhulls…of the future crowd around him."

Tilton continued to lecture, but he was no longer the firebrand reformer of old. He made enough money to afford a life of contented self-imposed exile in Paris, moving there in 1883 and living on the Isle de France for years, then moving to more fashionable quarters. Authors have characteristically portrayed him as a lonely recluse writing, as one said, "bad poetry." Far from it. In 1894 he was described as "one of the most alive men in Paris. You are sure to see his massive head" towering above

everyone at every opening art exhibit. "He is considered one of the finest looking men in Paris. The lines in his face give him character and his
white hair makes a fitting frame for his face," wrote an obvious admirer.

He wrote essays, published books of his poetry, and entertained some
of the most remarkable figures of the nineteenth century, among them
Stanton and Frederick Douglass. Civil War animosities were forgotten as
he frequently played chess with the former secretary of state for the Con-
federacy, Judah P. Benjamin. Tilton "has become quite a man of the world
in Paris, and is often seen in the most fashionable salons." Even the *Eagle*
gushed in awe over the former "Brooklynite," now respectable as an exotic
Parisian, who sat for his portrait by a well-known artist. Tilton died at
seventy-one, in 1909, outliving Beecher by twenty years. His page-one
obituary in the Paris *Herald-Tribune* had to explain to a different generation who he was, once a major force in politics and letters who had figured
in the most infamous trial of a different century.

The sisters were struggling to survive both during and following the trial.
Despite the many who thought Beecher guilty, few were in the mood to
embrace the women who had first exposed the scandal. In addition, they
were bludgeoned in a scurrilous tract that accused everyone in the family,
including their old mother, of prostitution. In the summer of 1874, in the
midst of the Tilton–Beecher–Plymouth Church uproar, Joseph Treat, a
disgruntled former writer for the *Weekly*, self-published a venomous rant
that should have been ignored as the incoherent ramblings of a deranged
mind. In it, he admitted his unrequited love for Woodhull and said that
she "gave herself to the embraces of others" when she needed money.

Treat later admitted that he was broke and wrote the pamphlet for
money "to make a living." His sensational story included Buck taking
Tennie to Greene Street, which was lined with the worst brothels, "and
bade her get her living there"; Tennie's "most painful illness last spring,"
he declared, "was a result of a sexual disease." The malicious Polly Sparr
allegedly told him the far-fetched tale that Tennie "has had ten men
visit her in one night and after each, she had bathed her, given her a new

night-robe and prepared her for the next"—and that Woodhull and Colonel Blood "made Tennie do it!" The mother and Meg Miles had also "lain under the piano, while Tennie has had a man in bed with her in the same room."

Perhaps because this calumny was so ludicrous, Woodhull decided to take the high road and not attack Treat, contrary to her custom when criticized. Although she vigorously wrote denials, a charge of libel and a subsequent rehashing in a trial would have been beyond their financial means and would only spread the story. Yet it was a mistake. While some major papers pummeled Treat, others gave the pamphlet currency and flogged the sisters. They were called "black as ravens" by the *New York Herald* and advocates of "harlotry" by the *Chicago Times*. Hundreds of Treat's pamphlets, a gift to Beecher's supporters, Woodhull claimed, turned up outside the halls where she was speaking. Eventually Colonel Blood brought libel charges. Treat was arrested in August 1876, but the courts took so long that he died before the trial, in February 1879. As Treat's tirade spread across the land and even to Europe, it became the final blow to the sisters' reputation. Woodhull cried out, "They [the press] follow me up and down the earth as if I were a pestilence to combat, willfully misrepresenting all my acts and views." She was weary of the fight. "I am worn out. Constant drippings wear the hardest stones."

Woodhull spoke no longer of free love, instead reaching more and more for the Bible and enveloping her speeches in religious passages. Her religiosity had a Spiritualist bent: she studied the Bible looking for "secrets she believed she could decipher through her Spiritualist aspirations," wrote biographer Underhill. She left the American Association of Spiritualists and came down hard on quacks in the field, but retained the belief that legitimate phenomena occurred: "Manifestations are accepted as evidence that there is life beyond the grave." She now embraced the Bible as a wondrous adjunct to her spiritualism, with its mutual message of life after death.

Tennie and Victoria once again became vagabonds, traveling with their mother and Victoria's daughter, Zula, and forced to make a living on the grueling lecture circuit. Woodhull's sedate performances played well in the South, but those who came out of curiosity drifted away. The Bible was no match for free love.

Colonel Blood showed up less and less on these journeys. In June of 1876, the *Weekly* folded, and with it, Woodhull's marriage to Blood. It was amazing that a radical paper had lasted six years, through arrests and jail, trials and destroyed presses, illness and financial strain, and a nation-wide depression. Now the very backbone of Victoria and the Colonel's relationship was gone.

If Woodhull no longer loved Blood, she practiced what she preached, and dissolved a loveless union. She applied for a divorce in September 1876 on the grounds of adultery, and later critics sniffed at the fact that she, of all people, was claiming adultery. But that was the only ground possible in New York—and remained so far into the twentieth century.

Blood moved on, remarrying a woman wealthy enough to help him on a misguided adventure to Africa in search of gold. He disappeared into the wilds and was pronounced dead on December 29, 1885. No one ever heard him say a bad word about Woodhull, and he once remarked, "The grandest woman in the world went back on me."

As for Tennie, there is little record of her private life in 1876. At the end of the trial the sisters advertised duo performances, lecturing at the Brooklyn Academy of Music on the "Prophetic Vision of the Destiny of the World," with Zula reciting Shakespeare. Busy lecturing and orchestrating her sister's lecture career, she may not have had much time to herself. Whether she continued her relationship with Johnny Green, the *Sun* editor, is unknown.

Of all those involved in the scandal, Beecher fared the best, continuing his profitable life of lecturing, preaching, greeting his flock, jaunting to Europe, holding forth in unperturbed fashion. He died on March 8, 1887. Flags across Brooklyn were dropped to half-staff, City Hall was draped in black crepe, businesses closed, and fifty thousand stood in line to view his casket. One wonders if Tilton and Woodhull smiled when they heard him eulogized as "America's Demosthenes." Many thought that a "Great Man" had died, but the shadow of the trial absorbed future generations more than his genius, so he is remembered mostly as the brother of the woman who wrote *Uncle Tom's Cabin* and as the preacher who probably committed adultery.

Mark Twain moaned to a friend at the time of Beecher's death, "What a pity that so insignificant a matter as the chastity or unchastity [*sic*] of an Elizabeth Tilton could clip the locks of this Samson and make him as other men, in the estimation of a nation of Lilliputians creeping and climbing about his shoe-soles."

While that was a popular outpouring at the time of his funeral, history shows that there was far more to it than the "insignificant matter," as Twain put it. It has been described nearly a century and a half later as one of those transformative trials that serve as a "barometer" for cultural anxiety and change. The trial revealed a national preoccupation and social upheaval, with factions violently disagreeing over proclaimed moral values and what others saw as pretenses. Endless fascination in "this page of domestic history," as Elizabeth Cady Stanton termed the trial, went beyond prurience and the specific cast of characters. Those battling for a religious and marital status quo needed to retain a belief in the Great Preacher. Even though he had disturbed religious orthodoxy by espousing a relaxed gospel of love, those fearing further cultural upheaval had to believe he was innocent. On the other hand, reformers such as Stanton looked at the exposure as a way of defining "great principles of social ethics. The true relations of man and woman," Stanton wrote, "the foundation of the family and home, are of more momentous importance than any question of State, or Church, can possibly be." A "fearless investigation of our present social evils," rather than the Beecher travesty, was needed, she said. Although no one was making this parallel at the time, there were indeed quieter echoes of the sisters' outspoken call for openness and social revolution.

As for Beecher, his discredited legacy was not because of adultery charges but his shameful conduct when cornered: his willingness to sacrifice everyone and everything to save himself, and to live the rest of his life without an apparent moment of guilt. Despite Beecher's genius and forceful leadership in transforming religion into a more progressive force, he could not escape, as author Paxton Hibben termed it, his "shabby and obscene compact with dishonor."

ACT FIVE

CHAPTER TWENTY-THREE

The Siege of London

By the end of 1876 the sisters were desperate for a new beginning. Lecture demands were scarce, and the death of the *Weekly* had left them voiceless. Even the scandal sheets seemed to have forgotten them. They were back living hand to mouth in the squalor of a family home that included their dreadful and battling sister Polly Sparr. In 1875, after their successful acquittals, they had appealed to Congress for $500,000 in compensation for damages, citing their wrecked printing operations, the loss of income from the *Weekly* and from lectures while incarcerated, and damaging publicity that kept them from continuing to earn money. Their statement charging that these damages had caused their complete collapse, while certainly a major factor, was not entirely true. The sisters' decline had started before their Beecher publication and imprisonment, noticeably in their having to suspend the *Weekly* and give up the mansion in the spring of 1872. Yet they had a fair argument about the unlawful wreckage of their office and damages, including extended imprisonment and financial loss. However, they were awarded nothing.

Vanderbilt died on January 4, 1877, and the world heralded his monumental role in creating America's transportation revolution as if a head of state had died: a "self-made chief executive of a country that he himself had invented, rather like a cross between George Washington and Genghis Khan," wrote biographer T. J. Stiles.

As the Commodore was laid to rest, his heirs squabbled sensationally, contesting the will in a very public trial that went into years. When Vanderbilt left 97 percent of his fortune to his eldest, William, the latter's nine seething siblings brought into court anyone who would testify that Vanderbilt was senile when he signed his will. Among these were magnetic healers, Spiritualists, a felon, and two men willing to say that Vanderbilt had reneged on a promise to marry Tennie. One was a Cincinnati book dealer and the other was good old, reliable Buck. They never testified, as the judge ruled such testimony irrelevant to any senility charge.

The sisters were far away in London when the trial began in November 1877, having set sail in August. Rumors buzzed through Manhattan that William Vanderbilt had paid them $100,000 to forget about testifying at the trial. Woodhull denied any such payment, but they did not travel steerage. Tennie, Victoria, mother Annie, Zula, and Byron took over six first-class double staterooms, trailed by a "bevy of newly hired servants." One distant Vanderbilt descendant, author Arthur T. Vanderbilt, stated flatly that William Vanderbilt "gave them more than $100,000 on condition they make themselves scarce during the trial."

In May, Tennie had made headlines when she demanded $100,000 from William, claiming that the $10,000 she had given Vanderbilt in 1871 to operate within railroad stocks and securities was now worth $70,000 plus compounded interest. She alleged that through the years, whenever she or Victoria wanted to acquire some of that money, Vanderbilt had treated them "like children," saying he could handle their money better. "There were some facts that I knew, and that he [William Vanderbilt] did not wish to be made public," Tennie hinted. Victoria added her threat: "If I was to tell you all I know, it would be worse a great deal than the Beecher case...but our lips are sealed." William Vanderbilt called Tennie's claim "too ridiculous to seriously discuss." Whatever had happened, by the end of 1877, they were comfortably settled in England, far away from the trial.

After their arrival in London, Tennie was still pursuing her Vanderbilt claim. Hearing that William was arriving in London, she wrote him a letter requesting to see him, and ended it with a warning: She was certain that "when I have satisfied you of the justice of my claim it will not be necessary for me to return to New York as advised by Scott Lord"—one of the high-powered lawyers retained by William's siblings. When she tried to corner William on a London street, he brushed her off, saying he was about to leave for New York. She wrote her father, who was still in New York, asking him to continue her fight. Whether she received any money from William Vanderbilt is unknown, but in a few years Tennie's life would change so drastically that she would never have to hound anyone for money again.

Before the sisters left for England they had decided to use draconian measures to sanitize their image. They would simply kill off their past. Victoria had said she wanted to eclipse her tarnished reputation to spare her daughter. Victoria still smarted from the rebuke of a private school that had barred Zula during Woodhull's free love era. Left behind in New York was a visceral reminder, an evil Victoria, cast in wax and viewed by carnival gawkers in Bunnell's New American Museum in the Bowery. Along with figures of Tweed, Beecher, and Gould, Woodhull writhed in an eternal Dante's *Inferno* wax tableau.

Yet it was no better across the Atlantic. "God only knows what we have suffered since we have been in England," cried Tennie in a letter to her father. "The lies slanders & filth are worse here than ever in America. It is a wonder that we were allowed to live." Tennie blamed Andrews: "The atmosphere was poisoned, & all on account of that rotten stinking moral leper Stephen Pearl Andrews pollcat [*sic*] free love doctrines which so blasted our entire family.... V never wanted that part of the Beecher article, which is so filthy, published in the paper. All she wanted were the facts." Completely reversing herself on free love, Tennie was blaming Andrews for Woodhull's ardent defense of "amative" relations in the article, because some of it was written by Andrews. The "filthy practices" now referred to free love liaisons, not hypocrisy.

As astonishing as it seems, both sisters felt they could not just bend the truth but smash it to pieces. Despite her many proud public avowals of free love—broadcast from stage to stage and in newspapers across

America—Victoria now flatly denied she had ever advocated the doctrine, and Tennie had shelved her harangue about women who marry for money being no better than prostitutes. They remained true to a softer chastising of the sexual double standard, which exonerated wandering males while reviling female partners. They painted themselves as traditional women's rights advocates and touted their interest in the eugenics craze, stressing that only physically and mentally healthy couples should bear children.

The sisters recast their advocacy as centering on the "teaching and elevation" of their sex. They wanted to join the British suffragists, but Susan B. Anthony blistered that move, cautioning their major leader, Millicent Garrett Fawcett, that "Both sisters are regarded as lewd and indecent. I would advise against any contact."

That the sisters could so thoroughly deny all that they had honored for years left their followers shattered and their adversaries hooting. In a revealing speech, Tennie expressed her deep despair about how tough their proselytizing radical road had been. "You may credit us with insanity, if you will; but I pray you, along with it, to also give us credit for honesty of purpose." The press said "that we are simply notoriety seekers...Do people usually invoke upon themselves continuous persecution, merely to obtain notoriety? Do they consciously invoke the terrible power of the press to crush them, to brand them before the world by every vile and detestable epithet? Do they seek the hoots and jeers of the common multitudes, and the sneers, and upturned noses of the select few wherever they go? Do they purposely render themselves friendless, and homeless and distressed in all possible ways merely to become simply notorious? Nay, my friends!...It requires stern conviction of duty, undying devotion to principles, and an unswerving faith...We sometimes almost fainted by the way side; It was almost a greater sorrow than we could endure...if the public knew what it has cost us in sleepless nights, ill heartaches and laceration of the soul to be able to perform our duties." Now, facing poverty, having discarded that brutally hard road, with its few rewards and constant ridicule, seemed the right move. Still, such disavowal of what the sisters had labeled their "undying devotion" to free love principles earned them lasting contempt from disillusioned followers.

The sisters had compelling private reasons for becoming chaste chameleons in their desperate dash for respectability. Soon after they arrived in England, they met men of great social distinction and wealth. Giving up their flaunted independence, they now sought a life unlike any they had ever known. If free love was the victim, so be it. After the pummeling they had received from the American public and press—and the lack of support from free lovers, Spiritualists, and suffragists when they were in prison—the sisters felt they had no allegiance to anything but their own happiness. Woodhull would forever refer to her "persecution" in America. But it would be long, desperate years before she and Tennie would get these desirable Englishmen to the altar.

Tennie had a slight encumbrance. The man she chose—one of the richest and most esteemed in England—was married. It is unclear how they met or how they shared their life before they wed. For once in her life, Tennie was the soul of discretion. There was no boasting to the press or, apparently, to her crazy, blackmailing family about her relationship with Francis Cook, considered in 1869 one of the three richest men in England. Tennie and Cook met sometime between 1877 and 1880. When Tennie turned thirty-five in October 1880, Cook was sixty-three. Because of the age difference, many dismissed the union as Tennie's fortune-hunting move, of exchanging one rich, old man (Vanderbilt) for another, but this is a shallow assessment. Letters between the couple reveal a closeness with one another, despite his family's being less than charmed at Tennie's arrival.

Cook was no Vanderbilt self-made semiliterate. His father had started a company that became England's major importer of fine silks and linens, and Cook had continued to build it into the highly successful Cook, Son & Co. He was well traveled, a lover of music, and an extraordinary art collector. His works included Roman and Etruscan sculptures and paintings by masters such as Van Eyck, Rembrandt, Velázquez, and El Greco.

He owned a castle near Lisbon called Monserrate with enormous acreage that encompassed even a small village. From the windows of Monserrate, one could see the vast rolling lawn and the "most noble and beautiful landscape garden in the world," as the London *Times* claimed at the time Tennie was in residence there.

Cook was vigorously prepossessing—"tall, long bearded, strikingly handsome"—and exhibited an intriguing combination of "old worldliness" and a "briskness of manner and absence of ceremony." Despite his colossal wealth, he liked to twit upper-class snobs by carrying brown paper parcels through the streets and walking to and from the railroad station. In a discussion, he could appear reticent, but he would then end it firmly, quietly, and politely: "That subject will not bear further discussion." It was certain that neither Francis nor Tennie had ever met anyone like the other, and both were entranced. Cook became a friend to both sisters and tried to help Victoria in her frustrated courtship with John Biddulph Martin, a prominent member of a banking family, whom Victoria wanted desperately to marry.

One December evening in 1877, John Martin was driven to hear Victoria Woodhull's lecture in St. James's Hall. He was still mourning the one sibling he cherished, a sister named Penelope, who had died in 1873 after giving birth. Her strong feminist views echoed in his thoughts as he went to hear the woman who had impressed him from afar. Victoria was thirty-nine and Martin thirty-six, a banker in the prestigious family firm on Lombard Street in London. Moneyed and Oxford-educated, Martin had been a star athlete and had kept his trim, handsome good looks.

Woodhull's six-month lecture tour had begun in towns such as Liverpool and Manchester and was ending in St. James's Hall for several performances. She was met with mixed success. Two thousand attended her well-publicized opening night, but the audience dwindled precipitously afterward. Londoners felt, as one critic said, that the American substituted "sentiment for fact and anecdote for scientific reasoning." Many papers ignored the lecture, and the London *Telegraph* criticized Woodhull's indulging in "somewhat flatulent rhetoric." But a minister who heard Woodhull praised "the boldness of that woman's intuition and the incisiveness of her fervent eloquence." Equally fascinated was Martin, who said to himself that if Woodhull wanted him, "I would certainly make her my wife."

Now on her march to respectability, Woodhull emphatically disavowed free love in her speech. Laws and social attitudes had not changed; nonetheless, marriage no longer enslaved women and was now, she said, a "sacred institution." Her earlier adamant praise of the Oneida, New York, colony where monogamy was harshly discouraged was now a part of her "consistently misrepresented" views. She had always praised true love "monogamic [*sic*]" unions, she swore, carefully picking out lesser lines in past speeches that were overshadowed by her anti-marriage riff back then. Painful howls erupted from disgusted past followers. After reading one of Woodhull's strenuous denials of "free lovism," a former *Weekly* reader spoke for many: her words had probably "never been exceeded" in their "barefaced mendacity." A *Brooklyn Eagle* tongue-in-cheek editorial mocked the transition: "We had all been 'misled.'" Woodhull now "stands revealed as pure and lustrous as an electric light in an alabaster vase."

But Victoria did not care. She would do anything to gain the peace, security, and respectability she saw in Martin. One family descendant feels that Martin was determined in his desire to marry her. "They seduced each other." He felt Woodhull's drive to be seen as respectable stemmed less from some fortune-hunting goal and more because of her real love for Martin. John was "very much a part of the establishment," writing esteemed papers, lecturing, and being an active partner in a centuries-old banking house. "She wanted to fit in with that; didn't want to let him down. If he had been an artist, it wouldn't have mattered. She wanted so much to help him and not embarrass him."

Both sisters also repeatedly insisted that they had at last found men who believed in their strong views on women's freedom, and thus were following their adherence to marrying for love, not money. With husbands so rich, few in the cynical press believed them, but both husbands did support their views, Sir Francis by publishing Tennie's writing, and Martin by becoming a partner in Woodhull's magazine, *The Humanitarian*.

Martin's brave impulse regarding marrying Victoria was stalled, however, by his family's horror at the thought. Woodhull collapsed into pitiable desperation when he pulled back. Several months after her speech, Martin had visited Woodhull at the Claflins' Warwick Road home, but shyly made no more moves for a full year, as he was dealing with a romance that ended in failure. He cryptically wrote in his diary that "I should certainly have asked E H" [the initials of an unnamed love] to be my wife" had not the "old obstacle intervened." Impotency seemed to be the "old obstacle." He began to spend nights with Victoria, marked with red dots in his diary. Thanks to Victoria's "forbearance in this regard," his "old enemy" vanished.

By February 1880, he had rented a house on Warwick Road for the two of them to escape from the Claflin bedlam next door. The smell of money had wafted overseas, and more of the America clan arrived in 1878: Buck, sister Meg Miles, and Meg's two daughters.

Despite his initial hesitation, Martin remained forever besotted with Victoria. "She was more alive than anyone I ever met," he told a friend. "When you were with her everything became so thrilling, so worthwhile. You looked at the world through her eyes and you saw miracles all around you...She believed that people were interesting and wonderful and they became it. She wanted people to be happy and she made them happy." Yet Martin was stuck. All his life, the litany of upper-class breeding was drummed into him: the centuries of banking esteem, the eleven family members in Parliament, the impeccable name.

In the spring of 1880, Victoria anxiously pushed Martin about marriage. He was "very upset" at a ruined outing when "the great question came up," and she pursued the subject of honorable intentions. Martin fled to Spain but could not forget Victoria. In August they reconciled but broke up again over her demands that Martin take her to Overbury, the Martin country estate, to meet the family. By November, Martin was still trying to get up the courage to tell his parents about the relationship. The whole family was pressuring him to break things off with Victoria. On December 1, 1880, he wrote, "Dear Momma. I am very sorry that any of you should feel anxiety on my account when I feel none." He would not write Victoria's name but said, " 'She' was very unhappy this morning & said that she was sure" that "none of you like her except for my sake, & that she would not come between me & my people but I hope we shall get over that. I hope I shall find you all friends on Friday. I shall not meet her in the meantime, as I have to go & make speeches tonight."

It sounds as if he was terrified of the prospect, leaving Victoria to enter the lion's den without him, accompanied by his older married sister, Julia Henty, whom he knew sharply disapproved. On December 2, Victoria went to Overbury. His older brother, Richard, grilled Woodhull and decided he liked her. Yet digging into this upstart American's past, Richard and his brother-in-law discovered Joseph Treat's pamphlet and confronted John with an "appalling story of V's antecedents."

John obeyed his mother and broke off relations with Victoria during intense, sobbing, hysterical meetings. Woodhull resorted to a bit of legal pressure, prevailing on Francis Cook to meet with Martin. Breach of promise was vaguely alluded to. The high-strung Woodhull was so devastated at the thought of losing Martin that she teetered on the edge, once again, of a breakdown. She paced, pleaded, and pursued.

As 1880 ended in "chaos," as Martin noted, a frantic Woodhull rushed to create a suitable makeover. She changed her name to Woodhall, with an *a*, in order to claim an English heritage. In a country where one's pedigree is judged in centuries, Woodhull invented an esteemed lineage: The sisters were "descended on their father's side from the Kings of Scotland and England" and also from German royalty on their mother's side. Somehow they were thus related to Alexander Hamilton.

There is something sad and pathetic in proud Victoria's departure from much she had once professed, to the extent of inventing royal antecedents—and something odious in her need to traduce Andrews and Blood. Years ago, Woodhull had stitched into her dress sleeves a biblical passage decrying "lying lips" and a "deceitful tongue." Now all her boasts of truth-telling, her "Yes, I'm a free lover!" claim, were being sacrificed as she faced a bleak future. In January 1881, when all seemed lost with Martin, she printed one issue of a *Woodhall* [with an *a*] *and Claflin's Journal* that blamed Stephen Pearl Andrews and Colonel Blood in poisonous terms. She had discovered Blood in an "adulterous" embrace, she wrote, using the same melodramatic phrases she had used against her first husband. She had once said, of Blood, "a nobler man never lived"; now she even suggested he might have written the Treat pamphlet. Ever-loyal Tennie, who had often said Blood treated her with kindness and "saved her" from ruin, now called him "that bad man Blood." Andrews had sullied their paper with his foul doctrine while she was out of town lecturing, claimed Victoria. She denied writing the Beecher article that she now called "obscene." She dissembled to an amazing degree, claiming "during no part of my life did I ever favor free love, even tacitly." While it is true that both sisters kept to one tenet of free love (that one should marry only for love), they spoke no more of love outside a legal marriage. The sisters' makeover consisted of doctoring the tough caricatures that the *Days' Doings* had drawn of them, even painting a row of ruffles on their skirts to cover the ankles they had so proudly revealed when they opened on Wall Street. "For over a century only the revised images" appeared in literature about the sisters, wrote Amanda Frisken, a writer who examined the before and after illustrations. Even after death, the sisters succeeded in recasting an unfavorable image.

In her frantic pursuit of Martin, Victoria was not shy about using the kind of pressure she would have abhorred years ago in an attempt to force him into a legal marriage. When Martin told her he was going abroad, she appealed to Cook again to talk to John's brother, Richard, stating that if Martin did not "fix a day" for marriage, she might "claim damages." This threat was not for money. She wanted a husband. Throughout months of frenetic onslaught Martin remained in love, but hesitant.

Victoria and John were finally married on October 31, 1883, six years after they met. The bride was now forty-five. Tennie, Annie, and Zula were present. There were no Martins. Brother Richard said he would not receive her. Sister Julia said she would see her in private but would not "insult" her friends by introducing them to Victoria. Julia sneered at her "weak" brother ensnared by the "harlot" Woodhull.

John did not tell his parents until after the fact, first through a telegram and then a long letter written three days after the wedding. Unlike his crisp, sure writing in less personal matters, this letter is smudged, with words crossed out and rewritten: "My Dear F & M, I think that my telegram will have led you to guess what I have to tell you. I am, & have long been [clearly meant in spirit rather than fact], married to Victoria. It is impossible to keep such a secret forever...I have to regret that I have had to keep anything hidden from you." He acknowledged "bitterness in my heart" because of those who tried to "wreck our happiness." He hoped "this will now fade away." He added a note to his mother: "I have a letter from you written long ago in w[hich] you said that you should not depart until you had seen all your children happy. You know how much unhappiness...has been visited on me." It had "made my life at times almost unbearable. I am looking forward to more happiness in the future, & your love will help us to attain it."

As for Tennie, hers would be a longer wait.

CHAPTER TWENTY-FOUR

Lady Cook

Despite family coolness, Victoria and Martin were enraptured newlyweds in their new home at 17 Hyde Gate Park in bustling London. Good breeding had won out, at least with John's mother, who decided to properly, if coolly, receive her daughter-in-law.

The following August of 1884, Francis Cook's first wife died. Three weeks later he told Victoria and John Martin about his intention to marry Tennie. The next spring Victoria and Martin visited Cook's Doughty House, tacitly giving their support to his relationship with Tennie. Martin was deeply impressed with Cook's magnificent art collection.

As months went by after the death of Cook's first wife, a patient Tennie finally reached a solution; according to legend, she told Francis Cook that she had communed with the late Mrs. Cook, who had blessed their union. Tennie became a happy bride on October 1, 1885, a few weeks before her fortieth birthday and a year after the death of the first Mrs. Cook. Sir Francis was sixty-eight when they took their vows in St. Mary's Abbot—"the finest church in Kensington," said Tennie. One of Buck Claflin's last acts was to give away his youngest daughter. In an attempt to present a proper family to their esteemed British partners—and probably to stave off possible blackmail from relatives about their life in the United States—the sisters had hidden their family squabbles. They now presented Buck as a noble father, although there had been little reference to him for several years. He had stayed behind in New York for some time before joining them. He died at eighty-nine of a stroke three weeks after Tennie's wedding. New York papers wrote about the wedding, dredging up tidbits about the sisters' notoriety. Victoria blamed the continued "persecution" by the press for her father's death.

Marrying a year after the death of a first wife was considered rather hasty in Victorian upper circles. "I have no doubt Cook and she were happy. He was too powerful and distinguished a man to marry her one year after his first wife died if he had not cared for her a great deal," remarked a British historian who had studied the Cooks. Sir Francis wrote longing letters when Tennie traveled. Huddled in Doughty House during a fierce snowstorm, he wrote, "My darling Tennie...the house is very lonely without you & I shall be counting the days for your return. I sincerely hope the trip backwards and forwards will do you good, but it is a great sacrifice for your poor husband. God bless Little Wifey and send her back to me" in good health. "Yours, forever, Frank."

The couple had been married less than a year when Queen Victoria created a baronetcy for Francis in 1886. Tennessee, a scruffy child of no fixed address, who had grown up in hovels and was called a prostitute, became the immensely wealthy Lady Cook for the rest of her life.

She brought new life to Doughty House in Richmond Hill, with its sweeping view overlooking the Thames, described as the finest view in London. The Georgian home was no ordinary one inside, filled with art from many periods and countries. Cook had even hung a sixteenth-century Italian painting measuring eight by sixteen feet on the hall ceiling, and visitors looked upward to see nymphs and cupids cavorting.

Tennie delighted in organizing grand garden parties for as many as a thousand on the flowing lawns behind the house, worked hard on charities, and hosted Cook's famed Sunday afternoon concerts. The most renowned musicians came to play, and the gallery resounded with the sound of an organ on which was carved in gilded letters across the frame, IF MUSIC BE THE FOOD OF LIFE—PLAY ON. The child fortune-teller, who would not have known a masterpiece from a fake, now discussed art treasures with her guests—among them, the world-famous art critic and historian Bernard Berenson. Tennessee talked rapidly, with her American intonation, pointing out such masterpieces as the *Adoration of the Magi*, by Fra Angelico and Filippo Lippi; Van Eyck's *Three Marys at the Sepulchre*; Rembrandt's *Portrait of a Boy*; Velázquez's *Old Woman Cooking Eggs*.

To be sure, Tennessee retained her ability to shock with straightforward openness. "To hear the strong and unfamiliar accents of the United States and to hear the problems that Americans discuss eagerly and familiarly—and England passes over in shuddering silence—and to see the slight, alert, restless and intellectual face of this fiery-souled American woman by the side of this stately old Englishman and in the framework of old art and English landscape was one of those surprises and contrasts that show how startling life can be," recounted one London visitor. Her scandalous past, however, was nowhere present when she became known as the wholesome "matchmaker"—"proper" young men and women often found good marriage partners at the fashionable dances she gave.

Vera Ryder, Francis's great-granddaughter, used to play among the art collection as a child and felt "some slightly sinister influence creeping through the gallery...I came to realize from whispered insinuations and shocked expressions" that there was a "shadow of my step great-grandmama." Ryder revealed a "mutual interest in Spiritualism" that formed a bond between Sir Francis and Tennessee. A more subdued Tennie nonetheless shocked the family by leaving pamphlets and tracts about suffrage, divorce reform, and equal rights around the gallery and slipped into catalogues. Condoned by her husband, Tennie's views were still appalling to many upper-class English. Tennie striding into ballrooms and galleries, extending her hand in the all-American handshake, talking away rapidly—all easily shattered stiff Victorian correctitude. For many years she was well protected from criticism, by her husband. She never forgot her crusade for women's rights, but as a bride, Tennie was busy meeting lords and ladies and, spectacularly, the future king and queen of England.

Sir Francis received his baronetcy for his charitable work, the major example being Alexandra House, which was named for Her Royal Highness, the Princess of Wales. Here young women of limited means could study art, literature, and music, "protected from harm" in a lavish home that housed one hundred and fifty and had cost millions to build. Sir Francis began the construction of Alexandra House in 1884. Tennie soon became an influential champion. With all the pomp of royalty, Alexandra House was officially dedicated in the spring of 1887 by His Royal Highness the Prince of Wales, who would become King Edward VII on the death of his mother, Queen Victoria. The handsome building occupied the entire block opposite Albert Hall and contained a concert hall, a ninety-foot-long dining room, a drawing room, a counsel room, a library, a gymnasium, and an "American elevator."

Carriages lined up for the afternoon opening ceremony, dispatching the archbishop of Canterbury and a collection of princes and princesses and lords and ladies. A red carpet led into the spacious main hall. Sir Francis and Lady Cook led the royal family on a tour that ended in the concert hall, with the audience cheering as the future king praised Sir Francis, whose name would live on through Alexandra House. Among the finely dressed women, a visitor noted that Lady Cook, "the little American beauty" in a suit of blue trimmed with gray sable, leaning on her husband's arm, was "the nicest dressed and prettiest woman in the hall." Only four years older than Tennie, the party-going Prince of Wales must have found her fetching; he had collected several mistresses, among them the celebrated actress Lillie Langtry.

Despite the lure of London, Tennie was happiest in her castle in Portugal, called Monserrate—an exotic pink-and-white confection reminiscent of the romantic Mughal era, with towers, cupolas, rose marble pillars, and arched windows. Walking through the castle corridors was like strolling through a Persian palace filled with arches and walls filigreed in delicate lacey patterns. On special occasions, Sir Francis and Tennie draped the large domed center from above with red cloth, which reflected a soft pink on the guests below. The chandeliered dining/ballroom looked out through arched windows to the terrace banked with dazzling flowers.

Tennie loved it all, walking in sunlight on the terrace, listening to a fountain spilling water in the center of the castle, warmed on chilly nights by elaborate fireplaces. Her bedroom was in one of three towers, and her second-story arched window held a breathtaking view of the garden, where fern trees grew eight feet tall and flowers of every conceivable species perfumed the paths. Waterfalls, glistening ponds, and an ancient chapel lay hidden behind a curtain of flowers, plants, and trees imported from all over the world and successfully transplanted after Sir Francis built the first irrigation system in Portugal. Cook, who employed vast numbers in the village on his estate, was so economically vital to the country that the king of Portugal titled him Viscount de Monserrate. The view was a thing of beauty long before Sir Francis Cook purchased the property in 1858. Lord Byron wrote of its splendor and was inspired to write *Childe Harold* there. A twelfth-century Moorish knight was buried high on a hill.

Tennie's letters back to Victoria in England bubbled with joy in her wonderland. "I am very much in love with Cintra [spelled *Sintra* today]… the Promenades are full with Tourists. I am out all day & as happy as a bird." She was busy decorating Monserrate and "should be pleased if you would give us a call. Our cook is perfection & we have two big fires going all the time." Tennie scrawled in the margins a sentiment she repeatedly expressed in letters to Victoria: "I have every thing that heart could wish & perfectly happy & contented with my precious husband."

Tennie shocked visiting British royalty by treating the villagers as equals, inviting them to her parties. She fed and clothed the half-starved children and started schools. She later recalled, "the Queen [of Portugal] and priests came to me, fearing I was going to interfere with their religion but I said: 'You look after their souls. Let me look after their bodies.' The schools were a great success." And Lady Cook and the Queen became friends. When strangers asked the students who they belonged to they would respond "we are the contessa's [Tennie's] children."

An American friend visiting Tennie in 1894 was astounded as their carriage neared Monserrate. Rockets shot up in the air, musicians played, and she was "nearly smothered with flowers, thrown by the natives." A laughing Tennie told her guest "this is all in honor of your arrival." Sir Francis met them at the entrance. Flags of every nation floated from the turrets and in front of the castle; most prominent was "Tennie's own Stars and Stripes," Sir Francis remarked as he led them into the palace.

Over time, all was not bliss, however, as Tennie dealt with her hectoring mother, a sex scandal involving Sir Francis, and her own severe illnesses.

In an undated letter written in 1890, when Tennie was in her mid-forties, she pleaded with Victoria to come to Monserrate. "My dear husband is doing all in his power to make me happy, but he cannot help me from having turn of life. Now Victoria if I am your darling sister & you love me so much[,] *now* [she underlined] is your time to show it." She was writing about her menopausal traumas and slightly chastised her older sister. "When you were passing through your time of life I was with you & came to you at every call no matter who I sacrificed. Now I am in a very weak and nervous condition. I have wiped out the last persecution in America & our fighting is finished. Now it is my life that I am fighting for. Monserrate is lovely, quiet and beautiful & indeed a Paradise, but I am in a terrible, nervous & melancholy state & I need someone with me that will sympathize and comfort me." Sir Francis wrote a postscript: "Dear Victoria, I add a few lines to urge you and Mr. Martin to come. In her present distressed condition she really requires your sisterly sympathy and support, so do come... Wire soon and say you are coming. Yours sincerely, Frank Cook." There is no indication whether Victoria came, but she at various times wrote impassioned and caring letters about Tennie's health, which became worse after menopause.

From the beginning of Tennie's marriage, mother Annie was up to her manipulative tricks. "Mother has written some awful letters to Sir F———," Tennie wrote Victoria. Her mother took pains to tell Tennie in a rambling, wheedling letter that she must return to Doughty House to care for "your dear old mother," now a widow. Since she still could not read or write, Annie dictated to a friend. Her paranoia seemed apparent when she noted that the letter was being written in secret, behind a locked door. "I prefer Doughty house *much* before Monserrat" [an accepted spelling at that time]. At Doughty she could be happy "if I lived to be as old as old Methusala [*sic*]...I think you must have been as blind as a bat," she remarked about Tennie's first visit to Doughty House. "Otherwise you would have seen what a lovely place it was." A dig at the possibility of Tennie's becoming high hat followed. "It is too often the case that those that done [*sic*] the good will be forgot [*sic*] when the glory comes but I hope that will not be the case with my darling angel...Now would you not think it best for you to come home and take a little comfort with your mother before she dies?" She was now calling Sir Francis "your darling husband." Annie would be around for four more years, until 1889. She got her way, dying at Doughty House.

In 1893, eight years after Tennie and Francis were married, a woman stepped out of the past to claim that Sir Francis had promised to marry her. She had been a housekeeper in Cook's home while his first wife was alive. She testified in court that Victoria had paid £30 for letters from Sir Francis to her. Sir Francis admitted the liaison but that he had never promised to marry her. He paid nominal damages.

The next year, a small item was headlined: A SOCIETY SCANDAL. A BARONET CHARGED WITH SEDUCTION: "An action for breach of promise of marriage has been brought against Sir Francis Cook by a young woman named Miss Frances Susans. The plaintiff states that the defendant seduced her and afterwards induced her to assent to abortion. Sir Francis Cook, who is in his 77th year, is a wealthy merchant." An exonerating article immediately followed, stating that the woman's lawyer had quit the case and that a verdict was in favor of Sir Francis." This clearly was a blackmail attempt, but Victoria scolded her sister on her husband's "libertine" ways.

Victoria seemed torn between disliking Cook and wanting to remain close to Tennie. Her huge scrawl took up a whole page for just a few words: "My darling sister...I am impelled to write you and ask you if your heart is satisfied with the man that stands by your side as husband. Is he worthy of the precious charge in his keeping? I fear not when I think what you have endured since he called you wife. My heart fails to believe you are content. The richness of that noble nature has never been satisfied with the scant appreciation his soul has given you. *Oh*, my sister, a hungry heart is not easily satisfied. You are going in company with a man who openly insults you and boasts of it and you are forced to bow your head and murmur not. Why? Because the one who should resent is a party to it. Write me a line."

A more agreeable letter invited the couple to visit: "Darling sister, I have just shown Johnny your letter. He says when you come in tomorrow you must stop with us." This had to have been after their mother had died in 1889. "We are all that is left in England. I have been sad unto death all day—you are *sad* as you can be. No we must have no more unnatural conduct." The provocative phrase is not explained but may have referred to free love. "We have suffered enough. *God* knows we deserve some happiness my precious sister. We will settle all our difficulties and enemies. Now only be brave and get well." A stab of fear for Tennie's health followed: "You know it would kill me to lose you now." Halfway down the page Martin wrote in his fine script, urging them both to come.

After Sir Francis's death, Victoria wrote a frenetic memo in crayon, partly about her daughter, Zula, and also as an apology to her: "I want to free my soul of its agony. My sister became the wife of Cook who was an *old* libertine. She took on his *conditions*. I, trying to save her from going to pieces, allowed her to bring his conditions into our sweet home... My child, how I regret your ever coming in contact with one of what the worlds call family—you are not of their world...she [Zula] was forced to live in the congested atmosphere of Ignorance of the old world's decrepitude which would not nor could not advance. The regret is why did I allow our lives to be affected by it. My daughter has never said one word of anger or a look that is not Love."

This letter leaves more questions than answers. Does this mean that at his advanced age Cook was a philanderer? What did the phrase "unnatural conduct" mean? Free love? Or was Victoria just dramatizing or speculating? Tennie's "taking on his conditions" sounds possibly like a venereal disease, but there is no record for confirming this. Why did Victoria have to save Tennie from "going to pieces"? Both sisters wrote often to one another about their extreme nervousness, which could—emphasis only on "could"—have been a symptom of such disease.

It is clear that unspecified serious illnesses frequently plagued Tennie. In an undated letter, which had to have been written before 1897, Tennie frantically wrote, "If we are both going to die at once I want to leave a name & put ourselves right before the world & no time is to be lost. We must get decent photos, have truthful interviews in the paper & an elaborate & correct account of our great work & our success & our true worth." She was as fixated on leaving a grand legacy as Victoria. "Our husbands might give us the money that they said they had left us, to spend now in putting us right before the world. I mean bis [*business*] I have suffered to [*sic*] much to die out & give my crown" to anyone who had not appreciated "us until to [*sic*] late." Monserrate was the place "to work out our future destiny. It is Paradise, everything is lovely, fruits of all kind, abundance of flowers & everyone in love with me & the climate grand. I am improving fast & have a big appetite. My bowels move every day & I sleep well & my complexion is beautiful. I am sure we will both get well here if you come. Cable quickly."

There is no record of whether Victoria visited.

Tennie's illnesses point to an ebb and flow: she had considerable energy to travel and lecture at times, and then would collapse and become bedridden. In 1920, when she was seventy-five, she felt near death while enduring great pain. Her doctor "now decided that I have a bad fistula & that I must have it treated & seen to & as soon as my nerves will permit I must have an operation performed. He says I must be put under chloroform but I dread that. Tomorrow morning at ten o'clock I have got to have another little operation to enlarge the hole & keep the wound open...I am very feeble & I am thinking more of my health & meeting my god... in my state of health I prefer to be alone & keep very quiet."

The site of the fistula, with an opening that needed to be drained of infection, was never mentioned. A fistula—an abnormal connection between an organ, vessel, or intestine as the result of injury or surgery or from infection—can occur in several places in the body: between an artery and a vein; the skull and nasal sinus; the bowel and vagina; or in the stomach, lung, and bowels. It is impossible to know where Tennie's was located. However, she knew about vaginal fistulas, and a decade before, at age sixty-five, she was still mesmerizing large audiences and, judging from the applause, hitting a nerve with scathing lectures about men "sowing their wild oats" only to give virgin brides pain, venereal diseases, and damaged children.

The specter of sexually transmitted diseases regarding the sisters has surfaced in biographies of Vanderbilt, Woodhull's claims of her first husband's constant whoring, and the scurrilous gossip of the unreliable Joseph Treat ("Tennie's most painful illness...was a result of sexual disease"). One doctor treating Vanderbilt stated that his enlarged prostate "was likely the result of gonorrhea or 'excessive venery' "—too much sex. Since gonorrhea was not seen as serious as syphilis at the time, Vanderbilt possibly could have infected Tennie, if they were lovers, with unforeseen results. Venereal disease can cause sterility, and Tennie had no children. It can also cause mental defects, such as those that afflicted Victoria's son, Byron. Yet any such connection is pure conjecture.

Still, the subject must be addressed, as it concerns theories regarding the sisters and Vanderbilt. A biography of Vanderbilt by Edward Renehan Jr. splashed on its flap cover that "unreleased archives" showed Vanderbilt was in the throes of syphilitic dementia when he met the sisters. Renehan concluded that Vanderbilt's relationship with them proved he was demented by the disease at the time. However, T. J. Stiles skewered Renehan's unreliable claim as fraudulent in a subsequent Vanderbilt biography.

CHAPTER TWENTY-FIVE

Love and Libel

At age forty-five, Victoria Claflin Woodhull Blood Martin was madly in love. Her interest in Martin may have begun out of a frantic need for redeeming respectability, but she actually found herself in a legalized marriage with a soul mate—something she had scoffed at being nigh impossible in her lectures and writing fifteen years before.

Their letters to one another are a study in contrast. Hers are filled with frenzied neediness and great outpourings of emotions, etched in large letters with jabbing underlines for emphasis and the *T*s crossed nearly through whole words. His are quieter, loving, but circumspect. Hers run on in haste without punctuation. His are dotted with commas and semicolons in all the right places.

Their physical intimacy was obvious: "I need your precious arms around me this moment," she wrote. She called him her boy, and he signed "Your loving boy," but John, three years younger, was her anchor. Without him she seemed adrift. "I am so lonely...darling husband my heart is very sad tonight." And in another: "My darling husband—I am dreadfully nervous—I cannot endure being away from you—I got up at 4 this morning—I cannot get to sleep until I hear [your] precious lips murmur God bless my dear wife...you must love me very much & wire me the moment you get this."

During their marriage Martin was away on short but frequent business trips or speaking engagements, yet her letters sound as if their separations were forever. "I am lonely tonight—without thee my heart cries aloud for your kiss—sometimes I think I shall end it all before you return— this cold unsympathetic atmosphere has at last chilled me through [she was not talking about the weather]. Deceptions, low cunning trickery all going to make up what this world calls life." Victoria "longed for the sympathy [from him] which I know lies stored up for *me* when all else fails."

She ruminates about those who had done her wrong, and levels digs at Martin's family. In 1897 Victoria was still writing caustically about his brother, Richard, who so disapproved of her: "I have just been listening to the story of *Richard* working to get a Baronetcy. *He* [twice underscored] will get it. Money buys all." Her private neediness would have startled audiences who witnessed her independence onstage, yet a hint at Victoria's success in capturing the devotion of successful men is revealed in her letters. The "feminine" rather than "feminist" side of dependence on men was beguiling and flattering, and threaded through her male relationships. Gen. Benjamin Butler eagerly prepared her appearance before Congress; Theodore Tilton played the gallant rescuer who introduced the little woman at her free lover speech; Stephen Pearl Andrews wrote her ringing words; and Colonel Blood constantly administered to her needs.

John responded to her pleas. "God bless you darling. You know that my heart is with you every minute." In his letters, such as this one, written eleven years after their marriage, he attempted to reassure his "DARLING WIFE...I cannot bear to think that you are sad in our home while I am away."

He also was needy. "Dearest little wife," he wrote on September 1, 1887, "I was so sorry not to find any letter or message from you this morning." In another he wrote, "Make me feel every minute that your heart is with me as much as mine is with yours."

Victoria seemed to vacillate between attempting to seek his parents' love and rejecting his pleas to visit them at Overbury. Martin was especially upset in 1896, thirteen years after their marriage, when she refused to come to Overbury while he visited his "gouty" father and his mother, but Victoria continued to feel unwelcome. Several letters from Martin in May and June of 1896 reveal a continuing rift. In June he sadly noted, "Yesterday was my birthday. Nor did anyone, not even my little wife, send me greetings."

Her litany of us-against-the world complaints must have worn on him, but Martin faithfully replied, "Be strong & brave, little wife, & trust in God & your husband whose love will put down all that would do you evil."

Surprisingly Victoria and John's mother had a few intimate moments. Two years after their marriage and within days of Victoria's father's death in 1885, she wrote to her mother-in-law and tried to patch up differences with Richard. "Darling Mother," she wrote, "Many thanks for your loving letter...My dear husband has become a thousand times dearer to us all...I love you and father because you are his parents. If you would only let me show how much I love you but I am always hurt because I feel you do not care to have me with you."

Six years later her mother-in-law confessed a secret to Victoria that she would not tell her own daughter, about how wounded she had been by a romance of her husband's. "I will not be dead a month before that woman has married [John's father] & is trotting him round the country," she exclaimed. John's mother so feared "gossip & scandal" that she would not "speak openly about it even to her children," despite the "tears of pain & distress" a Miss Fritsch had caused her. She revealed a letter to Victoria that "contained her wishes about Miss Fritsch." Presumably Miss Fritsch was sent packing; there are no other references to her.

In their life together, the couple visited museums, went to the opera and theater, played lawn tennis, and took a fancy to the new bicycling craze.

Friends from the movement days visited: Elizabeth Cady Stanton and Isabella Beecher Hooker, who also saw Tennie and was entranced by her new life. On one of their many trips abroad, Victoria finally met Frederick Douglass, in Rome in 1887. She walked across the hotel lobby and introduced herself. "She frankly—and I thought somewhat proudly—told me that she was formerly Mrs. Victoria Woodhull," wrote Douglass in his diary, noting that she was a woman of "very fine appearance. I am not sure that I quite concealed my surprise." Douglass made no reference to the fact that their names had been linked in a presidential campaign fifteen years before. He was in "no position to think poorly of her for her espousal of free love," commented a Douglass biographer who noted that Douglass had divorced his first wife and was now married to Helen Pitts, a white woman. At the time they met, Victoria was a matronly married woman who no longer spoke of free love. "I do not know that she is not in her life as pure as she seems to be," wrote Douglass. "I treated her politely and respectfully—and she departed apparently not displeased with her call."

After more than a decade of marriage, Victoria had grown restless and wrote a snappish letter to John expressing her need to return to the public. "When I realize how for 12 years I have allowed my soul to remain in a lethargic sleep while others were [profiting] by the work that I almost yielded up my life for I feel that now I must not be idle a moment longer." She needed him "to help me instead of [either he or she] being secondary to a dozen different things which amount to nothing."

The result was a magazine, *The Humanitarian*, which tackled politics and women's rights issues, but with a new emphasis on theology, scientific farming, eugenics, and health. As prescient as the *Weekly* had been, *The Humanitarian* was even more forward-thinking, calling cigarettes lethal to one's health. It also promoted Woodhull, running admiring biographies of her. With Martin's money, they were able to circulate it widely. Victoria had shrewdly contracted experts to write for the magazine and fought for astounding changes in society that did not happen for decades: Laboratories should analyze food and drink for impurities. Doctors should examine children in schools. The poor should be provided government services. Birth control was a necessity. Her emphasis on a form of eugenics, stirpiculture, took Darwinism to an odious level by today's standards, arguing that there should be "selective breeding" as in livestock, with only the physically and mentally "pure" allowed to bear children. In her era, however, this was in fact tried, at Oneida Community, with mates selected for their superior qualities. Before forced sterilization occurred in America, followed by Hitler's grisly evil design, breeding only healthy children was a popular idea. H. G. Wells (*War of the Worlds*) wrote admiringly of Victoria and her views.

Both Woodhull (she had given up the affected spelling "Woodhall") and Martin were excited about their magazine. Editorial proofs were passed back and forth when they were apart, although she did not take kindly even to his smallest criticisms.

Before they produced *The Humanitarian*, Martin's love for Victoria meant fighting highly publicized battles that surely embarrassed his family and, in the long run, merely kept alive the image of a scandalous Victoria. Martin seemed as obsessed as Victoria about hunting down blackmailers and slanderers. The couple even hired an agency to find Colonel Blood, thinking he may have spread stories. A circuitous chase ensued until the detectives traced him to his death in Africa; Blood had been declared dead on December 29, 1885.

Martin also attacked the esteemed Henry James because of a risqué character in his 1883 novel *The Siege of London*, Nancy Headway. The American fortune hunter sounds like a brash composite of Tennie and Victoria. Headway is "enormously divorced" when Sir Arthur Demesne wants to marry her, which his mother opposes. Demesne ignores friends who tell him she is not respectable, and he marries her anyway. When asked if Headway was based on a real person, James ducked with an evasive answer: "nobody has the right to say the character is actually drawn from real life." Balderdash, said the New York *World*. "It is an open secret that the heroine" is Woodhull, describing the character as a "scheming widow whose past reputation will not bear investigation." Historians widely assume Woodhull was also the model for James's trance medium Verena Tarrant in *The Bostonians*, although Verena is a pale version of Victoria. Probably aware of Martin and Victoria's litigious bent, the novelist was cordial and acquiescing when the two paid him a call. He wrote a letter for Martin stating that in no way was he "representing or suggesting" Woodhull in the novel *The Siege of London*.

In 1890, Victoria, Martin, Tennie, and even Sir Francis took on the legendary, toughest, and most ruthless cop in the world, New York's Thomas Byrnes. The Irish immigrant and superintendent of the New York City Police, with a worldwide reputation, was all brass knuckles. He coined the term the *third degree* for his new kind of interrogation, which included torture. His power was "feared by crooks and honest men alike."

The sisters and their husbands were livid over an article signed by Byrnes and published in 1889 that characterized the sisters as "adventuresses of the broadest and most comprehensive type." The article recycled the history of Buck, who would "do anything to make a dollar," and stated that Victoria's former and then-current husband had lived "under the same roof" in the Claflin household. Tennie, the article claimed, was married to a New York journalist, which would make her a bigamist. Sir Francis Cook (consistently misspelled "Cooke") was "a titled imbecile" whose family had tried to dissolve the marriage.

The Martins and Tennessee set sail for America, and in January 1890, headlines blared that Martin planned to sue Byrnes for "defamation of his wife and of her sister." Victoria fumed that the Byrnes article was "broadcast throughout England, mailed to almost every friend of my husband" in the "basest attempt" to damage them. Sir Francis offered £5,000 to anyone who could name those who were trashing the sisters.

After visiting Byrnes in New York, Woodhull told a reporter that the detective had apologized and "agreed to set her right before the world," and therefore she would drop the suit. The reporter went to Byrnes for confirmation. The crafty Byrnes held off saying anything until Victoria's comment about his having apologized appeared in print. Then Byrnes denied it—"I made no apology," a boast that ran in newspapers across the country. Thus he received the publicity he craved, as the press labeled Victoria a liar. Byrnes had sandbagged her. When the reporter told her of Byrnes's ploy, Victoria angrily cried persecution and raved "like a mad woman...And then she burst into a strain of impassioned eloquence that I have never heard equaled by man or woman since." The reporter sided with Woodhull: "Byrnes would not hesitate to sacrifice the truth."

Byrnes's rule came to an end in 1895 when a young man named Theodore Roosevelt, the new president of the New York City Police Commission, forced him to resign in his sweep to clean up police corruption.

Martin gave an amazing excuse for their plight. "There were any number of people who traveled under the names of Victoria Woodhull and Tennie Claflin, and we were made the scapegoats of all their misdeeds."

Tennie lashed out, saying that her husband, "a man who has made millions" and continued to oversee his business, was no imbecile, and the charge that she was a bigamist was slander. "The circulation of these vile rumors about me and my sister is epidemic. It is rumor that is killing us. The handle is in New York, but the blade is all over the world. It is cutting us to pieces."

Helping to cut them to pieces were brother Hebern Claflin and sister Polly Sparr. While the sisters were presenting a new face, Polly made headlines by exhuming her daughter's body. Rosa Burns, the daughter by Polly's first husband, Ross Burns, had died of stomach cancer in 1883. She had fled her mother's "boarding house" years before to live with a decent family. Polly now charged that Rosa had been poisoned, hoping to void her daughter's will, in which she had left $40,000 to the family with whom she was living and nothing to Polly. The widower and daughter who had supported Rosa countered that Polly had tried to blackmail them and that Rosa was "too pure to mix with the set with which her mother was surrounded."

Rosa had received the money, now in her will, from her father, a successful lawyer out west, whom Polly had said was dead but with whom Rosa had become reunited. The press once again dragged in the sisters, citing them as relations of Polly, a woman willing to wreck her dead daughter's reputation. Ross Burns had held little love for any of the Claflins. "I hope those cusses will never return to America."

Tennie, however, had attempted to deflect Polly's fights, writing in 1880 to the man who was taking care of Rosa and thanking him for kindness shown to Victoria and her, Tennie: "You may rest assured that if we can aid to brighten your future Vic and I will do so, for I am satisfied that you have taken good care of Rosa, who is the flower of our family." (Polly Sparr got not one cent of her daughter's will, as the courts ruled against her.)

Ten years after Tennie wrote that letter against Polly, the older sister was still causing trouble. Brother Hebern and Polly "have kept it very hot here for me" with blackmail threats, Tennie wrote to Victoria from Monserrate in 1890. She had brought Hebern and his wife to Monserrate, as "I wanted them to see me in my sane state & to let them feel I never should be played upon any longer." Yet Hebern continued to make trouble, trying to link his sisters and their aristocratic husbands in a bogus claim of acreage in the "heart of New York City, said to be worth $200,000,000." Martin sent Victoria the *Chicago Tribune* piece about it that he had received from "your 'worthy' brother." He instructed a New York lawyer to tell reporters that he and Victoria knew nothing about it, "but it will be better still if possible to say nothing."

In the midst of her battles to clear her name, Victoria decided to run for president of the United States again, in 1892. It was her "destiny," certainly an idea that had to come from spirits gone daft. She had tried an abortive run in 1882, and now, twenty years since her first attempt, she had no base in America. *The Humanitarian* was published in the States to advertise her campaign. She gathered a small group of old Victoria League members, called in the press, and went to Washington, DC, where a remnant of the Equal Rights Party nominated her for president. She did not have the backing of suffragists.

When Martin and Woodhull traveled to Chicago in May 1892, to stir up interest in her presidency, headlines hit them head-on. The publisher of the *Chicago Daily Mail*, a scandal rag, had assured detective Byrnes when he was writing his opus on the sisters two years before that a detective "could unearth a quantity of unsavory and ill-smelling" information on the sisters. When Woodhull and Martin got off the train in Chicago, the Byrnes story of two years before was facing them again, recycled by the *Daily Mail*. The paper railed that Victoria was unfit to represent women or run for president. When the sisters and Martin threatened a lawsuit, no one was more pleased than the publishers. The *Mail* threw everything it had on the sisters into the following edition: the details of con artist Buck's scams, their alleged brothel enterprises, claims of black-mail. Nearly thirty years after the fact, the public learned about Tennie's manslaughter indictment in the death of the Ottawa, Illinois, cancer patient. Woodhull and Martin learned the hard way the old adage "Never do battle with a man who buys ink by the barrel." Loathing the publicity of a trial, they dropped the suit, as well as Victoria's incipient candidacy.

Back in England, Victoria and Martin became the first people ever to sue the British Museum, that august archival repository. Following the Claflin tradition of taking their battles to court, Victoria acted with amazing audacity, even for her. She argued that the museum library harbored libelous material about her on its shelves—even material that she herself had written, dictated, or authorized. John Martin baldly stated that an article in an obscure magazine, in fact a reprint of the Tilton biography of Woodhull, "contains a gross and false libel on Mrs. Martin's parents and family," even though this was the very same material Victoria had provided Tilton in the biography she proudly distributed widely in 1871.

When Woodhull took the stand in January 1894, the fully bewildered British counselors sought yes and no answers. Did Tilton "not publish a biography" of her? Woodhull's mystifying answer: "If he did it is quite true. My memory did not follow it."

Trying to find out if she wrote the Beecher article unleashed a torrent of words, everything but an answer to the question she was asked ("Did you write it, yes or no?"). Woodhull answered in a 361-word circuitous tease, wandering back into the history of the scandal prior to the article, using the words *persecution* or *persecuted* several times, until the agitated judge broke in: "I think we are going beyond the point."

Woodhull's lawyer stated that her Beecher article had been "perverted and garbled by the wretched man Pearl Andrews" and that she had denounced these concepts on 250 platforms while lecturing. A British Museum lawyer showed that "no such 'denunciation' had been produced from her writings and speeches." He noted that *Woodhull & Claflin's Weekly* had even reprinted the entire article in 1873. (The British lawyers may not have known that the sisters spoke of it with pride as well as republishing it.)

The Martins' lawyers cited as "gross libel" the twenty-year-old *Chicago Times* story about Tilton being Victoria's lover, reprinted in a pamphlet. Woodhull stated, as she had previously, that the interview never happened. Other alleged libels in a pamphlet reprint of the Beecher trial testimony included a *Brooklyn Eagle* editorial that called her "the queen of prostitutes." The museum argued that the materials had been placed in the library according to its rules and regulations and without malice.

The museum lawyers made a major error when they ridiculed Woodhull. When asked if she had told Tilton, "My spiritual vision dates back as early as my third year," she said, "I have no recollection of stating that," but added unconcernedly, "My spiritual vision does date back further than that." The British Museum counselor read from Tilton's fulsome passages several lines about Demosthenes. When asked if he was her spiritual guardian, Woodhull said, "I do not think I shall tell you who he is or what he was." As the counselor continued to badger her, he cut her answers off in midsentence until Martin's lawyers objected. When asked if an apparition had appeared to her, Woodhull looked at the esteemed counselors and judge and said wryly, "There is one appearing at me now." The judge asked, "Not a ghostly apparition, I hope?" Woodhull shot back, "I do not know. I am waiting to see what your conclusions are." Laughter filled the courtroom. In his summation, Woodhull's counselor, sensing the feeling in the courtroom, asked, "Why was the poor lady kept for four hours on the rack and tortured with questions and insinuations" that had nothing to do with the case?

This seemed to hit a nerve with the jury. In 1894, Victoria was no longer a sexually intriguing young woman but a fifty-five-year-old distinguished matron, covered in bulky layers of Victorian dress, and the possessor of an esteemed and influential husband. The jury returned with a split decision. The documents were libelous, but the museum defendants bought, catalogued, and circulated the books as a duty. It was not their duty to know that the books contained libels, so they were not guilty of negligence, but, the jury stated, they should have used more care.

The judge ruled in favor of the British Museum. The couple declined to appeal, stating that Victoria's character had been "thoroughly vindicated," since the jury had said the material was libelous. Woodhull got what she called a victory: an apology from the British Museum for "annoyance which had been caused to them." Martin had to pay court costs. The London *Times* called for an act "to prevent the British Museum from being Bowdlerized; the Martins had found a defect" in their rules. Six years later, in 1900, Parliament passed a bill that exempted public library authorities from liability in legal proceedings "in respect of libellous matter" in books in their libraries. Thus Woodhull succeeded in forcing the British Parliament to rewrite the nation's library rules. Victoria would always call this battle a victory. "I did not dare to hope that I would live to the turn of the tide but we have," she ecstatically wrote Tennie in the fall of 1894. "The 21 years was up [since their 1873 battle] last spring when the papers came out & said 'persecution & insult has ended.'"

CHAPTER TWENTY-SIX

Widows

In the bitter English winter of 1897, John Martin developed a severe cold and decided to recoup in the Canary Islands. He did not rest long, leaving posh hotels for grueling hikes in remote territory. He had clearly rebelled against the stultified life he had known before Victoria. "This is far more to my taste than the Grand Hotel...where they play lawn tennis & golf, dress for dinner & are as dull as anywhere else, & the ladies more homely than any...I ever met."

At first his letters to Woodhull sound like a jolly travelogue. "I am · marching about five hours a day with a guide...it is the strangest country that I ever saw; nothing but lava-beds, extinct volcanoes, & devastation. I get along without eating meat, of which there is none; but on the other hand no fleas have eaten me, as they [villagers] do not use garlic, so things could be worse." He wondered if she would get this letter, written on February 1, as "I am out of the world." A mule carrying mail would take days.

Their correspondence reveals a tragedy of urgent messages not received on time or at all. He had not received many loving letters sent in January and February. A hurt John pleaded, "Why have you not written or cabled to me to say where you are going?" However, Victoria had explained in a letter two weeks before, on January 29, "Darling husband I am very unwell and must fly tomorrow to some warmer place. I cannot throw off this horror." On January 15 she had written, "Your dear letter lies next to my heart and it breathes to me of love and fidelity." Again she wrote, "My darling husband... worrying about you... Oh how lonely our dear home is but thank God you are in more sympathetic climate than London." Two days later she cabled: "Not able to take voyage—you must get well—don't worry."

Then came an urgent telegram in February to Martin's Las Palmas hotel: PRECIOUS HUSBAND LIVE FOR MY SAKE MY HEART IS BREAKING—MY SOUL IS WITH YOU—ARE YOU BETTER. Then another on February 25: WHEN COMING HOME [STOP] HEART ANXIOUS.

He did respond to that telegram, as she noted on the twenty-sixth: "Darling husband I have just received your cable and my heart went out searching through space for your answer to the wish of my heart—listening to hear your blessed voice." Even under such dire circumstances, Victoria could not stop obsessing about feeling persecuted: "Oh could we but live our life over again. Those who made us suffer so intensely might attempt in vain to disturb the tranquility of our hearts—I cannot bear to see them or hear their voices. Get well and we shall yet see some happy days together." In a "world of treachery and hollowness," he was "one who cares if I am... in despair." She did note that if he wanted her to come, to wire, "and if I am able to endure the long fatigue of the voyage I will do so."

On March 6, Martin responded that since his sick father was recovering at the Overbury estate, he would remain and "sail tonight for the most remote of all the Islands, Lanzarote." He would be away "from the world for 10 days," returning to Las Palmas on the sixteenth, hoping to catch the next steamer and "be back to you and to our dear home before the end of the month... Keep your dear heart happy, & all will be well." On March 18, his brother, Richard, wrote: "My dear Johnny... my [not "our"] father died last night... He was getting dressed for dinner... and quietly passed away." The family was shocked, as he had been "so much better." Richard assumed that Victoria had cabled John the news. He then critically noted: "I have written several times to Victoria but I have heard nothing from her. I urged her to go... to you at once as probably careful nursing is what would do you more good than doctors."

Victoria never forgave his family for the slights she felt. She was sending a friend to the island with a letter "that I may know the truth—I know your family do not *love* me—and I do not trust them—they did not care for us when we were well—how is it possible that they should *now*—hear me call you this moment—my soul speaks to you—live for my sake—we may be happy yet." On March 18, the same day his father died, a telegram was sent to Victoria from the Canary Islands: MARTIN VERY ILL BUT NO IMMEDIATE DANGER–WILL WIRE AGAIN.

A flurry of cables followed, from doctors: March 19, 11:10 a.m.: MARTIN WORSE—IN DANGER—FOURTH DAY ILLNESS; that afternoon, 5:50 p.m.: PLEURO—STILL DANGEROUSLY ILL—WRITING AGAIN; March 20, 11:00 a.m.: AFRAID MARTIN SINKING—NO USE COMING—; that afternoon, 5:34 p.m.: YOUR DEAR HUSBAND DIED THIS AFTERNOON. John Martin never knew that his father had died just three days before him.

The next day, Sunday, March 21, Martin's doctor, Brian Melland, wrote a three-page letter to Victoria about "your husband's terribly acute and sudden illness." Martin was on Lanzarote Island when he was taken ill on Sunday, March 14, "with rigors and very severe pain at the base of the right lung as if a knife were there." Martin managed to get on the boat to Las Palmas on Monday night and "was delirious all that night and never took off his clothes." When the boat landed at Las Palmas on Tuesday, bearers carried Martin from the boat to the hospital. Martin told Dr. Melland that he had a "frightful pain in his liver." He urgently hoped to be well enough to catch the boat for England on Friday, the nineteenth. "I saw he was very ill and that he had got Pleuro-Pneumonia...His breathing was very difficult on Friday morning." The doctor removed fluid from his lungs, and Martin "was rather better on Friday...but in the evening he was feeling short of breath again...On Saturday morning he became delirious and unconscious and passed away at 3 in the afternoon having made a most gallant fight for life." Martin was only fifty-five. The doctor told Victoria details her husband had kept from her in his letters. He had been having "shivering fits," had little to eat in mountain villages, and had endured severe cold. He had also fallen into water and ridden in wet clothes back to his Spanish Fonda. "It made all our hearts bleed not to be able to get him through his terrible illness for he was a very noble man."

Letters containing the harsh reality of sudden death followed—embalming arrangements, authorization of payment to ship Martin's body home. Victoria received a formal letter from his brother, Richard, concerning a request from the Canary Islands regarding the remains. "I am proposing to wire the following '—Return [the body]—Having learned all particulars Victoria remains here.' If you have anything to add perhaps it will be as well to do so in a separate telegram. I shall always be pleased to be of use. Yours very sincerely, Richard B. Martin." He followed with "Dear Victoria: have you made arrangements with an undertaker or agent to meet the body and convey…Let me know if I can help you."

After Martin's death she wrote bitterly to Tennie about "my family": "Dear Sister, In the divine aroma of my dear husband's old library I am now at midnight and going over all that I have suffered. I have seen Johnny's tears flow as he would tell me how my family persecution had unnerved him. And he would turn to me with a face white as death, saying who will take care of my dear wife when I am no longer able to *shield* her from their malignant ignorance & venom…my heart has been rent asunder by it all. Be *happy* [twice underlined]. We may never meet again on earth. We [no doubt Zula and Byron with her] leave London tomorrow morning. How long or where they may take me I do not know or care. I only know that my life has been made wretched by them all."

Apparently Tennie had been with her, perhaps at a memorial for Martin, but, unfortunately, all Victoria's letters are undated. She alluded to past coolness between her and Tennie, slightly apologized, and blamed Martin's family. Victoria's earlier hostility to Sir Francis Cook, whom she had called a "libertine," and the rumors about the sisters that had scandalized the Martin family, were indications of how visits from Tennie—despite her "Lady Cook" title—must have been discouraged. "When I said goodbye to you today with my heart not with my lips," Victoria wrote, "I realized that we both were nervous wrecks and that those who caused it all were utterly unworthy…Try and you may succeed in being happy with those who stand by you," she continued. "My family have [*sic*] done all they could to kill me as they did Johnny."

Four years later it was Tennie's turn to wear widow's weeds. Headlines emphasized Sir Francis Cook's philanthropy as he lay ill in February 1901: LIFE OF GOOD DEEDS DRAWING TO A CLOSE. "His riches are said to amount to tens of millions, and he has spent enormous sums in philanthropy and in aiding persons of moderate circumstances."

His death on February 17 was covered by papers in the United States because he had married an "American Girl." In this new century, obituary writers viewed Tennie and Victoria as quaint artifacts who had "attracted notice soon after the Civil War by advocating Spiritualism and clair-voyancy [*sic*] and their public utterances on woman's rights and other subjects." Vanderbilt was always mentioned. Some referred to Tennie's appointment as colonel of the colored veteran guards. Father Buck was transformed into a "well known New York merchant." A massive turnout of retainers mourned outside Monserrate, where Tennie would no longer be welcome.

Yet, in Claflin fashion, this was not to be a quiet and distinguished death. Six weeks later, Lady Cook requested that her husband's body be exhumed so that she could answer "rumors that Sir Francis died an unnatural death and owed his demise to me, the conspirators hoping in this fashion to blackmail me. Had I not been a woman of worldwide repu-tation, I could have afforded to let these calumnies die. My own health is extremely poor. Should I die now these lies might go on forever. I have therefore resolved to refute them now. False stories have been circulated by a person not related to Sir Francis, but who was disappointed at not being remembered in his will." "Harrowing as it is, I shall not flinch," vowed Tennie regarding exhuming the body. "My husband was beloved by me and I by him; and these iniquitous slanders shall be stamped out." Once again, screaming headlines in cities in the United States as well as London accompanied her actions: SHE WANTS TO SHOW THE WORLD SHE DIDN'T KILL HER HUSBAND. British officials decided that the stories were "so evidently absurd and so manifestly without foundation that they couldn't think of letting the sorrowing widow open her husband's grave."

However, John Henry Wallace, former personal secretary to Sir Francis and Lady Cook, alleged that her remarks, which did not name him, were enough to identify him as the person she said had circulated stories of her murdering Sir Francis. Said to be bitterly upset at not being mentioned in the will, two years after Sir Francis died Wallace sued Tennessee for $50,000 for libel and slander.

Wallace testified in January 1903 that he had acted as Tennessee's private detective and had trailed Sir Francis beginning in 1897, when Lady Cook "accused her husband of 'carrying on' with a certain lady." Wallace said he followed him for four years until just before Sir Francis's death at age eighty-four, being paid his regular salary by the very man he was spying on. He said he found nothing. Lady Cook's counsel said her press statements did not refer to Wallace and charged that this was a blackmailing action, gambling on Lady Cook's making "any sacrifice" rather than have the matter dragged into court. The jury thought otherwise and in March awarded Wallace £550.

Upon hearing the verdict, Tennie jumped up, "waving her arms and screaming." When an usher took her arm to escort her from the court, she cried out, "Don't pull me out. I'll walk out. I am a sorrowful woman. I have done more for England and America than anybody else has done and my reputation is ruined." As she left, she cried, "Cruel, cruel." On June 13, Tennessee was granted a retrial. The Court of Appeals ruled in her favor, characterizing the Wallace suit as a blackmailing action.

This saga ended most strangely when a doctor was called to Wallace's home to attend his sick wife the next month. He found her dead, having died from natural causes. Nearby was Wallace, bleeding from razor wounds to his throat. The doctor bound up his wounds and called the police, who charged him with attempting to commit suicide. While in the dock, he was seized with a fit. The case was adjourned, and Wallace was "remanded to the Kingston Workhouse."

Following tradition, Sir Francis's first-born son, Frederick, one year older than Tennie, inherited a fabulous fortune—all the estates in Portugal and two-thirds of his father's other property, including Doughty House. The second son, Wyndham, received the remaining third. Tennessee received £25,000 and the income for life from an investment of £50,000. Cook's daughter received £25,000 and income from an investment of £100,000. His famous collection was left in trust for Frederick and his heirs, and kept in the Doughty Gallery. If Tennie was bothered by not receiving any of the art collection, she never said so publicly. Frederick was not the devotee of fine art that his father was. It was said by family that he "preferred his Madonnas in the flesh."

Tennie, now in her late fifties, began a wandering life again, but this time as a very wealthy widow. She traveled the world in her crusade to aid women in whatever cause came to mind.

As for Victoria, the spirits could not have divined an eerier act of fate that left her, however lonely and unhappy, very wealthy. Because her father-in-law had died three days before her husband, she inherited the family home at Bredon's Norton and its surroundings and property elsewhere in England, plus their house in Hyde Park Gate and most of its contents. She also became the largest shareholder in Martins Bank. Had Martin's father outlived his son by even a few hours, she would have inherited only £100 from her father-in-law upon his death. His handsome bequest in his will for son John would not have passed to her.

After several months of mourning, Victoria, with Zula now her devoted caregiver, concentrated on publishing *The Humanitarian* until giving it up in 1901. In 1900, Victoria had begun her retreat from London, moving with Zula and Byron to her country home, Norton Park, in the village of Bredon's Norton. It was not far from the place she had always hated to visit, Overbury. Despite her wealth, Victoria spoke mostly of her lonesomeness. "Wealth only shows the falsity of life." People "flock to you for material things," compared to "those way back who came to you because they understand the truth and your mission. What does one gain if they get the world and lose soul power?"

CHAPTER TWENTY-SEVEN

Moving On

In 1901, Victoria turned sixty-three, and Tennie, fifty-six. Neither was in good health but Tennie kept up a world-jaunting life, staying in a residential hotel in Kensington while in London. She never complained about the loss of Monserrate or Doughty House, but neither did she mention ever seeing Sir Francis's children.

Despite her deep mourning, Victoria had spent four busy years in London, not entertaining as lavishly as she and Martin had, but attending such gatherings as the Duchess of Westminster's reception for Lord Salisbury. Yet Victoria was happiest in the company of thinkers, entertaining professors, and scientists who contributed to *The Humanitarian*.

She became more and more querulous and paranoid, threatening Martin's family after having imagined that they contemplated suing her and demanding to know what had been done with her husband's ashes. Her one friend in the family, nephew Robert, patiently informed her that he had buried them at sea as requested.

Victoria left London in 1901, escaping to an idyllic village 109 miles from London, in the rolling green fields at the edge of the Cotswolds. Her 1,200-acre estate outside Bredon's Norton featured an enchanted walled garden near the front of her ivy-covered Tudor-style home. A wide, circular gravel drive led to the entrance. The center hall resembled a cozy hunting lodge, with a diamond-patterned floor of black slate and pale gray stone, antlers looking down from thirteen-foot-high walls, dark wood paneling, and a huge fireplace. To the right, a large dining room sat across from Victoria's study, with windows looking out to the Malvern Hills. On the inner entrance stained-glass door, Victoria had inlaid her favorite word, KISMET, on the bottom. Above bedroom doorways, she had inscribed the names of poets, such as Tennyson.

Zula Maude, now forty, had replaced Tennie, Colonel Blood, and then Martin as the devoted caretaker for an emotionally needy Victoria. Six years before, when Zula was thirty-four, she made the decision to be a submissive member of her mother's entourage, forsaking the kind of freedom her mother had so seized in her youth. A family row back then had made the newspapers when Victoria tangled with her niece Ella (daughter of sister Meg) and Ella's husband, Dr. Charles Stuart Welles, over Zula. Victoria had hired Welles as the American agent for *The Humanitarian* and to look after Zula, who ran the American publication. Under a three-year contract, the Welleses were living with Zula in a Manhattan residence leased by Victoria in her daughter's name. In 1895, when Victoria heard that Zula had fallen in love, with a man Victoria presumed was after her daughter's money, she furiously blamed Welles for not rigidly overseeing her daughter. Zula joined her mother's suit against the Welleses to get sole possession of the house. In turn, Welles sued Victoria for back pay. Meg Miles, who had apparently remarried, as she was now called Margaret O'Halloran, unloaded on her sister Victoria, who had attacked *her* daughter Ella Welles, telling the whole story to the *New York Times*: "All this trouble arose over Zula Woodhull's falling in love." O'Halloran said her famous sister went on an eight-day siege to burn all that was "cursed" belonging to the Welleses, including seven trunks' worth of dresses, children's toys, and small furniture items. The rest of the furnishings she gave away. "There is no language that can describe the rascality of Victoria," who has now tried to "clear out my daughter," cried Meg.

From then on, Victoria extracted a promise from Zula never to marry; in exchange, she would inherit her mother's vast wealth. So Zula Maud, thirty-four at the time, gave up her last chance to find a life of her own.

Victoria, the legendary free lover in her youth, emphasized a decorous life for Zula. The latter returned to England with her mother and, when Martin died in 1897, devoted her life to caring for Victoria as well as Byron. Zula's attempts at individual expression, outside of her *Humanitarian* work, included writing a play, but were met with little success. She had none of her mother's looks or complicated charisma.

Tennie had stayed out of the fight over Zula Maud and had continued a close friendship with the Welleses' daughter, her grandniece Utica. When Utica's father, the Dr. Welles with whom Victoria had fought, secured a high post in the U.S. embassy in London, Tennie arranged for grandniece Utica to be presented to Queen Victoria. In 1903, Utica married Thomas Beecham, heir to a pharmaceutical fortune and later famously known as Sir Thomas Beecham, the founder and conductor of the London Philharmonic. Utica was the first of his three wives. Beecham had numerous affairs, including a liaison with the infamous Lady Cunard, known as Emerald. Although separated for years, Utica, unlike her great aunts Victoria and Tennie, did not believe in divorce. Beecham finally divorced her in 1943. Throughout her life, Tennie, a.k.a. Lady Cook, played a motherly role to grandniece Utica, Lady Beecham. Contrasting Victoria to Tennie, sister Meg chastised Woodhull for not being more like Lady Cook, "who is honored and loved for her charitable work in London and Portugal."

With Zula's help, Victoria continued to publish *The Humanitarian* for four more years after her husband's death, abandoning the nine-year venture at the end of 1901. She continued to travel often with Zula, but never lectured. Her last attempt, in America in 1893, was a failure. Her fiery oratory of the past had been dimmed by duller words spoken by a woman in her mid-fifties wearing glasses to read. Now, nine years later and passionate about motorcars, Victoria zoomed through London and the countryside in her 20 horsepower Mercedes Simplex; she and Zula Maud were reportedly the first women to drive through England to France and back again, in 1903. Sometimes she was driven by a chauffeur, who received numerous citations for driving, at Victoria's insistence, above the 20 mph speed limit.

When she busied herself with local issues, Victoria was far from popular with Bredon's Norton villagers, who were suspicious of her newfangled ideas and hostile to her imperious ways.

Victoria halted a charity that provided clothing and a ton of coal for every village family each winter, sacked servants, and refused to participate in "indiscriminate charity," which fueled outrage. After she made village improvements that included the installation of streetlights, vandals systematically smashed the glass lanterns and ripped out equipment. A few years later, a chastened Victoria played Lady Bountiful, providing warm clothing for the needy at her Christmas parties and working with the local church to help families.

Victoria never stopped trying to sanitize her past. In 1893 an anonymous pamphlet appeared in London depicting her as having been a "gentle home-loving wife" before she embarked on a career. Later she hired a writer to create and send letters to the local papers that stretched the truth beyond belief: Victoria had been "all but elected" president of the United States, despite Grant's landslide victory. In 1902 she told a magazine reporter that Buck was a "well known figure of the Ohio bar."

Zula and Victoria tried a "back to the land" collective, encouraging local women to grow vegetables. It was not a success. Backward education committees refused to back their next move: a progressive school that would start with prekindergarten. In addition to basics, they would emphasize painting, music, carpentry, sewing, cooking, basket making, and physical education. They would also provide swings and seesaws, unheard of in rural schools. When the school board refused to participate, Victoria and Zula started the school with their own money. By 1908 it was attracting children from three miles away. However, the two-year experiment crashed in 1909 after a board of educators refused to give the school a "Certificate of Efficiency." One editorial summed up a general feeling: pupils were going to mourn the loss of this "natural" education that "made the world a wonderful place" and a return to schools bound by rules and "copy-book maxims." Still, parents were warned that they could be prosecuted if they did not remove their children from Victoria and

Zula's school and return them to a school holding the required Certificate of Efficiency.

It is no wonder that Woodhull, despite her "Fairy Godmother" donations, remained aloof from this community and concentrated on her at-home salon, frequented by international and London visitors.

It may have surprised those who witnessed Woodhull as the prominent sister in the 1870s, but Tennie now took center stage, surpassing her older sister in carrying on their crusade for women's rights. She spoke to queens, presidents, and would-be presidents. She lectured twice to crowds of seven thousand cheering, applauding fans at Royal Albert Hall.

In this new century, Tennie used her influence and celebrity as Lady Cook to garner headlines in her fight for women's rights in England, France, Portugal, Italy, and the United States—wherever she was asked, and sometimes where she was not. At age fifty-nine, in January 1905, she looked the epitome of a Lady Cook, her short, curly silver hair crowned with a fussy, frilly hat tied in a bow at the chin. Just as she had entranced the British as an American novelty, she was now fascinating the press back in her homeland three decades later as a titled woman of note. Her views were now more staid than startling. Did she believe in communities raising children? "No indeed! Home is heaven where the father and mother work together in trust and sympathy. There is no holier word in our language" than *mother*, and the world needed "pure fathers" as much as the virtuous mother.

She was the press's favorite dowager. At a New Year's Eve party ushering in 1905, Tennie was the attraction in a luxurious, crowded room filled with the sound of soft dance music. Regal in sapphire velvet and ancient lace, "a woman of slight figure and with a face like an ivory miniature crowned with silvery hair," Tennie was surrounded by admirers. To younger women, it seemed impossible that she had been jeered at and thrown out of hotels thirty-five years before. "She is seen everywhere—in exclusive drawing-rooms and at famous clubs. Everyone asks. 'Who is the lovely white-haired lady?'"

Tennie fit in with the "progressive woman of today who...says anything she likes...penetrates the foulest slums to study social questions...

addresses legislatures without a tremor...travels around the world alone...
enters every trade and profession unchallenged...speaks boldly on every
issue under the sun." This was a rosy description of emancipation in 1905,
but at least by comparison, women could not dream of the restrictions of
1870. When the sisters "invaded Wall Street thirty-five years ago...No
epithet was too foul to be applied to them." It was "improper for a woman
to walk on Broadway alone," to be out on evenings alone, or to be seen in
Wall Street "even in a carriage, unless the blinds were drawn."

Tennie returned to America repeatedly to fight for the vote. In February of 1907, she sat down with President Theodore Roosevelt at the
White House. She told the president, "By putting us on the same plane
of suffrage with our servants and our former black slaves, you could rise
to the greatest height in the world." At a press conference afterward in
the Willard Hotel, where Tennie first sought legislative help thirty-seven
years before, she laughed. "I told him the women would elect and re-elect
him until he was too old to continue as President." He had not vowed to
take the issue up with Congress, however. The president "told me he did
not see that much good had come as a result of giving women the voting privilege...notably in Colorado and other States." He told her the
vote alone would not be "their redemption"—an argument the sisters had
made decades before with their cry for economic independence.

Tennie was supportive of the more militant British *suffragettes*, a new
term coined to distinguish their militancy from the comportment of *suffragists*, a general term for men and women who sought the vote. Led by Emme-
line Pankhurst, the suffragettes chained themselves to fences, smashed
windows, and endured forced feeding in prison. Pankhurst drew five hundred thousand suffragettes to one protest rally in Hyde Park. Tennie spoke
passionately about England's suffragettes who "brave mobs, court arrest and
suffer imprisonment for the cause we know to be just." Perhaps it was time
for "my American sisters" to do the same. It would take another nine years,
until 1916, before Alice Paul would lead American suffragists in marches and
demonstrations, picket the White House, and go on hunger strikes in prison
after some demonstrators were beaten unconscious by police.

In the fall of 1908, Tennie was now being praised as "one of the earliest and best known suffragettes in America." She announced from Paris that she would again return to the United States, this time to stump for William Jennings Bryan in the last days of his presidential race. "Lady Cook is convinced that Bryan will take a more active interest in her ideas than Roosevelt," a reporter wrote. "If he will agree with me on woman suffrage and the improvement of the marriage law," said Tennie, "I shall spend plenty of money working for him." Bryan lost to William Howard Taft.

While in America in 1908, Tennie once again tried to vote, receiving large headlines: THEY WOULDN'T LET LADY COOK VOTE. A crowd collected when an automobile disgorged Tennie and friends in front of a Manhattan registration site. "Keep in line, ladies," shouted a policeman, who was ignored. The registrar looked at Tennie and said, " 'Not eligible.' 'On what grounds?' asked Lady Cook in an unruffled tone…'only male voters are allowed to register.' " Tennie tried humor: "But I am a male and more—I am a FEmale." The registrar shot back, "Just leave off the 'fe' and you can vote." Lady Cook said pleasantly, "I shall have to take this matter to congress as I did in 1871," taking credit for Victoria's famous memorial to the Judiciary Committee. Her voting attempt was the "first small gun fired… They say women will get suffrage when they want it," she declared. "I am going to try to arouse the women so that they will see that millions want it."

Tennie was now routinely acclaimed as a brave and feisty veteran of the suffrage war, worthy of honor, not calumny. A large contingent of American suffragettes rode out in tugboats to greet Tennie the next year, 1909, when her ocean liner arrived in New York. She now vowed to spend her total fortune—$1 million, she said—to get the vote. She planned to meet with President Taft "to see if I cannot get him to do what Lincoln did, but by peaceable measures… The constitution says only idiots, the insane, and convicts may not vote and I want to know if that bars women." Whether she met with Taft or gave money to the cause is unknown, but the fight for the vote dragged on for another eleven years.

Her titled name was used in all headlines: LADY COOK IN HER OLD CELL. On that 1909 visit, Tennie cheerfully took reporters on a tour of the Ludlow Street Jail, pointing out, scratched on the wall of the cell but faded after thirty-seven years, TENNESSEE CLAFLIN AND VICTORIA CLAFLIN WOODHULL, WE WILL NOT COME HERE AGAIN. The jail official, not sure how to greet a jailbird turned nobility, bowed deeply. Tennie explained to a throng waiting outside, "My sister and I in 1872 were publishing a suffrage magazine... We didn't say anything in it which would now be considered very harmful... Arrested on a charge of publishing 'obscenity,' we were locked up in the jail... We found the jail ill-kept, malodorous and hideously dirty, but we survived it."

Not all the press was good. In 1910, Tennie was plagued by two strange incidents. Her sister Polly applied for a writ of habeas corpus ordering a newspaper friend of Tennie's and his wife to "produce in court the body of Tennessee Claflin Cook, known as Lady Cook." Sparr claimed that Tennie was "old, feeble, of advanced years," and, most important to Sparr, a woman of "large means." She alleged that the couple was holding Tennie captive, as she had not visited her. In fact, Tennie was willingly staying with these friends. She won over reporters with humor: "Well you've seen the body at any rate." She laughed about being held against her will: "I have never signed even a check that I didn't want to. Mrs. Sparr is a good deal older than I am, and we do not get along very well together, and that is all there is to it." A few months later, a shyster lawyer made headlines by parking an ambulance outside a New York courtroom "in anticipation of Lady Cook feigning a fit." She was inside, defending herself from a "breach of contract" suit brought by a writer who said she had verbally told him she would pay him $30,000 to write her biography. The suit was thrown out.

For the most part, however, Tennie was considered an oracle on all things relating to women. At sixty-eight, she announced, "Do you know if I had the vote I wouldn't go across the street to cast a ballot for any man; there isn't one good enough—not yet." In 1913, headlines trumpeted LADY COOK HANDS A STIFF JOLT TO CLOTHES CRANKS. She supported modern dress and blasted the "shameless revelations of women's anatomy which the old-time crinolines made... the wind blew those huge skirts around—well it was awful. And then came the great bustles, which weighted down the body and brought weakness…Puny, sickly babies by the hundreds were one result of the bustle monstrosity" and "tight corsets, which squeezed in the waist." She added: "Trailing outer skirts, which gathered up all the microbes on the street and carried them through the house, were more prolific of disease…among women than anything else that could be named." The woman of today, "with her light-weight, outer skirt, one thin petticoat, low-heeled comfortable shoes and skirts short enough to clear the ground…are gowned a hundred times more sensibly than they have been since the days of Grecian draperies."

Tennie kept to an amazing schedule, hopping from Paris to Naples, then back to the United States and England to lecture in major halls in New York, Chicago, Philadelphia, Albany, Pittsburgh, Leeds, Manchester, Sheffield, Birmingham, and London. Yet she wrote Victoria from New York on January 31, 1911, about her nervous stage jitters before a Carnegie Hall performance. "My dear sister, By the time you receive this my lecture will be over and I shall be very glad…I feel that it will be a success…early all the boxes and reserved seats are taken…but I will be glad when it is over."

Tennie seemed impervious, however, once onstage. At Carnegie Hall she drew laughs when she tailored her speech to an American audience. "Why, I love the American men, for they trust their wives." Pause. "Some of them trust their wives so much that when they want to evade payment of a debt or avoid business trouble, they put their property in their wives' names."

She was a huge success when she faced vast audiences at Royal Albert Hall in December 1909 and then again in May 1910. She was but one of several speakers at the December mass meeting organized by England's Women's Freedom League, yet she stole the show. One observer at her December performance marveled that she had delivered her lengthy lecture "without the assistance of a single note." While Tennie spoke "with the force of a mountain torrent, the immense audience listened as if petrified with admiring amazement." This critic praised her "ever-present humour" and her shift to "beautifully modulated tones." She brought tears to her audience when she addressed the "hapless condition of her sisters in all countries and under all forms of government, going back to Biblical time." Tennie's performance was the "most stirring plea for women's equality ever enunciated in a building which has vibrated to the notes of the world's greatest singers and musicians and to the fervent addresses of our Salisburys, Balfours, and Chamberlains." She received a "hurricane of applause."

On May 6, 1910, the stage was hers alone. Fans wondered how she would fare; "it was held to be impossible that one solitary woman, no matter who she might be," could attract and hold an audience of upward of seven thousand in that vast structure. In addition, a grim obstacle loomed. Gloom was hanging over London as bulletins reported that King Edward was near death. Thousands were streaming into the hall when news came from Buckingham Palace that the end was imminent. It was too late to postpone the lecture. Tennie faced the audience alone onstage. She expressed sadness over the death of the monarch who had opened the Alexandra House twenty-five years before: "I had prepared a special lecture for you; but on learning that our beloved King is now, perhaps, in the death struggle, it has grieved me very much, and I am sure everyone in this great hall to-night shares that feeling. But I hope you will bear with me in what I have got to say." (The King died just before midnight.)

The sympathetic audience interrupted Tennie's speech constantly with applause and laughed at her light asides. "Although she has to her account some four decades of incessant and strenuous work, she retains the personal charm, extraordinary vitality and activity, and invincible courage in the enunciation of her unchangeable opinion." Lady Cook, however, had indeed modified her opinion since her days as Tennie Claflin. Her Albert Hall speech of more than seven thousand words quoted the Bible, endlessly praised Jesus Christ and God, but circled back repetitiously to her main theme: "the purity of the sexes" and the necessity of mothers to teach their sons to respect women. Like her sister, Tennie now exalted marriage.

While extolling "Our Savior, the best friend that women ever had," Tennie still could sting. She blasted the teaching of priests, ministers, and other religious leaders as an explanation for "why women have been treated like slaves and worse than beasts during the last few centuries."

She quoted from a popular "Guide for Priests," which contained anti-female passages: "She is the gate by which the devil enters, the road that leads to sin." She attacked the Inquisition, which burned thousands of women as "witches": "How can you expect much from women in the face of such treatment?...a Galician Bishop declared that she was not human. At the Council of Macon the Bishops debated whether she had a soul." The audience cried, "Shame, shame," after she mentioned that a judge had recently said, " 'When women go into the witness-box they will swear to anything.' It is about time," Tennie cried, "we called for our sons to give us back our good name." Huge applause followed.

Her repetitive call to teach sons respect for women was laced with arguments for birth control and eugenics, demands for the women's vote, and attacks on the promiscuity that led to venereal disease. Churches should open their doors to events for "young people to meet in a pure and holy place" and maybe eventually marry. "Yes, I am a matchmaker, and I believe in it." Applause and laughter ensued.

She edged into the topic of birth control by opposing large families. "It is not quantity we want. We want quality." She assailed those who "breed like flies." The populace of insane asylums and jails were the "offspring of ignorant mothers, and of debased, debauched, and diseased fathers...The women have got to act, and they can stop it in one or two decades by stopping the supply." Her sympathy for prostitutes, whom she had characterized in her youth as victims of economic poverty, was long gone in her Albert Hall lecture. Prostitution "creates our degenerates, and it is the cause of over a million children dying every year before they reach the age of one with infantile syphilis and other causes." Now, in an age when the effects of sexual diseases were confirmed, Tennie dismissed the plight of prostitutes. Despairing of men who "sowed their wild oats" and then contaminated pure brides, she suggested that those men remain with people they had been "debauching and living with." She no longer talked about women exercising sexual freedom, and she swore that she had never advocated free love and now termed it *free lust*. In her youth she had shown compassion for an unmarried woman "following the instincts of her nature and the dictation of her soul." Now she sanctioned "purity" before marriage for both sexes.

(In a less public arena, however—a one-on-one interview five years before—Lady Cook did sound like the Tennie of old when she derided the "society mother" who holds "the theory that marriage is instituted for the purpose of getting daughters 'well provided for'—in other words to live the lives of drones. This is all wrong and false." And she defended poor prostitutes. "I hold that the woman who offers herself in the streets is a lesser offender than one who sells herself at the altar for a fortune or a title.")

A harsh eugenics warning from Tennie was followed by cries of "Hear! Hear!" from the thousands in Albert Hall: "Over a million children die every year before reaching the age of twelve months. They ought never to come into the world at all. We want to bring forth pure and healthy children, and then we shall not have to make war to kill off the mob of the unfit." With appalling insensitivity, she said, "If they only killed off the unfit we would not mind, but when you have a war you take the flower of our flock. You take our best and healthiest children, while you leave the degenerates and the paupers to breed, and we have to pay the taxes for their keep."

She remained serious about fighting to change marriage laws, and to get the vote, but she added an astonishing premise, given her feisty cries in the past: "We only want to put some decent men into Parliament... We do not wish to go there ourselves."

CHAPTER TWENTY-EIGHT

Last Acts

War made Tennie's 1872 battle cry to be a Joan of Arc willing to fight in combat less revolutionary. In the slaughter of World War I, Tennie sought to mobilize in three months a combat-trained army of 150,000 British women "wearing khaki uniforms, just like men, with the possible addition of knee-length skirts." Her Amazon Army was not ridiculed, and the *New York Times* wrote, "Lady Cook, pointing out the fact that the women would be the logical defenders when men were sent abroad, said 'I am going to rouse the women of England to defend their homes, to resist invaders, fight for their homes, their honor, their children.'" Britain had entered the war less than two weeks before, on August 4, 1914, in a mood of grand optimism that the fight would be over by Christmas. Tennie, who had rattled through a ravaged, war-torn country on a fortune-telling wagon as a teenager, was not so sure.

She started her mission by visiting Buckingham Palace and leaving a letter for Queen Mary: "Women have been brave in the past. We aren't all dolls." She praised the women for "knitting socks and doing Red Cross work," but England also needed women trained in arms. The War to End All Wars soon brought home to Britain the horrors of modern combat: aerial bombs screaming from the sky, trench warfare slaughter. The Battle of the Somme, in 1916, still stands as an appalling bloodbath, with the British army alone suffering nearly sixty thousand casualties in one day of the five-month siege. On the home front, British civilians were vulnerable to war's new destruction: aerial bombardment. In 1917 a bombardment on London killed 162 civilians, 18 of them children, when one bomb hit a school.

Britain was never invaded, but the fear was palpable as the war dragged on. Tennie's plan to arm women went nowhere, but British women did lobby for rifle training. Having no success with the male Home Defence forces, they were luckier when the Women's Defence Relief Corps was organized. Despite a major outcry that women should be seen as "gentle mothers" who did not bear arms and were designed to "bear armies," the Women's Defence Relief Corps organized a semimilitary section of women trained in drills, marching, scouting, and the use of arms.

The sisters were pleased to see women finally taken seriously as an economic force, although both decried the war as the reason. They had lived to see a new era for women—in the United States, too, but especially in Great Britain. Some eighty thousand British women served in the forces as noncombatants, and nurses served in combat areas. The need for women in the workforce hastened the collapse of domestic service, as maids left in droves for radical new employment opportunities, becoming bus conductors and civil service clerks, joining trade unions, and working in munitions factories. However, employers circumvented wartime equal-pay regulations by employing several women to replace one man.

Although women found out after the war that they were dispensable and quickly replaced by returning veterans, Britain's rigid class culture was dealt a blow, and in 1918, two years before the United States, British women got the vote, albeit for women age thirty and older. When asked if the age should be lowered, Victoria said that twenty-five would be low enough. Tennie never gave up her fight for women's rights and in old age was honored by younger as well as older suffragettes, who stood around her as she sat in the center of a group of them for a photograph, wearing a wide suffragette sash. Although American citizens, the sisters elected to stay in England throughout the war. Victoria hated the war, but as a supporter of Anglo-American alliance, she was deeply upset that the United

States stayed out until 1917. When the troops did arrive, she wrote, "Night after night, as I hear the rumble of the trains bearing the American boys to the front my heart turns—to the mothers who sent them, some to return, some to stain the earth with their blood freely given."

She sat in her study in Norton Park scrawling on scraps of paper her vivid and strong reactions. She "hoped to live until I could see...England's victory over savagery." She slashed her pages with underlines as she penned eloquent antiwar sentiments, written in such a rush of anger that she no longer cared about misspellings: "The Christmas bells can no longer ring out the message 'Peace on earth and good will to men.' Is it not hell on earth and death to men?—Is it not time to take stock of our souls *and* question the environment that led us blindfolded into this awful slaughter...? What is this awful quarel [*sic*] *over*? When the roar of cannon is heard *no* more, then hearts that have given loved ones on the alter [*sic*] of slaughter will demand an answer....The Church...has outlived its funcion [*sic*]...You are no longer your brothers [*sic*] keeper. He is toiling up the hill of investigation, blood stained and rebellious. No sophistry will answer what made this *hell* on earth possible."

At war's end, critics echoed her views. President Wilson admitted that the war happened "because Germany was afraid her commercial rivals were going to get the better of her." Warren G. Harding successfully rode into the White House on this message: "From the very beginning it was a lie to say this was a war to make the world safe for democracy."

Illness finally caught up with Tennie. In 1916 she wrote to Victoria, hoping to leave London: "My darling Sister, I want to come and stay with you at once and stay a good while, with whom should I love to be but yourself, when all the years of our youth we were so much to each other. We must be so now towards [either the "evening" or "ending"] of our lives."

It is unknown if she visited Victoria, but two years later she wrote a letter dated November 19, 1918. She requested that Victoria send someone to help her for a day or two and then "bring me right on down to you for there is no where I shall be so happy as with you. I must stay sometime

with you & get thoroughly better." Now without raids, "there is nothing
to fear with the war being over thanks [*sic*] God."

Whether Victoria, who had just turned eighty, ignored her sister's
pleas is not known. Tennie did not have someone like Zula to collect her
memorabilia; therefore few letters written *to* Tennie remain. Tennie sent
a telegram on September 4, 1919: YOU & I MUST HOLD TOGETHER IN OUR
OLD AGE. WE HAVE FEW OTHER PLEASURES LEFT NOW BUT OUR LOVE FOR
ONE ANOTHER & OUR MEMORIES OF THE PAST.

Then came Tennie's frightening letter, a year later, in 1920, about her
fistula and another operation. Her writing was now a difficult scribble.
Age and illness had all but obliterated the fun and fancy-free woman of
another time. The doctor "was annoyed to think I had got up today. Says
I must not leave the house for several days now...I am very feeble and
thinking more of my health and meeting my God."

Tennie hung on until the beginning of 1923, dying on January 18,
at the age of seventy-seven. She was not with Victoria, dying suddenly
while visiting her grandniece Lady Beecham at the home of Sir Thomas
Beecham. Her obituary in the *New York Times* twinned the sisters as "the
most widely-known women in the country fifty years ago." It retraced the
familiar milestones with a sarcastic edge: "They dabbled in spiritualism,
took up finance, and with the supposed aid of Commodore Vanderbilt
founded a brokerage house in Broad Street, sponsored eugenics and equal
rights, and generally impressed themselves on the public. Then they both
went to England and married men with large fortunes." Even in death,
Tennie could not escape dismissive smirking in a paper that had hounded
her and Victoria a half century before. The *Times* quoted extensively and
unfairly banker Henry Clews's scathing comments about Tennie. Slightly
kinder in March, the *Times* described her as a "woman writer and pioneer
of woman's suffrage," noting that she left property valued at £149,540,
worth millions today. Tennie left no will, granting letters of administration to Victoria. Polly Sparr argued that she was an heir. There is no
record of what Victoria Woodhull did with her sister's fortune.

Unsigned jottings in family archives mentioned that Tennie would be "buried at Norwood in the Cook's vaults." The writer wished to reassure others that Tennie did not suffer: "very peaceful & happy & talked so sincerely & lovingly of Mrs. Martin" (Victoria). The intriguing mystery is to whom the next sentence was referring. The note stated that Tennie's grandniece and dear friend Lady Beecham "will see that message is put with Lady Cook." Who still living was so close that a message would be placed in the casket with Tennie? It seems likely it was Victoria who had once written to Tennie so passionately, "I have loved thee with an everlasting love; with a love that passeth understanding. Your sister Victoria."

Victoria continued to foster Anglo-American alliances, flying both flags and meeting with English and American dignitaries who gladly visited the *grande dame* at her country estate. Her hostile treatment by the villagers had long evaporated, and she was praised for her beneficence, despite her aloofness. She had transferred her love of automobiles to the airplane. She announced she would give $5,000 to the first man or woman who flew across the Atlantic. Charles Lindbergh made his solo flight just weeks before she died, with no time for a reward from the ailing Victoria.

To the end, Victoria was unquestionably a seeker of knowledge, an eclectic hoarder of the written word: scraps, snippets, scrawls, poems, biblical passages; gushingly sentimental sayings mingled with bitter comments and some surprisingly witty observations, given her few excursions into humor. One spoke to her bitter treatment by writers: "It is well to remember that a dead diarist is also a dead liarist." She remained loyal to eugenics, clipping a sermon in which the pastor said he would marry only people who produced a doctor's certificate that stated they were free of venereal disease. And Spiritualism: "No where in the Bible does God condemn genuine seership...A knowledge of psychic phenomena is therefore the key to the understanding of the bible."

She collected lofty phrases that she felt pertained to her: "Martyrs today and heroes tomorrow." And underlined: "noble souls are sacrificed to ignoble man." Her love of mankind in her progressive phase seemed gone, according to this salty phrase: "Many people are not human beings. They are conditions, if they were my books I would discard *them*."

Victoria lashed out at family, perhaps both Claflins and Martins who had snubbed her. Save for Robert Holland-Martin, the nephew with whom she was close, there had been little communication. "I give all my shares and interests in the Martins [B]ank to my daughter Zula Maud Woodhull, to use as she wishes. I hope that *none* of what the *world calls family will* in any *way* make her any trouble or annoyance as she has *no* sympathy or desire to have them take any part in her life."

As she aged, Victoria grew more eccentric, refusing to shake hands as she obsessed about "microbes" dragged into houses by trailing skirts. She slept upright in a chair. She could be dictatorial with Zula, but upon her death, her daughter sobbed a tribute to a "darling" mother "who was comrade and friend... My heart is desolate... to go on is a terrible problem... it is like awakening on a different planet... where for am I called upon to endure this agony. I cannot reason with my heart."

Victoria outlived her enemies. She died in her sleep on June 9, 1927, having lived eighty-eight years, eight months, and sixteen days. As she requested, her ashes were scattered at sea, to symbolize the alliance of the two countries across the ocean. Stabs at an autobiography went unfinished, and Zula, who lived until 1940, never completed the task. (Zula's last burden, Byron, ended with his death in 1932.)

Nor had the sisters penned their collaboration. Yet in death they were twinned once again. In Victoria's obituary, Tennie got top billing in the London *Times*, which stressed her marriage to Sir Francis and praised her "vigorous championship of what used to be called women's rights." Exaggerations included Tennie's studying "law, medicine, and surgery and finance and banking." The *Times* article astoundingly positioned Victoria as one who "contented herself with banking" and later "scientific agriculture." She was characterized second as an orator: "like her sister, she became an excellent platform speaker." There was no mention in the *Times* article of Victoria's bid for the presidency, nor of Henry Ward

Beecher and the scandal that had so consumed America a half century before and had led to the sisters' astonishing final chapter in England.

Among Victoria's scrawled notes was a rare sentence of self-examination: "My life has been a long struggle to do right to the best of my ability, and God knows, if I have failed in many things, no one regrets it more than I *do*." In another sentence she is not far afield from her long-ago spirit guide expressions in the Tilton biography of her: "From my early childhood," she felt herself "being lifted above the earthy conditions by which I found myself." She called herself a "faithful servant" who never penned the opus that would "put me right before the world & for the coming generation."

The sisters left this world without the final imprint of their version of who they were and what they had accomplished. Victoria and Tennie belonged to the ages, which must now puzzle over and debate their worth, which continues to change with passing generations and shifting attitudes about women.

Well-Behaved Women Seldom Make History

Victoria Woodhull and Tennessee Claflin always said they were a hundred years ahead of their time, but one hundred and fifty would be more like it—and then some. Case in point: Society should leave "the love affairs of the community to regulate themselves, instead of trusting to legislation to regulate them." This is not a modern-day activist cheering the U.S. Supreme Court's 2013 overturning of the Defense of Marriage Act as unconstitutional, but Woodhull in 1871. "Put a woman on trial for anything—it is considered as a legitimate part of the defense to make the most searching inquiry into her sexual morality, and the decision generally turns upon the proof advanced in this regard." These words are not a contemporary comment on the disparaging treatment of victims of domestic violence or rape—one of the reasons 54 percent of rapes go unreported today—but rather, Tennie Claflin speaking out in 1871.

If the sisters were alive today, they would find many of the same problems they railed against over a century and a half ago, sometimes on issues unheard of back then, but dovetailing with their sense of personal freedom. As soon as the Supreme Court ruled on DOMA in 2013, opponents vowed to fight state by state against further legalizing of same-sex marriage. Other issues, familiar to the sisters, continue to be fought with new and sometimes appalling twists. Politicians argue over the existence of "legitimate rape" and swear that rapes resulting in pregnancy are "very low." They sponsor legislation involving vaginal probes, and mandate ultrasounds for women seeking abortions. Right-wing "Family Values" politicians are caught in adultery scandals. Corporate crime on Wall Street and corruption on Capitol Hill seldom shock anyone anymore.

The Tea Party extremist War on Women, infused by right-wing political action committees, continues at a ferocious pace, most noticeably in their battle against pro-choice, which is always a polarizing force in political campaigns. In the summer of 2013, the mostly male GOP-dominated House passed the most severe anti-abortion bill in a decade that would nationally ban abortions after twenty weeks, knowing full well that the Senate would not pass it, but determined to send a message.

Just like the generations born after *Roe v. Wade*, Victoria and Tennessee grew up in an era of relaxed views on abortion. Not until their adulthood and the 1873 rise of Comstockery did abortion become a serious crime. Today *Roe v. Wade* has been whittled away to an alarming degree. Some 145 years after the sisters fought to give women the right to own their bodies, many states severely restrict reproductive rights, with some proposing laws that would make a fetus a person at the moment of fertilization. Anti-choice opposition has forced the closing of Planned Parenthood clinics across the country, while politicians continually vow to end *Roe v. Wade*, which would once again criminalize abortion. Some states also impose limitations on access to contraception, making it harder for women who do not want to conceive. Texas governor Rick Perry led the battle in draconian achievements, and his legislation has so slashed Planned Parenthood funding that an estimated 200,000 women, especially poor women, have lost or could lose access to contraception, cancer screening, and basic preventive care.

As for sex education in schools—a goal of the sisters in the Victorian Age—ignorance rules the day across the nation; legislators in at least seven states last year fought to clamp down on comprehensive "medically accurate" sexual education. Some have banned Planned Parenthood representatives from teaching sex education and continue to push anti-abortion, abstinence, or creationism content.

A loud rallying cry to fight this ignorance was Senator Wendy Davis's abortion filibuster in 2013 against a harsh Texas abortion bill. The Fort Worth senator, who once lived in a trailer and worked her way through Harvard Law School, so galvanized the social media last June that a growing pro-choice backlash to the anti-choice backlash is festering among young women who felt complacent about gains made long in the past. Davis talked for eleven hours—not allowed to sit, lean on a desk, eat, drink, or take a bathroom break. Davis warned that if the bill were passed, more clinics would have to close. She also noted that men who did not "have the equipment" were legislating against women who did. Davis's filibuster temporarily halted Perry's male minions who passed the bill. Davis is now running for Texas governor in 2014.

While the battle against pro-choice remains the fiercest, dismissive treatment of other women's rights are appalling. Recently, Republican congressmen fought to roll back the Violence Against Women Act (VAWA) and eventually tried to kill it entirely. President Obama finally renewed the law in March 2013. When Congresswomen Pat Schroeder and Louise Slaughter sponsored the original legislation in 1993, a woman was raped every sixteen seconds in the United States and one was beaten every fifteen seconds, recalls Slaughter, noting a reduction in violence against women since the law was passed in 1994. In 2012, she said, "It took years to get to where we are today and yet we are again fighting some of these same battles. Shameful doesn't even begin to describe it."

Schroeder, the longest-serving female member of the House (1973–1996), was one of the few voices in Congress in the 1970s calling for women's rights. She battled for the Equal Rights Amendment (ERA), pro-choice and pro-contraception legislation, and equal pay for equal work, in addition to pushing for women in top corporate and political positions and for laws against domestic violence and rape, much as the sisters had done one hundred years before.

"Woodhull was amazing," Schroeder said. "I could go on forever about how things have stalled," she said, sighing. "I refused to go to the twentieth anniversary of my Family Medical Leave bill because no one has done one thing to expand it. I thought it was pathetic after we had to water it down. We are still the country that does the least for families." In fact, Schroeder said, the United States is one of only three countries, out of 177 nations, that do not mandate paid parental leave. The other two? Papua New Guinea and Swaziland.

House Republicans closed down the U.S. government in their 2013 fight to repeal Obamacare. The Affordable Care Act has already provided vital assistance to millions of women, giving them access to women's health services, wellness care, and protection from gender discrimination.

But rather than tackle such important women's issues, the twenty-first-century media have been awash with arguments about the Mommy Wars, with entire books written on the subject, and women agonizing about why their feminist mothers made them think they "could have it all." Those who did it without any safety net years ago can sympathize, but media-centric fights about whether it is better for mothers to stay at home than to work tend toward elitist debates of little significance to the vast number of mothers who *have* to work. As Schroeder says, "If women can find a way to stay home and like that, great. Who cares? Can you imagine men having such a debate? The problem is 90% of women don't have the opportunity for such a debate either. They must work. The media grinding away on such issues makes the women's movement look elitist.

"Here are some horrors we should be more concerned about: Single women with children make less than single women or married women. And women still make $0.77 to the dollar that men make, with some women making much less. Paid sick leave, family medical leave, etc., are still not guaranteed," Schroeder adds. Even a college degree—with women attending comparable schools, enrolling in the same major, and choosing the same profession—doesn't help. After one year out of college, a 2012 study found, women on average were making $7,600 less than their male counterparts, or 82 cents on the dollar. A half century after passage of the Equal Pay Act in 1963, "women continue to earn less than men do in nearly every occupation." That the sisters, during their labor activist days, sought equal pay for equal work in Victorian-era America is nothing short of a miracle.

They were, of course, the epitome of the slogan "Well-behaved women seldom make history"—but then, any woman who fights the status quo, from the suffragists to Eleanor Roosevelt, Bella Abzug, Betty Friedan, Gloria Steinem, Hillary Clinton, Ann and Cecile Richards, and Wendy Davis, has to go against the grain. When Pat Schroeder, a Harvard Law graduate, ran for office in 1972, the headlines read "Housewife" or "Mother" runs for Congress. When facing one indignant male colleague after another who demanded how she could be both a member of Congress and a mother, she said, "Because I have a brain and a uterus and both work."

As for the sisters' legacy, Tennessee is now seldom mentioned, as if her fight for women's equality, and especially her long battle for the vote, years after her Manhattan notoriety, never happened. I hope that this book will help remedy that. When Tennie faced wide-scale ridicule for attempting to become an honorary colonel and called for women in the military, little did she know that women would not be allowed to serve fully in combat until well into the twenty-first century—although this equality has been coupled with rampant sexual assault by male colleagues. Subsequent arguments would have seemed familiar to Tennie: for example, Tea Party congressman Allen West, in his argument against Senator Kirsten Gillibrand's battle to remove military sexual assault cases from the chain of command, linked sexual assaults to the problem of women being allowed in combat areas. Gillibrand noted that victims made such comments as "I could survive the rape but what I couldn't survive was my commanding officer not having my back." Gillibrand said, "Right now the person who is going to decide the case is her boss," noting that "out of 3,000 who reported sexual assaults, 62% said they were retaliated against. That there were 26,000 cases of sexual assaults and rapes last year and less than 1 percent prosecuted is outrageous."

Historians have been debating the worth of Tennie's sister Victoria well into the present. In the last years of the twentieth century, historian

Andrea Kerr argued that the Stanton-Anthony "misalliance" with Wood-hull "did incalculable harm" to the women's movement. "While present-day historians may sympathize with Woodhull's radical politics," wrote Kerr, the embrace of an "exotic, blackmailing, free-love advocate" was a "political disaster" for suffragists, leading to a "purity crusade" by Lucy Stone to protect "the family." Historian Ellen Dubois disagrees. Wood-hull's historic petition before the Judiciary Committee did incalculable good, not harm, and made the fight a principled battle involving the right of citizens to vote, rather than women "begging" for the "privilege." This New Departure did galvanize the not-so-well-behaved women to fight for state laws and to invade polling precincts. Unfortunately, conservative factions of the movement, who, as I point out, had tangled with the more progressive wing well before the sisters entered the picture, watered down such militancy, and the vote was not achieved until 1920.

Certainly family scandals and the sisters' adultery charge against Rev-erend Beecher, a darling of conservative suffragists, rocked the women's movement, especially because newspapers aligned the suffragists with the sisters in order to denigrate them. However, claims that the two women set the vote back twenty years are simply untrue. Their time in the suf-fragist movement lasted less than two years, and even the radical wing welcomed them for but a brief time. The Beecher fallout could have been repaired, especially after respectable critics later felt that testimony in the 1875 trial gave credence to Woodhull's charges of the preacher's adultery.

The ruinous rift among suffragists began post–Civil War and con-tinued for decades, until 1890. Both sides were stiff-necked, and Stone refused reconciliatory overtures from Anthony. More damaging than the sisters were these two groups duplicating time, money, and effort trying to woo the same segment of women—a minority at that, as most women remained anti-suffrage. The leaders of the movement, including Stanton, mentioned Woodhull's memorial or petition to the congressional Judiciary Committee, but otherwise ignored her in their massive *History of Woman Suffrage*, begun by Stanton, Anthony, and several others in 1881. But Woodhull got her reward posthumously, when she was inducted into the

National Women's Hall of Fame at Seneca Falls, New York, in 2001. Current feminist websites have discovered both sisters, lauding them as heroes.

It is tempting to ponder what might have happened had other suffragists joined Stanton and the sisters to decry the sexual, political, corporate, medical, and clerical subjugation women endured. Even after the sisters left the scene, the movement's timidity on any women's issue except the vote held women back for generations.

Stanton was one of the few contemporaries who refused to blame Woodhull for wrecking the women's movement. In 1876 she predicted that Woodhull "will be as famous as she had been infamous, made so by benighted or cowardly men and women." She would eventually have a "high place" in the "annals of emancipation." Catharine Beecher and her anti-vote battalion in the 1870s had its rebirth a hundred years later, in the anti-ERA movement led by Phyllis Schlafly. She succeeded in making a large segment of housewives think they would lose their financial rights as wives if the ERA passed, and predicted there would be unisex bathrooms, which made one wonder if she had ever ridden on an airplane. The mostly male legislatures defeated the Equal Rights Amendment.

Today the desire to upend *Roe v. Wade*, ban same-sex marriages, and curb the availability of contraception is once again coming from the religious right, just as religious curtailment of social freedoms held sway in the sisters' era. Victoria and Tennessee said that one's private life was none of anyone's business, especially the clergy and lawmakers. Activists say the same today, but the fight goes on. However, in spite of these roadblocks, many of the sexual freedoms the sisters called for in their younger days have finally become widely accepted cultural norms. By 2012 a new record low in marriages was reported; barely half of the adult population over age eighteen was married, with cohabitation, single parenthood, and same-sex relationships all growing more prevalent.

It is, at last, time to take a look at what the sisters were accused of—keeping in mind the far different standard held for Victorian males. On blackmailing and extortion, the record of wrongdoing remains slim.

There was a threatening article, which did not run, written on the possible adultery of women in the movement as payback against those who had denigrated Victoria and Tennie as tramps and prostitutes; a threatening letter to Henry Ward Beecher and a possible one to Challis, both of whom the sisters saw as sexual hypocrites; and comments from Tennie and Victoria threatening William Vanderbilt about their relations with his father, the Commodore, unless he gave them money they said was owed them. While I am not defending these actions, they were a far cry from the brazen thievery, corruption, bribery, and shady deals made by men on Wall Street and in politics at the time. The sisters fabricated and they lied, trying to advance themselves with fake personas in the rigid Victorian class structure. They were viewed as unscrupulously ambitious—as if male leaders were free from this trait. However, how many men of wealth worked as tirelessly as the sisters did for the working class and poor during their Yankee International days, or how many women fought for the advancement of women in every arena, from sex to politics?

Such onslaughts as repeated incarceration for minor offenses before being acquitted, and ridicule and hatred from every direction, eventually broke the sisters' will and resolve. Their turncoat lies about free love showed how flawed their avowals of truth were, but even friends such as Stanton and Hooker—who deserted them while in prison—came to understand their motives and visited them in England. And Tennie's long and stalwart march for women's suffrage and women's rights during this final period showed true conviction. By the time the two were elderly, their views on marriage seemed truly to have mellowed, a not unusual pattern as young radicals in all fields sometimes turn more conservative.

Of course, no discussion of the sisters or politicians, then and now, would be complete without a look at sex and scandal. More men than women have asked what seems to them to be the crucial question: were they prostitutes? As Tennie always said, look at the double standard. "You never hear a man called a prostitute...even the President of the United States, a governor of a state and a pastor of the most popular church, president of the most reliable bank, or of the grandest railroad corporation, may constantly practice all the debaucheries known to sensualism [*sic*] ... and he, by virtue of his sex, stands protected and respected." When a woman is involved in a sexual situation "newspapers make it their special business to herald her shame... utterly forgetting that there was a man in the scrape."

Illicit sex has been one of the least lofty but enduring cornerstones of American politics, from Thomas Jefferson on. Victoria knew what she was talking about when she shocked audiences by charging that lobbyists distributed money to brothel madams in order to secure influence with their customers in the house and senate; "I say it boldly, that it is the best men of the country who support the houses of prostitution!"

One could fault her phrase, "the best men of the country." Her observation of rampant sex among politicians, coupled by Tennie's anger at a double standard are as familiar now as they were in Victorian times. Political sex scandals fill newspapers, websites, and talk shows.

A recent spate of tawdriness kept the public spellbound once again in 2013, and this time some constituents didn't give a damn. At least that is the message surrounding former South Carolina governor Mark Sanford. He famously used taxpayers' money in 2009 to walk out of his office and trek off to see his Argentine mistress, while he was decidedly married. Undeterred, even by such misuse of his office, "family values" Republicans in this red state elected the "fiscal hawk" Sanford over Democrat Elizabeth Colbert Busch for Congress in 2013. Demonstrating that women continue to have an uphill battle in politics, *Slate* magazine surmised that two Democratic women actually helped elect Sanford: Republicans in South Carolina don't like Nancy Pelosi, the House Minority Leader, and "they couldn't stomach sending her an ally in Colbert Busch."

However, voters were not so forgiving of two sex-tainted New York pols: former congressman peter tweeter Anthony Weiner, as the comedians named him for once again sexting explicit photos of himself, and former Luv Gov Eliot Spitzer, who resigned as New York governor after being caught patronizing prostitutes. Tennie's ancient fight to change the double standard echoed in the actions of federal prosecutors who never charged Spitzer. They "traditionally didn't prosecute prostitutes' clients." Spitzer lost the 2013 race for the minor post of city comptroller and Weiner was trounced in his run for mayor. Meanwhile Bob Filner, mayor of San Diego, was forced to resign after nineteen women claimed sexual harassment.

Back to the question of whether the sisters were prostitutes. After reading everything available, I am inclined to think they may have been occasionally for sale when they were under their father's devious rule and possibly when they came out of prison destitute and tried to keep the *Weekly* and their various causes afloat. Still, it is conjecture, and authors who make it otherwise are using hearsay to create a sensational "fact." Better to look at the obstacles they faced and the names they were called, the humiliation they endured and their courage in trying to accomplish radical change. Sexism was rampant, but what was more chilling, I found during research, was the deep misogynist strain of contempt for women in all realms of Victorian life. Furthermore, men who supported women's suffrage, let alone free love, were commonly mocked as unmanly.

As for women in business, the glass ceiling has only cracked and is far from broken. Some 145 years ago Tennie said of the rough treatment she received on Wall Street from the male clique, "the real objection to me was that I was attempting to stand upon an equality with them, to transact business, while these other women [cleaning women who were allowed in their offices] were their slaves, to wipe up their vile tobacco puddles." When she attacked Wall Street colleagues, their response was to tar her with sexual slurs. Corporate women today still complain of being shunned, derided, and passed up for promotion by male colleagues.

In politics, women are still more likely than men to be asked why they are running for office. And their egos are often viewed as excessive, while no one questions a man's personal ambition. Woodhull was thought insane for running for president, even though her reason was symbolic: to stress parity for women. Both sisters were regarded as viciously ambitious, and therefore abnormal, tough, mannish, "strong-minded," unsexed—

but, conversely, viewed as prostitutes. Nearly 140 years later, Hillary Clinton faced an incredible barrage of degrading and dismissive name-calling in her serious 2008 quest for the presidency and again, in 2013, was viciously targeted by the Tea Party while still an undeclared candidate.

In the end, we come full circle, back to 1870 when the sisters argued that the vote alone was not enough; women need to be elected and in positions of power. Only then can women change not only attitudes but the laws that matter. As of now, there are more elected women than ever before, but they are far from a critical mass, and real change happens only when there is a critical mass. Women make up half the United States, but there are only twenty in a Senate of one hundred. As Pat Schroeder says, "20 percent is *not* a critical mass." Let's support and nurture more young women who are "seldom well behaved" and who are following in the line of uppity others, from Tennessee Claflin and Victoria Woodhull onward. They will make the history that matters.

Bibliography

Archives

Chicago History Museum.

Cook Collection. Richmond Local History Collection, London.

Hooker, Isabella Beecher, Collection. Stowe-Day Library, Hartford, CT.

Hooker, Isabella Beecher, Correspondence. Ashton Willard Papers. Vermont Historical Society, Montpelier, VT.

National American Woman Suffrage Association Collection. Library of Congress, Washington, DC.

New York Public Library.

Original Documents on Martin & Wife vs. British Museum. Trustees of the British Museum, 1894; Royal Courts of Justice, 1894. Transcript.

Stanton, Elizabeth Cady, Correspondence. New York Public Library Manuscript Collection, New York.

Tucker-Sachs Correspondence. New York Public Library Manuscript Collection, New York. (Previously unpublished material included.)

Whitelaw Reid Collection. Library of Congress, Washington, DC.

Woodhull, Victoria Claflin (Martin), Papers. Southern Illinois University [SIU] Special Collections. Morris Library, Carbondale, IL.

Woodhull, Victoria (Martin), Papers. Boston Public Library. Courtesy of the Trustees of the Boston Public Library/Rare Books.

Newspapers

Adelaide (Australia) Advertiser
Anglo-American
Atlanta Constitution
Baltimore Sun
Cedar Falls Gazette
Chicago Daily Mail
Chicago Daily Tribune
Elmira (NY) Gazette
(Washington, DC) Evening Star
(Washington, DC) Evening Times
Grey River Argus
Los Angeles Times
Monticello Express
Newark Sunday Call
Newport Daily
New York Chronicle
New-York Daily Tribune
New York Herald
(NY) Sun
New York Times
Ohio Democrat
Ottawa (IL) Republican
Philadelphia Inquirer
San Francisco Chronicle
Springfield Daily Republican
St. Petersburg Index
(London) Times
Washington Post
Woodhull & Claflin's Weekly

Manuscripts, Periodicals, and Websites

Andrews, Stephen Pearl, Henry James, and Horace Greeley. "Love, Marriage and Divorce: A Discussion." New York: Stringer and Townsend, 1853.

"The Beecher Trial: A Review of the Evidence." Reprinted from the *New York Times*, July 3, 1875.

"The Case of Henry Ward Beecher." Opening address of Benjamin Franklin Tracy. New York: George W. Smith and Co. Publishers, 1875. Reprinted by University of Michigan Library, 2005. Can be found at http://quod.lib.umich.edu/m/moa/AJK2284.0001.001?.

Claflin, Tennessee. "Sexual Equality Speech." Published in 1871. Woodhull & Claflin's Weekly Co. Collection.

Clark, Edward H. G. "The Thunderbolt." New York, Albany, and Troy: n.p., May 1873.

Danziger, Elon. "The Cook Collection, Its Founder and Its Inheritors." *The Burlington Magazine* 145, no. 1215 (July 2004): 444–58.

———. "The Cook Collection, Its Founder and Its Inheritors." *Jardim Formoso*. August 12, 2009.

Darewin, G. S. "Synopsis of the Lives of Victoria C. Woodhull, Now Mrs. John Biddulph Martin, and Tennessee Claflin, Now Lady Cook: The First Two Lady Bankers and Reformers of America." London: n.p., 1891.

The Humanitarian: A Monthly Review of Sociological Science. New York and London, vols. 1–19 (1892–1901).

Kisner, Arlene. "*Woodhull & Claflin's Weekly*: The Lives and Writings of the Notorious Victoria Woodhull and Her Sister, Tennessee Claflin." Times Change Press, 1972.

Legge, Madeleine. "Two Noble Women, Nobly Planned." London: Phelps Brothers, 1893.

Luckhurst, Gerald. "Friends of Monserrate." *Jardim Formoso*. June 26, 2010.

McCrimmon, Barbara. "Victoria Woodhull Martin Sues the British Museum for Libel." *The Library Quarterly* 45, no. 4 (Oct. 1975): 355–72.

"Mrs. Satan." *Harper's Weekly*. February 17, 1872.

The Selected Papers of Elizabeth Cady Stanton and Susan B. Anthony. vol. 3, 1873–1880. Rutgers, NJ: Rutgers University Press, 2003.

Shearer, Mary. *Victoria Woodhull & Company*, at http://www.victoria-woodhull.com. Provides information about Woodhull, articles by and about her, pictures, and historical matter.

Stanton, Elizabeth Cady, and Susan B. Anthony. "Wall Street Aroused." *Revolution*, February 24, 1870.

———. "What Can Women Do?" editorial, *Revolution* (March 24, 1870): LoC, vol. 5, January–June 1870, 188.

———. "The Working Woman." *Revolution* (March 10, 1870).

Stern, Madeleine B. "Notable Women of 19th-Century America." *Manuscripts* 34, no. 1 (Winter 1982): 119 (autograph of Woodhull).

Tilton, Theodore. "Victoria C. Woodhull, A Biographical Sketch, Mr. Tilton's Account of Mrs. Woodhull." New York: *The Golden Age*, tract 3, 1871.

Treat, Joseph, M.D. *Beecher, Tilton, Woodhull, and the Creation of Society: All Four of Them Exposed, and If Possible Reformed and Forgiven, in Dr. Treat's Celebrated Letter to Victoria C. Woodhull.* Self-published. New York, 1874.

U.S. Congress. Senate. "Memorial of Victoria C. Woodhull, Praying the Passage of a Law Carrying into Execution the Right Vested by the Constitution in Citizens of the United States to Vote, without Regard to Sex." 41st Cong., 3d sess. S. Mis. Doc. 16. Washington, DC: Government Printing Office, 1870.

Woodhull & Claflin's Weekly, New York. May 14, 1870–June 10, 1876 (publication suspended from June through October 1872).

Woodhull, Victoria Claflin. "Tendencies of Government." *New York Herald*, April 16 and 25; May 2, 9, 16, and 27; June 4 and 19; July 4, 1870. Probably ghostwritten by Stephen Pearl Andrews.

———. (Mrs. John Biddulph Martin). "Manor House Causeries." Bredon's Norton, near Tewkesbury, n.d.

Books

Ackerman, Kenneth D. *Boss Tweed: The Corrupt Pol Who Conceived the Soul of Modern New York.* New York: 1st Carroll and Graf ed., 2005. Falls Church, VA: Viral History Press, 2011.

———. *The Gold Ring: Jim Fisk, Jay Gould, and Black Friday, 1869.* New York: 1st Dodd, Mead and Company ed., 1988. Falls Church, VA: Viral History Press, 2011.

Anonymous. *The Gentleman's Companion. A Vest Pocket Guide to Brothels*, 1870. Reprinted in the *New York Times*, January 26, 2011.

Applegate, Debby. *The Most Famous Man in America: The Biography of Henry Ward Beecher.* New York: Three Leaves Press, 2007.

Auchincloss, Louis, *The Vanderbilt Era: Profiles of a Gilded Age*. New York: Charles Scribner's Sons, 1989.

Baker, Jean. *Sisters: The Lives of American Suffragists*. New York: Hill and Wang, 2006.

Barker-Benfield, Graham John. *The Horrors of the Half-Known Life: Male Attitudes Toward Women and Sexuality in Nineteenth-Century America*. New York: Routledge, 1968.

The Beecher-Tilton War: Official original documents, letters and statements, University of Michigan Historical Reprint Series: MPublishing. Print on demand print service through Amazon.com.

Brandt, Allan M. *No Magic Bullet: A Social History of Venereal Disease in the United States since 1880*. New York: Oxford University Press, 1985.

Braude, Ann. *Radical Spirits: Spiritualism and Women's Rights in Nineteenth-Century America*. Boston: Beacon Press, 1989.

Brodie, Janet Farrell. *Contraception and Abortion in Nineteenth-Century America*. 1st Cornell paperback ed. Ithaca, NY: Cornell University Press, 1997.

Brody, Miriam. *Victoria Woodhull: Free Spirit for Women's Rights*. New York: Oxford University Press, 2004.

Brough, James. *The Vixens: A Biography of Victoria and Tennessee Claflin*. New York: Simon and Schuster, 1980.

Broun, Heywood, and Margaret Leech. *Anthony Comstock: Roundsman of the Lord*. New York: Boni, 1927.

Burrows, Edwin G., and Mike Wallace. *Gotham: A History of New York City to 1898*. New York: Oxford University Press, 1999.

Byrnes, Thomas. *1886 Professional Criminals of America*. Reprint of 19th Century Rogues' Gallery of Criminals. New York: The Lyons Press, 2000.

Carpenter, Cari M., ed. *Selected Writings of Victoria Woodhull: Legacies of Nineteenth-Century American Women Writers*. Lincoln: University of Nebraska Press, 2010.

Chesterton, G. K. *Eugenics and Other Evils*. London and New York: Cassell, 1922.

Claflin, Tennessee, Lady Cook. *Essays on Social Topics*. London: The Roxburgh Press, c. 1895.

Clews, Henry. *Fifty Years in Wall Street*. New York: Irving Publishing, 1908.

Constitutional Equality of the Sexes. New York: Woodhull & Claflin's Weekly Co., 1871.

Darwin, Charles. *On the Origin of Species.* Cambridge, MA: Harvard University Press, 1979.

Donnelly, Mabel Collins. *The American Victorian Woman: The Myth and the Reality.* Contributions in Women's Studies no. 71. New York: Greenwood Press, 1986.

Douglass, Frederick. *The Autobiographies of Frederick Douglass, Narrative of the Life of Frederick Douglass, an American Slave.* Library of America, Series. 1994.

———. *Narrative of the Life of Frederick Douglass: Authoritative Text, Contexts, Criticism.* 1st Norton Critical ed. New York: W. W. Norton and Co., 1996.

Doyle, John E. P. *Plymouth Church and Its Pastor: Or Henry Ward Beecher and His Accusers.* St. Louis: Bryan, Brand and Co., 1875. Digital U-M, Cornell University collaboration.

Drabble, Margaret. *For Queen and Country: Britain in the Victorian Age.* 1st American ed. New York: Seabury Press, 1979.

Edel, Leon. *Henry James: The Conquest of London.* Philadelphia: J. B. Lippincott, 1961; New York: Avon Books, 1978.

Edwards, Rebecca. *New Spirits: Americans in the "Gilded Age," 1865–1905.* 2nd ed. New York: Oxford University Press, 2011.

Edwards, Stewart. *The Communards of Paris, 1871: Documents of Revolution.* Ithaca, N.Y: Cornell University Press, 1973.

Ellington, George (pseudonym). *The Women of New York: Or, Social Life in the Great City.* 1870; repr. New York: General Books, 2009. Original title: *The Women of New York: Or, the Underworld of the Great City.*

Foner, Eric. *Frederick Douglass on Women's Rights.* New York: Da Capo Press, 1992.

———. *Reconstruction: America's Unfinished Revolution, 1863–1877.* New York: Harper and Row, 1988.

Fox, Richard Wightman. *Trials of Intimacy: Love and Loss in the Beecher-Tilton Scandal.* Chicago and London: University of Chicago Press, 1999.

Frisken, Amanda. *Victoria Woodhull's Sexual Revolution: Political Theater and Popular Press in Nineteenth-Century America.* Philadelphia, PA: University of Pennsylvania Press, 2004.

Gabriel, Mary. *Notorious Victoria: The Life of Victoria Woodhull, Uncensored.* Chapel Hill, NC: Algonquin Books, 1998.

Gardner, Augustus K. *Conjugal Sins against the Laws of Life and Health, and Their Effects Upon the Father, Mother and Child.* New York: J. S. Redfield Publisher, 1870. Available at http://hdl.handle.net/2027/hvd .32044009948563.

Geisst, Charles R. *Wall Street: A History.* New York: Oxford University Press, 1997.

Ginzberg, Lori D. *Elizabeth Cady Stanton: An American Life.* New York: Hill and Wang, 2009.

Goldsmith, Barbara. *Other Powers: The Age of Suffrage, Spiritualism, and the Scandalous Victoria Woodhull.* New York: HarperPerennial, 1998.

Gordon, John Steele. *The Great Game: The Emergence of Wall Street.* New York: Touchstone, 2000.

———. *The Scarlet Woman of Wall Street: Jay Gould, Jim Fisk, Cornelius Vanderbilt, the Erie Railway Wars, and the Birth of Wall Street.* New York: Weidenfeld and Nicolson, 1988.

Griffith, Elisabeth. *In Her Own Right: The Life of Elizabeth Cady Stanton.* New York: Oxford University Press, 1984.

Hale, William Harlan. *Horace Greeley, Voice of the People.* 1st ed. New York: Harper, 1950.

Harper, Ida Husted, *The Life and Work of Susan B. Anthony*, chapter 22, vol. 1 Project Gutenberg ebook version, 2005. www.gutenberg.org.

Hays, Elinor Rice. *Morning Star: A Biography of Lucy Stone, 1818–1893.* 1st ed. New York: Harcourt, Brace and World, 1961.

Hibben, Paxton. *Henry Ward Beecher: An American Portrait.* New York: Press of the New York Readers Club, 1942.

Hobsbawm, E. J. *The Age of Capital, 1848–1875.* 1st Vintage ed. New York: Vintage Books, 1996.

Holbrook, Stewart Hall. *The Age of the Moguls.* Garden City, NY: Doubleday, 1954.

Holzman, Robert S. *Stormy Ben Butler.* New York: Macmillan, 1954.

Horowitz, Helen Lefkowitz. *Attitudes toward Sex in Antebellum America: A Brief History with Documents.* Boston: Bedford/St. Martin's, 2006.

————. *Rereading Sex: Battles over Sexual Knowledge and Suppression in Nineteenth-Century America.* 1st ed. New York: Vintage Books, 2003.

Houghton, Walter E. *The Victorian Frame of Mind, 1830–1870.* New Haven, CT: Published for Wellesley College by Yale University Press, 1957.

Howells, William Dean. *Years of My Youth.* New York, Harper and Co., 1916. BibioLife reproduction, 2008.

————. *Impressions and Experiences.* Ulan Press reprint of pre-1920s books, Unlimited Publishing LLC. Vantage Press.

Hoyt, Edwin Palmer. *The Vanderbilts and Their Fortunes.* Garden City, NY: Doubleday, 1962.

James, Henry. *The Bostonians.* New York: Macmillan, 1886; New York: Penguin, 1983.

————. *The Great Short Novels of Henry James: The Siege of London.* New York: Dial Press, 1944; New York: Penguin, 1983. ("The Siege of London" first appeared in *Cornhill Magazine,* January–February 1883.)

James, William. *The Varieties of Religious Experience: A Study in Human Nature, Being the Gifford Lectures on Natural Religion Delivered at Edinburgh in 1901–1902.* New York: Random House, Modern Library, n.d.

Johnson, Gerald W. *The Lunatic Fringe.* Philadelphia: J. B. Lippincott, 1957.

Johnston, Johanna. *Mrs. Satan: The Incredible Saga of Victoria Woodhull.* New York: G. P. Putnam's Sons, 1967; London: Macmillan, 1967.

Josephson, Matthew. *The Robber Barons: The Great American Capitalists, 1861–1901.* New York: Harcourt, Brace and Co., 1934.

Kaplan, Justin. *When the Astors Owned New York: Blue Bloods and Grand Hotels in a Gilded Age.* New York: Viking, 2006.

Keller, Allan. *Scandalous Lady: The Life and Times of Madame Restell, New York's Most Notorious Abortionist.* 1st ed. New York: Atheneum, 1981.

Kerr, Andrea Moore. *Lucy Stone: Speaking Out for Equality.* New Brunswick, NJ: Rutgers University Press, 1992; paperback, 1995.

Kerr, Howard. *Mediums, Spirit-Rappers, and Roaring Radicals: Spiritualism in American Literature, 1850–1900.* Urbana: University of Illinois Press, 1972.

Kessler-Harris, Alice. *Out to Work: A History of Wage-Earning Women in the United States.* New York: Oxford University Press, 2003.

Klein, Maury. *The Genesis of Industrial America, 1870–1920*. 1st ed. Cambridge, UK: Cambridge University Press, 2007.

———. *The Life and Legend of Jay Gould*. Baltimore, MD: Johns Hopkins University Press, 1986.

Krull, Kathleen, and Jane Dyer. *A Woman for President: The Story of Victoria Woodhull*. New York: Walker and Co., 2004.

Leach, William. *True Love and Perfect Union: The Feminist Reform of Sex and Society*. New York: Basic Books, 1980.

Leonard, Todd Jay. *Talking to the Other Side: A History of Modern Spiritualism and Mediumship*. Bloomington, Indiana: iUniverse, 2005.

Lewis, R. W. B. *Edith Wharton: A Biography*. New York: Harper and Row, 1975.

Lubetkin, John M. *Jay Cooke's Gamble: The Northern Pacific Railroad, the Sioux, and the Panic of 1873*. Norman: University of Oklahoma Press, 2006.

Lutz, Alma. *Created Equal: A Biography of Elizabeth Cady Stanton, 1815–1902*. New York: John Day, 1940.

MacPherson, Myra. *All Governments Lie!: The Life and Times of Rebel Journalist I. F. Stone*. New York: Scribner, 2006.

———. *The Power Lovers: An Intimate Look at Politicians and Their Marriages*. New York: G. P. Putnam's Sons, 1975.

Maines, Rachel P. *The Technology of Orgasm: "Hysteria," the Vibrator, and Women's Sexual Satisfaction*. Johns Hopkins Studies in the History of Technology new ser., no. 24. Baltimore, MD: Johns Hopkins University Press, 1998.

Marberry, M. M. *Vicky: A Biography of Victoria C. Woodhull*. New York: Funk and Wagnalls, 1967.

Marcuse, Maxwell F. *This Was New York: A Nostalgic Picture of Gotham in the Gaslight Era*. New York: LIM Press, 1969.

Marshall, Charles F. *The True History of the Brooklyn Scandal*. Philadelphia, PA, and Chicago, IL: National Pub. Co., 1874.

Martin, John Biddulph. *The Grasshopper in Lombard Street*. London: Simpkin Marshall Hamilton Kent and Co.; New York: Scribner and Welford, 1892.

McFeely, William. *Ulysses S. Grant: A Biography*. New York: W. W. Norton and Co., 1982.

Meade, Marion. *Free Woman: The Life and Times of Victoria Woodhull*. New York: Alfred A. Knopf, 1976.

Messer-Kruse, Timothy. *The Yankee International: Marxism and the American Reform Tradition, 1848–1876.* Chapel Hill: University of North Carolina Press, 1998. http://search.ebscohost.com/login.aspx?direct=true&scope=site&db=nlebk&db=nlabk&AN=41504.

Morris, Charles R. *The Tycoons: How Andrew Carnegie, John D. Rockefeller, Jay Gould, and J. P. Morgan Invented the American Supereconomy.* New York: Henry Holt and Co., 2005.

Morris, Lloyd R. *Incredible New York: High Life and Low Life of the Last Hundred Years.* New York: Random House, 1951.

Murphy, Cait N. *Scoundrels in Law: The Trials of Howe and Hummel, Lawyers to the Gangsters, Cops, Starlets, and Rakes Who Made the Gilded Age.* 1st ed. New York: Smithsonian Books/HarperCollins, 2010.

O'Brien, Patricia. *Harriet and Isabella: A Novel.* New York: Touchstone, 2009.

O'Neill, William L. *Everyone Was Brave: The Rise and Fall of Feminism in America.* Chicago: Quadrangle Books, 1969.

Powers, Ron. *Mark Twain: A Life.* New York: Free Press, 2005.

Ratnikas, Algis. *Timelines of History*, vol. 8: 1850–1870. Edited by Algis Ratnikas. 2nd ed. Self-published, 2012.

Renehan Jr., Edward J. *Commodore: The Life of Cornelius Vanderbilt.* New York: Basic Books, 2007.

Rhodes, James Ford. *The History of the United States from the Compromise of 1830*, vol. 7. New York: Macmillan, 1920.

Robinson, Jane. *Women Out of Bounds.* New York: Carroll and Graf, 2003.

Rose, Phyllis. *Parallel Lives: Five Victorian Marriages.* London: Chatto and Windus, 1984.

Ross, Ishbel. *Crusades and Crinolines: The Life and Times of Ellen Curtis Demorest and William Jennings Demorest.* New York: Harper and Row, 1963.

Rutherfurd, Edward. *New York: The Novel.* Reprint. New York: Ballantine Books, 2010.

Ryder, Vera. *Little Victims at Play. Reminiscences of Doughty House by Great-Granddaughter of Sir Francis Cook, Tennessee Claflin's Husband.* London: Robert Hale Ltd., 1974.

Sachs, Emanie N. *"The Terrible Siren": Victoria Woodhull, 1838–1927.* New York: Harper and Brothers, 1928.

Sante, Luc. *Low Life: Lures and Snares of Old New York*. Farrar, Straus and Giroux, 1991.

Scott, Joan Wallach, and American Council of Learned Societies. *Gender and the Politics of History*. Rev. ed. *Gender and Culture*. New York: Columbia University Press, 1999.

Sears, Hal D. *The Sex Radicals: Free Love in High Victorian America*. Lawrence: Regents Press of Kansas, 1977.

Shaplen, Robert. *Free Love and Heavenly Sinners: The Story of the Great Henry Ward Beecher Scandal*. London: Andre Deutsch, 1956.

Sherr, Lynn. *Failure Is Impossible: Susan B. Anthony in Her Own Words*. 1st paperback ed. New York: Times Books, 1996.

Sherwin, Richard K. *When Law Goes Pop: The Vanishing Line between Law and Popular Culture*. Chicago: University of Chicago Press, 2000.

Smith, Arthur D. *Commodore Vanderbilt: An Epic of American Achievement*. New York: Robert M. McBride and Co., 1927.

Stansell, Christine, and American Council of Learned Societies. *City of Women: Sex and Class in New York, 1789–1860*. 1st ed. New York: Alfred A. Knopf, 1986.

Stanton, Elizabeth Cady, Susan B. Anthony, Matilda Johnson Sage, and Ida Husted Harper. *History of Woman Suffrage, 1861–1876*, vol. 2, part 2. 1881; repr. Whitefish, MT: Kessinger Publishing, 2013.

Stern, Madeleine B., and Paul Avrich Collection (Library of Congress). *The Pantarch: A Biography of Stephen Pearl Andrews*. Austin: University of Texas Press, 1968.

Stiles, T. J. *The First Tycoon: The Epic Life of Cornelius Vanderbilt*. New York: Alfred A. Knopf, 2009.

Stinchcombe, Owen. *American Lady of the Manor Bredon's Norton: The Later Life of Victoria Woodhull Martin, 1901–1927*. Self-published, 2000.

Stoehr, Taylor, and Paul Avrich Collection (Library of Congress). *Free Love in America: a Documentary History*. New York: AMS Press, 1979.

Stowe, Harriet Beecher. *My Wife and I, or, Harry Henderson's History*. New York: J. B. Ford and Co., 1872.

———. *Uncle Tom's Cabin*. New York: Wordsworth Editions Ltd., 1999.

Streitmatter, Rodger. *Voices of Revolution: The Dissident Press in America*. New York: Columbia University Press, 2001.

Swanberg, W. A. *Jim Fisk: The Career of an Improbable Rascal.* New York: Scribner's, 1959.

Tilton vs. Beecher: Action for Criminal Conversation. Verbatim Report by the Official Stenographer. 3 vols. New York: McDivitt, Campbell and Co., 1875.

Titone, Nora. *My Thoughts Be Bloody: The Bitter Rivalry between Edwin and John Wilkes Booth That Led to an American Tragedy.* New York: Free Press, 2010.

Tone, Andrea. *Devices and Desires: A History of Contraceptives in America.* New York: Hill and Wang, 2001.

Underhill, Lois Beachy. *The Woman Who Ran for President.* Bridgehampton, NY: Bridge Works Publishers, 1995.

Vidal, Gore. *1876: A Novel.* New York: Random House, 1976.

Wallace, Irving. *The Nympho and Other Maniacs.* New York: Simon and Schuster, 1971.

Wharton, Edith. *The Age of Innocence.* New York; Toronto: Collier Books; Maxwell Macmillan Canada; Maxwell Macmillan International, 1992.

Wheeler, Marjorie Spruill, ed. *One Woman, One Vote: Rediscovering the Women's Suffrage Movement.* Troutdale, OR: NewSage Press, 1995.

Woodhull, Victoria C. *Lady Eugenist: Feminist Eugenics in the Speeches and Writings of Victoria Woodhull.* Inkling Books, 2005.

———. *The Origin, Tendencies and Principles of Government: Or, A Review of the Rise and Fall of Nations from Early Historic Times to the Present; with Special Considerations Regarding the Future of the United States as the Representative Government of the World and the Form of Administration Which Will Secure This Consummation.* New York, Woodhull & Claflin's Weekly Co., 1871.

———. *The Victoria Woodhull Reader.* M&S Press, 1974.

Woodhull, Victoria Claflin (Mrs. John Biddulph Martin). *A Fragmentary Record of Public Work Done in America, 1871–1877.* London: G. Norman and Son, 1887.

Woodhull, Victoria Claflin (Mrs. John Biddulph Martin), and Tennessee C. Claflin (Lady Cook). *The Human Body, the Temple of God; or The Philosophy of Sociology.* Self-published. London, 1890.

Acknowledgments

Obviously I could have not accomplished anything without the mountain of Victorian history—books, periodicals, newspapers, letters, and archived papers—that I devoured in order to write about the seven incredible decades of the Scarlet Sisters and the major characters who figured in their lives. Yet a great deal of thanks goes to those very alive people who personally contributed to making this book possible. I'm deeply indebted to my major research assistant, Terumi Rafferty-Osaki, who was invaluable, endlessly culling newspapers and periodicals at the Library of Congress before many were digitized, including the massive collection of bound volumes of *Woodhull & Claflin's Weekly*. Later, when I read an 1872 *New York Times* article on my phone, sent by Terumi on his phone, it seemed like pure magic to someone who remembers torturous hours copying material while writing previous books. Lauren Santangelo researched material at the New York Public Library, and Amy Langford tracked down permissions for photos and drawings. Karen Mylan not only found ancient and valuable letters but was a whiz at helping me translate the sometimes murky handwriting of Tennessee and Victoria contained in the Victoria Claflin Woodhull Martin Papers in the Southern Illinois University Special Collections. I am also indebted to the staff at the Boston Public Library who generously helped me research the Victoria Woodhull Martin Papers in the library's rare books division.

In London, the staff at the British Museum provided me with a desk and a large leather-bound volume, unaware of the thrill I felt reading the precise penmanship of someone who 120 years ago copied the testimony of Victoria when she and husband John Martin sued the Trustees of the British Museum.

To flesh out Tennessee as Lady Cook, only briefly touched on in biographies of Woodhull, I found a large volume of unpublished and revealing letters in the SIU and the Boston Public Library collections. Many newspapers of the period were consumed with covering Lady Cook well into her final years, producing a treasure trove not featured in books about Victoria. I am incredibly grateful for the gracious help from Gerald Luckhurst, historian, landscape architect of the magnificent Monserrate gardens, and consultant to Parques de Sintra at Monserrate. He located articles and material on Sir Francis and Lady Cook and gave me a personal upstairs-downstairs tour of the palace and gardens, shortly after Prince Charles and Camilla had been there to christen a new rose garden. Unfortunately the magnificence of the interior, garden, and grounds was relegated to mere paragraphs in order to keep the story of the sisters moving. I recommend further photographs and websites on Monserrate and Gerald's monumental book when it is completed.

Sir Francis and Lady Cook's Doughty House has been long neglected, but Andre Metaxides, the owner who was restoring it in 2011, was so knowledgeable and helpful when I visited that he captured a vision of it for me as it once was.

Debby and David Booth, the delightful owners of Norton Park since 2003, showed me around Victoria's lovely final home. Perhaps I am the only visitor to have been gored by a very dead antler there. As I stared at the high-ceilinged main hall and the ancient antler heads that hung there in Victoria's time, I walked into one on the floor that was being remounted. The sharp prick made me wonder, was Victoria, the Spiritualist, sending a message to do right by her? Debby also took me to Tewkesbury Abbey, to see the plaque commemorating Woodhull, placed there by daughter Zula Maud. I also appreciate the help of Robin Holland-Martin, the grandson of Robert Holland-Martin, Woodhull's nephew, for giving me more background to Victoria's life in England and guiding me to the Booths.

Historian Ken Ackerman, author of *The Gold Ring* and *Boss Tweed*, kindly read the chapters on Wall Street and high finance among the robber barons, making vital suggestions and improvements. At the beginning of my research I was helped immeasurably by the Library of Congress Women's History Discussion Group (WHDG).

I am of course indebted to biographers and authors who came before me; the most reliable and well-researched biographies on Victoria Woodhull were Lois Beachy Underhill's *The Woman Who Ran for President* and Mary Gabriel's *Notorious Victoria*. Amanda Frisken's more recent book, *Victoria Woodhull's Sexual Revolution*, added a new dimension with its vital examination of the drawings of both sisters in the tabloid-style papers, which contributed to a racy public image that galvanized Victorian-era prejudice against them. I disagree with books that take the Tilton as-told-to biography at face value, and I feel Woodhull's agenda explains why that version cannot be taken as fact. Also I find it factually inaccurate that some authors ignore or disregard Tennie.

Newer books, such as T. J. Stiles's Vanderbilt biography, *The First Tycoon*; Richard Wightman Fox's *Trials of Intimacy*, on the Beecher-Tilton scandal; and Debby Applegate's Beecher biography, *The Most Famous Man in America*, add new insight to landmark books by Robert Shaplen and Paxton Hibben and earlier Vanderbilt biographies. One of the best examinations of the trial occurred while it was still in progress. The *New York Times*'s critical summation of Beecher's testimony convinced me that he was guilty of perjury at the very least.

My agent, Dan Green, a gift from our mutual late friend, Molly Ivins, helped me imagine the story and came up with the *Scarlet Sisters* title. Jon Karp bought the book for Twelve; Cary Goldstein provided organizing suggestions; Libby Burton was excellent at fine-tune editing; and the new and encouraging team at Twelve—Deb Futter, publisher; Sean Desmond, editor-in-chief; and Brian McLendon, associate publisher; along with Libby Burton, made *The Scarlet Sisters* a reality.

Friends and family put up with my grousing despair. I am particularly grateful to my son, Michael Siegel, a fine writer who made suggestions as he listened sympathetically. So did a group of author friends—Thom Racina, Joe Drape, Nicholas Von Hoffman, Molly and Jim Dickenson, Bill McPherson, George Wilson, Lou Dubose, Ellen Sweets, and Pat O'Brien, who wrote the novel *Harriet and Isabella*, based on the Beecher family friction over Woodhull. Other friends and family nudged me along—Mary Bradshaw, Barbara Blum, Richard Rymland, Janet Donovan, Ruth Noble Groom, Katy and Alan Novak, Grace Mark, Marcy and Ed Saddy, Jennifer Roberts, Eric Loehr, Jonathan Gordon and Melanie Sommers, Susan Vodicka, Margaret Kempel, Margie Haley, and a host of others who said, "When are you going to get that darn book finished?"

About the Author

MYRA MACPHERSON is the award-winning, best-selling author of four previous books, including *The Power Lovers*, an examination of political marriages, the Vietnam War classic *Long Time Passing*, and *All Governments Lie!*. She was a highly regarded journalist at the *Washington Post* for many years, and has also written for the *New York Times* and numerous national magazines and websites. She lives in Washington, DC.

Notes

Guide to Abbreviations

BPL = Victoria Woodhull Martin Papers, Boston Public Library

ECS = Elizabeth Cady Stanton

IBH = Isabella Beecher Hooker

JM = John Biddulph Martin

MM = Myra MacPherson

SBA = Susan B. Anthony

SIU = Victoria Claflin Woodhull Martin Papers, Southern
Illinois University

TC = Tennessee Claflin

Tucker-Sachs = Correspondence between Benjamin Tucker and Emanie
Sachs, New York Public Library

VW = Victoria Woodhull

WCW = *Woodhull & Claflin's Weekly*

Introducing Two Improper Victorians

xiii. **gold is cash:** Lois Underhill, *The Woman Who Ran for President* (Bridgehampton, NY: Bridge Works Publishing, 1995), p. 128, mentions it was a
Tennie comment in the *New York Herald*, n.d.

xvii. **families of the dead cannot sue:** Sachs's comment in private correspondence with Benjamin Tucker, 1927–28, New York Public Library
collection.

xviii. **Two recent biographies of the sisters' friend:** Edward J. Renehan Jr., *Commodore: The Life of Cornelius Vanderbilt* (New York: Basic Books, 2007). Renehan made the charge, and T. J. Stiles skewers it in *The First Tycoon: The Epic Life of Cornelius Vanderbilt* (New York: Alfred A. Knopf, 2009). For further details see chapter 24 in this book, *The Scarlet Sisters*, endnote on pp. 383–84: "Stiles skewers Renehan's unreliable claim."

xviii. **Henry James and Harriet Beecher Stowe:** Richard Wightman Fox, *Trials of Intimacy: Love and Loss in the Beecher-Tilton Scandal* (Chicago; London: University of Chicago Press, 1999), pp. 302–5, also takes on Barbara Goldsmith, *Other Powers: The Age of Suffrage, Spiritualism, and the Scandalous Victoria Woodhull* (New York: Alfred A. Knopf, 1998), for her "fictionalized storytelling," especially her unsubstantiated premise that Elizabeth Tilton had an abortion: "It is worth examining this story…about the possible abortion," Fox writes, "since it illuminates the ongoing process of mythmaking about the scandal…One author draws on and extends the already inventive work of earlier writers…Goldsmith's assertion of a Beecher pregnancy and possible abortion is false." Although Fox terms Woodhull's 1872 account of the scandal "scattershot allegations," she merely says that Tilton told her there was a "great probability" that Elizabeth was "enceinte by Mr. Beecher instead of himself." In light of Lib Tilton's testimony of her husband saying he doubted he was the father, Woodhull probably accurately repeated Tilton. She never hinted at an abortion.

Opening Scene: Arriving

xxi. **Nor would it again:** In 1965 Julia Walsh became the first woman to enter the American Stock Exchange. Muriel Siebert became the first woman to earn a seat on the New York Stock Exchange, in 1967.

xxii. **GENTLEMEN WILL STATE THEIR BUSINESS:** *(NY) Sun*, Feb. 13, 1870, p. 7.

xxii. **vile bunches of hair:** Arlene Kisner, *Woodhull & Claflin's Weekly: The Lives and Writings of the Notorious Victoria Woodhull and Her Sister Tennessee Claflin* (New York: Times Change Press, 1972), p. 24.

xxiii. **exquisite figures:** *New York Herald*, Feb. 6, 1870, p. 3.

xxiii. **talking with a rapidity and fluency:** *(NY) World*, Feb. 8, 1870, p. 5.

xxiii. **gouty old war horses:** *New York Herald*, Feb. 6, 1870, p. 3.

xxiii. **"without any signs of headaches.":** Ibid.

xxiii. **'Before call 94 ½.':** *(NY) Sun*, Feb. 7, 1870.

xxiii. **ladies can be wise and discreet:** Ibid., Feb. 13, 1870, p. 7.

xxiii. **Woodhull tartly replied:** Ibid.

xxiii. **What do present profits amount to:** *New York Herald*, Jan. 22, 1870, p. 10.

xxiii. **working-class poor made $200:** An average worker's annual salary in a good year in the 1870s was about $375 for a sixty-hour week. See http://www.digitalhistory.uh.edu/historyonline/us26.cfm. Americans in the manufacturing labor force who participated in the census of 1870, following 1869's Black Friday, reported they earned $129 per year.

xxiii. **lost it mainly in speculation:** From Susan B. Anthony interview, quoted in the women's rights journal *The Revolution*, Feb. 24, 1870.

Chapter One: Vicky

3. **construction of the Ohio and Erie Canal:** The most thorough information on the Claflin parents is in Underhill, *The Woman Who Ran for President*. I have used historical information given on pp. 12–15.

4. **To avoid arrest:** Sachs, *The Terrible Siren*.

4. **after the Bible was read:** Underhill, *The Woman Who Ran for President*, p. 16.

4. **passions aroused by religious ecstasy:** Goldsmith, *Other Powers*, p. 17. As in several disturbing instances, Goldsmith cites no original source. She states that Buck dragged his wife "to the back of tent, where he threw her down and forced himself into her…Thus, *according to her own account*, was Victoria Woodhull conceived." However, there is no such description or account in Woodhull's autobiography dictated to Tilton. Goldsmith offers no other source. The tale should therefore be considered questionable.

5. **damning memorial of his father's wrath:** Unless otherwise indicated, the information in this chapter is from Theodore Tilton's "Victoria C. Woodhull, A Biographical Sketch" (New York: *The Golden Age*, 1871).

6. **the 'Dutch Hummels':** *Chicago Daily Mail*, May 9, 1892.

6. **The Claflin house:** Ibid.

6. **sink down in front of the altar:** Ibid.

6. **Never spent one year:** *Atlanta Constitution*, 1876; mentioned in a website dedicated to facts on Woodhull, http://www.victoria-woodhull.com/index.htm.

7. **Beds were everywhere:** *Chicago Daily Mail,* May 9, 1892. Also Sachs, *The Terrible Siren.* Sachs does not attribute any of her accounts, but the description of unmade beds probably came from Thankful Claflin, a cousin who lived with the family. Sachs wrote a friend (see Tucker-Sachs) that Thankful was "willing to spill the beans."

7. **"terrible sins.":** Sachs, *The Terrible Siren,* p. 4.

7. **'out of the body.':** *Chicago Daily Mail,* May 9, 1892.

8. **the money was gone:** Ibid.

9. **escape from the parental yoke:** Despite Buck Claflin's many faults, one uncorroborated inference regarding sexual abuse of Victoria reveals how a phrase can be stretched and miscast into a leap of sensationalism: Goldsmith, in *Other Powers,* writes, "Vickie *often* intimated that he sexually abused her" (pp. 51–52). This comes only from a half sentence. Wrote Goldsmith, "Later Victoria would say that Buck made her a 'woman before her time.'"—hence the incest. Not only did Victoria not say this, but there was no "often" involved, nor was it about incest. In his biography of Victoria, Tilton surmises that both her parents were willing to marry off a daughter "whose sorrow was ripening her into a woman before her time." Her "sorrow" and "woman before her time," phrases penned by Tilton, not quotes from Victoria, were never described as having to do with incest. Both parents championed a child-bride marriage because they wanted one less mouth to feed and saw Canning as a "catch." Victoria also told suffragist Lucretia Mott, "All that I am I have become through sorrow." Goldsmith cites this as clinching her incest assumption. But this was Victoria's mantra, stemming from Tilton's creation of her "sorrow-stricken" childhood and early bad marriage, not from incest.

11. **sincere maternal affection:** Tucker-Sachs.

12. **"ultimately affect her ruin.":** When a beautiful Manhattan cigar girl, Mary Rogers, was brutally murdered in 1841, her death became a journalistic and literary cause célèbre. Her customers included famed literary giants James Fenimore Cooper, Washington Irving, and Edgar Allan Poe. Daniel Stashower, *The Beautiful Cigar Girl: Mary Rogers, Edgar Allan Poe and the Invention of Murder* (New York: Dutton, Penguin Group, 2006).

Chapter Two: Tennie

14. **Margaret's marriage ended:** Goldsmith, *Other Powers*, p. 50; no original attribution.

14. **"insane on spiritualism.":** *New York Herald*, May 17, 1871; and the *(NY) Sun*, May 16, 1871.

15. **"I love her dearly anyway.":** *New York Herald*, May 17, 1871.

15. **Ads were placed in local papers:** The "Wonderful Child" ad was first published in an 1859 Columbus, Ohio, paper; it was used for years as Buck fudged on Tennie's age.

16. **the Fox sisters were authentic:** Ann Braude, *Radical Spirits: Spiritualism and Women's Rights in Nineteenth-Century America* (Boston: Beacon Press, 1989).

16. **her younger sister, Kate:** Different sources say that Maggie was either fourteen or thirteen and that Kate was either ten or twelve. Ibid. See also Howard Kerr, *Mediums and Spirit-Rappers and Roaring Radicals: Spiritualism in American Literature, 1850–1900* (Urbana: University of Illinois Press, 1972).

16. **crowds stormed Barnum's hotel:** Ibid.

16. **Mark Twain's editor William Dean Howells:** Howells, *Years of My Youth* (New York, Harper and Co. 1916 BiblioLife reproduction, 2008), p. 106.

17. **Utopians, many of whom advocated free love:** Braude, *Radical Spirits*, p. 296.

17. **They held forth as lecturers:** Ibid.

17. **Spiritualist churches embraced women's rights:** Ibid., p. 3.

17. **"science of the metaphysical":** Timothy Messer-Kruse, *The Yankee International, 1848–1876: Marxism and the American Reform Tradition* (Chapel Hill: University of North Carolina Press, 1998), p. 15n21.

18. **inventions transformed Manhattan:** John Steele Gordon, *The Scarlet Woman of Wall Street: Jay Gould, Jim Fisk, Cornelius Vanderbilt, the Erie Railroad Wars, and the Birth of Wall Street* (New York: Weidenfeld and Nicolson, 1988).

18. **any sort of millennium:** William Dean Howells, *Impressions and Experiences* (Ulan Press reprint of pre-1920s books, Unlimited Publishing LLC, Vantage Press), p. 11.

18. *The Spiritual Telegraph*: Todd Jay Leonard, *Talking to the Other Side: A History of Modern Spiritualism and Mediumship* (Bloomington, Indiana: iUniverse, 2005), p. 216.

18. **The astounded soldier swore:** J. E. P. Doyle, *Plymouth Church and Its Pastor, or Henry Ward Beecher and His Accusers* (St. Louis, MO: Bryan, Brand and Co., 1875), p. 440.

18. **334 Spiritualist churches:** Leonard, *Talking to the Other Side*, p. 222.

19. **development of therapeutic hypnotism:** Leonard, *Talking to the Other Side*.

19. **magnetic healing followers:** Google "magnetic therapy" and more than 12 million results come up, including many advertising modern day practitioners, ads for magnetic bracelets, and other paraphernalia.

19. **magnetic healing became popular:** *Talking to the Other Side*, pp. 55–57.

19. **I was a very good doctor:** Quoted in "The Working Woman," *Revolution*, March 10, 1870. LoC vol. 5 (Jan-June 1870): pp. 154–55.

19. **children under five:** Gordon, *Scarlet Woman*, p. 45; additional period background is from Lloyd R. Morris, *Incredible New York: High Life and Low Life of the Last Hundred Years* (New York: Random House, 1951).

19. **Some 750,000 soldiers:** In April 2012, the *New York Times* reported that historian and demographer J. David Hacker, using newly digitized census data, had recalculated the death toll and increased it by 20 percent from the time-honored statistic of 618,222. Guy Gugliotta, "New Estimate Raises Civil War Death Toll," *New York Times*, April 3, 2013, p. D1, http://www.nytimes.com/2012/04/03/science/civil-war-toll -up-by-20-percent-in-new-estimate.html?pagewanted=all&_r=0.

20. **a flashing dandy named John Bortel:** Underhill, *The Woman Who Ran for President*, p. 49; some biographers misspell his name as Bartels.

20. **a self-proclaimed doctor:** Goldsmith, *Other Powers*, p. 104; no original attribution.

20. **Cancers killed and extracted:** Ottawa, Illinois, newspaper ad, 1863.

21. **"recommends" her cancer treatment:** *Chicago Daily Mail*, May 9, 1892.

21. **an imposter, and one wholly unfit:** Ottawa *Republican*, repeated in ibid.

21. **dying and unfed patients:** Ibid.

21. **intent to cheat and defraud:** Ibid.

22. **preposterous lie:** Any comparison between money in 1870 and today is, by its nature, extremely vague and inexact. The financial systems were starkly different. There are many more differences than just inflation. For instance, in 1870 there were no credit cards and very little credit; banks were embryonic, unregulated, and loaned money only to the rich. Very few people except the rich had

savings accounts (or savings to put in them) or insurance policies, so there were none of the financial "multiplier effects" feeding the economy that we take for granted today. A good wage in 1870 was one dollar per day, which meant you never had a spare penny and nothing got saved. Ken Ackerman, author of the *Gold Ring*, from e-mail to MM, May 20, 2013.

22. **The age of wonders:** Tilton, "Victoria C. Woodhull."

22. **her name was changed:** To avoid confusion, I have used "Zula" rather than "Zulu" throughout the rest of the text.

25. **whether this was a legal act:** Victoria Woodhull website; Mary Shearer, who has collected a large array of Woodhull information, including copies of marriage certificates; plus various testimony accounts by Woodhull and Blood.

26. **official records of arrests:** *Chicago Daily Mail*, May 9, 1892. Sachs did not tell her readers these were rumors, not fact.

26. **Some of the first people in Cincinnati:** *San Francisco Chronicle*, May 26, 1871, p. 1; *New York Herald*, May 17, 1871.

Chapter Three: Wall Street Warriors

31. **directors of the Erie Railroad:** Information for this chapter comes from several books: W. A. Swanburg, *Jim Fisk: The Career of an Improbable Rascal* (New York: Scribner, 1959); Stiles, *The First Tycoon*; Gordon, *The Scarlet Woman*, and his *The Great Game: The Emergence of Wall Street* (New York: Touchstone, 2000). Above all, Kenneth Ackerman, *The Gold Ring: Jim Fisk, Jay Gould, and Black Friday, 1869* (New York: Carroll and Graf, 2005). Ackerman additionally assisted MM in May 2013 e-mail interviews.

32. **The Commodore quickly bought:** E-mail interview with Ken Ackerman, May 18, 2013.

33. **all he wants of Erie:** Swanburg, *Jim Fisk*, p. 41.

33. **no closer to controlling the company:** Ackerman to MM, May 18, 2013.

33. **creating a panic:** Gordon, *The Great Game*, p. 117.

33. **would be ruin for him:** Swanburg, *Jim Fisk*, p. 44.

33. **stuffed millions in carpetbags:** Gordon, *The Great Game*, p. 118.

34. **If you don't lend the Commodore:** Ibid.; and Ackerman, *The Gold Ring*.

34. **thousand-dollar gratuities:** *New York Herald*, April 15, 1868, p. 186; Gordon, *The Scarlet Woman*.

34. **hungry legislators and lobbymen:** *New York Herald*, p. 59; Swanburg, *Jim Fisk.*

35. **half a million in stockholders' money:** Swanburg, *Jim Fisk*, p. 63.

35. **He soon was back in the game:** Ibid., p. 66. Regarding the bribing of legislators: Stiles's 2009 biography of Vanderbilt contends that "contemporaries and historians alike have carelessly lumped Vanderbilt together with Gould, Fisk and the Erie board in their accusations of bribery." Stiles states that investigations "found little evidence of corruption by Vanderbilt and his agents" as opposed to the gang of three. Stiles also questions whether the notoriously corrupt Judge Barnard ever received a bribe from Vanderbilt (p. 469). However, Gordon's *The Scarlet Woman* states, "While the Commodore's forces perhaps had not yet begun wholesale bribery, they had been most active in the Assembly's Railroad Committee, and the *Herald* reported a rumor that half a million dollars had been spread around the committee to kill the bill. Whatever the sum, it proved quite adequate, for on March 27th, the committee reported out the bill unfavorably" (pp. 185–86).

35. **many notorious Wall Street operations:** Ackerman to MM, May 18, 2013.

36. **he was never a liar:** Stiles, *The First Tycoon*, p. 455.

36. **never launched a war of aggression:** Ibid., p. 455.

36. **fascination for Spiritualism:** Ibid., p. 412. Vanderbilt once admitted some skepticism but added that he felt "there was a skill and acuteness" to Spiritualism.

36. **prescriptions from a Spiritualist healer:** Stiles, *The First Tycoon*, p. 363; Howard Kerr, *Mediums and Spirit-Rappers and Roaring Radicals: Spiritualism in American Literature, 1850–1900*, p. 413; ibid., p. 484.

36. **Vanderbilt was definitely ready:** Tilton's biographical sketch of Woodhull says that "the sisters won the good graces of Commodore Vanderbilt—a fine old gentleman of comfortable means." Father Buck, with his well-honed instinct for a pigeon, may have made the Commodore's acquaintance.

37. **"magnetic physicians and clairvoyants":** Stiles, *The First Tycoon*, p. 484.

37. **Why don't you do as I do:** Stiles, *The First Tycoon*, p. 505; *(NY) Sun*, Sept. 25, 1870; *New York Herald*, May 17, 1871; *New-York Daily Tri-*

bune, May 17, 1871. This anecdote is a staple of all books on Tennie and Vanderbilt.

37. **she sat on his lap:** Every account of Vanderbilt; no original attribution, as it has been used and repeated as fact for more than a century.

38. **indicted for manslaughter:** Stiles, *The First Tycoon*, p. 225.

38. **a matter of taste:** Ibid., pp. 503 and 593n78. Stiles argues against previous books repeating rumors as fact regarding Vanderbilt and Tennie.

38. **communication from Jim Fisk:** *New-York Daily Tribune*, Oct. 16, 1878, p. 4.

39. **New York Gold Exchange's:** The Gold Exchange was created during the Civil War after the New York Stock Exchange refused to allow gold trading under its roof, deeming it unpatriotic. This forced gold traders to set up a separate organization. Ken Ackerman to MM, May 18, 2013.

39. **Hysterical sobbing filled the Street:** Ackerman was a major source for this information. See also Swanburg, *Jim Fisk*; Stiles, *The First Tycoon*; Gordon, *The Great Game*; and Maury Klein, *The Life and Legend of Jay Gould* (Baltimore, MD: Johns Hopkins University Press, 1986).

39. **"I came out a winner!":** *New York Herald*, Jan. 22, 1870, p. 10.

Chapter Four: The Bewitching Brokers

40. **the posh Hoffman House:** Although several biographers mention a full-length nude painting adorning the bar wall of the sisters' temporary residence, this was not a part of the hotel fixture until the 1880s.

40. **higher floors were prized:** Justin Kaplan, *When the Astors Owned New York: Blue Bloods and Grand Hotels in a Gilded Age* (New York: Viking, 2006), p. 25.

41. **mantle of the genial old Commodore:** *New York Herald*, Jan. 22, 1870, p. 10. All quotes in this section are from this article.

41. **Tennie was less discreet:** *New York Herald*, Feb. 5, 1871.

42. **200 horses died daily:** Edwin G. Burrows and Mike Wallace, *Gotham: A History of New York City to 1898* (New York: Oxford University Press, 1999), pp. 931–32.

42. **The first L train:** Ibid.

42. **It closed three years later:** See "Alfred Ely Beach: Beach's Bizarre Broadway Subway," at http://www.klaatu.org/klaatu11.html.

42. **a thousand tons of manure:** For the figures on New York City's horse population, see Gordon, *The Scarlet Woman*, p. 37. A second source (Burrows and Wallace, *Gotham*) used a different number: "40,000 horses each working day produced some four hundred tons of manure and twenty thousand gallons of urine daily" (p. 948).

43. **"the heart of a shark.":** Burrows and Wallace, *Gotham*, p. 912.

43. **He who sells what isn't his'n:** Gordon, *The Great Game*, pp. 84 and 61.

43. **the immorality of his time:** Swanburg, *Jim Fisk*, text on jacket cover.

43. **Tennie was the Jim Fisk:** Doyle, *Plymouth Church and Its Pastor*, p. 436.

44. **an object lesson to the whole world:** SIU.

44. **the Commodore had aided:** Henry Clews, *Fifty Years in Wall Street* (New York: Irving Publishing, 1908). Reprinted in the *Wall Street Journal*, Aug. 11, 1927. Stiles, *The First Tycoon*, states that there was no evidence that Vanderbilt contributed anything to their enterprise. However, contemporaneous recollections by Clews and Jay Gould, and reaction on the Street, indicate that his initial assistance was crucial.

45. **Vanderbilt soon shunned them:** Stiles, *The First Tycoon*, pp. 501–8.

45. **Rather neat finesse:** Jay Gould quoted in the *Wall Street Journal*, Aug. 11, 1927.

45. **the wall gave the Financial District:** Gordon, *Scarlet Woman*, p. 10.

46. **Monday: I started my land operations:** George F. Train, *Young America in Wall Street*. Reprint of books in public domain, Nabu Press, through Amazon, 2012, p. 209.

46. **The Williams and Grey firm:** *(NY) World*, Feb. 8, 1870; Thomas Byrnes, *1886 Professional Criminals of America*. Reprint of 19th Century Rogues' Gallery of Criminals (New York: The Lyons Press, 2000), p. 313.

46. **boldness, spirit, grandeur and enterprise:** *New York Herald*, Feb. 5, 1870.

47. **They are the salt of the earth:** Underhill, *The Woman Who Ran for President*, pp. 70 (quoting Matthew Hale Smith's contemporaneous account) and 71.

47. **cosmetics, the toilet, fashion and vanity:** *New York Herald*, Feb. 6, 1870, p. 3.

47. **the younger woman's candor:** "The Working Woman," *Revolution*, March 10, 1870. LoC vol. 5, January-June 1870, pp. 154–155.

48. **part of the regular machinery:** Ibid.

48. **hung in effigy:** Jean Baker, *Sisters: The Lives of American Suffragists* (New York: Hill and Wang, 2006), p. 63.

48. **delirium of unreason:** *Brooklyn Eagle*, Jan. 10, 1870.

49. **a stop on the social evils:** "The Working Woman," *Revolution*, March 10, 1870.

49. **without asking men's leave:** Ibid.

49. **show in financial matters:** "What Can Women Do?" editorial, *Revolution*, March 24, 1870: LoC vol. 5, January–June 1870, p. 188.

Chapter Five: *Woodhull & Claflin's Weekly*

50. **We propose revolution:** *New York Herald*, Feb. 13, 1870, p. 7.

51. **"Now for victory in 1872.":** *New York Herald*, April 2, 1870.

51. **The blacks were cattle:** Underhill, *The Woman Who Ran for President*, p. 79.

52. **"to teach the illiterate Negro.":** Madeleine B. Stern, *The Pantarch: A Biography of Stephen Pearl Andrews* (Austin: University of Texas Press, 1968), p. 54.

53. **Andrews slammed James:** Ibid., p. 83.

53. **who was the husband or wife:** Ibid., p. 85.

53. **the ongoing repression of women:** Timothy Messer-Kruse, *Yankee International, Marxism and the American Reform Tradition, 1848–1876.* (Chapel Hill: University of North Carolina Press, 1998), p. 110.

54. **subtle echo of sameness:** Stern, *The Pantarch*, p. 105.

54. **vigorous police raid:** Ibid., p. 89.

54. **"addicted to disorder.":** *Brooklyn Eagle*, May 5, 1875.

56. **dined with Vanderbilt:** *(NY) World*, Sept. 24, 1870, p. 5.

56. **ideas of "radical progress.":** *Brooklyn Eagle*, May 5, 1875.

57. **I hope to see tomorrow:** VW to Reid, Jan. 26, 1870; TC to Reid, Feb. 6, 1870. Some biographers feel Tennie's letter said she hoped to see him in the "a.m."; the abbreviation is difficult to read and could be "p.m.," which adds a sexual overtone. Whitelaw Reid Collection, Library of Congress, Washington, DC.

57. **penmanship of Colonel Blood:** Underhill, *The Woman Who Ran for President*, p. 73. Underhill postulates that Blood may have been a procurer for Tennie, but there is no evidence except his writing this letter.

57. **figured in American history:** Robert S. Holzman, *Stormy Ben Butler*. (New York: Macmillan, 1954).

57. **the Civil War Yankee general:** New Orleanians do not forget. Information from their Louisiana State Museum, the Cabildo, states that the nickname "Beast" reflects local sentiments even today.

57. **which end of them looks best:** Holzman, *Stormy Ben Butler*, pp. 84–88.

57. **As Edith Wharton said:** Edith Wharton, *The Age of Innocence* (New York; Toronto; New York: Collier Books; Maxwell Macmillan Canada; Maxwell Macmillan International, 1992), p. 100.

58. **descended from Jews:** Kaplan, *When the Astors Owned New York*, pp. 29–31 and 53.

58. **"indescribably pretentious" trappings:** Ibid., p. 30.

59. **the Selfridge Merrys:** Wharton, *The Age of Innocence*, p. 215.

59. **one can't make over society:** Ibid., p. 111.

Chapter Six: "Madam, you are not a citizen, you are a woman!"

60. **support the houses of prostitution!:** VW in *Tried as by Fire or, the True and the False, Socially* (essay and speech) (New York: Woodhull and Claflin, 1874).

61. **championed the vote for women:** Holzman, *Stormy Ben Butler*, pp. 4 and 171.

62. **I hope to snuggle you closer:** Baker, *Sisters*, p. 75.

62. **her naked person:** The Butler "naked" anecdote is repeated as fact in twentieth-century biographies. However, biographer Sachs's "source," Benjamin Tucker, actually told her he was repeating rumor. Sachs used the naked comment as truth, not printing Tucker, who'd said flatly, "About Ben Butler's relations with Victoria I knew nothing. I believe this to be a total lie." Tucker-Sachs.

62. **"I went at night":** SIU.

62. **open the [judiciary] committee:** Ibid.

62. **dip into my husband's pockets:** IBH to JM, at SIU.

63. **"on her own.":** Ibid.

63. **Mrs. Woodhull's talent and personality:** Ibid.

63. **very ably debated:** Ibid.

63. **servitude of the hardest kind:** Elizabeth Cady Stanton, Susan B. Anthony, Matilda Johnson Sage, and Ida Husted Harper, *History of Woman Suffrage, 1861–1876*, vol. 2, part 2, 1881 Reprint (Whitefish, MT: Kessinger Publishing, 2013), p. 456.

64. **women as citizens should be included:** Woodhull's memorial available in many books and on numerous websites including *An American Time Capsule: Three Centuries of Broadsides and Other Printed Ephemera*, Library of Congress, Rare Books and Special Collections division; and Cari M. Carpenter, *Selected Writings of Virginia Woodhull* (Lincoln: University of Nebraska Press, 2010).

64. **the question to be argued:** *(Washington, DC) Daily Morning Chronicle*, Jan. 11, 1871, p. 2.

64. **"You are a woman!":** Underhill, *The Woman Who Ran for President*, p. 99, and several other accounts.

65. **makes her logic irresistible:** *Evening Star*, Jan. 11, 1871, p. 1.

65. **Hooker became a fervent follower:** IBH to JM, at SIU.

66. **picture of the advanced ideas:** *Daily Patriot*, Jan. 11, 1871.

66. **found to contain ice:** *Philadelphia Press*, Jan. 22, 1871.

66. **Hooker thought she would fall:** IBH to JM, at SIU.

67. **the fourteenth amendment is good enough:** *Daily Morning Chronicle*, Jan. 14, 1871, p. 4.

67. **made news when they tried to vote:** When the sisters and several women friends burst into the polling place, a Democratic inspector told them that Boss Tweed's Tammany Hall had given him orders not to receive the votes of women. Woodhull's eyes flashed. "Is it a crime to be a woman?" she asked. The inspectors ignored her question. Curious onlookers crushed into the polling place to see how this "new thing was going to work." Tennie addressed the crowd before the inspector pushed her hand away as she tried to vote. The women vowed to bring a suit against the inspectors, noting that Wyoming Territory and Michigan had both accorded women the right to vote. *New York Herald*, Nov. 8, 1871, p. 4.

67. **ramifications of an amendment:** *Daily Morning Chronicle*, Jan. 14, 1871, p. 4.

67. **the irresistible Tennie!:** *Philadelphia Press*, Jan. 14, 1870, p. 1.

68. **"masculine coat-tails":** Gabriel, *Notorious Victoria*, p. 75.

68. **the woman we are after:** Sherr, *Failure Is Impossible: Susan B. Anthony in Her Own Words*. 1st paperback ed. (New York: Times Books, 1996), p. 222.

68. **"in which I have no voice.":** *WCW* reprinted speech, March 4, 1871, p. 8.

69. **a government of righteousness:** Ibid.

69. **fluttering of white handkerchiefs:** Gabriel, *Notorious Victoria*, p. 87.

69. **"A masterly argument,":** Underhill, *The Woman Who Ran for President*, p. 112.

69. **help strike the chains:** Stanton letter to Woodhull, in *WCW*, SIU.

Chapter Seven: Free Love, Suffrage, and Abolition

70. **women should grovel in the mire:** Anthony to Laura Deforce Gordon, Feb. 9, 1871, Stanton and Anthony Papers; Goldsmith, *Other Powers*, p. 255.

70. **the woman must be sacrificed:** Stanton to Stone, Nov. 24, 1856; William O'Neill, *Everyone Was Brave: The Rise and Fall of Feminism in America* (Chicago: Quadrangle Books, 1969), p. 2.

71. **the adult traits Stone shared:** Andrea Moore Kerr, *Lucy Stone: Speaking Out for Equality* (New Brunswick, NJ: Rutgers University Press, 1992; paperback, 1995), pp. 15 and 251n.

71. **deepen this disappointment:** Ibid., p. 11.

71. **a healthy woman has as much passion:** Mabel Collins Donnelly, *The American Victorian Woman: The Myth and the Reality* (Westport, CT: Greenwood Press, 1986), p. 47n13.

72. **wives could refuse sex:** Baker, *Sisters*, p. 109n34.

72. **man master, woman slave:** O'Neill, *Everyone Was Brave*, p. 21.

72. **in a word Free Love:** 1871 letter, Stanton to Anthony; Baker, *Sisters*.

73. **a crack-brained harlequin:** Elisabeth Griffith, *In Her Own Right: The Life of Elizabeth Cady Stanton* (New York: Oxford University Press, 1984), p. 130.

73. **I should have said Amen!:** Marjorie Spruill Wheeler, ed., *One Woman, One Vote: Rediscovering the Women's Suffrage Movement* (Troutdale, OR: NewSage Press, 1995), p. 68.

73. **men and women were slaughtered:** Lori D. Ginzberg, *Elizabeth Cady Stanton: An American Life* (New York: Hill and Wang, 2009), p. 125.

73. **get out of the terrible pit:** Eric Foner, *Frederick Douglass on Women's Rights* (New York: Da Capo Press, 1992), p. 33.

73. **ignorant negroes and foreigners:** Ibid., p. 90.

73. **an order for a mule:** Ginzberg, *Elizabeth Cady Stanton*, p. 141.

74. **Patrick and Yung Fung:** Griffith, *In Her Own Right*, p. 152.

74. **fearful outrages on womanhood:** Foner, *Frederick Douglass on Women's Rights*, p. 33.

74. **'Sambo…and the bootblack.':** Ibid., p. 87.

74. **an urgency to obtain the ballot:** Ibid., p. 33.

74. **it is true of the black woman:** Ibid., p. 87.

75. **"Battle-him of the Republic.":** *Brooklyn Eagle*, Jan. 10, 1870.

76. **five thousand anti-suffragists:** *Anglo-American*, Feb. 11, 1871.

76. **unsuited to their physical organization:** Gabriel, *Notorious Victoria*, p. 83.

76. **let men drive the nails:** Gabriel, *Notorious Victoria*, p. 92; Quoting Stanton to Mott, April 1, 1871.

77. **work for her own enfranchisement:** Letter to Milo A. Townsend, April 5, 1871, letter no. 41 in Peggy Jean Townsend and Charles Walker Townsend III, eds., *Milo Adams Townsend and Social Movements of the 19th Century*, 1994, at http://www.bchistory.org/beavercounty/book lengthdocuments/AMilobook/23Woodhull.html.

77. **assume to be better than I:** VW to IBH, quoted in Gilbert, *Notorious Victoria*, p. 90; no original attribution.

77. **every gossip of every revolutionist:** Letter from SBA to IBH, in Lynn Sherr, *Failure Is Impossible: Susan B. Anthony in Her Own Words*, 1st paperback ed. (New York: Times Books, 1996), p. 220.

78. **all the scandals afloat:** Ibid., p. 221.

78. **A lady in every sense:** Gabriel, *Notorious Victoria*, p. 98; and letter from Isabella Hooker to VW: SIU.

79. **at the expense of any ambition:** *New-York Daily Tribune*, May 12, 1871, p. 2.

79. **such rivers of blood:** Gabriel, *Notorioius Victoria*, p. 94.

80. **rhetoric on privacy rights:** *New-York Daily Tribune*, May 12, 1871, p. 5. More than a hundred years later a Florida senator, Jack D. Gordon, managed to pass a Florida state constitutional amendment assuring the right to privacy, thus protecting individual rights such as sexual relationships from government interference. Florida was one of a few states to pass such an amendment. In a Republican Florida Senate, Gordon's privacy amendment—"right to privacy" would have been called "free love" in the sisters' era—was stripped of much of its power by a subsequent conservative amendment.

80. **what terrible rough seas:** Goldsmith, *Other Powers*, p. 275.

80. **The paper then excoriated:** *Brooklyn Eagle*, May 19, 1871, p. 2.

Chapter Eight: All in the Family: "Never a wholly sane mother"

81. **[U]pon affidavits of Annie Claflin:** *New York Herald*, May 16, 1871, p. 3.

81. **"disprove the charges against me.":** *Brooklyn Eagle*, May 8, 1871, p. 10.

82. **Byron's Dadu electrified:** Ibid.

82. **they "were not compatible.":** TC and VW were incredibly advanced on divorce reform; incompatibility as of 2010 was still not a ground for divorce in New York, although no-fault divorce had been instituted.

82. **get $10,000 or $15,000:** *Brooklyn Eagle*, May 8, 1871, p. 10.

83. **the parties behind your mother:** Ibid.

83. **They were accustomed to trouble:** Tucker-Sachs.

84. **meet these persons face to face:** *Brooklyn Eagle*, May 8, 1871, p. 10.

84. **the firm's "silent or 'sleeping partner'":** *New York Herald*, May 16, 1871, p. 3. The biased headline: ASTONISHING REVELATIONS BY OLD MRS. CLAFLIN—BLOOD THREATENED HER LIFE.

84. **living example of immorality and unchastity:** *(NY) World*, May 22, 1871, p. 3.

85. **takes care of him:** *New York Herald*, May 16, 1871, p. 3.

85. **divers wicked and magic arts:** Ibid.

86. **Counsel: "[W]ould you really do that?":** Ibid.

86. **silver-tongued Tennie:** *New York Herald*, May 17, 1871, p. 10.

86. **she would have him in the Penitentiary:** Ibid. The entire description of Woodhull and Claflin testimony is from the *New York Herald*, May 18, 1871, p. 10, unless otherwise indicated.

87. **make money to keep these deadheads:** *San Francisco Chronicle*, May 26, 1871, p. 1; *New York Herald*, May 17, 1871, p. 10.

87. **COMMODORE VANDERBILT KNOWS MY POWER:** Ibid.

88. **you are only making yourself conspicuous:** Ibid.

89. **She hates Colonel Blood and Vicky:** *New York Herald*, June 8, 1871, p. 6.

89. **The fond and fierce mother:** Tilton, "Victoria C. Woodhull."

89. **these brittle tenements:** *WCW*, June 8, 1871.

89. **the one had me taken off:** *Chicago Tribune*, May 27, 1871, p. 1.

89. **shoot her down in the streets:** *Chicago Tribune*, June 11, 1871.

90. **"poor old mother, Pa and Polly,":** *(NY) Sun*, June 9, 1871, p. 1.

90. **"kicked about the corpse":** *Brooklyn Eagle*, June 9, 1871.

90. **the social subordination of woman:** Stanton letter to VW, June 21, 1871, published in *WCW,* July 15, 1871.

90. **a fair representative of the movement:** Goldsmith, *Other Powers,* p. 279, cites the *Cleveland Leader,* no date provided; M. M. Marberry, *Vicky: A Biography of Victoria C. Woodhull* (New York: Funk and Wagnalls, 1967).

91. **one who has two husbands:** *New-York Daily Tribune,* May 20, 1871.

91. **Mr. Greeley's home:** *WCW,* May 27, 1871.

91. **shouldn't be associating with such folks:** *New-York Daily Tribune,* May 21, 1871.

91. **I believe in public justice:** VW letter to the *New York Times* and the *(NY) World,* May 20, 1871.

Chapter Nine: Sex and the City, circa 1871

92. **the stream will disappear:** *Tried as by Fire,* Cari M. Carpenter, ed., *Selected Writings of Victoria Woodhull (Legacies of Nineteenth-Century American Women Writers).* (Lincoln: University of Nebraska Press, 2010).

93. **"improper sexual commerce":** Ibid.

93. **sink such morality!:** Ibid.

94. **saying nothing about the men:** Ibid.

94. **that great good to the human family:** Reprint of TC speech, in Doyle, *Plymouth Church and Its Pastor.*

95. **a worshipped belle of New York:** Doyle, *Plymouth Church,* p. 90; TC's sexual equality speech published in *WCW* Co. collection.

95. **those who are called prostitutes:** *Tried as by Fire.*

95. **Transplanted impoverished southern belles:** Diary of George Templeton Strong (1869 comment). Reprinted in George Ellington (pseudonym), *The Women of New York, or the Underworld of the Great City* (c. 1870; reprinted as *The Women of New York or, Social Life in the Great City,* New York: General Books LLC, 2009), p. 42. *The Women of New York* different edition (New York: Arno Press, 1971), p. 243.

95. **These women paraded on Broadway:** Ellington, *The Women of New York.*

96. **could not procure elsewhere:** *The Gentleman's Companion New York City* (1870; reprinted in the *New York Times,* Jan. 28, 2011). All grammatical and spelling errors are repeated as in original.

96. **likely to engage in the sex trade:** Christine Stansell and the American Council of Learned Societies, *City of Women Sex and Class in New York, 1789–1860*, 1st ed. (New York: Alfred A. Knopf, 1986), p. 167.

96. **sixty percent of women workers in 1870:** Alice Kessler-Harris, *Out to Work: A History of Wage-Earning Women in the United States* (New York: Oxford University Press, 2003), p. 141.

97. **degradation and bodily injury:** *WCW*, February 1871.

98. **when the sluts are out:** Kerr, *Lucy Stone*, p. 25.

99. **Neither teachers, parents or priests:** *WCW*, April 26, 1875. Amazingly they broached sex education that was taboo well into the twentieth century and among some religious groups today. The sisters would have been shocked to know that, 140 years later, this battle was still being fought. In 1980, opposition from religious groups and school board members defeated a city mandate approved for a sex-education curriculum. Thirty years later, in 2011, mandatory sex education in New York City was instituted despite protests. Still, parents can keep their children out of sex-ed classes; many public schools have "opt out" options for parents. Despite protests, the mandate calls for sex ed to be taught starting in the sixth and seventh grade, in coed classes like those the sisters championed. "Sex Education Again a Must in City Schools," *New York Times*, Aug. 10, 2011, p. A-1.

99. **simplistic and incoherent solution:** *Tried as by Fire*. For further reading, Cari M. Carpenter's introduction to *Selected Writings of Victoria Woodhull: Legacies of Nineteenth-Century American Women Writers* (Lincoln: University of Nebraska Press, 2010), discusses Victorian sexual attitudes.

100. **we prate of the holy marriage covenant!:** *Tried as by Fire*.

100. **backlash against an "age of debauchery,":** Margaret Drabble, *For Queen and Country: Britain in the Victorian Age*. 1st American ed. (New York: Seabury Press, 1979), p. 16.

100. **women were supposed to be horrified:** Ibid.

100. **Anthony resisted until she tired:** Baker, *Sisters*, p. 55.

101. **he will know what woman's dress is:** Ibid., p. 56.

101. **man whose wife "wears the britches.":** Ibid.

101. **Fashionable clothes were "absurd...ridiculous":** TC's sexual equality speech, pp. 93 and 94.

101. **While women remain mere dolls:** Ibid.

101. BEAUTIFUL WOMEN, **beckoned one:** *WCW,* July 12, 1873, p. 15.

102. **wash their face after application:** Ellington, *The Women of New York.*

102. **Plumpness was so admired:** Ibid.

103. **removing the clitoris:** Graham John Barker-Benfield, *The Horrors of the Half-Known Life: Male Attitudes Toward Women and Sexuality in Nineteenth Century America* (New York: Routledge, 1968).

103. **"concealed beneath its deceptive exterior.":** Taylor Stoehr and Paul Avrich Collection (Library of Congress), *Free Love in America: A Documentary History* (New York: AMS Press, 1979), p. 357.

103. **its founder, John Humphrey Noyes:** "Histories of the free love movement written by men reflect the same sexism that existed in such communes and did not take women like Woodhull as seriously as men. Male concerns, such as ejaculation were considered central, while female sexual concerns—such as contraception or female orgasm—were peripheral." HNet website, "Feminism and Free Love." http://www.h-net .org/~women/papers/freeloveintro.html.

103. **too much education was unhealthy:** Several sources, including Drabble, *For Queen and Country*; Janet Farrell Brodie, *Contraception and Abortion in Nineteenth-Century America*, 1st Cornell paperback ed. (Ithaca, NY: Cornell University Press, 1997); Barker-Benfield, *The Horrors of the Half-Known Life*; Allan M. Brandt, *No Magic Bullet: A Social History of Venereal Disease in the United States since 1880* (New York: Oxford University Press, 1985).

104. **a relief from manual stimulation:** Rachel P. Maines, *The Technology of Orgasm: "Hysteria," the Vibrator, and Women's Sexual Satisfaction*, Johns Hopkins Studies in the History of Technology, new ser., no. 24 (Baltimore, MD: Johns Hopkins University Press, 1998).

104. **By the 1870s, gynecologists had also begun:** Barker-Benfield, *The Horrors of the Half-Known Life*, p. 83. Note: I am indebted to this well-researched book and its examples of the practices of nineteenth-century gynecologists. MM.

104. **an enormous tax on a young doctor:** Ibid., p 89.

104. **Mrs. H. couldn't stand it:** Ibid., p. 95.

105. **her masturbation eternally damned her:** Barker-Benfield, *The Horrors of the Half-Known Life*, p. 121.

105. **the cheek of sweet sixteen:** Ibid., p. 124.

105. **tractable, orderly, industrious and cleanly:** Ibid., p. 115.

105. **'they know too much to have babies.':** Ibid., p. 242.

106. **unwillingness of our women:** Brodie, *Contraception and Abortion*, p. 272.

106. **"reproduction of the race.":** Clerical objection to contraceptives was such a powerful force that even one hundred years after the sisters, one Long Island man was jailed merely for giving out birth control information (MM article on Bill Baird, *Washington Post*, December 9, 1968). Major news in the 2012 U.S. presidential election, termed the "War on Women," covered GOP attacks on everything from federal funding for contraception to definitions of rape.

106. **Contraceptive devices were called:** Brodie, *Contraception and Abortion*, p. 212.

106. **"Vegetable Compound and Uterine Tonic,":** Ibid., p. 214.

107. **abortion is the choice of evils:** TC, *WCW*, Sept. 23, 1871. Reprinted in Carpenter, ed., *Selected Writings*.

107. **pills touted to induce miscarriage:** Brodie, *Contraception and Abortion*.

107. **Pills with a promise of producing abortion:** Anonymous, *The Gentleman's Companion: A Vest Pocket Guide to Brothels* (1870; reprinted in *New York Times*, Jan. 26, 2011).

107. **a death rate 15 percent higher:** Brodie, *Contraception and Abortion*.

108. **an "evil murderer.":** Alan Keller, *Scandalous Lady: The Life and Times of Madame Restell, New York's Most Notorious Abortionist*, 1st ed. (New York: Atheneum, 1981).

108. **said to be worth $1.5 million:** *New York* magazine, April 9, 2012, p. 36.

108. **constituted a special danger:** Brandt, *No Magic Bullet*.

109. **no "inducement" to battle sexual diseases:** TC's sexual equality speech.

109. **How many Social Evil bills:** VW in *Tried as by Fire*.

109. **syphilis was much more dangerous:** Brandt, *No Magic Bullet*. Brandt cites original works: Alfred Fournier, *Syphilis and Marriage*, trans. Prince A. Morrow (New York: Appleton, 1881); L. Duncan Bulkley, *Syphilis in the Innocent* (New York: Bailey and Fairchild, 1894); and Prince A. Morrow, "The Relations of Social Diseases to the Family," *American Journal of Sociology* (March 1909).

110. **a woman frequently gives gonorrhea:** Brandt, *No Magic Bullet*, p. 212n14.

110. **the "glorious clap.":** Nora Titone, *My Thoughts Be Bloody: The Bitter Rivalry between Edwin and John Wilkes Booth That Led to an American Tragedy* (New York: Free Press, 2010), p. 278.

110. **a serious venereal malady:** Brandt, *No Magic Bullet*, p. 10.

110. **90 percent of sterile women:** Ibid., p.11.

110. **"flatten" his member:** Ibid., p.12.

110. **5 to 18 percent of all males:** Ibid.

Chapter Ten: Confessions of Sin and Battling the Beechers

115. **the lips of Mrs. Tilton:** Full account in *The Selected Papers of Elizabeth Cady Stanton and Susan B. Anthony*, vol. 3: 1873–1880 (New Brunswick, NJ: Rutgers University Press, 2003), pp. 95–97. Recounted in an interview, extensively reported in the *Chicago Tribune*, July 28, 1874; *WCW*, Aug. 8, 1874; and credited to the *Brooklyn Daily Argus*, July 27, 1874.

116. **at least twenty of his mistresses:** Victoria said she heard this from an anonymous man in the corridors of the Capitol Building in Washington, DC, in January 1870, a year and a half before Stanton relayed the Tilton gossip. More than likely, the thought came from Theodore Tilton, with whom she had a cozy alliance. Months before Woodhull would have heard it at the Capitol, Elizabeth Tilton complained in similar fashion in a letter to her husband: "when you say...Mr. B. preaches to forty of his mistresses every Sunday." Richard Wightman Fox, *Trials of Intimacy: Love and Loss in the Beecher-Tilton Scandal* (Chicago; London: University of Chicago Press, 1999). This and numerous other letters involving the Beecher scandal are contained in *Trials of Intimacy* appendix p. 340; ET to TT.

116. **full rights of American citizenship:** *WCW*, Jan. 14, 1871.

116. **"domineering, querulous and eccentric" autocrat:** Baker, *Sisters*, p. 46.

117. **Victoria's dramatic version:** *WCW*, May 17, 1873, p. 15. Woodhull's is the only depiction, modified through the years by biographers.

117. **hapless victim of malignant spirits:** *New-York Daily Tribune* and the *(NY) Sun*, March 1873, republished in *WCW*, May 17, 1873.

118. **waiting for her to cool down!:** Feb. 6, 1871, Isabella Beecher Hooker letter, published in Ida Husted Harper, *The Life and Work of Susan B. Anthony*, chapter 22, vol. 1 (Project Gutenberg ebook version, 2005) www.gutenberg.org.

118. **writing letters to the Hartford papers:** *WCW*, May 17, 1873.

118. **a good clip with a shovel:** Johanna Johnston, *Mrs. Satan: The Incredible Saga of Victoria Woodhull* (New York: G. P. Putnam's Sons, 1967; London: Macmillan, 1967), p. 126.

118. **her roman à clef, *My Wife and I*:** Harriet Beecher Stowe, *My Wife and I* (New York: J. B. Ford and Co., 1872).

119. **in the matter of libel suits:** *(NY) World* and the *New York Times*, letter by VW, May 20, 1871.

119. **the "propriety of delay.":** Woodhull, *WCW*, May 17, 1873.

119. **I am a savior:** Ibid.

120. **charmed with sparkling conversation:** *Chicago Times*, July 9, 1874.

120. **little lady who started the war:** This legend in various forms has become a historic "truth."

120. **homely as a singed cat:** Debby Applegate, *The Most Famous Man in America: The Biography of Henry Ward Beecher* (New York: Three Leaves Press, 2007), pp. 372–73.

121. **smashed the stereotype:** Ibid., p. 212.

121. **reeked of sensuousness:** *WCW*, Nov. 2, 1872.

121. **dressed in virginal white:** Applegate, *The Most Famous Man*, p. 284.

121. **loosen her hair:** Paxton Hibben, *Henry Ward Beecher: An American Portrait* (New York: Press of the New York Readers Club, 1942), p. 136.

121. **Shall she go out free?:** Applegate, *The Most Famous Man*, p. 284.

121. **Beecher shouted, "Who bids?!":** Hibben, *Henry Ward Beecher*, p. 136.

121. **He dragged out heavy iron slave-shackles:** Ibid.

122. **"true kindred" souls to "love":** Applegate, *The Most Famous Man*, p. 291; Fox, *Trials of Intimacy*.

122. **everything he'd ever hated:** Applegate, *The Most Famous Man*, p. 213.

122. **flowers overflowing the altar:** Information from Applegate, *The Most Famous Man*, and Hibben, *Henry Ward Beecher*.

122. **His rolling-thunder voice:** Applegate, *The Most Famous Man*, p. 211.

123. **their deep love as soul mates:** Fox, *Trials of Intimacy*.

123. **one of the fairest pairs:** Applegate, *The Most Famous Man*, p. 308.

124. **"Philadelphia Nigger Convention.":** On the *Brooklyn Eagle*'s racism, see Applegate, *The Most Famous Man*, p. 285.

124. **ugly and deformed child:** Ginzberg, *Elizabeth Cady Stanton*, p. 118.

124. **He did a lot of good:** Tucker-Sachs.

124. **he was "no vestal virgin.":** Ginzberg, *Elizabeth Cady Stanton*, p. 118.

Chapter Eleven: "Yes, I am a free lover!"

126. **Hastily T.T.:** Beecher trial documents in Charles F. Marshall, *The True History of the Brooklyn Scandal* (Philadelphia, PA; Chicago, IL: National Publishing Co., 1874); letters published in the *(NY) Sun* at time of the Beecher trial, May 17, 1875, p. 3.

126. **most extraordinary woman:** Robert Shaplen, *Free Love and Heavenly Sinners: The Story of the Great Henry Ward Beecher Scandal* (London: Andre Deutsch, 1956), p. 144.

127. **the ruin of my church:** *WCW*, Nov. 2, 1872.

127. **What I shall or shall not say:** Marshall, *The True History*.

127. **I may take my own life:** *WCW*, Nov. 2, 1872, p. 12.

128. **announcing Victoria's speech:** *Chicago Tribune*, Nov. 24, 1871.

128. **their expression by a lady:** *New York Times*, Nov. 21, 1871.

128. **I haven't come here for nothing:** *New York Herald*, Nov, 21, 1871.

128. **Free Love ladies and gentlemen:** Ibid.

129. **Woodhull paced, cheeks burning:** *WCW*, May 17, 1873, recounting the event.

130. **I have the honor of introducing:** *Chicago Tribune*, Nov. 24, 1871.

130. **most astonishing doctrine:** *New York Herald*, Nov. 21, 1871.

130. **rule the female citizens:** *WCW*, May 17, 1873; portions of the lecture text not used by newspapers are included, from the full text.

131. **his shouts were hissed down:** *New York Herald*, Nov. 21, 1871.

131. **come into this world without knowing:** Newspapers all carried variations of what was said: "[H]ow could you expect to be recognized in society unless you knew who your father or mother was?" (*New York Herald*, Nov. 24, 1871); "Would you like to come into this world without knowing who your father or mother was?" (*Chicago Tribune*, Nov. 24, 1871); and "[H]ow would she like to have come into this world without knowing who was her father?" (*Baltimore Sun*, Nov. 24, 1871).

132. **Utica sat back down:** *New York Herald*, Nov. 21, 1871.

132. **at race-horse speed:** Ibid.

132. **"Are you a free lover?"**: *Chicago Tribune*, Nov. 24, 1871. Contemporary reports and subsequent books confuse the manner in which she uttered the famous phrase. Some dramatize it as an extemporaneous response when someone shouted from the audience, "Are you a free lover?" Others contend it was a scripted part of her speech. Tilton confused the issue by testifying that the written speech was not inflammatory, just the extemporaneous parts, but his reason for saying so was self-serving. The contemporary pamphlet printed by Woodhull, Claflin and Co. contains the quote. The *New York Times* and the *Baltimore Sun* did not even use it. The *Herald* stated that she uttered it without prompting, but perhaps extemporaneously. An eyewitness, Benjamin Tucker, who worked at the *Weekly*, claimed it was in the text and that he had heard her deliver it soon after "with great calmness in Boston." This declaration "was planned and plotted in advance, to be flung into the teeth of the hostile." He fought with Emanie Sachs, Woodhull's first biographer, to correct her high-drama account. She did not, and others followed suit.

133. **this form of slavery:** *WCW*, May 17, 1873. Reprinted the entire text.

133. **The Tilton relationship remains a probability:** One source, who had an axe to grind, Benjamin Tucker, claims that Woodhull told him she had had sex with both Tilton and Beecher.

135. **kiss my ass:** Tucker-Sachs.

Chapter Twelve: From Spirit Ghosts to Karl Marx

136. **read aloud at the meeting:** Underhill, *The Woman Who Ran for President*, p. 169.

137. **the most mystical and ethereal type:** Tilton, "Victoria C. Woodhull."

138. **"The Queen of Quacks":** *(NY) World*. Reprinted in the *Chicago Tribune*, Sept. 17, 1871, p. 6.

138. **If apples are wormy:** For a century this quote has been attributed to *Harper's Weekly*, but a Harper's website states that the magazine reprinted it from the *New York Tribune*, September 11, 1871, http://nastandgreeley.harpweek .com. Note: one hundred years later, women were still battling for political recognition and failed in the passage of the Equal Rights Amendment.

138. **the first American publication to print:** Messer-Kruse, *The Yankee International*, p. 170.

139. **few holding all the wealth:** *New York Times*, March 16, 1872; *WCW*, March 16, 1872.

139. **plant the Flag of women's rebellion:** *WCW*, Oct. 18, 1873, quoted in Miriam Brody, *Victoria Woodhull: Free Spirit for Women's Rights* (New York: Oxford University Press, 2004), p. 35.

139. **English-language organ:** Messer-Kruse, *The Yankee International*, p. 106.

139. **"highly-interesting" paper:** Ibid., p. 106.

140. **an embarrassment:** Messer-Kruse, *The Yankee International*, p. 197.

140. **only religious sect in the world:** National American Woman Suffrage Association Collection, Library of Congress, Washington, DC.

140. **soul of the American International:** Messer-Kruse, *The Yankee International*, p. 107.

140. **The Communards called for:** Stewart Edwards, ed., *The Communards of Paris, 1871*. Documents of Revolution series (Ithaca, NY: Cornell University Press, 1973).

141. **"Let us kill no more!":** Alistair Horne, *The Terrible Year: The Paris Commune, 1871* (London: Phoenix, 2004 paperback edition), p. 137. Estimates of the numbers of Parisians slaughtered vary wildly between 6,000 and 40,000. "Reliable French historians" placed the figure at between 20,000 and 25,000, although revisions continue. p. 139.

141. **murderous mobs:** Messer-Kruse, *The Yankee International*, p. 101.

141. **lowered the American flag:** *(NY) World*, Dec. 18, 1871, p. 1.

141. **forged a compromise:** *(NY) Sun*, Dec. 18, 1871, p. 1.

142. **exerted themselves like Trojans:** Ibid.

142. **All the spectators stared:** *New York Herald*, Dec. 18, 1871, p. 3. Some biographers argue that Victoria was in a carriage in back the entire time, but contemporary newspapers clearly mention the sisters marching in front, although they may have retired to a carriage along the parade route.

142. **the sisters wore:** *(NY) Sun*, Dec. 18, 1871.

142. **Tennie led the women's group:** *Baltimore Sun*, Dec. 18, 1871.

142. **she had to give up the banner:** *New York Herald*, Dec. 18, 1871, p. 3.

142. **THE WORLD IS OUR COUNTRY:** *(NY) World*, Dec. 18, 1871, p. 1.

142. **his Christian solution:** Ibid.

143. **denunciation of capitalist power:** Speech, New York Academy of Music, Feb. 20, 1872; Boston Music Hall, Feb. 1, 1872.

144. **abuse of men:** "A Lamp Without Oil," *New York Times*, Feb. 22, 1872.

145. **comparison with Mr. Astor:** *WCW*, March 1872.

145. **damaging tag of Mrs. Satan:** Amanda Frisken, *Victoria Woodhull's Sexual Revolution: Political Theater and Popular Press in Nineteenth-Century America* (Philadelphia: University of Pennsylvania Press, 2004), pp. 46–48.

Chapter Thirteen: Being Tennie

146. **"Soup for three,":** JM files, at SIU.

146. **That there should be two:** *New York Times*, May 16, 1872, p. 4.

147. **not a person to trifle with:** Tucker-Sachs correspondence.

147. **unnerved the visitor:** Tucker-Sachs.

147. **"Oh that Tenn, Tenn, Tennessee.":** Marberry, *Vicky*, p. 5.

148. **childlike and unsophisticated innocence:** Ibid.

148. **"Draw your own conclusions.":** Ibid.

148. **referring to his private parts:** Tucker-Sachs.

148. **made Tennie a cover girl:** Frisken, *Victoria Woodhull's Sexual Revolution*.

148. **Tennie Claflin's name:** Ibid., p. 78, quoting from *The Days' Doings*, June 8, 1872; and *(NY) Evening Telegram*, May 15, 1872.

148. **the low-class portrayal:** Marberry, *Vicky*, p. 27.

149. **her upholstered derriere:** *(NY) Sun*, March 21, 1870.

149. **denies all knowledge of her:** Stiles, *The First Tycoon*, p. 504; *(NY) Sun*, March 26, 1870.

150. **This silly illustration:** Amanda Frisken's *Victoria Woodhull's Sexual Revolution* is a valuable addition to the sisters' lore; Frisken examines the "sporting news" scandal periodicals. The cartoons described here are *Days' Doings* illustrations reproduced in Frisken's book.

150. **a twinlike personality:** Frisken, in her admirable examination of the sporting news treatment of the sisters, develops this concept.

150. **We have queer theories:** *Brooklyn Eagle*, May 8, 1871, p. 10.

150. **make a solo splash:** *WCW*, July 8, 1871.

151. **passing us by without recognition:** *WCW*, Dec. 16, 1871.

152. **Each bewitching gypsy:** Underhill, *The Woman Who Ran for President*, pp. 34–35.

153. **kept her voice in check:** *WCW*, Nov. 28, 1874, p. 9.

153. **the love that she inspired:** Tucker-Sachs.

154. **large lithograph of Tennie:** *(NY) Sun*, Aug. 12, 1871, p. 1; entire recount of the meeting.

155. **two engines on the same track:** Swanburg, *Jim Fisk*, p. 209.

155. **decided to extort money:** Kenneth D. Ackerman, *Boss Tweed: The Rise and Fall of the Corrupt Politician Who Conceived the Soul of Modern New York* (New York and Berkeley: Carroll and Graf Publishers, 2005), pp. 283–84.

155. **night that Abe Lincoln was shot:** Ibid., p. 284.

155. **without moral sense:** Ibid., p. 284.

156. **loudest professing saint:** *WCW*, Feb. 3, 1872.

156. **occasion incredulity:** *(NY) Sun*, May 15, 1872.

156. **the metaphorical stars of Col. Fisk:** *New York Times*, May 16, 1872, p. 4.

156. **admire Miss Claflin's logic:** *New York Times* distorted her *(NY) Sun* letter to make her seem more arrogant; republished in *WCW*, June 1, 1872.

156. **erratically riding a horse:** Frisken, *Victoria Woodhull's Sexual Revolution*, p. 78; illustration in *The Days' Doings*, June 8, 1872.

158. **outfit the six-hundred-man regiment:** *(NY) Sun*, June 14, 1872, p. 1. Entire coverage of event is from this source.

158. **cosmetics of the Caucasian woman:** *New York Times*, June 16, 1872.

158. **respect of New York's black community:** Messer-Kruse, *The Yankee International*, p. 204.

158. **was never commissioned:** There was no follow-up account. Some biographers contend that she was never commissioned because the regiment demanded uniforms up front, which she could not supply.

159. **a five or six-inch skirt:** *New York Times*, June 16, 1872.

159. **select a mule to ride on:** *(NY) Evening Telegram*, May 15, 1872, quoted in Frisken, *Victoria Woodhull's Sexual Revolution*, p. 78.

159. **mob of ten thousand persons:** *(NY) Sun*, March 30, 1872, p. 1.

160. **POLLUTION OF THE ACADEMY:** *(NY) World*, March 30, 1872.

160. **free to turn the tables:** *New York Herald*, March 30, 1872, p. 5.

160. **even at typesetting:** *(NY) Sun*, March 30, 1872.

160. **their vile tobacco puddles:** Her speech quoted in Ibid.

161. ***reputations to lose:*** *New York Times*, March 31, 1872.

Chapter Fourteen: Future Presidentess

163. **the woman we are after:** Underhill, *The Woman Who Ran for President*; *WCW*, Jan. 27, 1872.

163. **resorted to blackmailing:** Underhill, *The Woman Who Ran for President*, p. 226.

163. **I shall not hesitate:** *WCW*, April 2, 1873.

163. **whose souls are black with crimes:** Paulina Wright Davis letter to Victoria Woodhull, December 1872, quoted in Goldsmith, *Other Powers*, p. 317.

164. **the two best girls in the world:** *(NY) Sun* quoted in Gabriel, *Notorious Victoria*, p. 165, n.d. given for newspaper.

165. **turn out all the gaslights:** Ida Husted Harper, *The Life and Work of Susan B. Anthony*, chapter 24, vol. 1 (Project Gutenberg ebook version, 2005) www.gutenberg.org.

166. **"demoralizing" embrace of Woodhull:** Ibid.

166. **"heterogeneous gathering that assembled in any city in any age.":** *(NY) World*, May 11, 1872.

166. **speeches lasting until 4:00 p.m.:** *(NY) Sun*, May 11, 1872.

167. **the usual masculine shortness:** *(NY) World*, May 11, 1872.

167. **justice, though the heavens fall!:** *New York Herald*, May 11, 1872.

167. **"blood-stained document.":** *(NY) Sun*, May 11, 1872.

167. **the honor you have conferred:** *New York Herald* and the *(NY) Sun*, May 11, 1872.

168. **nominate a "heathen Chinese.":** *(NY) Sun*, May 11, 1872, p. 1; and AP wire service, May 11, 1872.

168. **ugly minstrels:** Frisken, *Victoria Woodhull's Sexual Revolution*, p. 69.

168. **little money to offer:** The Equal Rights Party was financially doomed. In a country locked into the two-party system, opinion makers traditionally view even well-financed third-party efforts as futile. They are either ignored or ridiculed, and voters are warned to resist voting for windmill-tilting dreams. This was especially so in 1872, when populist challenges to the capitalistic status quo were weak in numbers.

169. **this pettifogging pretender:** *WCW*, March 2, 1872.

169. **whittled to a "toothpick.":** Griffith, *In Her Own Right*, p. 153.

Chapter Fifteen: Down and Out in Manhattan

173. **"guessing wrong more often than right,":** Underhill, *The Woman Who Ran for President*, p. 128.

173. **"The loss is immeasurable,":** *The Autobiographies of Frederick Douglass, Narrative of the Life of Frederick Douglass, an American Slave* (Library of America, Series, 1994), p. 709. [no publication location given].

174. **boisterously ratified the nomination:** *WCW*, June 15, 1872.

174. **the constitution needs improvement:** *WCW*, Feb. 24, 1872.

174. **Brown would rob them:** *WCW*, May 25, 1872.

174. **denounces the greatest of all reforms:** *WCW*, Nov. 2, 1872.

175. **"barefaced attempt to misrepresent":** Kerr, *Lucy Stone*, p. 172; and *WCW*, June 1872.

175. **nothing to do with Stone's AWSA:** Kerr, *Lucy Stone*, p. 173.

176. **calling him a fallen despot:** Messer-Kruse, *The Yankee International*, pp. 175–76.

176. **bridging America's racial divide:** Ibid., p. 205.

176. **found Zula Maud and Byron:** *WCW*, Nov. 2, 1872.

177. **frighten away all their family boarders:** Even though she was willing to run for office with a black man, an absolutely amazing concept in her day, and could speak righteously about social reform, Victoria was not free from racial prejudices. In attacking free love critics who thought women freed from marital bondage would chase after any man, Woodhull responded. Would these critics not say "that even negroes would not escape the mad debauch of white women?" Woodhull both invoked the Reconstruction era's explosive hatred of miscegenation and also belittled as ludicrous the notion that a white woman could be attracted to a black male. Carpenter, *Selected Writings*, introduction, quoting the "Scare-crows of Sexual Slavery" speech by VW.

177. **because we publish a paper:** TC, *WCW*, Nov. 2, 1872.

177. **Will you lend me your aid:** Ibid.

178. **if it brings trouble:** Tilton-Beecher trial records in Marshall, *The True History*.

178. **"persecution she was to suffer.":** *The Beecher Trial: A Review of the Evidence.* Reprinted from the *New York Times*, July 3, 1875, with some revisions and additions (New York: 1875), p. 332.

178. **"my own circle of friends.":** *WCW*, Nov. 2, 1872.

179. **denunciatory, fiery and scandalous:** Hibben, *Henry Ward Beecher*, p. 99; *WCW*, Nov. 2, 1872; and *Memphis Appeal*, Nov. 6, 1872.

Chapter Sixteen: Unmasking Beecher and a Masked Ball Rape

180. **"a poltroon, a coward and a sneak.":** *WCW*, Nov. 2, 1872.

181. **the fruit of my wife's infidelity:** Ibid. Richard Fox in his painstaking *Trials of Intimacy* dismisses VW's version as highly fabricated. However, I feel her source for such embellishment was Tilton, who was capable of histrionically exclaiming that Beecher had impregnated his wife; particularly if Elizabeth Tilton's tales of his jealous fits were true. Her inclusion of "orgies" in front of the Tilton children is, of course, far-fetched and has the stamp of her recklessness, but Tilton may have been capable of spreading that. Other writers have incorrectly used Woodhull's story to manufacture an abortion, which she never claimed, and that Lib carried a six-month-old fetus; Woodhull was guilty of peddling that second rumor, claiming suffragist sources, who then denied they told her. However, the *central* story of adultery charges, backed by Elizabeth Cady Stanton as "substantially" true and probably embellished by Tilton in talks with VW, remains solid. Fox analysis pp. 159, 300–5.

182. **hasten a social regeneration:** Ibid., pp. 10–11.

182. **this harlequin and absurd way:** Ibid.

182. **inquiry into her sexual morality:** Ibid. It remains staggering that sexual attitudes toward rape and abuse continue in this century, 150 years later, with defense attorneys badgering victims in trials and questioning their dress, sexual conduct, and character.

184. **the men who inflict them:** TC in *WCW*, Nov. 2, 1872.

184. **with liquor and its own beastliness:** *(NY) World*, Dec. 24, 1869. Does this not conjure up the 1991 Tailhook scandal, more than a century later, when eighty-three women charged that they were forced to run the gauntlet of drunken servicemen in hotel corridors at the U.S. Navy and Marine Las Vegas convention? In the aftermath, protest demonstrations, outrage, and investigations resulted in the scuttled careers for three hundred aviation officers and fourteen admirals. Women in the armed services reported sexual harassment still in 2013. (See *The Invisible War*, the 2012 award-winning documentary on women in the military.)

185. **debauch these young girls:** *WCW,* Nov. 2, 1872.

185. **make her debut as Portia:** Ibid.

185. **like buttered hot cakes:** *Chicago Times,* July 9, 1874. There remains a problem regarding the veracity of this reporter's account; it was published two years after the fact. He states the sisters were dwelling in a "first-class, English basement, four-story private house, well-furnished...on the eve of their arrest." However, they were destitute and boarding with a sister at a different address. VW letter to *Brooklyn Eagle,* March 27, 1875, p. 3.

185. **as much as forty dollars:** *WCW,* Dec. 28, 1872, p. 10.

186. **an arrest warrant for the sisters:** Heywood Broun and Margaret Leech, *Anthony Comstock: Roundsman of the Lord* (New York: Boni, 1927).

186. **the damning issue of the *Weekly*:** *New York Times,* Nov. 3, 1872, p. 1.

Chapter Seventeen: Jailbirds and the Naked Truth

187. **flushed like a rose:** *Brooklyn Eagle,* Nov. 5, 1872, p. 8.

187. **she could look commonplace:** Tilton, "Victoria C. Woodhull"; and the *New York Herald,* Nov. 4, 1872, p. 8.

187. **a newly chopped onion:** Cait N. Murphy, *Scoundrels in Law: The Trials of Howe and Hummel, Lawyers to the Gangsters, Cops, Starlets, and Rakes Who Made the Gilded Age,* 1st ed. (Washington, DC: Smithsonian, 2010).

188. **indecent and obscene publications:** *New York Herald,* Nov. 4, 1872.

188. **inmates refrained from smoking:** Ibid.

188. **severely tempted by Satan:** Quotes and background on Comstock, unless otherwise noted, are from Broun and Leech, *Anthony Comstock.*

189. **steals away the elastic step:** Ibid.

189. **gave birth to a naked baby!:** Ibid.

190. **untrue in every particular:** *The Selected Papers of Elizabeth Cady Stanton and Susan B. Anthony*: vol. 3, 1873–1880 (2003, Rutgers, the State University of New Jersey) Nov. 6, 1872, p. 14; her remark was sent out nationwide. ECS let it stand until January 1873.

190. **He is foolish—but young:** Goldsmith, *Other Powers,* p. 348.

190. **They did not flinch:** *New-York Daily Tribune,* Nov. 9, 1872, p. 2.

191. **Jeering laughter filled the room:** *New York Herald,* Nov. 10, 1872, pp. 10 and 11.

191. **her father's damaging testimony:** Ibid.

192. **particulars of the "terrible debauchery,":** *New-York Daily Tribune*, Nov. 9, 1872, p. 2.

192. **judge ruled that he was complicit:** *New York Times*, Nov. 20, 1872.

192. **she swore that Jesus had visited:** *WCW*, May 1873.

193. **"those vile jailbirds":** Goldsmith, *Other Powers*, p. 363.

193. **he had collected the twelve copies:** Broun and Leech, *Anthony Comstock*.

193. **the passengers would be safe:** *(NY) Sun*, Jan. 9, 1873.

194. **her hair tumbling down:** *WCW*, Feb. 8, 1873.

194. **a cell in the American Bastille:** From "Moral Cowardice and Modern Hypocrisy—the Naked Truth—Thirty Days in the Ludlow Street Jail," speech in Carpenter, ed., *Selected Writings*.

194. **torrent of burning, glowing words:** *WCW*, Feb. 8, 1873.

196. **they could not give bail:** *(NY) Sun*, Jan. 22, 1873, p. 1.

196. **pile of bastard Egyptian:** Charles Dickens, *American Notes*, 1842.

196. **recently arrested Boss Tweed:** *New York Times*, Jan. 23, 1873, p. 8.

197. **"Yes, even so," said Comstock:** This portion of the trial is from Murphy, *Scoundrels in Law*.

197. **a law more narrow and oppressive:** *Brooklyn Eagle*, Nov. 7, 1872.

197. **let the suit be pressed:** *(NY) Commercial Advertiser*, Jan. 14, 1873.

198. **a living skunk with a dead lion:** *WCW*, Feb. 8, 1873.

Chapter Eighteen: Life and Death

199. **Woodhull's face was ashen:** *(NY) Sun*, June 7, 1873.

200. **DEATH OF THE GREAT REFORMER:** *Chicago Tribune*, June 7, 1873.

200. **sat beside her throughout the night:** *(NY) Sun*, June 7, 1873.

200. **it is very much regretted:** *WCW*, June 21, 1873, p. 3.

200. **hoax to garner sympathy:** *Chicago Tribune*, June 7, 1873.

201. **signed a tripartite covenant:** *New York Times*, May 30, 1873, p. 5.

201. **nearly like ravishment:** Marshall, *The True History*, p. 314; *Daily Graphic*, Sept. 11, 1874.

201. **denied that he had violently assaulted:** Ibid. When the Proctor story appeared in the newspaper the *Daily Graphic*, Bowen sued the editor, and Proctor vociferously denied the whole thing and sued attorney Frank Moulton for raising the tale during testimony.

201. **he shared Tilton's ideas:** Applegate, *The Most Famous Man*, p. 364.

202. **loveless marriages should be dissolved:** Ibid., p. 400.

202. **"an obscene newspaper.":** *New York Times*, May 30, 1873, p. 4.

204. **she might cooperate with him:** This entire account of Bowen and the sisters is found in the *Brooklyn Eagle*, June 26, 1873.

204. **an "Inglorious Failure.":** *Brooklyn Eagle*, June 27, 1873, p. 4.

204. **the "Irish smut dealer.":** Broun and Leech, *Anthony Comstock*, p. 17.

205. **"stories and rumors" are "utterly false,":** Beecher letter to the editor, *Brooklyn Eagle*, June 30, 1873.

205. **affect the public against me:** *New York Times*, July 1, 1873, p. 5.

205. **she was a raving maniac:** *New York Herald*, July 11, 1873.

206. **Cut off at thirty-one:** *WCW*, July 26, 1873, p. 9.

206. **"a nobler man never lived.":** Ibid., p. 10.

206. **rotten with sexual disease:** Ibid.

207. **plain hearse and four carriages:** *(NY) Sun*, July 14, 1873.

207. **they are going to the bad:** Gabriel, *Notorious Victoria*, p. 214.

207. **"Birthplace of Modern Spiritualism.":** *WCW*, Nov. 22, 1873, p. 16.

208. **the charms of the sex:** *Chicago Daily Tribune*, Sept. 17, 1873, p. 5.

208. **Address by the Presiding Genius:** Ibid.

209. **I have braved the penitentiary:** *WCW*, Oct. 15, 1873, pp. 5–6.

210. **submit sexually for money:** Ibid.

210. **insure that no such exigency:** Ibid.

210. **going to help yourselves?:** *Chicago Daily Tribune*, Sept. 19, 1873.

211. **of a character to be published:** Ibid., p. 5.

Chapter Nineteen: Panic and Victory

212. **the country's leading banker:** John M. Lubetkin, *Jay Cooke's Gamble: The Northern Pacific Railroad, the Sioux, and the Panic of 1873* (Norman: University of Oklahoma Press, 2006), p. 3.

213. **caused a "veritable paralysis":** James Ford Rhodes, *History of the United States from the Compromise of 1850 to the McKinley-Bryan Campaign of 1896*, vol. 7 (New York: Macmillan, 1920), p. 110. Now on openlibrary.org http://archive.org/stream/histusacomp07rhodrich#page/n5/mode/2up.

213. **done on credit:** *(NY) Sun*, Sept. 19, 1873.

214. **And in America!:** *New York Herald*. Reprinted in *WCW*, Nov. 29, 1873, p. 13.

215. **Friday evening, October 17:** *WCW*, Oct. 23, 1873. Publishing date was October 23, but the issue was on the street before their October 17 speech.

215. **Applause and hisses followed:** *(NY) Sun* and the *New York Herald*, Oct. 18, 1873.

215. **"Queen of the Rostrum":** Frisken, *Victoria Woodhull's Sexual Revolution.*

215. **back and forth on the stage:** *New York Herald*, Oct. 18, 1873.

216. **worn-out song of Christianity:** *(NY) Sun*, Oct. 18, 1873, p. 2.

217. **power of her oratory:** Newspapers reprinted in *WCW*, March 7, 1874, p. 11.

217. **the wing of Tammany Hall:** Tucker-Sachs.

217. **asked that bail be reduced:** *WCW*, March 21, 1874, p. 10.

218. **tried to gavel them down:** Gabriel, *Notorious Victoria*, p. 226.

218. **could not be found to testify:** *WCW*, March 21, 1874.

218. **wipe up the vomit:** Tucker-Sachs.

219. **jurors were locked up:** *New-York Daily Tribune*, March 14, 1874, p. 5.

219. **ashamed of the jury:** Gabriel, *Notorious Victoria*, p. 228; *(NY) Evening Telegram*, n.d. Reprinted in *WCW*, March 28, 1874, p. 10.

219. **had reasonable doubt:** *(NY) World*, March 15, 1874, p. 5.

219. **the woman that unsexes herself:** *Brooklyn Eagle*, March 14, 1874, p. 4.

220. **fill it with beer:** Tucker-Sachs.

220. **half the regular fare:** Ibid.

Chapter Twenty: The Star Chamber

221. **a sweet-savored trio:** Robert Shaplen, *Free Love and Heavenly Sinners: The Story of the Great Henry Ward Beecher Scandal* (London: Andre Deutsch, 1956), pp. 179–80.

221. **"slandering" Beecher:** Shaplen, *Free Love and Heavenly Sinners*, p. 176.

221. **the words *knave* and *dog*:** Fox, *Trials of Intimacy*, p. 53.

222. **all this smoke of scandal:** Ron Powers, *Mark Twain: A Life* (New York: Free Press, 2005), p. 326.

222. **"greater in plot, development and effect.":** Shaplen, *Free Love and Heavenly Sinners*, quoting *Frank Leslie's Illustrated Newspaper*, n.d., p. 193.

222. **whom his children belonged to:** Plymouth Church investigation testimony from Marshall, *The True History*, p. 198.

222. **"giving up his religious faith,":** "Mrs. Tilton's Statement," Marshall, *The True History*, p. 197.

223. **With Mr. Beecher I had:** Ibid., p. 197.

223. **"indecorous or improper proposal.":** *The Beecher-Tilton War*: Official original documents, letters and statements, University of Michigan Historical Reprint Series: MPublishing. Print on demand print service through Amazon.com, p. 29.

224. **crush out Beecher:** Ibid.

224. **"not been a bad boy.":** *New York Herald*, July 31, 1874, p. 3.

224. **bankrupt in reputation:** Marshall, *The True History*, pp. 257 and 258.

224. **thrust her affections upon me:** Ibid., pp. 264–65.

224. **did not refer to adultery:** Ibid., p. 282.

224. **after long moral resistance:** *The Beecher-Tilton War*: Official original documents, letters and statements, University of Michigan Historical Reprint Series: MPublishing. Print on demand print service through Amazon.com, p. 6.

225. **end abruptly and in disaster:** Marshall, *The True History*, p. 264.

225. **a monstrous conspiracy:** *New-York Daily Tribune*, Aug. 14, 1874; other comments compiled in the *Brooklyn Eagle*, Aug. 20, 1874.

225. **three months in my arms:** *Chicago Times*, July 9, 1874, p. 2.

227. **"The *Chicago Times*?" "Yes.":** *The Beecher-Tilton War*, University of Michigan Historical Reprint Series: MPublishing, p. 62.

227. **Mrs. Woodhull was not safe:** Ibid., p. 35.

227. **criminal is the word:** *Chicago Daily Tribune*, Aug. 2, 1874, p. 4.

228. **the woman gets blamed:** *Chicago Daily Tribune*, Oct. 13, 1874.

228. **spare us the reputation of Susan:** *New York Herald*, n.d. Reprinted in the *Brooklyn Eagle*, Aug. 24, 1874.

228. **'deluded' and 'weak-minded.':** The letter was written in August 1874 but was not printed until October 1, 1874, in the *Chicago Daily Tribune*.

229. **last despairing effort for peace:** Marshall, *The True History*, p. 310.

229. **to Moulton!:** Goldsmith, *Other Powers*, p. 403; no attribution.

229. **investment hangs by the eyelids:** Stanton letter to the *Chicago Daily Tribune*, Oct. 1, 1874.

229. **Said Beecher, "the Voice of the Nation:** Shaplen, *Free Love and Heavenly Sinners*, p. 206.

Chapter Twenty-One: Wickedness in High Places

231. **halting the trial:** Shaplen, *Free Love and Heavenly Sinners*, p. 216; Fox, *The Trials of Intimacy*, p. 89.

232. **Bowery saloon performance:** Fox, *Trials of Intimacy*, p. 90.

232. **disliked Moulton's looks:** Applegate, *The Most Famous Man*, p. 448.

232. **a libertine:** Shaplen, *Free Love and Heavenly Sinners*, pp. 219–20.

232. **often contemplative, Tilton blushed:** *Brooklyn Eagle*, Jan. 15, 1875, p. 4.

232. **"the mother of Uncle Tom.":** Shaplen, *Free Love and Heavenly Sinners*, p. 207.

233. **one man in Brooklyn:** Ibid., p. 212.

233. **four hundred thousand copies:** Fox, *Trials of Intimacy*, p. 56.

233. **her libertine husband and friend:** *New York Herald*. Reprinted in *WCW*, May 29, 1875, pp. 2–3.

233. **can't make Beecher white:** Shaplen, *Free Love and Heavenly Sinners*, p. 240.

233. **the filthy kiss of Victoria Woodhull:** *Brooklyn Eagle*, Feb. 25, 1875, p. 4.

234. ***filthy kiss* expunged:** *The Case of Henry Ward Beecher: Opening Address of Benjamin F. Tracy* (New York: George W. Smith and Co. Publishers, 1875). Reprinted by University of Michigan Library, 2005, and found at http://quod.lib.umich.edu/m/moa/AJK2284.0001.001?.

234. **the voluble Tracy speechless for once:** *(NY) Sun*, May 13, 1875. Reprinted in *WCW*, May 29, 1875, pp. 2–3.

234. **of the prosecution:** *New York Herald*, May 13, 1875.

235. **Victoria's face flushed:** Ibid.

235. **an anxious, half despairing look:** *Brooklyn Eagle*, May 12, 1875.

235. **a bright glitter grew:** *New York Herald*, May 13, 1875.

235. **When Woodhull was excused:** *New-York Daily Tribune*, *New York Herald*, *(NY) Sun*, and *Brooklyn Eagle*, reprinted in *WCW*, May 29, 1875, pp. 2–3. Woodhull's court appearance was May 12, 1875.

236. **as if going to sleep:** Applegate, *The Most Famous Man*, p. 430; *Brooklyn Eagle* full transcript, February 19–20, 1875, p. 1.

236. **his suicidal plans:** *Brooklyn Eagle*, full transcript, Feb. 19, 1875, p. 4.

236. **my last Sunday:** Marshall, *The True History*, pp. 280–82.

237. **contrast of fiction and fact:** *New York Herald*, April 25, 1875.

237. **"uncertainty, forgetfulness, or evasion,":** Shaplen, *Free Love and Heavenly Sinners*, p. 220.

237. **his own former admissions and letters:** *The Beecher Trial: A Review of the Evidence*, p. 22.

237. **happily reprinted these opinions:** For reprint of out-of-town negative editorials on Beecher, see *WCW*, May 8, 1875, p. 6.

237. **adverse to Mr. Tilton:** *New York Times*, April 25, 1875. Reprinted in *WCW*, May 8, 1875, p. 6.

238. **perjury and probably adultery:** *The Beecher Trial: A Review of the Evidence*.

239. **every one of them crushes:** Ibid.; paragraph is a reprise of *Times* summation.

239. **The defense's purpose was to show:** *Brooklyn Eagle*, April 27, 1875, p. 2.

239. **prostitutes for his own pleasure!:** *Brooklyn Eagle*, June 21, 1875, p. 4.

240. **preparations for retiring at night:** *New York Herald*, March 26, 1875; *WCW*, April 19, 1875, p. 10.

240. **cannot well be left out:** *New York Herald*, March 27, 1875. Reprinted in *WCW*, April 10, 1875, p. 6.

240. **to crush him in this case:** Ibid.

241. **this immensely damaging assault:** *New York Herald*, March 29, 1875; *WCW* April 10, 1875.

241. **Mr. Beecher is as much responsible:** Shaplen, *Free Love and Heavenly Sinners*, p. 241.

241. **if he should live to grow up:** Woodhull's letter, *New York Herald*, March 29, 1875; *WCW*, April 17, 1875.

242. **repair the wrong that I have suffered:** *New York Herald*, March 29, 1875; *WCW*, April 17, 1875, p. 3.

242. **impersonal justice, with self expunged:** *New York Herald*, March 30, 1875; *WCW*, April 17, 1875, p. 3.

243. **ignominy that would have paralyzed:** Shaplen, *Free Love and Heavenly Sinners*, p. 245. Quoting the *Newark Sunday Call* interview with ECS, Jan. 2, 1876.

Chapter Twenty-Two: Beecher's Revenge

244. **"clerical kangaroo court":** Hibben, *Henry Ward Beecher*, p. 284.

244. **Bowen "knows nothing.":** *Brooklyn Eagle*, April 1, 1876, p. 4.

245. **denials or protestations or oaths:** Hibben, *Henry Ward Beecher*, p. 285.

245. **adultery, perjury and hypocrisy:** *Independent*, Feb. 10, 1876.

245. **witness to a lie:** *New York Times*, March 3, 1876.

245. **the finger of scorn:** *Brooklyn Eagle*, May 24, 1876, p. 2.

245. **the cause of truth and justice:** *New York Times*, April 16, 1878.

246. **wrong in her mental operations:** *Brooklyn Eagle*, April 17, 1878, p. 2.

246. **the couple was reuniting:** *Chicago Daily Tribune*, April 2, 1878; *(NY) Sun*, March 14, 1878.

246. **price she pays for a reconciliation:** *Elmira (NY) Gazette*, April 16, 1878.

246. **believed she was protecting a saint:** *New York Times*, April 17, 1878.

246. **world-wide as the lie:** Debby Applegate, *The Most Famous Man*, p. 455.

246. **Christian charity and fortitude:** *Brooklyn Eagle*, April 3, 1897.

247. **love of her children:** *Brooklyn Eagle*, April 15, 1897.

247. **un-American idea of any third term:** undated newspaper, Brooklyn Public Library.

247. **at any time in Brooklyn:** *Brooklyn Eagle*, Oct. 1, 1875, p. 2.

247. **the Woodhulls...of the future:** Ibid.

248. **a fitting frame for his face:** *Brooklyn Eagle*, April 22, 1894, p. 21.

248. **the former "Brooklynite," now respectable:** *Brooklyn Eagle*, June 24, 1894.

248. **gave herself to the embraces:** Underhill, *The Woman Who Ran for President*, p. 263.

248. **money "to make a living.":** Frisken, *Victoria Woodhull's Sexual Revolution*, p. 180, chapter note 67.

249. **Tennie has had a man in bed:** All Joseph Treat's accusations are from a self-published pamphlet, Aug. 6, 1874.

249. **of "harlotry":** Underhill, *The Woman Who Ran for President*, p. 265.

249. **drippings wear the hardest stones:** Ibid., pp. 266–67.

249. **decipher through her Spiritualist aspirations:** Ibid., p. 268.

249. **there is life beyond the grave:** Ibid., p. 268; no attribution for quote.

250. **The grandest woman in the world:** Tucker-Sachs.

250. **the Destiny of the World:** Ad for lecture, *Brooklyn Eagle*, June 27, 1876.

251. **climbing about his shoe-soles:** Applegate, *The Most Famous Man*, p. 468.

251. **"barometer" for cultural anxiety:** Richard K. Sherwin, *When Law Goes Pop: The Vanishing Line between Law and Popular Culture* (Chicago: University of Chicago Press, 2000).

251. **our present social evils:** *Chicago Daily Tribune*, Oct. 1, 1874.

Chapter Twenty-Three: The Siege of London

255. **George Washington and Genghis Khan:** Stiles, *The First Tycoon*, pp. 563–66.

256. **irrelevant to any senility charge:** Ibid., p. 504.

256. **make themselves scarce during the trial:** Arthur T. Vanderbilt II, *Fortune's Children: The Fall of the House of Vanderbilt* (New York: William Morrow, 1991), p. 61.

256. **"too ridiculous to seriously discuss.":** *New York Times*, May 13, 1877, p. 12.

257. **advised by Scott Lord:** TC letters, SIU.

257. **Dante's *Inferno* wax tableau:** Luc Sante, *Low Life: Lures and Snares of Old New York* (New York: Farrar, Straus and Giroux, 1991), p. 97.

257. **"filthy practices" now referred to:** TC letters, SIU.

258. **advise against any contact:** Underhill, *The Woman Who Ran for President*, p. 278.

258. **perform our duties:** Doyle, *Plymouth Church and Its Pastor*, pp. 438–39.

259. **the three richest men in England:** Elon Danziger, "The Cook Collection: Its Founders and Its Inheritors," *The Burlington Magazine* 145, no. 1215 (July 2004): 444–58.

260. **noble and beautiful landscape garden:** *(London) Times* quote in Danziger, "The Cook Collection."

260. **absence of ceremony:** *House Beautiful: Making of an American Project* (Chicago: Herbert S. Stone and Company), reproduction of a book published before 1923.

260. **not bear further discussion:** Ibid.

261. **"somewhat flatulent rhetoric.":** Correspondent for the *Brooklyn Eagle*, commenting on VW's reception by British reporters. Dec. 24, 1877.

261. **her fervent eloquence:** Gabriel, *Notorious Victoria*, p. 247.

261. **certainly make her my wife:** John Biddulph Martin obituary, *New York Press*, BPL, March 24, 1897.

261. **their "barefaced mendacity.":** Gabriel, *Notorious Victoria*, p. 254.

261. **an electric light in an alabaster vase:** *Brooklyn Eagle*, Jan. 18, 1881.

261. **marrying for love, not money:** *New York Times*, Oct. 23, 1909, p. 20.

262. **his "old enemy" vanished:** Underhill, *The Woman Who Ran for President*, p. 280.

262. **she made them happy:** SIU.

262. **litany of upper-class breeding:** In 1699 the first Martin joined a banking firm that had reigned from the early fourteenth century. In all, thirteen family members served as members of Parliament between 1741 and 1885. John Biddulph Martin, *The Grasshopper in Lombard Street* (London: Simpkin Marshall Hamilton Kent and Co.; New York: Scribner and Welford, 1892).

263. **feel anxiety on my account:** BPL.

263. **"appalling story of V's antecedents.":** Underhill, *The Woman Who Ran for President*, p. 282.

263. **related to Alexander Hamilton:** G. S. Darewin, "Synopsis of the Lives of Victoria C. Woodhull (Now Mrs. John Biddulph Martin) and Tennessee Claflin (Now Lady Cook): The First Two Lady Bankers and Reformers of America" (London: n.p., 1891).

264. **"lying lips" and a "deceitful tongue.":** Tilton, "Victoria C. Woodhull."

264. **favor free love, even tacitly:** Underhill, *The Woman Who Ran for President*, p. 283.

264. **only the revised images:** Frisken, *Victoria Woodhull's Sexual Revolution*, p. 148.

265. **ensnared by the "harlot" Woodhull:** Underhill, *The Woman Who Ran for President*, p. 285.

265. **& your love will help us:** Martin correspondence, Nov. 3, 1883, at SIU.

Chapter Twenty-Four: Lady Cook

267. **cared for her a great deal:** John Somerville e-mail to MM, May 30, 2011.

267. **"Yours, forever, Frank.":** SIU.

267. **nymphs and cupids cavorting:** Andre Metaxides, owner of Doughty House, in June 2011, who provided MM with a photo of the painting.

267. **Sunday afternoon concerts:** *New York Times*, May 17, 1914.

268. **pointing out such masterpieces as:** *Jardim Formoso*, Aug. 12, 2009.

268. **how startling life can be:** *The Burlington Magazine*, July 2004.

268. **leaving pamphlets and tracts:** Vera Ryder, *Little Victims at Play: Reminiscences of Doughty House by the Great-Granddaughter of Sir Francis Cook, Tennessee Claflin's Husband* (London: Robert Hale Ltd., 1974).

269. **an "American elevator.":** Fragment of article, at SIU.

269. **prettiest woman in the hall:** *Omaha Daily Bee*, May 29, 1887, p. 4.

270. **titled him Viscount de Monserrate:** The palace and garden are now a national monument and a favorite destination for tourists. Gerald Luckhurst, Monserrate's landscape architect, led MM on a fine tour of this magnificent site. In 2011, Prince Charles and Camilla, Duchess of Cornwall, christened a new rose garden at Monserrate.

270. **contented with my precious husband:** SIU.

270. **the contessa's [Tennie's] children:** *Atlanta Constitution*, Jan. 22, 1905.

271. **"Tennie's own Stars and Stripes,":** Ibid.

271. **Yours sincerely, Frank Cook:** SIU.

272. **calling Sir Francis "your darling husband.":** Ibid.

272. **He paid nominal damages:** Underhill, *The Woman Who Ran for President*, p. 295; no original attribution.

272. **in favor of Sir Francis:** *(Adelaide, Australia) Advertiser*, March 18 and 20, 1894.

273. **Write me a line:** VW to TC, undated letter, at SIU.

273. **wrote in his fine script:** VW and JM to TC, undated letter, at SIU.

273. **a look that is not Love:** SIU.

274. **Cable quickly:** TC to VW, undated, in ibid.

274. **alone & keep very quiet:** Ibid.

275. **a result of sexual disease:** Joseph Treat, *Beecher, Tilton, Woodhull, the creation of society*. Self-published pamphlet, 1874.

275. **gonorrhea or 'excessive venery':** Stiles, *The First Tycoon*, p. 557.

275. **Stiles skewered Renehan's unreliable claim:** Stiles challenged Renehan to produce what Stiles charged were nonexistent diaries from a Vanderbilt doctor. Renehan never answered or refuted Stiles. The latter's credibility was further muddied when he was sentenced to eighteen months in federal prison for pilfering letters written by George Washington, Abraham Lincoln, and Theodore Roosevelt from the Theodore Roosevelt Association, and selling them for $100,000, while he was acting director of the association (*[NY] Sun*, June 23, 2008). Renehan said he was suffering from bipolar disorder at the time, which was also while he was writing the Vanderbilt biography. Renehan did not respond to my attempts to reach him. A request for an explanation from his publisher, Basic Books, resulted in this e-mail: "My recollection is that we asked the author to review this matter and to submit any necessary changes... publishers rarely if ever are in the business of fact-checking their authors' man-

uscripts. It's neither financially feasible, nor is it contractually required." The Renehan biography remains prominent on Amazon, without changes. Stiles argued that Vanderbilt remained mentally alert to the end and showed none of the symptoms of physical or mental tertiary syphilitic dementia. Even the doctor who said Vanderbilt may have had gonorrhea testified that Vanderbilt was a most clearheaded man, able to transact business until the end.

Chapter Twenty-Five: Love and Libel

276. **your precious arms around me:** Unless otherwise indicated, the correspondence in this chapter between VW and JM is from BPL.

278. **bicycling craze:** Underhill, *The Woman Who Ran for President*, p. 301.

279. **not displeased with her call:** William S. McFeely, *Frederick Douglass* (New York, W. W. Norton and Co., 1991), p. 333; Douglass diary, Feb. 1887 in *The Autobiographies of Frederick Douglass, Narrative of the Life of Frederick Douglass, An American Slave* (Library of America, Series, 1994).

279. **Birth control was a necessity:** Underhill, *The Woman Who Ran for President*, p. 292.

280. **reputation will not bear investigation:** Marberry, *Vicky*, pp. 227–228; Quotes the *(NY) World*, n.d.

280. **"representing or suggesting" Woodhull:** Underhill, *The Woman Who Ran for President*, p. 288, no attribution.

281. **crooks and honest men:** *New York Herald*, April 24, 1892, p. 5.

281. **"a titled imbecile":** *Brooklyn Eagle*, Nov. 19, 1889, p. 7.

281. **"I made no apology,":** *Washington Post*, May 5, 1890.

281. **hesitate to sacrifice the truth:** *New York Herald*, April 24, 1892, p. 5.

282. **scapegoats of all their misdeeds:** *Los Angeles Times*, May 4, 1890, p. 4.

282. **It is cutting us to pieces:** *Brooklyn Eagle*, May 4, 1890, p. 20.

282. **too pure to mix:** *New York Times*, Sept. 4, 1883.

282. **the flower of our family:** *New York Times*, Sept. 8, 1883.

283. **see me in my sane state:** TC to VW, at SIU.

283. **"your 'worthy' brother.":** JM to VW, July 23, 1891, at SIU.

283. **if possible to say nothing:** JM to lawyer, Sept. 23, 1892, at SIU.

284. **going beyond the point:** Royal Courts of Justice, Tuesday, January 28, 1894; handwritten transcript of the *Martin v. British Museum* trial, MM, British Museum, June 23, 2011.

284. **reprinted the entire article in 1873:** *(London) Times,* Jan. 24, 1894, p. 13; reporting on lawsuit: *Martin and Wife v. Trustees of the British Museum and Edward Maunde Thompson,* the principal librarian.

285. **called her "the queen of prostitutes.":** *(London) Times,* Jan. 24, 1894, p. 13.

285. **according to its rules and regulations:** Ibid.

285. **four hours on the rack:** Ibid.

285. **should have used more care:** Barbara McCrimmon, "Victoria Woodhull Martin Sues the British Museum for Libel," *The Library Quarterly* 45, no. 4 (October 1975): 355–72.

286. **"annoyance which had been caused to them.":** *(London) Times,* March 5, 1894, p. 3, col. 3; *(London) Times,* April 20, 1894, p. 13, col. 3.

286. **Martins had found a defect:** *(London) Times,* Feb. 28, 1894, p. 9.

286. **"in respect of libellous matter":** McCrimmon, "Victoria Woodhull Martin Sues the British Museum for Libel," p. 228.

286. **'persecution & insult has ended.':** SIU.

Chapter Twenty-Six: Widows

287. **I ever met:** Unless otherwise indicated, all letters from JM to VW during his Canary Island journey and her replies to him are from BPL.

288. **do you more good than doctors:** Richard Martin to JM, Ibid.

290. **arrangements with an undertaker or agent:** Ibid.

290. **my life has been made wretched:** SIU.

291. **kill me as they did Johnny:** Ibid.

291. **spent enormous sums in philanthropy:** *Chicago Daily Tribune,* Feb. 17, 1901, p. 11; special cable from London, Feb. 16, 1901.

291. **"well known New York merchant.":** *Baltimore Sun,* Feb. 19, 1901, p. 2.

291. **not being remembered in his will:** *London Constitution,* April 4, 1901, p. 1.

291. **slanders shall be stamped out:** *Washington Post,* April 5, 1901; and *New York Times,* April 5, 1901, p. 6.

291. SHE DIDN'T KILL HER HUSBAND: *Baltimore Sun,* April 5, 1901, p. 2.

292. **the sorrowing widow:** *Atlanta Constitution,* Dec. 14, 1902, p. 3.

292. **awarded Wallace £550:** *(London) Times,* March 4, 1903, p. 3.

292. **she cried, "Cruel, cruel.":** *Chicago Daily Tribune,* March 4, 1903, p. 3; *Baltimore Sun,* March 4, 1903, p. 8.

292. **a blackmailing action:** *New York Times,* June 14, 1903; *(London) Times,* July 16, 1903, p. 10.
292. **"remanded to the Kingston Workhouse.":** *(London) Times,* July 16, 1903, p. 10.
293. **kept in the Doughty Gallery:** *New York Times,* March 14, 1901, p. 9.
293. **His handsome bequest in his will:** Owen Stinchcombe, *American Lady of the Manor, Bredon's Norton; The Later Life of Victoria Woodhull Martin, 1901–1927* (self-published, 2000), available at http://www.amazon.co .uk/American-Lady-Manor-Owen-Stinchcombe/dp/B000KGMI5O.
293. **get the world and lose soul power:** Gabriel, *Notorious Victoria,* p. 286.

Chapter Twenty-Seven: Moving On

294. **he had buried them at sea:** Gabriel, *Notorious Victoria,* p. 287.
295. **inscribed the names of poets:** Norton Park MM visit; with owner, Debby Booth, June 25, 2011.
295. **tried to "clear out my daughter,":** *New York Times,* June 5, 1895, p. 2.
296. **to Queen Victoria:** Underhill, *The Woman Who Ran for President.*
296. **in London and Portugal:** *New York Times,* June 5, 1895, p. 2.
296. **Victoria's insistence:** Stinchcombe, *American Lady of the Manor.*
297. **halted a charity:** Ibid.
297. **"well known figure of the Ohio bar.":** Ibid., pp. 21, 27–28.
297. **"Certificate of Efficiency.":** Stinchcombe, *American Lady of the Manor,* pp. 50–55.
298. **white-haired lady:** "Lady Cook's Crusade," *Chicago Chronicle,* Jan. 1, 1905, in SIU.
299. **blinds were drawn:** Ibid.
299. **time for "my American sisters":** *Washington Post,* Feb. 2, 1907, p. 6.
300. **plenty of money working for him:** *Chicago Tribune,* Aug. 30, 1908, p. 1.
300. **see that millions want it:** *New York Times,* Oct. 11, 1908.
300. **only idiots, the insane, and convicts:** *Chicago Tribune,* Oct. 19, 1909, p. 5.
301. **malodorous and hideously dirty:** *New York Times,* Oct. 23, 1909.
301. **we do not get along very well:** *New York Times,* June 2, 1910.
301. **"breach of contract" suit:** *New York Times,* Sept. 17, 1910.
301. **isn't one good enough—not yet:** *Pittsburgh Press,* Oct. 12, 1913.
302. **the days of Grecian draperies:** Ibid.

302. **glad when it is over:** SIU.

302. **property in their wives' names:** *New York Times*, Feb. 4, 1911, p. 2.

303. **"hurricane of applause.":** *The Grey River Argus*, Jan. 21, 1910, p. 4.

303. **enunciation of her unchangeable opinion:** Unless otherwise indicated, her speech and comments are from her May 6, 1910, lecture, *The Need of Revising Morals and Laws* (London: Christy and Lilly, Ltd., n.d.).

305. **sells herself at the altar:** "Lady Cook's Crusade," *Chicago Chronicle*, Sunday Morning, January 1, 1905.

305. **decent men into Parliament:** May 6, 1910, lecture.

Chapter Twenty-Eight: Last Acts

306. **their homes, their honor, their children:** *New York Times*, Aug. 17, 1914.

307. **marching, scouting, and the use of arms:** Professor Joanna Bourke, writing for the BBC History World War One series *Women on the Home Front in World War One* and *Women and the Military in World War One*, available online. Bourke, a prize-winning historian and author, is professor of history, Birbeck College, University of London.

308. **their blood freely given:** SIU.

308. **No sophistry will answer:** Ibid.

308. **make the world safe for democracy:** MM, *All Governments Lie!: The Life and Times of Rebel Journalist I. F. Stone* (New York: Scribner, 2006), pp. 55–56; original source John Graham, *Yours for the Revolution: The Appeal to Reason, 1895–1922* (Lincoln: University of Nebraska Press, republished 1990), p. 285.

308. **We must be so now:** SIU.

309. **nothing to fear with the war being over:** Ibid.

309. **my health and meeting my God:** Ibid.

309. **Henry Clews's scathing comments:** *New York Times*, Jan. 10, 1923.

309. **granting letters of administration:** *New York Times*, March 22, 1923.

309. **Polly Sparr argued:** *New York Times*, March 8, 1923.

310. **she would give $5,000:** Stinchcombe, *American Lady of the Manor*.

310. **the understanding of the bible:** BPL.

311. **I would discard *them*:** Ibid.

311. **take any part in her life:** SIU.

311. **I cannot reason with my heart:** BPL.

311. **an excellent platform speaker:** Victoria Woodhull obituary, *(London) Times,* June 11, 1927.

312. **put me right before the world:** SIU.

Epilogue: Well-Behaved Women Seldom Make History

313. **54 percent of rapes go unreported:** For the statistics on rape, see Rape, Abuse, & Incest National Network (RAINN), the nation's largest anti-sexual violence organization, at http://www.rainn.org/get-information/statistics/reporting-rates. Out of one hundred rapes reported, only three rapists will ever serve any jail time.

314. **an estimated 200,000 women:** Jaeah Lee, "Charts: This Is What Happens When You Defund Planned Parenthood." *Mother Jones,* March 24, 2013.

315. **Shameful doesn't even begin to describe it:** Published May 16, 2012, on Congresswoman Louise M. Slaughter's website, http://www.louise.house.gov.

315. **longest-serving female member of the House:** U.S. Senator Barbara Mikulski (D-Md.) has served the longest of any female in history on Capitol Hill, first as a member of Congress and then in the United States Senate from 1986 until the present.

315. **I could go on forever:** E-mail interview with MM, March 24 and 31, 2013.

316. **Papua New Guinea and Swaziland:** "Landmark Family Leave Law Doesn't Help Millions of Workers," *Washington Post,* Feb. 10, 2013. Statistics quoted from McGill and Harvard University research.

316. **vital assistance to millions of women:** http://obamacarefacts.com/obamacare-womens-health-services.php.

316. **women continue to earn less:** Christianne Corbett and Catherine Hill, "Graduating to a Pay Gap: The Earnings of Women and Men One Year after Graduation," researched and written for the American Association of University Women (AAUW).

317. **linked sexual assaults to the problem:** http://mediamatters.org/blog/2013/06/06/foxs-allen-west-uses-military-sexual-assault-ep/194378.

317. **26,000 cases of sexual assaults and rapes:** Senator Kirsten Gillibrand interview on the *Daily Show,* Aug. 9, 2013.

318. **This New Departure did galvanize:** Wheeler, *One Woman, One Vote,* pp. 76 and 82.

319. **"annals of emancipation.":** *Newark Sunday Call,* Jan. 2, 1876; *The Selected Papers of Elizabeth Cady Stanton and Susan B. Anthony*; Goldsmith, *Other Powers,* p. 427.

319. **cohabitation, single parenthood, and same-sex relationships:** Pew Research, Social & Demographic Trends, "Barely Half of U.S. Adults Are Married—A Record Low," Dec. 14, 2011, at http://www.pewsocialtrends .org/2011/12/14/barely-half-of-u-s-adults-are-married-a-record-low.

321. **an ally in Colbert Busch:** John Dickerson, *Slate,* May 7, 2013.

Index

Note: The term "Sisters," applies to the "Scarlet Sisters." Abbreviations TCC and VCW refer to Tennessee Celeste Claflin and Victoria Claflin Woodhull, respectively.

ABOUT TWELVE

TWELVE

TWELVE was established in August 2005 with the objective of publishing no more than twelve books each year. We strive to publish the singular book, by authors who have a unique perspective and compelling authority. Works that explain our culture; that illuminate, inspire, provoke, and entertain. We seek to establish communities of conversation surrounding our books. Talented authors deserve attention not only from publishers, but from readers as well. To sell the book is only the beginning of our mission. To build avid audiences of readers who are enriched by these works—that is our ultimate purpose.

For more information about forthcoming TWELVE books, please go to www.twelvebooks.com.